Writing in the Irish Republic

Writing in the Irish Republic

Literature, Culture, Politics 1949–1999

Edited by

Ray Ryan

First published in Great Britain 2000 by
MACMILLAN PRESS LTD
Houndmills, Basingstoke, Hampshire RG21 6XS and London
Companies and representatives throughout the world

A catalogue record for this book is available from the British Library.

ISBN 0–333–73657–5 hardcover
ISBN 0–333–73658–3 paperback

First published in the United States of America 2000 by
ST. MARTIN'S PRESS, LLC,
Scholarly and Reference Division,
175 Fifth Avenue, New York, N.Y. 10010

ISBN 0–312–23153–9

Library of Congress Cataloging-in-Publication Data
Writing in the Irish Republic : literature, culture, politics 1949–1999 / edited by
Ray Ryan.
    p. cm.
Includes bibliographical references and index.
ISBN 0–312–23153–9
  1. Ireland—Civilization—20th century. 2. English literature—Irish authors–
–History and criticism. 3. English literature—20th century—History and
criticism. 4. Ireland—Politics and government—20th century. 5. Ireland—In
literature. I. Ryan, Ray, 1965–

DA959.1 .W75 2000
959.5082—dc21

                           00–033267

This book is printed on paper suitable for recycling and made from fully managed and sustained
forest sources.

10   9   8   7   6   5   4   3   2   1
09 08 07 06 05 04 03 02 01 00

Printed and bound in Great Britain by
Antony Rowe Ltd, Chippenham, Wiltshire

Contents

List of Tables

List of Contributors

Jonathan Allison is Associate Professor in the Department of English, University of Kentucky, Lexington. He is the author of many essays on twentieth-century Irish poetry, Assistant Director of the Yeats Summer School and editor of *Yeats's Political Identities*. He is currently working on *A History of Twentieth Century Irish Poetry* for Cambridge University Press.

Joe Cleary lectures in the English Department at the National University of Ireland, Maynooth. His book *Colonial Partitions: Literature and the Nation State in Northern Ireland, Israel and Palestine* will be published by Cambridge University Press in 2001.

Catriona Clutterbuck completed her D.Phil. at St. John's College, Oxford, and now lectures in Anglo-Irish literature at University College, Dublin.

Chris Morash lectures in the English Department at St. Patrick's College, Maynooth. His *Writing the Famine* was published by Oxford University Press in 1997. The author of many essays on nineteenth- and twentieth-century Irish literature and drama, he is currently working on *A History of Irish Drama* for Cambridge University Press.

Tom Garvin is Professor of Politics at University College, Dublin. He is the author of many articles on Irish and comparative politics. His books include *The Evolution of Irish Nationalist Politics* (1981), *Nationalist Revolutionaries in Ireland, 1858–1927* (1987), and *1922: The Birth of Irish Democracy* (1996).

Cormac ó Gráda is Professor of Economics at University College Dublin. His most recent works include *Ireland: A New Economic History*, *A Rocky Road: The Irish Economy Since the 1920s*, and *Black '47 and Beyond: The Great Irish Famine in History, Economy, and Memory*.

Richard Haslam, formerly Lecturer in Modern Irish Literature at the Institute of Irish Studies, University of Liverpool, is Assistant Professor at St. Joseph's University, Philadelphia. He has written several essays on Irish film, and is completing a book entitled *Apparitions: the Hermeneutics of Irish Fantastic Fiction* for the University Press of Kentucky.

Barbara O'Connor lectures in the Department of Communication, Dublin City University. She is editor, with Michael Cronin, of *Tourism in Ireland: A Critical Analysis* (Cork University Press, 1992), and, with Mary J. Kelly, *Media Audiences in Ireland: Power and Cultural Identity* (University College Dublin Press, 1997).

Michael Cronin is Director for the Centre of Translation Studies, Dublin City University. He is editor, with Barbara O'Connor, of *Tourism in Ireland: A Critical Analysis* (Cork University Press, 1992). His most recent book is *Across The Lines: Travel, Language, Translation* (Cork University Press, 2000).

Tony Canavan, a graduate of Queen's University, Belfast, was one of the founders of *History Ireland* and still serves on its Editorial Board. A former editor of *Causeway*, the cultural traditions journal, he now lives in Dublin working as an editor and reviewer.

John Horgan was Staff Journalist and Special Correspondent for *The Irish Times* between 1963 and 1973, and Editor of *The Education Times* between 1973 and 1976. A former Member of Seanad Éireann, he was a Member of Dáil Éireann between 1977 and 1987, and a Member of the European Parliament, 1981–3. He is now Professor of Journalism at Dublin City University. His recent books include *Sean Lemass: The Pragmatic Patriot* (Gill and Macmillan, 1997), *Mary Robinson: A President with a Purpose.* (O'Brien Press, 1997) and *Noel Browne: Taking No Hostages*, Dublin, Gill and Macmillan (in press). He is currently working on *A Critical History of Irish Media 1922–2000*, to be published by Routledge.

Patrick Hanafin lectures in the School of Law at Birkbeck College, University of London. He is the author of a number of books on medical law including *Last Rights: Death, Dying and the Law in Ireland* (Cork University Press, 1997), co-editor of a collection of essays, *Identity, Rights and Constitutional Transformation* (Ashgate, 1999) and writer of numerous articles on the interaction between law and cultural norms in Ireland. He is currently completing *Political Identity Formation and the Law in Post-Independence Ireland* (Forthcoming, Ashgate, 2001).

Colin Coulter lectures in the Department of Sociology, National University of Ireland, Maynooth. He has written extensively on various aspects of Irish politics and society, North and South. His *Contemporary Northern Irish Society: An Introduction* is published by Pluto Press.

Ray Ryan is editor of *Bullán: An Irish Studies Journal*. His *Region, State, and Nation: The Republic of Ireland and Scotland*, is forthcoming from Oxford University Press.

Acknowledgements

My first thanks are to Charmian Hearne, my exemplary editor at Macmillan and longtime friend not just of this project, but of Irish studies in general. Without her generous support from the outset, this book would not have been possible.

Karl Howe's professionalism ensured that this collection came to fruition. I'm extremely grateful to him, and to Sue, for the time spent preparing the manuscript.

Christina Zaba's contribution to this project has been immensely valuable and rewarding. I'm very grateful for her expert copy-editing and wise advice at various stages during the preparation of the script.

For generous advice and commentary on aspects of this book, thanks to John Kerrigan, Ben Levitas, Rónán McDonald, Shaun Richards, Matthew Campbell and Andrew Hadfield.

There were many individuals who gave indispensable support of many kinds during the preparation of this volume. I thank them all very warmly.

Finally, my thanks go to all the contributors in this volume for their patience and participation.

Introduction:
State and Nation: The Republic and Ireland, 1949–99

Ray Ryan

> *A State is always disappointing, especially one that has issued from a high rhetoric of race and nation. It is bound to incur the sardonic note of disillusion.*
>
> Denis Donoghue, *The Parnell Lecture, Cambridge* (1997)

On Easter Monday 1949 the Republic of Ireland was born. Despite that resonant Easter Monday origin (falling just over mid-way between the 1916 Rising and its fiftieth anniversary in 1966) the events surrounding the Republic of Ireland Act of 1949 are undramatic and a little hazy. A series of haphazard and loosely co-ordinated political and diplomatic decisions accompanied the official birth of the state. There were no ringing declarations of the nation's geography, history or identity, no mention of the people, no heroic acts of defiance, parades, speeches or flags. The Republic was not brought into being by de Valera, the revered, iconic hero of 1916 and the War of Independence, but by John Costello, a mostly forgotten leader of Fine Gael and head of the Free State's first coalition government, formed upon the removal of Fianna Fáil from office in 1948 after sixteen years in power.

So relatively obscure are the events surrounding the passing of the act, compared to the familiar litany of nationalist and unionist commemorations, that they bear brief retelling here. Taoiseach John Costello promised to establish a Republic in 1948 while on a visit to Canada, partly in response to some mild provocation from the Canadian Governor General, Lord Alexander, a former Ulster Volunteer Force man, who refused to toast the Irish President at an official dinner. The following day, in an apparently spontaneous response to reporters' questioning, an irked Costello announced his government's intention to repeal the

External Relations Act, an act which allowed the British monarch to appoint and receive envoys and ratify treaties on behalf of the Irish Free State, and establish a Republic. That intention quickly became a reality. Sean McBride, Minister for External Affairs – like almost everyone else, stunned by Costello's announcement – now astonished Costello and infuriated civil servants by drafting a Bill to repeal the External Relations Act while Costello was still in Canada. Meanwhile, the British government, piqued by the announcement of the Republic, withdrew an invitation to the Dublin government to attend a meeting of Commonwealth ministers in London, an act that was 'tantamount to terminating Eire's ambiguous membership of the commonwealth'.[1]

After Indian independence, the Irish actions provided a further worrying example for the rest of the Commonwealth; so much so that rumours began to circulate of the British government's intention to forcibly repatriate the Irish Community in Britain. On his return, a distraught Costello offered his resignation. This was refused, and the government retrospectively approved his action in Canada, a move helped by the decision of the Commonwealth States to agree that, for trading purposes, the Irish State and its citizens would not be designated 'foreign'. The Republic of Ireland Act was signed by the President Sean T. O'Kelly in December 1948, but there was to be no instant drama for the new state. The act did not become law until Easter Monday 1949, when the Republic of Ireland was, at last, formally inaugurated.

Also in 1949, seven months after the Republic of Ireland Act was passed, the British government committed themselves to the principle of majority rule in the Northern State, a principle which still abides today. It guaranteed that Northern Ireland would not leave the United Kingdom 'without the consent of the parliament of Northern Ireland'.

In 1999 very few commemorated John Costello's achievements fifty years before. The reasons for this are probably connected to the messy local politics surrounding the Republic of Ireland Act of 1949, but perhaps mostly to conceptual difficulties with the very idea of a state as a corporate entity, and the dominant critical frames upon which Irish cultural studies currently rest. For compared to the nation, the qualities in a state's existence are peculiarly difficult to describe and commemorate. Once established, it undoubtedly exists, but where and how is it made manifest? Once founded, it becomes legitimate; but it does not then recognise any horizon beyond its own existence, except for the boundaries of other states. All other forms of polity it regards as potentially anarchic and threatening to itself. In Ireland, where the state was competing for sovereignty and legitimacy with the ancient nation that took the island as the absolute forum in which value and meaning should evolve, this situation was particularly acute. Patrick Hanafin's essay on the 1937 Constitution here examines some of the judicial aspects of that tension. Hanafin shows how de Valera's constitution, the foundational document for the 26-county state, has been modified and reinterpreted in response to a less restrictive model of Irish identity, and argues that it is 'the tension between the Gaelic romantic strand of the Constitution and the Irish Enlightenment strand that in effect holds the Constitution together'.

But as Chris Morash documents in his essay, '"Something's Missing": Theatre and the Republic of Ireland Act', in one sense the state born in 1949 already existed for Irish republicans: the idea of the Irish Republic did not require the ratification of legislation. To actually declare the Republic, as Morash notes, was for some a gross impertinence, for it suggested that it had not always been there. The state was the terminus and realisation of Irish Republican aspirations, but the 1949 Act simply acknowledged, belatedly, an ideal reality that, for Republicans in the Free State, had always existed in theory if not in fact. Morash quotes the then Sinn Féin President Margaret Buckley addressing her party's Ard Fheis. Buckley stated that the coalition government could not declare a Republic because 'the Republic was proclaimed in 1916, established in 1919, and it had never been deestablished.' For nationalists, the 26-county state's first sin is thus the Beckettian one of being born, for its existence testifies to a state of affairs that is not wholly natural, and so the yearning for a moment before its being was necessary still lingers.

The state, by contrast, conceives of itself as complete and autonomous, as having arrived at a political form that is the fullest expression of the people's soul. For a thinker such as Hegel, the state was the ultimate expression of the universal *and* the individual will: 'the embodiment of concrete freedom, in which the individual's particular interests have their complete development and receive recognition of their rights'. The state is the space for Hegel in which 'the world spirit', Absolute Knowing, finally grasps itself as absolute, and 'the series of spiritual forms is therewith for the moment concluded'.[2] In Francis Fukuyama's evocative phrase, which develops Hegel's notion, the state is thus synonymous with the End of History, with the concluding cadences of historical and political development. The present moment now 'casts aside its barbarity', all that preceded the state, and allows 'true reconciliation, which reveals the state as the image and actuality of reason to become objective'.[3] One point to note immediately about Buckley's rhetoric, however, is that it refuses to make just this kind of acknowledgement of the state as the expression of modernity. Ireland, according to Sinn Féin's logic, did not need to wait until 1949 to be fully realised. The nation had reached the best possible form of political organisation before the state arrived, and in this sense Buckley exemplifies the hostility the 26-county Republic attracted, and continues to attract, for not being coterminous with the nation that preceded its own existence. For once the Republic of Ireland as a state starts to compile its own history, for nationalists like Buckley it would seem to dramatically announce the end of nationalist Irish history. Tony Canavan's essay addresses the political pressures this introduces into the teaching of Irish history in schools, and the changes introduced into the curriculum by the state in response to the conflict in the north. It is highly unlikely of course, that the state would ever sanction a version of history that suggested its own existence was illegitimate or unjustifiable; but Canavan shows that even school textbooks on early medieval Ireland were affected by the political violence in Northern Ireland. Canavan also looks at the public attitude in the Republic to the debate surrounding the revision of Irish history, and addresses the way various broadcasting organs within the state developed an editorial policy with a sometimes stridently anti-nationalist tone.

But the Republic was not unique in facing a situation where it did not correspond with the nation's history. This is to some extent a feature of all states: once born, a state assumes that it has always immemorially existed, so that it cannot imagine a time when it did not exist, or any form of political organisation beyond statehood. A state, any state, cannot proclaim a spectral or millenarian relationship to history; it cannot enact a sudden, magical, divine intervention that would transform the existing order, which like the rebels of 1916 would forego mundane compromises and transform colonial dullness into exhilarating freedom (hence Denis Donoghue's perhaps too gloomy comments above on the advent of statehood). It conceives of itself as *sui generis*. The state does not exist within the state: it is not a world that can be mapped on the co-ordinates given by its own laws. In one reading, the idea of the state is boundless in that it asserts, on certain issues, ultimate claims over all the lives of those within it. In Hobbes's brutal and coercive terms, it induces the citizen to give up individual will and act freely, having taken this decision not to disobey: only when the citizen is prepared to abdicate this right to disobey can he or she enjoy freedom. Someone unfortunate enough to be excluded from the rule of the state, a stateless person, becomes in theory and practice a sort of non-person, a non-participant in the activity of governing, the activity whereby the individual is subjected to state power.[4] According to Hobbes, the state's primary reason for existence is to defend its authority and sovereignty, to ensure it continues to be. It is sovereign and perceives itself to be, like the laws of nature, natural; its function is to provide rational rules governing the behaviour between groups, rules which can, if necessary, be enforced when broken. The state as a concept, then, is a combination of rationality and universalism; by definition, it is to some degree authoritarian, and while it must exist within the territory it claims as its own, having rights and duties before the law, it is not a concept traceable to that particular world alone. But the state has no intrinsic relation to the territory it occupies at that moment: there is no absolute relation between the territory of the state of the Republic of Ireland and 26 or 32 counties.

A number of ironies and tensions arise from these features as they intersect with Irish history. Part of what makes Ireland distinct and different is its history of occupation, hunger, emigration and liberation, the catastrophic and irrational dimensions to the island's relationship with Britain. Over the last 500 years, the state has emerged as the most important means of organising ethnic and group identities into defined boundaries around the globe.[5] Its indifference to traditional territorial frontiers, and to the sacral and catastrophic dimensions of local histories, actually helped consolidate its position as *the* characteristic form of the modern polity. So while resisting assimilation into the boundaries of the British state is at the heart of Irish nationalist identity, since 1949 the Republic has moved ever closer to a European model of the state forged during the experience of colonial expansion, a model which must be to some degree authoritarian: it insists that there are limits to the forms of belonging the state can contain, so that individuals can be assimilated as its citizens.[6] For example, in a state you cannot claim the right to be entirely rootless or to march wherever you want, so impositions are placed on the travelling community in the Republic and the Orange Order in Northern Ireland to limit the mobility of both these groups. The state as a corporate entity brings these two communities into an intriguing coalition by designating certain forms of behaviour as incompatible with its own stability, and it does not recognise their appeal to histories and tradition that existed before it was born.

But this kind of curtailment on ethnic identities (the travellers) or political solidarities (the Orange Order) that challenge prevailing modes of being and authority – the status quo, in other words – makes the aspiration to statehood, for some, an entirely illusory form of emancipation. In David Lloyd's influential expression, the state is not the most perfect or fullest expression of men's will but 'an effective brake on the decolonising process':

> The adoption, virtually wholesale, of the State institutions of the colonizing power, and conformity to its models of representative democracy, poses what Fanon terms the 'sterile formalism' of bourgeois politics against the popular movements its institutions are designed to contain. The State, which represents the point of intersection of the nation with the unilaterally defined universality of the world economic order, becomes an effective brake on the decolonising process culturally as well as economically.[7]

Because a fundamental tenet of any state is that it alone has a monopoly on violence,[8] any 'popular movements' which threaten it are automatically delegitimised. The revolutionary energies Lloyd celebrates amongst nineteenth-century peasant organisations, for example, are terminated once the state comes into being: communal attachments to the land are superseded by the series of economic relationships the state sponsors. As a form of political organisation, the state tends to conflate its own identity with that of society, so that it is always in danger of assuming that its own disappearance means that all social life is threatened. Hence any form of representation, whether aesthetic or democratic, that threatens its self-identity is either banished completely or, just as effectively, absorbed within it. Examples of this process would be the Republic's appetite for censorship in the Fifties and Sixties, and its refusal today to extend voting rights to emigrants: in both cases, the state is decreeing that certain forms of representation are incompatible with the social order that best ensures its own continued stability. Certain books and certain potential voters are thus expelled or occluded from the polity, while previously demonised writers such as Joyce are repatriated and made emblematic of the state's identity: these days, an uncharacteristically avuncular Joyce adorns every Irish ten-punt note issued by the state's Central Bank. It is this kind of instinct for self-preservation that inspired Marx's general denunciation of the state in 'The German ideology'.

> Through the emancipation of private property from the community, the State has become a separate entity, beside and outside civil society; but it is nothing more than the form of organisation which the bourgeoisie necessarily adopts both for internal and external purposes, for the mutual guarantee of their property and interests.[9]

The political stability of the Republic since 1949, the ease with which it has accommodated European integration, is actually an indictment from the perspective of post-colonial and Marxist theory. To over-simplify these two complex strands of thought, the state insulates the property-owning bourgeoisie from the radical energies of a nationalist or class conflict that preceded its birth, and thereby perpetuates division, inequality and injustice.

There can be no doubt that since 1949 the Republic has played a major role in legitimising partition. The referendum on the 1998 Belfast Agreement, and the subsequent deletion of Articles 2 and 3 from the Constitution, is just the most visible element in this process. While all states define themselves as independent by delimiting their territory from neighbouring states, after the simultaneous referendums north and south of the border, one essential component of the Republic's self-identity became its independence from the northern state, despite the presence within Northern Ireland of a minority Republican and nationalist community. In denouncing this trend in the Republic, Declan Kiberd lamented the myopic political identity it generated:

> The rising generation did not speak with a single voice: and its members were too mobile to solidify into single schools. Some ... repudiated Irish nationalism and declared themselves positively uninterested in having a united Ireland. On the most urgent question facing the people, these took a line even more conservative than that favoured by the Dublin government.[10]

A sceptical response to this might ask how Kiberd knows the North to be the most urgent issue facing 'the people', while 'the people' remain obtusely focused on economics, housing, education – all those issues the Dublin government is actually responsible for. But what the state does with acts such as the referendum is remove sovereignty from 'the people' and abrogate it to itself; it becomes the sovereign author of its own destiny and henceforth is assumed to constitute a 'state of nature', over which no law or popular movement or definition of 'the people' can have a prior claim.[11]

To extrapolate from Kiberd's important criticism, there is no doubt that a project such as *Writing in the Irish Republic*, which must to some degree accept and address the Republic as a coherent cultural identity, participates in the thematics of division and partition. The overall project (though certainly not all individual contributions) must, of course, accept the 26-county State as the author of a substantial part of the contemporary Irish experience. In so doing, it to some extent legitimises and naturalises that experience, pushes it from the margins of Irish critical attention a little closer to the centre, makes the Republic canonical and, perhaps, marginalises the experience of smaller groups, such as Northern nationalists. As Joe Cleary puts it, in a pioneering examination of partition and state borders, such studies can prematurely accept and naturalise provisional state borders, acquiesce in a process which perhaps distorts the frameworks and periodisations available for critical debate.

> Partitions inaugurate the establishment of new states, and since most historiography is state-centric in its focus, the events that occur after partition tend to be assimilated to the career of one or other of the states involved. In other words, once state borders are established, academic disciplines such as history adapt themselves to them, taking the lineaments of the nation-state as the framework of their own investigations and analysis. As a result, 'after partition', the states thus established are treated as naturalised units of analysis, and the material consequences and functions of their borders tend either to be much less emphasised or to drop out of sight altogether.[12]

But because the Northern Troubles have produced a literature 'authenticated by crisis',[13] writing whose immediate political and cultural context facilitates the preoccupations of frameworks like post-colonialism and identity politics, the Republic has been largely abandoned by Irish cultural criticism, hidden because its writing did not directly address the conditions of violence.[14] Thus the way the state has facilitated, indeed enabled the kind of cultural myopia Kiberd criticises has never been addressed.[15] The first characteristic of any state, according to Anthony Giddens, is that 'All States involve the reflexive monitoring of aspects of the reproduction of the social systems subject to their rule.'[16] The Northern state, for example, systematically discriminated against Catholic citizens who did not accept the legitimacy of its own borders. In the Republic, as Tom Garvin's essay shows, political parties collaborated with Catholic dogma in order to monitor activities considered secular or anti-Catholic. These are obvious examples of Giddens's substantive point. But in the 'post-nationalist', secular Republic, it is still possible to discern the state's investment in the activity of monitoring the way meaning about the Republic is produced. The subscription to Giddens's 'reflexive monitoring' of the reproduction of meaning has not lapsed in the newly prosperous and liberalised Republic. As Richard

Haslam shows in his essay on the financing and production of Irish films, and as Barbara O'Connor and Michael Cronin show in their essay on Bord Fáilte and Irish Tourism, the state both actively intervenes in and even inaugurates narratives that produce meaning about itself. The extent of its activities becomes apparent only when we accept the Republic as something more than an artificial entity, a brake on the decolonising process, an illegitimate heir to a sovereignty that rightfully resides in 'the people'. And equally, as Catriona Clutterbuck argues in her essay on Irish women's poetry, the Republic may well be the most appropriate frame in which to analyse certain forms of writing. Clutterbuck claims that self-division and multiple allegiances are the inevitable characteristics of the woman poet in Ireland today. And it is these same qualities, she argues, that define the Republic as a state, thus making it the most appropriate frame within which to analyse the concerns of Irish women poets. The actual origin of women's poetry is less important than this shared inheritance, and we can, she suggests, better understand the Republic if we attend to the enabling disjunctions women poets feel between representation and reality, between myth and history, between formalism and form.

The present volume, then, has the standard critical aim of addressing the way the Republic has been represented in a variety of literary and political discourses. But alongside that aim, *Writing in the Irish Republic* should cast a cold, sceptical eye on the Republic's self-representation, on the forms of meaning and writing the state has facilitated and helped develop in order to naturalise its own sovereignty and territory. It should also show how the state can operate *within* cultural paradigms and ideological sites of contestation to develop a consensual stability. John Horgan's essay, for example, traces the role of the state in regulating the frenetic changes in the Republic's print, radio and television media since 1949. By that date, both main parties in the Republic, Fianna Fáil and Fine Gael, had their own newspapers, the *Irish Press* and the *Irish Independent* respectively, while the effectiveness of radio broadcasting in the Second World War, by the Allies and Germany, alerted all governments to the power of this still relatively new medium. In an era of globalisation and hugely powerful transnational satellite companies, the idea of a public service broadcasting may appear almost anachronistic. Horgan, however, relates many of the changes in the Republic's attitude to broadcasting legislation and deregulation to wider cultural and social changes in which, yet again, the North emerges as a crucial factor.

All commemorations are of course inevitably selective, designed to serve the political priorities of the present through dates which are, to some extent, always arbitrary: fifty years is not a period that has any intrinsic intellectual significance. But the flatly contradictory interpretations of events such as the 1798 Rising not only demonstrate the continually contested legacy of the past; they also demonstrate the enormous emotional significance which the act of commemoration entails. The politics of remembrance actually construct the collective memory bequeathed by the present to the future. While *Writing in the Irish Republic* is no exception, it does not try to simply advocate or celebrate the dramatic changes in the Republic since the Celtic Tiger was first found prowling Irish streets. But it does try to argue that the state should be recognised as an active agent in Irish cultural life; that the pervasive intervention of the state in people's cultural lives must be accounted for, for good and for ill; and that the best means of addressing this influence is through a genuinely interdisciplinary initiative. To account for the systematic way in which the state encourages citizens to identify its operations with modernisation, it is necessary to reach across intellectual boundaries and divisions. Barbara O'Connor and Michael Cronin here provide a powerful example of that methodology by analysing the state's sponsorship of tourism since 1949, and the version of modernisation which that particular discourse has produced.[17]

By signing the Belfast Agreement in 1998, Sinn Féin accepted the existence of the Northern state. At the time of writing, it appears that Irish nationalism has begun to accommodate the lineaments of the state borders on the island. Fifty years on from Buckley's haughty disdain for the 1949 Republic of Ireland Act, it is not impossible to imagine Sinn Féin as a minority coalition partner in a future government of the Republic. To imagine such a scenario, however, is not now to equate the state on its fiftieth birthday with modernity, to see it as the fullest expression of the people, north and south, with the nation forever associated with the strife that preceded the state's maturity. Throughout this volume, that predictable and tired opposition between modernity and backwardness, idealism and realism is interrogated, while contributors still try to account for the dramatic political economic and cultural transformations which the Republic has actually undergone. In his essay on Irish drama after 1949, for example, Christopher Morash asks what happens when the sense of tradition, modernity and memory that for so long has been tied to the utopian ideal of a single indivisible nation is suddenly terminated by the actuality of a 26-county State. He describes the 'post-utopian' sensibility that characterises much Irish theatre of the period, and reveals the extent of the engagement by playwrights and critics in the theme of partition.

Colin Coulter's essay shows how certain Unionist intellectuals have mobilised precisely these oppositions of modernity and tradition to portray the Republic perennially as an economically and socially backward, theologically driven State. If it is often hard to see the intellectual rather than the emotional power of these arguments, by placing them in the broader context of 'modernisation theory', Coulter shows the political ramifications of the economic 'analyses' proffered by a series of influential commentators. He claims that, for some unionist writers, the political divisions on the island represent 'nothing less than a boundary between a society that is modern/progressive/civilised and another that is traditional/regressive/primitive'. Joe Cleary's essay develops similar themes in several prominent literary texts from the Republic. Cleary argues that the *soi-disant* realism of writers such as Kavanagh, Friel, McGahern and McCabe leaves the pastoral ideology that underpinned the Irish Revival unmoved. The counter-revivalist response, Cleary claims, is not a shift from 'idealization to demystified actuality' but the displacement of one aesthetic by another, a displacement that 'leaves the modernizing philosophy embraced by the southern elite unchallenged'.

In contrast to some of the commentaries Coulter examines, Cormac Ó Gráda provides a detailed genealogy of the Republic's current economic prosperity, tracing the various attempts to formulate a coherent economic programme since 1949. Where Tom Garvin's essay traces the cultural impact of the political insularity in 1950s Ireland, and the brand of defensive nativism which it generated, Ó Gráda here examines the economic impact of that protectionist mentality and the policies it doggedly pursued during the decade. The consensus that indigenous industries should be cultivated at all costs finally relented as foreign capital was allowed in as a precursor to the Republic's unsuccessful application to enter the EEC in 1961. But even a decade ago, Ó Gráda notes, the case for the Republic being a failed economic entity was a powerful one. Now, if current predictions for economic growth are achieved, living standards in the Republic by 2010 will be as high as in all but the richest European economic countries. Ó Gráda, the leading authority on Irish economic history, documents the policy shifts which have led to this state of affairs, offering detailed comparative analysis between northern and southern states. And, like Coulter, he notes that claims for Northern economic superiority, which have served as a rationalisation of partition, now seem very dubious indeed.

One aspiration of cultural analysis must be to address accurately the way things are. This means accepting the Republic as a cultural entity and analysing its various disciplinary formats and designations. The construction and legitimisation of the state, its inscription through literary and political narratives, its impact on the vocabulary available for critical debate – these themes are most effectively scrutinised in a context which does not return us, again, to the old simplistic affirmation of difference and validation of difference. Or as Eiléan Ní Chuilleanáin beautifully puts it, 'A line is drawn across our experience, by an event in history or a pattern of nature, and we instantly find ourselves in a double life, cut in two by a line of bars.'[18] Jonathan Allison's essay explores the way in which Irish male poets have responded to this sense of division, analysing the various attempts to create poetic canons that account for 'southern' and 'northern' poetry, and the larger political claims inherent in such an exercise. The civic responsibilities of 'southern' poetry, he claims, are traceable to the way they manifest a sense of tradition, modernity and memory. Allison contrasts the work of Paul Durcan, Michael O'Loughlin and Eavan Boland with Heaney, Muldoon and a wide range of male poets throughout the century. My own essay takes up some of these themes by trying to account for the treatment of the Republic in various literary canons. I argue that the ostensibly 'liberal' post-nationalism these canons sponsor is actually exclusionary.

Many of these essays address areas and themes in Irish experience where the state, visibly and subliminally, draws lines across our experience. The exclusion of certain areas because of space is regrettable, and no claim for definitiveness is made. *Writing in the Irish Republic* should, though, constitute a detailed and coherent attempt to analyse the Republic of Ireland as a state since 1949 and what it means to use that very designation; and it should provoke as many questions as it tries to answer.

Notes

1 I draw here on Ian McCabe's 'Surprise Change of Status to Independent Republic', *The Irish Times*, April 5 1999. See also Charles Townshend, *Ireland: The 20th Century* (Arnold: London, 1999), pp. 132–59.
2 See the chapter entitled 'The State – the Consciousness of Freedom', in Shlomo Avineri, *Hegel's Theory of the Modern State* (Cambridge: Cambridge University Press), pp. 176–93.
3 Perry Anderson, *A Zone of Engagement* (London: Verso, 1992), p. 285.
4 'Every human agent now alive is held by at least one particular state to be subject to [a state's] obligations . . . there is no part of the world today in which a human being can confidently expect to escape the presumption of political subordination . . . nowhere . . . is there habitable space on earth which lies simply beyond the jurisdiction of state power. Virtually everyone in the modern world accordingly, is claimed as subject to political obligation.'

John Dunn, 'Political Obligation', in David Held (ed.), *Political Theory Today* (Stanford: Stanford University Press, 1991), p. 23. See also Rodney Barker, *Political Legitimacy and the State* (Oxford: Clarendon, 1990), p. 9.

5 See Thomas Bartlett, 'From Irish State to British Empire: Reflections on State-Building in Ireland, 1690–1830', *Études Irlaindais*, 21 (Winter 1995), pp. 25–37.

6 Christopher W. Morris, *An Essay on the Modern State* (Cambridge: Cambridge University Press, 1998), pp. 1–13.

7 David Lloyd, *Anomalous States: Irish Writing and the Post-Colonial Moment* (Dublin: Lilliput Press, 1993), p. 7.

8 See Anthony Giddens, *The Nation-State and Violence* (Cambridge: Polity Press, 1985), pp. 7–17.

9 Karl Marx, 'The German Ideology', in *The Marx-Engels Reader*, 2nd ed., ed. R. Tucker (New York and London: Norton, 1978), p. 187.

10 Declan Kiberd, *Inventing Ireland: The Literature of the Modern Nation* (Jonathan Cape: London, 1995), p. 610.

11 Or, as Hegel put it, 'Since the sovereignty of states is the principle governing their mutual relations, they exist to that extent in a state of nature in relation to one another.' Quoted in Morris, *An Essay on the Modern State*, p. 41.

12 Joe Cleary, *Partition and Postcolonial Studies: Literature and Politics in Ireland, Israel and Palestine* (Cambridge: Cambridge University Press, forthcoming).

13 John Kerrigan 'Hidden Ireland: Eiléan Ní Chuilleanáin and Munster Poetry', *Critical Quarterly*, 40 no. 4 (Winter 1998), pp. 76–100.

14 See Sean O'Brien, *The Deregulated Muse* (Newcastle upon Tyne: Bloodaxe, 1998), pp. 104–11. A notable exception to this is Terence Brown's *Ireland: A Cultural and Social History* (London: Fontana, 1984).

15 See Terry Eagleton, *Crazy John and the Bishop* (Cork: Cork University Press, 1998), p. ix: 'Scanning the bibliographies, an outsider might be forgiven for concluding that the Irish literary pantheon was populated more or less exclusively by Yeats, Synge, Joyce, Beckett, Flann O'Brien and Northern Irish Poetry.'

16 Giddens, *The Nation-State and Violence*, p. 17.

17 David Lloyd and Paul Thomas, *Culture and the State* (London: Routledge, 1998), p. 12: 'The concept [of wholeness] is prepolitical precisely insofar as the political stands for a division of the human into partialities.' Those partialities extend across a range of intellectual and social spheres.

18 Eiléan Ní Chuilleanáin, 'Borderlands of Irish Poetry', in Elmer Andrews (ed.), *Contemporary Irish Poetry: A Collection of Critical Essays* (Basingstoke: Macmillan, 1992), p. 25.

Part I
Literature

1
Irish Women's Poetry and the Republic of Ireland: Formalism as Form

Catriona Clutterbuck

My subject is the relationship between Irish women's poetry and the Republic. Self-evidently, Irish women's poetry is not containable by the term 'Republic of Ireland poetry', defined as such if a substantial part of the writing career of the poet has happened in the South or has been influenced by background in the South since 1949. These criteria exclude approximately fifteen women from the North out of the total of about 120 Irish women poets who have published at least one major poetry collection in the past 50 years[1] (though it includes writers like Heather Brett and Kerry Hardie, raised in the North but living in the South, who on this basis may also be called Northern Irish poets). On the very briefest consideration, a major figure like Medbh McGuckian who has lived all her life in Belfast challenges the Republic as a fitting frame for women's poetry on the island. As with most other areas of Irish cultural endeavour, in the field of women's poetry the result is that the 26-county Republic is not accepted in its function as criterion of identity – but neither is it actively rejected. Instead it is ignored. However, as I shall argue, most particularly in the case of Irish women's poetry, the existing Republic in fact offers itself as an invaluable construct allowing such island-wide writing to finally come into the kind of focus it has long required.

My basic contention is that, in the period since 1949, the undoubted stylistic and historical differences in the projects of women's poetry written from Southern Irish and from Northern Irish standpoints matters less than the fact of a common purpose for these two bodies of work. In a situation where migration of cultural traditions as well as people confers multiply-directed citizenship on everybody who has lived on the island of Ireland or been connected closely with someone who has, women's poetry currently leads Irish poetry in its role in prompting the people of this island towards recognition that accepting and celebrating difference is the truest basis of personal and group identity. The project of women's poetry island-wide therefore implicitly demands that we attend to the project of the existing Republic in a new way, especially in the wake of the recent referendum by which the Republic's claim to identity with the North of Ireland was altered from one of ownership to one of agreement (the effect of the 1995 referendum, which legalized divorce, upon the result of the 1998 referendum which dealt with Articles 2 and 3 of the constitution, remains to be examined). Although the Republic has been extensively investigated for the intricacies of its political, social and cultural construction,[2] it remains under-conceptualized as itself a form, an allegiance-commanding construct that is one of the primary current structures for group identity on the island.[3] As long as this is the case, the recognition of the value of difference mentioned above cannot come about. I will argue in this chapter that Irish women's poetry (in both North and South) helps us to understand the Republic in the way called for above because it shares with that territorial construct the positive results of being conditioned by the dynamics of formalism. By this I mean that the fact of disjunction between representation and reality – an integral criterion of formation for both the existing Republic and Irish women's poetry – can be more enabling than disabling in its effect.

In the period of the existence of the Republic, women's poetry island-wide has emerged from invisibility and near non-entity in 1949 to acquiring, in the late 1990s, the controversial status of most critically fashionable sub-division in Irish poetry – a baton that began to pass over from the 'Poetry of the Current Northern Troubles' around the late 1980s, when that body of writing began to be recognized as too diffuse in energy for ready categorization, and when socio-sexual issues began to dominate politics openly in the 26 counties.[4] According to a 1983 survey,[5] only 11 per cent of all Irish books published that year were by women, including 9 per cent by women publishing with the woman-oriented Dublin-based Arlen House Press; the remaining 2 per cent were published by mainstream presses. In the first 30 years of the Republic, 15 per cent of all Irish women poets who have published collections since 1949 emerged in book format. However, the 1980s saw an explosion in the publication of women's poetry, with over 35 poets beginning book publication in that decade; around the same number of new names reached the shelves in the first half of the 1990s alone. Jessie Lendennie's

Galway-based Salmon Press is a vital component of this growth, publishing the first books of about twenty-five of the approximately eighty Irish women poets who have emerged in the period in which it has published individual collections, that is, since 1985.[6] The editor of Gallery Press, the most influential publisher of poetry in the Republic since the early 1970s, testifies to the altered profile of women's poetry in Ireland: Peter Fallon argues (contentiously) that in the mid-1980s there were no substantial new women poets available for his list,[7] whereas at the end of the 1990s the work of the women poets published by Gallery 'tends to receive more attention than that of their male counterparts'.[8]

Beyond the obviously favourable impact which the Irish women's movement (reactivated in the Republic at the beginning of the 1970s) has had on general public receptivity to women's poetry, one reason for its popularity may be that women's poetry seems to offer a steadier basis for criticism than other categories in the quaking sod that is Irish poetry. The politics of Irish women's poetry tends to be directly equated with Irish feminism as a general politics of emancipation,[9] and is frequently read as properly defining itself, alongside that feminism, against territorial politics, most usually against nationalism.[10] This resistance-based feminism (and, by implication, women's poetry) is then implicitly assumed to be self-contained in a way that territorial politics on this island (and, by implication, the project of representation in poetry by men) stubbornly resists. This nexus of assumptions, based as it is on partial truth, produces the groundwork for simplified readings of Irish women's poetry as of Irish feminism. Poetry by women in Ireland has been too easily regarded as naturally antipathetic to nationalism because of the role played by this politics in silencing women's lived experience. This assumption prevails to the extent that the complexity of Irish women poets' substantial engagement with the theme of territorial politics has been under-read by critics.

For example, Steven Matthews offers the interesting assessment that Irish male poets' 'sense that their poetic must falter before extreme and violent events is ... at odds with hers' – that of the Irish woman poet, North and South, who understands that (quoting Eavan Boland) 'an inner world' can 'suffer the outer world so powerfully that history itself faltered before its gaze'. This is so, according to Matthews, because for the woman poet, '"reality" is that which ... remains outside "legitimized" historical discourses'; consequently, for her, 'poems represent an absolutely free space' in which 'the public is continuous with the private', allowing 'metaphorical directness' instead of the 'constructive methods' of 'male emblematizing'.[11] Matthews's understanding that for women poets the personal deconstructs and reconstructs the historical – in a way that allows poetry back into an Eden of unproblematic representation denied to male poets – pays insufficient attention to the fragmented and already historicized nature of the woman's 'inner world' once she takes on the task of speech.

The problem of legitimizing the authority to represent is more rather than less acute for the woman poet because of the condition Matthews describes, whereby her reality 'is outside "legitimized" historical discourses'. Matthews neglects the feminist insight that a woman's marginalization from official systems of representation will inevitably take place in terms of language itself as well as in terms of sociology, history and culture. This experience of alienation within language then prompts the woman poet to adopt 'constructive methods' as the only methods available to her, both as a woman and as an Irish person, in the project of representation. These methods, for the woman poet as for the male poet (though for additional reasons), are enablingly usable only through their patent falsity or inadequacy as well as through their potential visionary appropriateness. As a result, an Irish female poetics is not separate from an Irish male poetics, but dynamically intersects with it in teaching that the project of recovering or engaging with history is properly one of desire, not empirical achievement or non-achievement. In summary, more focus is needed on how, in terms of the problems of representation, Ireland's women poets register cross-border concern ('border' here referring to divisions of language, class, religion, sexual orientation, ethnicity, age or formal style as well as of territory) with a relationship of private to public realm that is conditioned by Irish culture's gendered unease about definitions of nation and state.

The recent growth in the popularity of women's poetry, therefore, does not necessarily mean that its revolutionary potential is being attended to. (Analogously, the recent surge in confidence in the Irish Republic, so marked in its sporting and economic achievement in the 1990s, does not mean that its revolutionary potential to exceed its own boundaries in new ways is being truly recognized – for example, by rendering its own border dynamically porous through celebrating the achievements gained through emigration and immigration.) The clearest indication that the challenge of a newly strengthened Irish women's poetry (and of a newly strengthened 26-county Irish Republic) is being circumscribed anew is the proliferation of reductive readings of the significance of domestic space. Mary O'Malley, in her piece 'Interior',[12] addresses such a critical practice, whereby the historical locus of a poem (or of a state) – that is, where it is situated – is emphasized to the neglect of the engaged vision of what poetry (or statehood) might do. Any historical matrix is properly both the occasion and invigilator of such a vision, but too often the realizing of place (and its corollary, position) becomes a criterion of success in itself. Through her motif of building a kitchen, O'Malley illustrates how this damaging interpretative assumption is assembled along with the uncritical revaluation of the local and the domestic:

> *'There is no domestic detail in her poems. . .'.*
>
> There is now. Two by fours
> And concrete slabs, the floors
> Littered with cigarette stubs.
>
> The timber supporting the new stairs
> Is stalwart. 'That won't shift'.
> It will of course and its all useless
>
> When the electrician's mate
> Kangoes through the live wire
> Playing a mean guitar.
>
> Good golly, Miss Molly. 'Draw a straight line
> Up from the switch, in your mind.
> That's called an image'. I told him
>
> But they're only interested in grouting
> And gulley risers, a consonance of solid things.
> Nuts and bolts men.

In abeyance since the theatre of the mid-century, the kitchen has come round again as building site of the Irish literary tradition. However, this time women are the builders, and as such they are testing the whole construction, in particular its claims to realism. By so doing, women poets signal that the hearth/history opposition beloved of earlier critiques of Irish poetry is, and always was, an empty binary.[13] Classically exemplified by the Gregory/Yeats play *Cathleen Ni Houlihan* in 1901, the hearth has long been the ground upon which, not for or with which, Irish history is worked out. The hearth as self-contained unit of energy has also, more subliminally, operated as a figure for individual artistic inspiration through which that history was mediated. Women poets in Ireland are leading the drive to redefine the Irish hearth (in its function as figure for both the dual private/public nature of the artist's material and the inspiration of the artist-activist) as no longer a cosily cohesive changeless catalyst of public transformation, but as a centre of skilled and variable local command of universal, co-operatively accessed energy in Irish culture. In other words, women's poetry is leading a re-cognition of the hearth as the heart of public civil space as well as of private communal space.[14] The absence of such a redefinition of the hearth in Irish history has given rise to a habit of negative focus on the inevitable, but resultingly deepening fault line between the concepts of 'nation' and 'state', the non-acceptance of which has led to the Irish Republic foundering in confidence as a culturally realized entity, 50 years into its existence.

That foundering is better exemplified by poetry than most other cultural enterprises in Ireland, since poetry has been peculiarly associated with the drive to unite nation and state and with challenges to that drive since well before the mid-nineteenth-century Young Ireland movement where such politicization of poetry is usually said to originate. The dominance of this association is demonstrated by the fact that the adjectives 'poetic' or (interchangeably) 'literary' entered Irish historiography in the late 1960s and 1970s as a cover-term describing all that was wrong with the methodology of present politics and earlier histories of Ireland alike.[15] However, critics who have made it their business to assess and contextualize this traditional conjunction between poetry and politics have neglected one part of their business in so far as they have ignored the specific impact of the 26-county Republic in its claim to be a viable political and cultural entity.

Post-colonialism and revisionism in their locked roles as a dominating binary, within which literary criticism with a geopolitical basis has been conducted on the island in recent years, have together been largely responsible for eliminating room for considering the 26 counties as a separable poetic base. This is because both post-colonialism and revisionism have attended more to the relation between the aspirant whole of a 32-county nation state and the defiant challenge of a 6-county 'cultural corridor'[16] than to the relation of either of these to a 26-county existing Republic, which tends to be represented in debate more symbolically than practically as either non-deserving of the status of Republic, over-complacent with it, threateningly dissatisfied with its own lack of completion, or any combination of the three. And while the North as declared base of regionalism in Ireland since the 1940s[17] may have influenced critics' decisions to re-create other areas as specific poetic locations, such as the border counties, the west of Ireland, Dublin and the south of the country, regionalism as an approach to Irish poetry remains almost invariably, if often silently, locked into debate with its polar opposite, national territorial poetics.

There seems to be a tacit assumption among poetry critics that the one geographical categorization beyond regionalism, beyond the old workhorse of the rural–suburban–urban divide and beyond the special status of the North as unignorably fraught socio-political locus – the existing Republic – should be avoided. Alternative models for registering a broken yet potentially whole tradition on the island include Thomas Kinsella's and Tom Paulin's offer of linguistic division and reconnection instead of the territorial variant.[18] A further alternative is offered by Stephen Matthews as the latest among a critical lineage including Michael Smith and Samuel Beckett, who argue that traditionalist versus modernist poetic form is the cake-slice that is truest to Irish experience North and South.[19] The echoes of Yeats's class-based dividing line for aesthetic significance continue to sound through these various national, regional, urbanist, linguistic and strict poetic formal alternatives for categorizing Irish poetry, and in all cases an island-wide context remains fixed and the Republic remains effectively ignored.

As regards the territorial unit of the Republic, only a small number of critics, including Terence Brown, Edna Longley and Sebastian Barry, have attempted to differentiate a state-wide poetic.[20] However, this poetry criticism is marked by common diagnoses of Southern poetry as either a privatized or publicized aesthetic – never the vital, tense, co-joining of public and private that is commonly celebrated as the basic force of poetry from the North of Ireland. For example, Terence Brown in his seminal publication *Ireland: A Social and Cultural History* divides Southern literature between 1922 and 1980 into two firmly separate categories: literature that was outward-directed up to the late 1950s (either for orthodox nativist or rebel-iconoclast reasons), and inward-directed and resistant to calls for relevance since then.[21] The categories of public and private are thus contained in separation from each other. Sebastian Barry, in *The Inherited Boundaries*, his controversial introduction to the 1986 anthology of writers from the Republic whose careers begin in the 1970s, supports Brown's findings in a brave announcement of a Southern poetical sensibility which emerges as intensely private through lack of clear identification: this sensibility is 'not-Northern', but is capable of being associated with a propensity to 'argue with ourselves' in a condition of cultural confidence about our 'uncluttered' non-colonial, non-provincial, non-parochial, non-aged and implicitly non-female citizenship of a place that is 'without definition' and therefore 'nowhere at all'.[22] This is the Republic projected as a personalized off-shore account named *Tír na nÓg*.[23]

Neglect of the Republic as a territorial unit worthy of serious consideration in poetry criticism may derive, then, from a sense of its non-entity
that is in turn predicated upon failure to notice the manner in which, in
the writing of the Republic as in that of the North, the private and public
elements of the poem are simultaneously present, and bear upon each
other in complex ways. The most important way in which the successful
Irish poem is public and private at the same time is the manner in which
aesthetic form operates within it both traditionally, as a buried or
'private' element of theme, and radically, as an explicit or 'public' element
of it. This particular conjunction of public and private is attended to in
relation to poetry from the North of Ireland in careful criticism of the
relation between poetic form and historical context; specifically, critics
and poets alike are preoccupied by internal variations and challenges to
the model of the well-made poem as an appropriate response to extreme
socio-cultural division and violence. Indeed, this has been the basis upon
which poetry from the North has been accorded its defining status.[24]

But similar issues of form rarely impede on the occasional specific
critique of the poetry of the Republic, and when they do it is often only
to suggest that the South does not measure up to the North in terms of
its aesthetic worthiness as a base for poetry. Edna Longley, who in her
essay 'Poetic Forms and Social Malformations' has produced the most
substantial consideration of the 26 counties as a unit-base for poetry,
works from the standpoint that Southern poets such as Brendan
Kennelly and Paul Durcan are engaged with a game of historico-cultural
liberation on such an open playing-pitch that there is no need in the
South for that close-wrought, tenser, and ultimately more challenging
linguistic aesthetic that more naturally belongs in the North of Ireland.[25] Hers is an informative assessment of Southern poetics from the
point of view of socio-political differences between North and South.
From the point of view of poetics and politics, however, it tends
towards foreclosure of linguistic tension as a Northern phenomenon[26]
in a way that neglects to take account of the Irish language's absence-
cum-presence as a shadow-theme in writing North and South, and
more importantly, fails to consider the potential of acknowledged formalism as a common factor in both poetries (as we shall see). Effectively,
Longley's argument rules that in Irish poetry Northern and Southern
themes rarely intersect in either substance or import.

Recently, as a function of its current emblematic status, women's
poetry rather than men's has become the agent of codifying territorial
aesthetics in Irish poetry criticism. Critiques of Irish women's poetry
which distinguish Medbh McGuckian's, Eiléan Ní Chuilleanáin's and

Nuala Ní Dhomhnaill's aesthetics from that of Eavan Boland, Ireland's highest-profile female poet, interestingly chime with Longley's 1988 distinction above of Mahon or Muldoon from Kennelly or Durcan. They suggest that in Irish poetry at large the division of aesthetic concentration and enabling problematizing of the representative function of language is being made not strictly along North/South but along non-or-pre-Republic/Republic lines. Clair Wills, for example, elects McGuckian over Boland as the more interesting writer (as she does, implicitly, Northern over the Republic's poetry) on the basis that Boland is writing out of an already secured political base and McGuckian is not. She associates Boland's poetics with a 'strategy of representation – of giving voice', and continues: 'the belief in the efficacy of such representation depends on a fundamental faith in representative politics, or more broadly the public realm of democratic politics... [and] the fact that what is being represented... forms a link between a personal and a public or national narrative... a poem constitutes a political demand, as it stands in for the demands of a marginalized community, in this case women. Hence representativeness does not necessarily entail a form of concurrence with existing modes of address, so much as a process of legitimization through shared modes of address'.[27]

The other three 'senior' Irish women poets, McGuckian as a Northern Irish writer, Ní Dhomhnaill in her choice both of the Irish language and an Irish iconic feminine apparently unequivocally rejected by Boland, and Ní Chuilleanáin in her poetics of obscurity, which recent critiques have linked to a Corkery-like hidden Ireland and the seventeenth-century counter-reformation Ireland,[28] are associated with a common poetics of secrecy which exemplifies Wills's alternative 'poetic strategy' adaptable by Irish poets. This is one which 'in its enigmatic refusal of clarity and interpretation, throws into question the notion of both representation and representativeness, and with it the dominant definition of the public realm'.[29] In other words, this is a strategy outside the remit of that achieved resolution of the representative function which the idea of a republic, and hence the Irish Republic, would apparently embody. But Eavan Boland (in explaining the current significance of Irish women's poetry) specifically focuses on the problems of power relations within the act of representation, and in doing so implies just such a questioning of the representative function – both poetically and politically – which Wills's analysis approves: 'some of the questions raised by women's poetry – questions about the voice and the self, about revising the stance of the poet and the relation of the poem to the erotic, to the unwritten, not to mention the crucial relation of the poet to the act of power – are also some of the questions which are at the heart of poetry right now'.[30] Through implicitly claiming for her own poetry this questioning of the representative function, Boland here challenges critiques of her work which condemn it as being too direct politically and too bland poetically.[31] As a corollary, her statement can be read as challenging the concomitant critical assumption that the Republic may no longer have political vitality since, in terms of its sense of statehood, it feels itself to be resolved and complete (however much lip service it pays to the ideal of a 32-county identity). Such an ascription of complacency to the existing Republic is misguided not because its territorial aspiration to the North of Ireland may be more important than it seems, but because irresolution is endemic in its condition as an Irish Republic of whatever size, since it cannot fulfil its claim to represent the nation. This is the case firstly because the nation exceeds the state through the diaspora, secondly because Irish nationality is spliced through with other nationalities, especially the Scottish and English ones, and thirdly because of the ever-increasing complexity of its relationship with the European Union.

My argument here has been that readings of the poetry of the Republic as limited reflect a reading of the Southern state (either as a republic *per se* or as an incomplete republic) as a limited matrix for grounding cultural achievement. However, the existing 26-county Republic should be recognized, like the North is now, as a vital construct which art contextualizes and by which that art itself finds meaning. Like the North, the Republic produces a variety of disjunctions of unreal and real, margin and centre, which are fundamental to the imaginative process itself. The 26-county Republic offers, as does the North, a peculiarly fructive combination of immediacy and incoherence, reality and idealism, truth and falsity as conditions within which poetry's purposes can be understood.

Irish women's poetry is like the construct of the existing Republic in that the basis of its achievement is acknowledged formalism. Irish women's poetry, juxtaposed with the 26-county state since 1949, represents one subdivision which has recently attained official status through being constantly spurred and challenged but also threatened by the idealism of its own formation, alongside another. Women's poetry is to Irish poetry today what the Republic is to the whole island. Initially this seems a preposterous contention. Firstly, as Eavan Boland has influentially argued, territorial criteria are precisely the condition of discouraging and rendering invisible poetry by Irish women as women – but as Boland herself has also argued, Irish women poets cannot afford to ignore the territorial constructs such as nationalism which have shaped their lives, because to do so is to ignore the history of the woman poet's own silence which must be confronted before her effective speech in poetry is possible.[32] Precisely because political geography and gender interconnect so extensively in Irish culture, it is important to find out how each operate as constructs, and this is best done by examining their parallel as well as their intersecting relationships.

However, many critics will argue that even if the fact of such a territorial analogy is valid, relative proportion should require that poetry by Irish men be equated with the Republic and poetry by women with the North of Ireland. Indeed, conflicts over the necessity or appropriateness of the category 'woman poet' do at first suggest a closer analogy with the North than the South of Ireland. This North–women alignment is broadly suggested in criticism of Irish women's poetry which considers the marginalization of women's poetry, as of women in general, as a prime example of the failure of 'post-independence Ireland' (that is, the Republic in waiting or in actuality) to treat all its citizens equally.[33] More specifically, critics link all-Ireland women's poetry to Northern poetry in order to celebrate distinctive achievement in one or both. For Edna Longley, women's poetry performs a revisionist function in relation to a monolithic concept of 'Irish' poetry;[34] for Clair Wills, women's poetry and Northern poetry are both engaged in 'rethinking the relationship between the lyric and history', producing 'alternative modes of remembrance, which can take account of absence and articulate a sense of loss without offering the poem as substitute or consolation for that loss'.[35] Implicitly, male poetry from the South is found wanting. More clearly, the temptation of women poets, in Eavan Boland's words, to feminize their perceptions rather than humanize their femininity under the pressure of urgently felt need to represent suppressed identities and socio-sexual violence[36] resonates with the well-documented pressure experienced by Northern Irish poets since 1969 to respond tribally to territorial violence.[37]

But it seems to me that the 26-county Republic, rather than the North of Ireland, still has one over-riding claim to operate as the more appropriate parallel for Irish women's poetry, at its present stage of development. This claim depends on the fact that the Republic exists, in political terms, as a self-governing democracy formed through compromise, with hope and history coming together in slant-rhyme. (The 1998 Good Friday Agreement and the formation of the Northern Ireland Assembly may gradually be challenging the distinction I make here between the forms of government in Southern and Northern Ireland.) The clear and (now officially) accepted gap between aspiration and reality in the constitutional identity of the existing Republic mirrors that within which Irish women's poetry works in its effort to fully represent female identity. The Republic of Ireland is one of the most useful figures available for an Irish women's poetry that, like the existing Republic, is a categorizing unit whose conditions dynamically unite confidence with insecurity. The 26-county Republic and Irish women's poetry are each constituted through a history of three types of presence: virtual, suppressed and actual. These operate simultaneously rather than consecutively in time. The result for both the Republic and women's poetry in Ireland is that a vital gap between aspiration and achievement is closed as well as dynamically resisting being closed. This historical condition is also an ontological condition of the two constructs under debate: with regard to both the idea of a republic and the idea of a women's poetry in the Irish context, the political reach to the Other (that which is not yet or fully represented) foregrounds a utopian reach to the ideal, which is an inherent characteristic of republics and of women's poetry. Whether or not the Irish Republic expands to become a 32-county state, and, equivalently, no matter how numerically strong Irish women's poetry becomes in the field of Irish poetry as a whole, their aspiration for completion can never be fulfilled. The Republic desires to fully represent or 'contain' both nation and individual together, and Irish women's poetry, both collective and individual Irish woman (whether we talk about 'woman' in the poem as poet, speaker, subject or formal or thematic gendered perspective). But no part of these compound aims can succeed. This failure invalidates neither the aspiration to complete representation by Irish Republic or woman's poem, nor the movement towards its realization, nor challenges to the assumptions of monolithic nationhood and monolithic gender identity which underlie such an aspiration. To summarize, then, the main argument (using the terms of the title of this chapter which are now to be investigated): the existing Irish Republic and Irish women's poetry are in analogous and hence mutually revelatory relation because, in each, form and formalism are in creative tension.

An important development in the South's official relation to itself as an independent political unit illustrates the relationship between formalism and form – or false and true representation – which I argue is central to the achievement of both the existing Republic as a construct, and Irish women's poetry. The *OED*'s definition of 'formalism' as both 'strict or excessive adherence to prescribed forms' and 'the manipulation according to certain formal rules of symbols that are intrinsically meaningless' informs this argument. In 1927 Fianna Fáil's entry to the Dáil meant that the oath of allegiance to the British crown (a condition of participation in the Dáil and therefore in the government of the Free State) changed from being a 'form of words' that was considered meaningful by the main political parties (who either accepted it and entered the Dáil, or not) to one that would henceforth be considered as enablingly meaningless in that it allowed for broader, hence truer, representation of the Irish people than before. This emptying of the oath of its substance is an example of a form becoming an enabling formalism: a working compromise between denying reality and being true to it. It is an example of linguistic expediency, questionable but politically purposeful. This is challenged by, but also has its parallels in, Irish poetry male and female, particularly in the period since the mid-1960s. It is the adoption of an openly false or fantastic position in relation to the materials or ideals one is representing, in order to truly represent them. The work of Paul Muldoon, Nuala Ní Dhomhnaill, Medbh McGuckian, Paul Durcan and the later Seamus Heaney, to name but a few, immediately springs to mind. It is a central drive in the aesthetic of Irish women poets and has been influentially theorized by Eavan Boland.

Boland's aesthetic makes a careful distinction between form and formalism.[38] 'Formalism'[39] is the use of those formal devices – images, metaphors, tropes and icons – which signal an inbuilt restriction of 'the full report of the reality conveyed to [the poet] by his awareness'[40] and which are 'manipulative to material'.[41] The primary example of formalism explored in Boland's aesthetic is the employment of women in Irish poetry as 'ornamental icons and figments of national expression',[42] damaging because, like the erotic object in a love poem, this iconography meant 'the ascribing of vision and perception to the speaker and only movement to the spoken-of'.[43] For Boland, formalism is marked by an antipathy between style and truth and an 'ornamental relation between imagination and image';[44] form is marked by an alliance between style and truth and an ethical relation between imagination and image: 'I suppose it is the nightmare of every artist that the form in which he works, the materials he moulds, has a double option. It can represent and it can misrepresent; it can be a force for truth and a method of distortion. I have always been aware of the dual possibilities within poetry'.[45] But exactly this 'dual possibility' is central to Boland's and other Irish women and men poets' achievements as writers.

Such dual possibility in poetry is present because it is a precise equivalent of a central tension in culture at large which women poets focus on. In the tradition of Mangan, Synge, O'Faoláin and Muldoon, women poets North and South explore the precariousness of ideals of a pure identity by investigating the danger that form (a fully present authentic identity) will yield to formalism (replicated aggression against the other), in the very act of defending its integrity. Mary O'Malley's 'Peasants'[46] challenges reflex antipathy to the colonial romanticization of Ireland by comparing native direct aggression to the kind indirectly practised through exoticization. The poem in total goes:

> Her uncle said they were all
> a shower of English feckers
> that should be shot. Useless
> to the earth and all that walked it.
> That shower
> thought we were still peasants.
>
> Isn't a peasant a bird,
> a lovely shiny bird
> that lives in trees
> and gets shot? Nor far off
> her uncle said.

As the poem wryly demonstrates, both sides threaten with guns. The uncle here might represent the kind of poet who Boland criticizes, who writes a poem which 'accrue[s] too much power to the speaker to allow that speaker to be himself a plausible critic of power'.[47] She summarizes the danger for Irish women of an Irish poetic tradition that has become reliant on formalism: 'the Irish poem ... demoted and suspected women's experience, exactly as the society it occurred in demoted and suspected that experience' so that there was 'a correlation between the conservative elements of [the] art-form and [the] society'.[48] The danger exists, by extension, for any Irish person whose group identity is used in an uncritically generalized manner either in the poem's direct content or as an aspect of its form.

But such formalism can be turned to the good through redefining the political poem, in Boland's words, as 'a rebalancing of the perceived relation of power between an inner and an outer world[49] ... so that the fracture in one annotates the wound in the other'.[50] Boland's aesthetic suggests this 'inner' world as both the silenced role of the poet in his or her poem on Irish history, and the equivalently silenced role of Irish women in that history. A rebalancing of silenced poet/woman with the history they annotate and are part of is most powerfully effected through metaphorically re-connecting each side through their joint experience of need and loss: 'the truths of womanhood [and of author-hood] and the defeats of a nation'.[51] Only such recognition of double negatives has the power to reverse form's collapse into formalism.

One of Boland's most famous and most controversial poems illustrates this paradox: in 'Mise Eire'[52] the speaker as female is simultaneously both the icon of Ireland (Mise *Eire*) that elides the suppressed elements of the country's history (such as the lives of its whores and emigrants), and herself what *is* elided (*Mise* Eire). Therefore the speaker at once models the mask demanded by nation, and the emptiness beneath it. However, this misrepresentation is resisted, not by taking off the forced disguise, but by splitting it into oppositional but equally stereotypical masks, such as those of garrison prostitute and emigrant mother: 'who neither/knows nor cares' that she functions here as 'a new language' that is 'a kind of scar' which 'heals after a while/into a passable imitation/of what went before'. This new language of stereotype is riskily like the old one but with one vital difference: it is 'a kind of scar' which heals, not into the pure flesh of historically lived experience, but into a 'passable imitation' of it. In other words, this is representation marking its own failure to represent, instead *enacting* the very tension between false and true representation which is endemic in the foundations of modern Irish culture, and arguing that only such a formalism counteracts form-alism: it is the turning of 'one flawed head towards another'.[53] Eiléan Ní Chuilleanáin in 'The Promise' uses the same trope of scar to similarly call for recognition of the mechanics of representation as a formalism which only in its open compromise of truth, paradoxically guarantees it:

> In retrospect, it was all
> A prelude to the embarkation.
> I watch the bones, and they begin to shine,
>
> Where, like a welded scar, we show
> Where we have split and healed askew –[54]

Northern Irish women's poetry demonstrates clear links with that of the Republic in recognizing the potential of formalism. Medbh McGuckian's early poem 'Slips'[55] in exemplifying this recognition, can be regarded as foundational in her aesthetic. The poem is an examination of studied artistic effects and the role of language in both creating and subverting them. The first stanza describes the perfect constructed artist's images such as 'The apple tree that makes the whitest wash'. The serpent in this study of Eden is presented as the unreliability of a woman's (this artist's) language: she 'forget[s] names, remembering them wrongly/Where they touch upon another name'. The poem then moves to a vital comparison of the insecure idyll of the artefact's created effect, with both the condition of remembered childhood and the national story: 'My childhood is preserved as a nation's history'. The poet suggests that all three of these forms for containing experience are 'favourite fairytales': useful provisional dwellings for an identity in the process of inventing itself, 'shells /leased by the hermit crab'. McGuckian implicitly compares the construction of the 'nation's history' to her own processes of control through artistic vision which allow her, likewise, the permission to reverse time and to enter, uninvited, worlds not her own. Thus the paradox of national aspiration is dramatized as both the preservation of the moment of her grandmother's or national mother's demise ('see[ing]' her death as 'a piece of ice') and the reversal of this stasis by the 'restor[ation]' of her (national) mother's 'slimness' to her. This paradox-constitued identity, recognized as such, is the only key which can be 'slotted' in the door of the sceptical reader or oppositional political tradition – the only fitting means of opening two-way access between their world and hers. Identity (personal, poetic and historical) operates as an ironic seduction which both requires the reader's complicity and insists on their awareness of that seduction as process through effects:

> Tricks you might guess from this unfastened button,
> A pen mislaid, a word misread,
> My hair coming down in the middle of a conversation.

The calculated innocence of seduction becomes a function of the genuine potential of formalism: of misreading as well as accurately reading the word at the same time.

Like Boland and McGuckian, Ní Chuilleanáin has developed an aesthetic of the enabling formalism that bears upon territorial identity: her volume *The Brazen Serpent* centres around the efficacy of any dominant icon of falsity to cure the damage done by falsity. In 'The Real Thing',[56] a nun exposes a relic of the old testament serpent as a paradoxical means of resisting the veiling of womankind in guilt and silence after the Fall: the 'torn end of the serpent' is 'the one free foot kicking/ Under the white sheet of history'. Nuala Ní Dhomhnaill's larger project is closely related to that of other Irish women poets dealt with here in that she dramatizes (most famously through the figure of the *Bean an Leasa* or fairy woman) how vital elements of the female or national psyche, once suppressed, become tools of formalism stalking the personal and communal unconscious; only the confrontation of these formalistic spectres of the self in their full threatening natures can allow the self to be reclaimed in an integrated way: again, only formalism cures formalism. Paula Meehan's poetry is related to Ní Dhomhnaill's in its exploration of the exchange of identities between women, or the witness to ideal identity which men and women offer each other, as moments of achieved willed balance between the forces of attraction and repulsion to pre-constructed patterns of identity (that is, to formalism), whereby those limitations are converted into sources of personal power. One such moment is that which concludes Meehan's most famous poem when the speaker describes her now-lost mother who in pentecostal terms teaches her that form can be wrested from formalism: 'Tongues of flame in her dark eyes,/she'd say, 'One of these days I must/teach you to follow a pattern'.[57]

Eavan Boland similarly wrests form from formalism in a central poem in any consideration of Irish women's poetry over the past fifty years. 'Lava Cameo'[58] claims the power of acknowledged formalism by demonstrating that truth in art is a function of language's arrangement of relation to itself rather than its power to uncover external 'reality': the quality of mimesis in a poem is dependent on its self-reflexive element. 'Lava Cameo' does this by presenting a speaker attempting to reclaim another woman lost in history, Boland's own grandmother who died at the age of 31 in a fever ward. The poem theorizes its own act of reclamation through poetry as follows:

> there is a way of making free with the past,
> a pastiche of what is
> real and what is
> not, which can only be
> justified if you think of it
>
> not as sculpture but syntax:
>
> a structure extrinsic to meaning which uncovers
> the inner secret of it.

Boland uses the word 'pastiche' here as she did 'passable imitation' in 'Mise Eire', inferring that both this poem (where she imaginatively re-assembles the scene of her unknown grandmother and grandfather's reunion after his sea voyage) and the lava cameo which the poet has made into that lost woman's emblem are examples of 'syntax' in operation, or what she later in the piece – and more harshly – describes as

> the obduracy of an art which can
> arrest a profile in the flux of hell.
>
> Inscribe catastrophe.

In her prose commentary on this poem, Boland describes the brooch carved on volcanic rock as 'an elaborate sarcasm' because it 'put[s] the stamp of human remembrance on the material of . . . random and unsparing destruction'.[59] The brooch and the poem both are a 'statement of irony and corruption' in their deploying of the material of historical loss, and each self-reflexively comments on the idea of being able to use history to order, so the speaker in the poem 'Lava Cameo' demands that the face in the artefact (a face which both she and the brooch-maker have made) 'look at me'. It is the 'looking', or consciousness of the process, whereby artefact holds up artist to exposure, rather than the testifiable 'accuracy' of the testimony to external reality which that artefact may offer, which is the source of its power.[60]

Similarly Rita Ann Higgins in her poem 'Remapping the Borders'[61] has artefact testing artist, but unlike Boland in 'Lava Cameo', she finds the artist wanting. Higgins's overall aesthetic can be characterized as one which precisely dramatizes moments when form yields to formalism in Irish culture. In her early work this happens through the individual becoming the victim of larger impersonal forces of patriarchal state control, but increasingly her poems suggest that the collapse of form into disabling formalism is dependent upon that individual's refusal to see the potential of acknowledged formalism. In 'Remapping the Border', the most famous instance of formalism of them all, Cathleen Ní Houlihan enters a Texas Irish writing conference ceilí as a woman dancing the Siege of Ennis. She has a voice, however, and uses it to inquire of the margarita-drinking speaker: 'Could you see my stocking belt/as I did the swing?' The disconcerted speaker refuses to acknowledge that she obviously has seen it – has registered the mechanics by which 'sheer' identity is offered by a national icon – an erotic 'slither belt,/with lace embroidered border/that was hardly a border at all' attaching covering to skin. The speaker, ironically, excuses her retreat from this open formalism by claiming her proper attention is on exposing lies: 'I was looking for the worm in my glass'. But this retreat from a falsity playfully theatricalizing itself (in the woman's question) leads directly to the prim speaker's unwitting collusion in formalism:

> I swear to you
> I saw nothing, not even the worm
> lying on his back
> waiting to penetrate my tongue.[62]

One of the terms used in culture to describe an enabling formalism is myth. Irish women's poetry over the past fifty years has entered vigilant accommodation with the mythology of achieved identity that the term 'Republic' both represents and challenges. Poetry, Eavan Boland says, 'enters at the point where myth touches history' and here 'a sense of place can happen . . . In the first instance [myth] there are the healing repetitions, the technology of propitiation. In the second [history] there is the consciousness of violent and random event. In the zone between them something happens. Ideas of belonging take on the fluidity of sleep . . . And here, on the edge of sleep, is a place in which I locate myself as a poet'.[63] This chapter, by relating Irish women's poetry to the construct of the Republic, has sought to show that Irish women poets similarly locate themselves on the border where myth touches history, where formalism touches form.

Notes

1 See Appendix. Special thanks to Joan McBreen for advice in the later stages of its compilation.

2 See for example Terence Brown, *Ireland: A Social and Cultural History 1922–1985* (rev. ed.), (London: Fontana Press, 1985); Anne Byrne and Madeleine Leonard (eds.), *Women and Irish Society: A Sociological Reader* (Belfast: Beyond the Pale Publications, 1997); Patrick Clancy *et al.* (eds.), *Irish Society: Sociological Perspectives* (Dublin: Institute of Public Administration, 1995); Dermot Keogh, *Twentieth-Century Ireland: Nation and State* (Dublin: Gill & Macmillan, 1994); Joseph Lee, *Ireland 1912–1985: Politics and Society* (Cambridge: Cambridge University Press, 1989); Ailbhe Smyth (ed.), *Irish Women's Studies Reader* (Dublin: Attic Press, 1993).

3 Although rarely focusing on the idea of a Republic and its relationship to the existing 26-county state, useful work on the South's changing self-image *is* offered in a variety of publications such as Dermot Bolger (ed.), *Letters from the New Island* (Dublin: The Raven Arts Press, 1991); Paul Brennan and Catherine de Saint Phalle (eds.), *Arguing at the Crossroads: Essays on a Changing Ireland.* (Dublin: New Island Books, 1997); Fintan O'Toole, *Black Hole, Green Card: The Disappearance of Ireland* (Dublin: New Island Books, 1994); John Waters, *Jiving at the Crossroads* (Belfast: The Blackstaff Press, 1991), and the

series of LIP pamphlets on gender in Irish society published by Dublin's Attic Press in the late 1980s and early 1990s.

4   See Catherine B. Shannon, 'The Changing Face of Cathleen ni Houlihán: Women and Politics in Ireland, 1960–1966', in Anthony Bradley and Maryann Gialanella Valiulis (eds.), *Gender and Sexuality in Modern Ireland* (Amherst: University of Massachusetts Press, 1997), pp. 257–74; also Ailbhe Smyth, 'States of Change: Reflections on Ireland in Several Uncertain Parts', *Feminist Review*, Special Issue: 'The Irish Issue: The British Question', 50 (Summer 1995), pp. 24–43.

5   This survey was conducted by Women in Publishing (WiP); its results are quoted in Patricia Ferreira, 'Claiming and Transforming an "Entirely Gentlemanly Artifact": Ireland's Attic Press', *The Canadian Journal of Irish Studies*, 19/1 (July 1993), p. 99.

6   At the time of writing, the comparable figure for Gallery Press is two newly emerged women poets since 1985: Vona Groarke and Kerry Hardie (Gallery publishes a number of other women poets some of whose careers began elsewhere). A much more extensive study of the conditions under which women poets *and* men poets have or have not been published in Ireland is needed than has yet been made available. As well as focusing on the impact upon Irish poetry of international publishers, little magazines, the poetry reading circuit, the proliferation of workshops, summer schools and competitions, and the diversifying effect of expatriot Irish poets and non-Irish poets resident in Ireland, such a study would investigate the complex conditions under which individual poetry publishing houses in Ireland share and create a market for poetry books. Patricia Boyle Haberstroh's book, *Women Creating Women: Contemporary Irish Women Poets* (Dublin: Attic Press, 1996), includes a valuable discussion of some of the Irish social, literary and critical tradition's attitudes which informs these conditions as they relate to women poets.

7   Peter Fallon describes being challenged by Eavan Boland 'twelve years ago' on the fact that Gallery didn't then publish many women: 'I asked her to name one poet who was a woman whose work should be published and wasn't. She said that wasn't her job. Nevertheless I repeated the question, and it was by then a question we both faced. Again she was evasive. I don't believe there was a woman who was being excluded, and I've often returned to the same question.' Peter Fallon, 'Notes on a History of Publishing Poetry', *Princeton University Library Chronicle*, 59/3 (Spring 1998), p. 557.

8   Ibid.

9   See, for example, Catherine Shannon's statement that 'the poetry, prose, drama, and painting produced by creative artists . . . reflect the growing solidarity of Irish women' ('The Changing Face of Cathleen ni Houlihan', p. 271), or Lia Mills's argument that women produce 'a poetic discourse which is . . . engaged in collapsing the space between women and poetry, giving women a discernible presence in the cultural life of the country, which is, in its turn, distinct from the 'nation'.' Lia Mills, "I Won't Go Back to It': Irish Women Poets and the Iconic Feminine', *Feminist Review* Special Issue – The Irish Issue: The British Question', 50 (Summer 1995), p. 70.

10   Edna Longley and Ailbhe Smyth respectively represent the anti-nationalist and pro-feminist emphases in this thinking. Longley 'compare[s] Irish Nationalism to bad poetry' on the basis of each one's disconnection of the

image of Irish woman from women's real life, arguing in the same essay that 'As a general rule: the more Republican, the less feminist' (Gerardine Meaney has sharply criticized this rule as reductive of feminism) and criticizing Eavan Boland for not recognizing the construct of nationalism itself 'both inside and outside poetry' as extremely damaging. Longley suggests: 'Perhaps the equivalent of advanced feminist 'troubling and subverting' is precisely what our nationalist and Unionist patriarchal straitjackets need'. In including Unionism in her critique, Longley's ideas interestingly link to those of Ailbhe Smyth. For Smyth, Irish women's poetry has been badly constrained within the discourse on territory to the exclusion of critical focus on concerns such as sexuality, childhood and lesbianism: 'Irish women's poetry is no more confined to, within or by national borders than sexuality within motherhood, or sex by love, or Irish women within the jurisdiction of Ireland by legal prohibition against abortion.' Edna Longley, *The Living Stream: Literature and Revisionism in Ireland* (Newcastle upon Tyne: Bloodaxe Books, 1994), pp. 186, 191, 188, 187. Gerardine Meaney, *Sex and Nation: Women in Irish Culture and Politics* (Dublin: Attic Press, 1991), p. 12; Ailbhe Smyth, 'Dodging Around the Grand Piano', in Vicki Bertram (ed.), *Kicking Daffodils: Twentieth-Century Women Poets* (Edinburgh: Edinburgh University Press, 1997), p. 61.

11 Steven Matthews, *Irish Poetry: Politics, History, Negotiation: The Evolving Debate, 1969 to the Present* (Basingstoke and London: Macmillan Press, 1997), pp. 36–44.

12 Mary O'Malley, *The Knife in the Wave* (Galway: Salmon, 1997), p. 4.

13 See Arthur McGuinness, 'Hearth and History: Poetry by Contemporary Irish Women', in Michael Kenneally (ed.), *Cultural Contexts and Literary Idioms in Contemporary Irish Literature*, (Gerrards Cross: Colin Smythe, 1988), pp. 197–220.

14 This argument is developed elsewhere, in Catriona Clutterbuck, 'Gender and Self-Representation in Irish Poetry: The Critical Debate', *Bullán*, 4/1 (Autumn 1998), pp. 43–58.

15 See Brown, *Ireland: A Social and Cultural History*, pp. 289–92, on the argument for empirical rather than poetic or literary scales of assessment of Irish goals and achievement.

16 Longley, *The Living Stream*, p. 195.

17 Edna Longley, 'An ABC of Reading Contemporary Irish Poetry', *Princeton University Library Chronicle*, 59/3 (Spring 1998), p. 519.

18 Thomas Kinsella, 'The Divided Mind', in Sean Lucy (ed.), *Irish Poets in English* (Cork and Dublin: The Mercier Press, 1972), pp. 208–18; Thomas Kinsella, *The Dual Tradition: An Essay on Poetry and Politics in Ireland* (Manchester: Carcanet Press, 1995); Tom Paulin, 'A New Look at the Language Question', in *Ireland's Field Day* (London: Hutchinson, 1985).

19 Matthews, *Irish Poetry: Politics, History, Negotiation*; Michael Smith, 'The Contemporary Situation in Irish Poetry', in Douglas Dunn (ed.), *Two Decades of Irish Writing: A Critical Survey*, (Cheadle: Carcanet, 1975); Samuel Beckett, 'Recent Irish Poetry' [1934], *Disjecta – Miscellaneous Writings and a Dramatic Fragment* (London: John Calder, 1983), pp. 70–6.

20 Brown, *Ireland: A Social and Cultural History*, pp. 312–25; Longley, *The Living Stream*, pp. 196–226; Sebastian Barry, 'Introduction: The History and

Topography of Nowhere', in Sebastian Barry (ed.), *The Inherited Boundaries: Younger Poets of the Republic of Ireland* (Portlaoise: The Dolmen Press, 1986), pp. 13–29.

21 Brown, *Ireland: A Social and Cultural History*, pp. 312–14.

22 Barry, 'Introduction', p. 16.

23 Nuala Ní Dhomhnaill's fourteen-poem sequence on a mysteriously appearing and disappearing island off the coast of Ireland titled 'Immram' (translated, appropriately, by Paul Muldoon) makes an interesting comment on Barry's Republic-as-no-place. Nuala Ni Dhomhnaill/Paul Muldoon, *The Astrakhan Cloak* (Oldcastle: The Gallery Press, 1992), pp. 72–103.

24 See Terence Brown, *Ireland's Literature: Selected Essays* (Dublin: The Lilliput Press, 1988), pp. 203–22; Longley, *The Living Stream*, pp. 196–226; Neil Corcoran, *After Joyce and Yeats: Reading Modern Irish Literature* (Oxford: Oxford University Press, 1997), pp. 140–53.

25 For example, Longley compares Paul Muldoon's and Thomas Kinsella's projects in producing anthologies of Irish poetry by remarking that 'Muldoon's politics . . . seem more intrinsically aesthetic than Kinsella's in that he favours [in selecting his contributors] a concentration akin to his own'. She does, however, note that these Muldoonian criteria 'bar John Hewitt as well as Brendan Kennelly'. *The Living Stream*, p. 201.

26 Longley argues that 'Belfast is Irish poetry's strangest port of call. Once damned as the antithesis of poetry, the city has become its locus and focus . . . Perfection and finality – not "closure" but words at their most intense moments – still attract poets from Northern Ireland, such as Muldoon, Carson and McGuckian.' 'An ABC of Reading Contemporary Irish Poetry', pp. 519, 525.

27 Clair Wills, *Improprieties: Politics and Sexuality in Northern Irish Poetry* (Oxford: Oxford University Press, 1993), pp. 47–8.

28 See John Kerrigan, 'Hidden Ireland: Eiléan Ní Chuilleanáin and Munster Poetry', *Critical Quarterly*, 40/4 (Winter 1998), pp. 76–100, and Dillon Johnston, '"Our Bodies' Eyes and Writing Hands": Secrecy and Sensuality in Ní Chuilleanáin's Baroque Art', in Bradley and Gialanella Valiulus (eds.), *Gender and Sexuality in Modern Ireland*, pp. 187–211.

29 Wills, *Improprieties*, p. 48.

30 Jody Allen-Randolph, 'An Interview with Eavan Boland', *Irish University Review*, 23/1 (Spring/Summer 1993), p. 130.

31 See, for example, Caitriona O'Reilly, 'Testaments of a native daughter', Review of Eavan Boland, *The Lost Land*, *The Irish Times* (Saturday 10 October 1998), Weekend p. 11.

32 Eavan Boland, *Object Lessons: The Life of the Woman and the Poet in Our Time* (Manchester: Carcanet 1995), pp. 123–53.

33 In the context of assessments such as Gerardine Meaney's that 'Women, in everything which is specific to them as women, are quite obviously not citizens of the Republic', Patricia Boyle Haberstroh argues: 'If we are to understand the marginalised woman poet we must first study the marginalised woman in Ireland'. Clair Wills defines Eavan Boland's poetic on this basis as a suffragette one: '[Boland] seeks not to challenge the basis of the poet's authority, but to widen the political constituency, adding women to the electoral rolls.' Ailbhe Smyth argues for abandoning any such effort to

negotiate with a national tradition: 'Irish poets – especially women – do not necessarily write Irish poems.' Geraldine Meaney, *Sex and Nation*, p. 8; Haberstroh, *Women Creating Women*, p. 13; Wills, *Improprieties*, p. 59, Smyth, 'Dodging Around the Grand Piano', p. 60.

34 The paucity of representation of women poets and debates on gender in the 1991 *Field Day Anthology* formed one of the main planks of Longley's castigation of that publication as nationalist literary hegemony. See also her assertion that Northern Ireland promotes a 'female, feminist, connective' web-like 'range of social relations rather than a single allegiance'. *The Living Stream*, pp. 34–6; p. 195.

35 Clair Wills, 'Modes of Redress: The Elegy in Recent Irish Poetry', *Princeton University Library Chronicle*, 59/3 (Spring 1998), p. 599.

36 Boland, *Object Lessons*, p. 245.

37 Lia Mills comes close to applying this pressure in her work on Irish women poets, arguing that 'There is a civil as well as an aesthetic aspect to the role of the poet within a community, which is well recognized . . . We demand more from our poets than art, as if their presence, their voice, their vitality is an essential part of the process.' For answer, Denis O'Driscoll's argument in relation to Northern poets working in a context of tribal violence speaks also to women poets in a context of misogyny: 'The poet must be faithful to the art of poetry as well as to the facts of the situation. A 'balanced' poetry would be bland, and a protest poetry would be unbalanced.' Mills, 'Irish Women Poets and the Iconic Feminine', p. 82; Denis O'Driscoll, 'Troubled Thoughts: Poetry Politics in Contemporary Ireland', *The Southern Review* 31/3 (July 1995), p. 645.

38 Boland first uses the term 'formalism' in an essay first published in 1989 to describe negative reactions among American critics to poets' use of the lyric as dooming poetry to 'inbuilt restrictions'. Eavan Boland, 'The Serinette Principle: The Lyric in Contemporary Poetry', reprinted in *PN Review*, 19/4 (March/April 1993), p. 23.

39 There is an interesting tangential relationship between Boland's concept of formalism and the theory developed by Sklovskij and the Russian Formalists between 1916 and 1930. Like the Formalists, Boland holds that technique and form are the means to artistic creation, but in the early part of her career, unlike the Russian theorists, she condemns form as the goal of that creation on the basis of art's resulting neglect of social and psychological reality. However (as the poems to be examined show), the later Boland, while still distant from Formalism's elevation of the literary over the mimetic, nevertheless sees the representative act of the poet as a vital part of content and thus can be said to adapt Formalist theory to her own purposes. She recognizes that reality can only be expressed in its complexity – that is, with due reference to its subjective as well as objective elements – if form is a goal as well as means of artistic creation, but one that exposes its own acts of subterfuge at the very moment of justifying itself.

40 Boland, citing Alan Tate, *Object Lessons*, p. 133.

41 Rebecca E. Wilson, 'Eavan Boland', in Gillean Somerville-Arjat and Rebecca E. Wilson (eds.), *Sleeping With Monsters: Conversations with Scottish and Irish Women Poets* (Dublin: Wolfhound Press, 1990), p. 81.

42 Boland, 'The Woman Poet in a National Tradition', *Studies* 76 (302), p.155.

43 Boland, *Object Lessons* p. 214. Boland's critique here is of Robert Herrick's 'Upon Julia's Clothes'.
44 Boland, *Object Lessons*, p. 152.
45 Eavan Boland, 'Religion and Poetry', *The Furrow*, 33/12 (December 1982), p. 748.
46 Mary O'Malley, *Where the Rocks Float* (Galway: Salmon Press, 1993), p. 6.
47 Eavan Boland, *Object Lessons*, p. 191.
48 Jody Allen-Randolph, 'An Interview with Eavan Boland', pp. 121/122.
49 Eavan Boland, 'P.B.S. Choice Spring 1994', *P.B.S. Bulletin*, 160 (Spring 1994), pp. 1/2.
50 Boland, *Object Lessons*, p. 190. The concept of fracture annotating wound is a synopsis of Boland's famous statement in her essay 'Outside History' (1987) where the intersection of the defeats of womanhood and the suffering of a nation are suggested as liberating. *Object Lessons*, p. 148.
51 Ibid.
52 Eavan Boland, *Collected Poems* (Manchester: Carcanet, 1995), p. 102.
53 Eavan Boland, 'The Scar', *The Lost Land* (Manchester: Carcanet, 1998), p. 19. Similarly, in Eiléan Ní Chuilleanáin's poem 'J'ai Mal à nos Dents', a nun in old age returns to her family to nurse her sister, saying 'Une malade à soigner une malade'. Eiléan Ní Chuilleanáin, *The Magdalen Sermon* (Oldcastle: Gallery Press, 1989), p. 29.
54 Ní Chuilleanáin, *The Magdalen Sermon*, p. 40.
55 Medbh McGuckian, *The Flower Master* [2nd. ed.] (Oldcastle: Gallery Press, 1993), p. 21.
56 Eiléan Ní Chuilleanáin, *The Brazen Serpent* (Oldcastle: Gallery Press, 1994), p. 16.
57 Paula Meehan, 'The Pattern', *The Man Who Was Marked By Winter* (Oldcastle: Gallery Press, 1991), p. 17.
58 Boland, *Collected Poems*, p. 195.
59 Boland, *Object Lessons*, pp. 34, 33.
60 Boland displays great awareness of the frailty of the poet within her poem. 'If [the lava cameo, object and poem] was a witticism in the face of terror, if it made an ornament of it, what else was memory? Yet in the end, in my need to make a construct of that past, it came down to a simple fact. I had no choice.' Formalism is here granted permission to own the potential to become form. *Object Lessons*, p. 34.
61 Rita Ann Higgins, *Higher Purchase* (Cliffs of Moher: Salmon Press, 1996), p. 38.
62 This poem's ironic relation to its speaker is related to that in Nuala Ní Dhomhnaill's more direct poem on the same subject, 'Caitlín'. Ní Dhomhnaill/Muldoon, *The Astrakhan Cloak*, p. 38/39.
63 Boland, *Object Lessons*, pp. 166, 172.

Permission has been received from Mary O'Malley to quote from her poem 'Interior' and to quote the poem 'Peasants' in full.

Appendix

Irish Women Poets with Dates of Main Collections of New Poetry, 1949–99
Allen, Dell (1975)

Archer, Nuala (1981, 1992, 1995)
Bardwell, Leland (1970, 1984, 1991, 1998)
Berkeley, Sara (1986, 1989, 1994)
Bleakney, Jean (1999)
Boland, Eavan (1967, 1975, 1980, 1982, 1987, 1990, 1994, 1998)
Boland, Rosita (1991)
Bourke, Eva (1985, 1989, 1996)
Bracken, Carmel RSM (1992)
Bradshaw, Máire (1988, 1992)
Brennan, Deirdre (1984, 1989, 1993)
Brennan, Lucy (1999)
Brett, Heather (1991, 1994)
Burke Brogan, Patricia (1994)
Byron, Catherine (1985, 1987, 1993, 1999)
Callaghan, Louise (1999)
Callan, Annie (1995)
Campbell, Siobhán (1996)
Canavan, Rosemary (1994)
Cannon, Moya (1990, 1997)
Carr, Ruth (1999)
Casey, Juanita (1968, 1985)
Charleton, Maureen (1990, 1997)
Cimino, Glenda (1988)
Cluysenaar, Anne (1971, 1982, 1997)
Coghill, Rhoda (1948, 1956)
Concannon, Helena (1953)
Connolly, Susan (1993)
Cowman, Roz (1989)
Crowley, Vicki (1992)
Cullen, Yvonne (1998)
Cunningham, Paula (1999)
Dáibhís, Bríd (1978, 1989, 1999)
de Fréine, Celia (1997)
de Valera, Sinéad (1961)
Donaldson, Moyra (1998)
Donovan, Katie (1993, 1997)
Dorcey, Mary (1982, 1991, 1995)
Dowdican, Anna-Marie (1998)
Duffy, Katherine (1998)
Evans, Martina (1995, 1998)
Fayne, Pauline (1979)
Fitzpatrick Simmons, Janice (1995, 1999)
Flynn, Anna Maria (1981)
Fyffe, Anne-Marie (1999)
Graham, Catherine (1998)
Greene, Angela (1993)
Greig, Rene (1999)
Groarke, Vona (1994, 1999)
Hardie, Kerry (1996)

Haverty, Anne (1999)
Higgins, Rita Ann (1986, 1988, 1992, 1996)
Hill, Nora (1968)
Holmes, Máire C. (1988)
Hurson, Tess (1997)
Jenkinson, Biddy (1986, 1988, 1991, 1997)
Kelly, Maeve (1986)
Kelly, Rita (1984, 1990)
Kennedy, Anne (1989, 1994)
Le Marquand Hartigan, Anne (1982, 1986, 1991, 1993)
Lendennie, Jessie (1988)
McBreen, Joan (1990, 1995)
MacCarthy, Catherine Phil (1994, 1998)
McCarthy, Patricia (1975, 1985)
McGuckian, Medbh (1982, 1984, 1988, 1991, 1994, 1998)
McKiernan, Ethna (1989)
McLoghlen, Diana (1972)
McPhilemy, Kathleen (1990, 1996)
Martin, Eilish (1999)
Martin, Orla (1996)
Maude, Caitlín (1984)
Medbh, Maighréad (1990, 1999)
Meehan, Paula (1984, 1986, 1991, 1994)
Mhac an tSaoi, Máire (1956, 1973, 1980, 1988)
Miller, Áine (1994, 1999)
Moran, Lynda (1985)
Morrissey, Sinéad (1996)
Murdock, Iris (1978)
Murphy, Lizz (1994, 1997)
Newmann, Joan (1995, 1998)
Nic Aodha, Colette (1998)
Ní Chuilleanáin, Eiléan (1972, 1975, 1981, 1989, 1994)
Nic Ghearailt, Máire Áine (1971, 1990, 1990, 1991, 1992)
Ní Dhomhnaill, Nuala (1981, 1984, 1991, 1992, 1993, 1998, 1999)
Ní Dhomhnalláin, Máirín (1997)
Ní Ghallchóir, Colette (1999)
Ní Ghlinn, Áine (1984, 1988, 1996)
Ní Mhóráin, Brighid (1992)
Ní Shúilleabháin, Siobhán (1999)
O'Brien, Jean (1997)
O'Callaghan, Julie (1983, 1986, 1988, 1991, 1998)
O'Connor, Clairr (1989)
O'Donnell, Mary (1990, 1993, 1998)
O'Driscoll, Kathleen (1980)
O'Hagan, Lily (1991)
O'Hagan, Sheila (1992, 1995)
O'Mahony, Nessa (1999)
O'Malley, Mary (1990, 1993, 1997)
Parkinson, Barbara (1995)

Paterson, Evangeline (1972, 1978, 1983, 1991, 1994, 1997)
Patten, Angela (1999)
Peters, Anne (1982)
Rowley, Rosemarie (1985, 1987, 1989)
Scales, Audrey (1983)
Scanlan, Patricia (1988)
Shanahan, Deirdre (1988)
Shepperson, Janet (1995)
Slade, Jo (1989, 1994)
Strong, Eithne (1943, 1961, 1974, 1980, 1980, 1983, 1985, 1990, 1990, 1990, 1993, 1998)
Sullivan, Breda (1992, 1998)
Taylor, Alice (1990, 1998)
Thompson, Kate (1992)
Tompkin, Diana (1959)
Uí Fhlatharta, Máire (1989)
Uí Fhoghlú, Áine (1999)
Uí Nuanáin, Máire (1998)
Vial, Noelle (1995)
Walsh, Catherine (1989, 1994)
Wichert, Sabine (1993, 1995, 1999)
Wingfield, Sheila (1938, 1946, 1949, 1954, 1964, 1977, 1978)
Wyley, Enda (1993, 1998)
Zell, Ann (1998)

Printed Sources

Hogan, Robert (ed.), *Dictionary of Irish Literature* (2 vols., rev. ed.; Westport, Connecticut and London: Greenwood Press and Aldwich Press, 1996).
McBreen, Joan, *The White Page/An Bhileog Bhán – Twentieth Century Irish Women Poets* (Cliffs of Moher: Salmon Press, 1999).
Weekes, Ann Owens, *Unveiling Treasures: The Attic Guide to the Published Works of Irish Women Literary Writers* (Dublin: Attic Press, 1993).

2

Acts of Memory: Poetry and the Republic of Ireland since 1949

Jonathan Allison

Edna Longley begins her study of twentieth-century poetry, *Poetry in the Wars*, with the observation that as she wrote her book, 'two themes converged: poetry's relation to public conflicts of the last seventy-five years; and the conflict between "traditionalism" and "Modernism" which has raged in its own backyard.'[1] Longley tends to associate the traditional with poets like Yeats, Hardy or Edward Thomas, rooted poets of place, and modernism with the international cosmopolitan poetics of Eliot and Pound. In *Poetry in the Wars*, the former are championed, while the cosmopolitanism of the latter is regretted. One might say that the tension between tradition and modernity is common to all modern enterprises, and merely reflects the need of the artist to deal with the inherent tension between tradition and the individual talent, by Eliotsian cultivation of a sense of the past, or Bloomian patricide, or by some other form of accommodation with history. Yet the dichotomy rears its two heads again and again in many accounts of modern and contemporary Irish poetry. For Richard Kearney, the division is inherent in modern Irish culture generally: 'In our century Ireland has witnessed a crisis of culture. This has often been experienced as a conflict between the claims of tradition and modernity.' Irish culture needs to effect a transition from past to future, and the task undertaken by numerous practitioners of the arts has been 'to narrate the problematic relationship between tradition and modernity'.[2] Every artist, for Kearney, is thus engaged in a dialogue with tradition. Those who tend to revive the past he dubs revivalist (uncontroversially enough), and those who repudiate or rewrite it, modernist. The artistic juggling between the two areas, the narration of this transition, obviously requires particular kinds of talent, based upon a hunger for innovation and a responsible awareness of the richness of the past and its resources.

Arguments similar to Kearney's can be heard from a variety of critical sources: Maurice Harmon, in his introduction to the anthology *Irish Poetry After Yeats*, writes: 'The concept of tradition, as an actual entity, to be drawn upon, to be extended, deepened, or reinterpreted, is also central.'[3] Harmon stresses, like Kearney, the way in which poets have borrowed or learned from, built upon, but hardly repudiated the various heritages to which they were heirs. The response of post-Yeatsian poets to tradition, and the Revival, is of course central to many accounts of modern poetry. Indeed, the dialogue between tradition and innovation has been dubbed one of the master-narratives of cultural history, and when we think of the late nineteenth-century inheritance that fed into the Celtic Revival ('and all that stir of thought', in Yeats's words), and the response to that inheritance after independence, it would be foolish to ignore this model entirely. Robert Welch's remarks in *Changing States* offer as ambitious a synthesis as Kearney's, and are equally compelling:

> We may sum up and say that the preoccupation with continuity in Irish culture and literature is linked to a desire for stasis and negation, a human desire, by no means confined to Ireland. Against this, in Irish culture, in culture generally, and continually begot by and begetting its opposite, there is a desire for variation and ceaseless change. A tension of this kind probably underlies all creative activity, and indeed probably lies at the root of language itself.[4]

For him, this characteristic tussle between kinesis and stasis, creativity and that which is inherited is fundamental to language and to culture itself. Clearly, Welch is partly influenced here by the Blakean doctrine, 'without contraries is no progression', and other modern dialectical systems, including Yeats's theory of the gyres or indeed his theory of poetry as the 'quarrel with the self'. Undoubtedly, the six aforementioned authors (Longley, Kearney, Harmon, Garratt, Johnston and Welch) each define tradition and modernity in slightly different ways, but many of them – with the exception of Longley, perhaps, who is interested in English forms of 'traditionalism' as well as the case of Yeats – construe Revivalism as a form of traditionalism, and the literature of the counter-Revival as a form of Modernism. Also, if this dichotomy may be applicable to a hundred years of literature, it is often applied to the Irish post-1949 period.

Irish poetry since 1949 certainly has been read in these terms. Patrick Crotty, for example, distinguishes between two main strains in modern

Irish poetry since the death of Yeats, in the course of his introduction to his recent anthology, *Modern Irish Poetry*: 'Austin Clarke, John Hewitt, Richard Murphy, Thomas Kinsella, John Montague, Seamus Heaney, Michael Hartnett, Eavan Boland, Tom Paulin extend a characteristically Yeatsian and Revivalist practice insofar as they approach the present through a heroising reading of the past.'[5] On the other hand, he argues, another significant group of writers (Kavanagh, Coffey, Beckett, MacNeice, Durcan, McGuckian) 'takes a stand on the primacy of the here-and-now'. They offer 'the indirect homage of counterstatement to the Literary Revival's premise that only a recovery of the past can effect liberation in the present'. This sense of a dichotomous history, with writers veering off in two opposite directions, has been delivered repeatedly. For instance, Robert Garratt and Dillon Johnston both published books in the 1980s predicated on the two antithetical Yeatsian and Joycean traditions (one mythological, recuperative, heroising, and the other quotidian, rooted in the present, ironical in relation to the past, and in a sense 'realistic').[6] As Crotty knows, he is using broad brush-strokes in his portrait of the period, and it is possible to think of moments in each of the aforementioned author's works when they don't quite fit the category, or indeed seem to share qualities with poets of the other, supposedly antithetical category. However, I wish to use the distinction as the basis for some remarks on postwar Irish poetry in relation to the ideas of memory and cultural memory, paying particular attention to Heaney, Durcan, O'Loughlin and Boland.

Maurice Harmon, again, in his introduction to *Irish Poetry After Yeats*, makes a similar sort of distinction: 'The diminishments of the Irish heritage, a constant factor throughout the modern period, results in two major directions: the extensions outward into European and other cultures and the extensions backward into the Irish past.' The terms aren't identical to Crotty's, though they do suggest opposing tendencies of the Neo-Revivalist backward look and the Euro-modernism of a counter-Revivalist internationalism.[7]

Paul Muldoon's prefatory matter, published in lieu of an introduction, to his *Faber Book of Contemporary Irish Poetry* takes the form of an old BBC dialogue between F. R. Higgins and Louis MacNeice, and similarly conveys this sense of dual origins for the period (whether we call those origins Revivalist and Modernist, Romantic and sceptical, essentialist and relativist, or nativist and cosmopolitan).[8] Higgins argues for lots of things that, by the standards of 1985 (the date of publication), sound romantic and anachronistic, and the reader readily applauds MacNeice's plea for common sense, rationality and a strategic poetic impurity. The preface might appear to some readers almost unfair in the way that Higgins, in his advocacy of what appears to be a rather moth-eaten, mystical nationalism, is clearly the straw man. He is merely, in the words of Neil Corcoran, 'fall guy to MacNeice'.[9]

For Higgins, Irish poetry is traditionally 'pure', modern, but 'not modernist,' expressive of spirituality, and a 'sense of magic'. Rooted in rural civilisation, it expresses the Irish racial character.[10] By contrast, MacNeice responds with a more self-consciously rationalist, cosmopolitan and urbane perspective. Seemingly bemused, but mildly irked by Higgins's words, he argues that modern poetry should be 'impure'; above all, it should be honest, and he is sceptical of Higgins's ideas of racial character and 'blood music', which seem to him chauvinist and mystical, if not indeed nonsensical – 'one's racial blood music ... may be left to look after itself'. The poet, for him, is merely a 'sensitive instrument designed to record anything which interests his mind or affects his emotions'. MacNeice's poet is secular, quasi-scientific, taxonomic, yet voracious, and open to experience.

As a preface to the volume, this was a peculiar choice on Muldoon's part, entailing as it did the complete absence of editorial commentary or judgement. Clearly, as with an epigraph, he expects the reader to intuit, or deduce, what exactly this all means in relation to the poetry collected in the book. The key issue is that there are two widely divergent but highly influential views on modern poetry and nationality being presented. Higgins's beliefs seems Yeatsian in some respects, notably in his stress on the crucial connection between poetry and national character, his interest in spirituality and rurality. MacNeice, on the other hand, seems post- or counter-Revivalist in tendency, and in many respects the dialogue echoes the dichotomy introduced by Crotty in his introduction to his anthology. It would appear, then, that this distinction between neo- and counter-Revivalism has become canonical, a reading of the period institutionalised by the editors of several recent anthologies.

Many proponents of the Literary Revival wished to revive through translation the Gaelic or Irish-language heritage that the ascendancy of the English language in Ireland since the eighteenth century had suppressed. As we have seen, this mentality lies behind the remarks of a Higgins or a Colum, and it can be traced from the *fin-de-siècle* period of translations from the Irish through the poetry of Austin Clarke, Thomas Kinsella, Seamus Heaney, Nuala Ní Dhomhnaill, Ciaran Carson and many others. This particular aspect of the Revival mentality was conveyed strongly by Kinsella in his edition of the *New Oxford Book of Irish*

Verse (1986). Kinsella's argument in his introduction to the volume, which is clearly pitted against the version of literary history fostered by Donagh MacDonagh and Lennox Robinson in their 1958 edition of the *Oxford Book of Irish Verse*, rests on the assumption that modern Irish literature is a gapped tradition, and it must be understood as a dual Gaelic and Anglo-Irish tradition, if it is to be understood properly.[11] Kinsella takes issue with the fact that the earlier anthology had, with very few exceptions, included only 'the glories of Anglo-Irish literature', i.e. work in the English language since the seventeenth century (beginning with Luke Waddington and Nahum Tate). 'It included, without specific comments, a tiny handful of translations from the Irish.' That phrase 'tiny handful' speaks volumes in itself. For Kinsella, the editors missed an opportunity, if not an 'obligation', to represent a body of Irish poetry that had 'served its people . . . for a thousand years before the curse of Cromwell fell upon them'. What could be more urgent? He speaks of the 'dual tradition' of Irish literature:

> It should be clear at least that the Irish tradition is a matter of two linguistic entities in dynamic interaction, of two major bodies of poetry asking to be understood together as functions of a shared and painful history. To limit a response to one aspect only, as is often done . . . is to miss a rare opportunity. (xxvii)

He puts this another way elsewhere:

> Irish literature exists as a dual entity. It was composed in two languages. The changing emphases between one language and the other reflect changing circumstances through the centuries . . . A dual approach is nonetheless essential if the literature of the Irish tradition is to be fully understood.[12]

And in an early poem, Kinsella has given us a stark image of this historic duality, which might stand for two cultures as well as two literary traditions: 'A black tree with a double trunk – two trees/Grown into one. . . . ' The point where they join is 'A slowly twisted scar', indicating the painful aspects of the encounter between the two traditions.[13]

For Kinsella, then, the canon-making or breaking potential of anthology editing makes the job gravely responsible, giving editorial choices considerable political and moral urgency. Clearly, for him, the editor's job is to excavate a heritage that has been buried for too long owing to the ascendancy of the English language. Good editing is an act of remembrance, retrieval. And Kinsella's stress on recuperation and loss may make him seem like a neo-Revivalist, in Crotty's view.

If anthologies are constructions of cultural memory, it is also the case that much contemporary Irish poetry, North and South, has itself been involved with invoking, describing, constructing cultural memory, as it is understood by individual poets. This is another way of saying that a dominant theme of this poetry has been the presence of the past – or, as with Kinsella, the re-assertion of a past that has been forgotten or suppressed. A *locus classicus* of such a procedure, in which the individual talent takes the measure not merely of the literary tradition but of the entire nexus of cultural and historical traditions that underlie the practices of the present time, is Heaney's 'Bogland'.[14]

'Bogland', though a northern poem, establishes a tradition and a history for all of Ireland, North and South. A meditation on the Irish landscape in notable contrast with the American frontier, and on the magical powers of peat water to preserve objects buried there, the lyric is a personal exploration of memory and an invocation of national memory. Furthermore, it attempts to combine the subjective with the public, the personal with the communitarian, by implying a connection between the depth of the creative self and the depth of the Irish landscape, and history.[15] Deeply in debt to the new wave of Irish archaeology of the late 1960s and early 1970s, the lyric presents an archaeological model of subjectivity, identity and nationhood, while implying that the cultural memory of the nation, like the memory of the individual subject, has a transcendent or noumenal value, an eternal quality, if you like: 'the wet centre is bottomless'. I think the poem illustrates the sort of recuperative aesthetic that Crotty associates with neo-Revivalism, and it is redolent of the effort of cultural retrieval that was current during the early century, and which has continued in various forms since. This poem is presumably one of those Kearney had in mind when he discussed the popular interpretation of Heaney as 'the poet of the patria . . . an excavator of the national landscape devoted to the recovery of national pieties'.[16] In fact, Kearney argues that this particular interpretation of Heaney is flawed as an account of the overall career. I agree, but I would say that the poem 'Bogland', as well as certain other of his poems from the early 1970s (Gaelic place-name poems like 'Broagh' and 'Anahorish' and so on) do indeed conform to this reading; however, they comprise only one part of his *oeuvre*, which has been continually expanding and transforming.

Heaney's poem imagines the land as a repository of the past, in which all that happened has been absorbed into and recorded by it; it resembles in this way Yeats's *anima mundi*, the storehouse of images in which human history is compressed. As I have said elsewhere, the poem is also exploring the same kind of territory as Louis Simpson's 'American Poetry', in which the literary tradition is 'like the shark', with a stomach capable of digesting the most difficult and unpleasant materials.[17] It is gigantic and omnivorous and it describes a poetic capable of representing a modern, industrial world. Simpson's poem attempts to reflect the eclecticism and modernity of American culture, and is also a poem about the literary past:

> 'Whatever it is, it must have
> A stomach that can digest
> Rubber, coal, uranium, moons, poems.'[18]

If this is, indeed, a poem about an American mythology, 'Bogland' is an 'answering myth', in Heaney's words, a poem that posits depth and history in place of American vigour, dynamism and space. In light of Simpson's poem, 'Bogland' might be titled 'Irish Culture'.

Paul Durcan could scarcely be more unlike Heaney as a poet. He is identified, by Patrick Crotty and others, with an antithetical gesture in Irish poetry, a quotidian aesthetic of the here-and-now. He is a comic satirist with considerable bite, a vernacular clown and a melancholy autobiographer. He is widely admired. Richard Kearney, who finds him subversive of the nationalist ideology, considers him 'one of the most innovative and iconoclastic of the younger generation of Irish poets'.[19] Anthony Thwaite called him 'the most surprising and idiosyncratic poet to emerge from the South in recent years'.[20] Neil Corcoran finds Durcan's satirical comedy political in implication: 'it offers a view of the north which flies in the face of all nationalist sentiment with a critique of the IRA and its apologists'.[21] His poetry displays no ambition to plumb the archaeological or indeed linguistic depths of a Heaney or the cultural history of Montague or Murphy, and he avoids the complexity and neo-Modernist obliquity of a Kinsella. Yet his plain style and self-denigrating social comedy are married to a capacity for surreal surprises and uncanny, even visionary poetic moments. In *Daddy, Daddy*, a powerful, elegiac book of bereavement, if also of satire and self-satire, he narrates a story of love for, disillusionment with and final reconciliation with his father, exploring a comparison between his father and the most uncompromising men of modern history, and between Ireland and Nazi Germany: 'Look into your Irish heart, you will find a

German U-boat.'[22] His account of Irish culture has a slightly cartoon-like quality, and is indebted to a highly personal reading of paternal authority as a mode of anti-democratic conservatism. His father's conservatism is projected onto a national screen, and the poet's reading of culture is rooted in his personal family relationships.

In one poem, 'Pine by the Sea', he appears to allude to the genre of Irish landscape poetry only to deride it; on the other hand, one might say he is invoking it to subvert, expand and transform it, to make it more inclusive of human agency and sexuality.[23] There are two subtexts to this poem, two inter-textual allusions. One is clearly the painting *Pino sul Mare* (1921), by Carlo Carra (the Italian Futurist and Metaphysical painter), invoked by the poem's title and the dedication to Carra; the other is Heaney's 'Bogland', which is surely at the back of Durcan's mind as he parodically echoes the phrase 'the wet centre is bottomless'. The painting in question is of a plain coastal scene, painted by Carra in Liguria, and delivered in a naïve and plain style. The side of a building is in evidence in the left foreground, with clean, straight lines reminiscent of the work of Carra's friend and rival, De Chirico. An unusual-looking beach cabin abuts the sea on the right, and the eponymous pine tree is in the centre foreground, portrayed in a very stylised fashion, almost branchless and bare in appearance. Beside this, a white shirt hangs to dry on a wooden trestle. All around is bare earth, punctuated by occasional tufts of grass. It has the unpeopled air of desolation suggested by Durcan's poem, and is signally lacking in any bare bottoms, despite the fantasy relayed in the Durcan poem. There is no pink clump in the painting, and indeed the Durcan fantasy bears little resemblance to the Carra picture. This painting is sometimes considered by critics to be 'metaphysical'.[24] It is interesting for the purpose of the present discussion that Carra described metaphysical painting as 'a search for a better relationship between reality and intellectual values; as such the ideas of modernity and tradition no longer form a dualism, but connect and merge. I understand tradition and modernity as two halves of the same sphere. The sphere turns and the half below comes to the top; in this way the revolutionary can become traditionalist and vice versa.'[25] Carra's thoughts on the matter may or may not have much to do with Durcan's views. However, they do have a bearing on the discussion so far. Carra argues that tradition and modernity are bound together symbiotically, feeding off and responding to one another. The sentiment is certainly in agreement with the Blakean idea of contraries in permanent tension, which underlies Welch's thesis, and throws new light on the dynamic relations between past and present, and helps to explain what

Kearney means by the narration of a transition from past to future. The future may only be forged by dialogue with the past. This Italian conclusion, it might be said, has a startling Irish dimension.

There are five points of similarity between the two poems that suggest deliberate intertextual reference. Whereas Heaney's poem is dedicated to T. P. Flanagan, famous Irish painter of bog landscapes, Durcan's poem is dedicated to Carlo Carra. There are several verbal echoes between the two poems, including references to 'horizons', to 'bottom', and 'bottomless', and there are in both poems references to important moments of visual perception ('My eye focusses on a pink clump/Swaying between the waves of heather,' in Durcan, and in Heaney: 'the eye concedes', 'the cyclops eye of a tarn', 'the sights of the sun'). In both cases, the scene is desolate, wild and apparently unpopulated – though the dramatic crux of the Durcan poem is the recognition of human life amid the gloom. The desolation and northern-ness of the place ('all that is visible is a Scots pine') recall Heaney's vista, though without the sense of archaeological richness found in 'Bogland'. This is, of course, deliberate, since such nationalist tradition-building is not at all a part of Durcan's aesthetic. The melancholia and pathos of the poem to this point, associated with the tone of solitariness, is undermined by the final note of surreal humour introduced by the image of a couple copulating, whose oscillating pink bottoms are conspicuous in the desolate landscape:

> 'I become aware that it is a human bottom
> And that there is a second human bottom underneath,
> A pair of human bottoms. . . .'

As a result of this bizarre scene, the philosophical conclusion attempted in the final ten lines can scarcely be taken seriously, and a series of fundamental words – 'bottomless', 'bottoms', 'bottomlessness' – conveys mockingly an echo of the epiphany closing 'Bogland' – 'the wet centre is bottomless'. Durcan's poem indicates a revisionary impulse to be found elsewhere in contemporary Irish poetry, in which the respect or near-reverence for history and landscape evident in early Heaney, for instance, and his attempt to make out of that emotion a national mythology, is derided and challenged by the younger author. The play with 'bottom' indicates a desire to people the landscape, vivify and eroticise it, and to suggest that the poet may have other things to do than ponder the dubious bottomlessness or otherwise of national culture. Paul Durcan's poem illustrates Fintan O'Toole's observation that, during the 1980s in Ireland, 'Tradition could be used only ironically. A thatched cottage on the stage of a new Irish play was not a static backdrop but something that would have to be immediately contradicted and subverted. . . . A landscape could be painted only to dissolve into a personal, subjective vision.'[26] Durcan's landscape, while commemorating those of Flanagan, Heaney, and Carra, dissolves into satire.

Declan Kiberd has written of the 1970s and 1980s that it 'became fashionable to rewrite the key documents of Irish nationalism in bitter acts of dismissive parody . . . it seemed that no aspects of national tradition would be left unscathed'.[27] Certainly, Durcan's parodic satires on an Irish Republic which bears resemblance, within the terms of his eccentric phantasmagoria, to Hitler's Germany exemplify this tendency as do, in different ways, many other texts of the period. What Sebastian Barry has said of Dermot Bolger might be said of several contemporary writers – 'an often fighting barer of an Ireland without historical resonance, the part that is at the same time most local (the crippled housing estates of North Dublin) and most European.'[28] In this regard, it would appear Bolger has much in common with the poet Michael O'Loughlin. Born in Dublin, though now resident in Amsterdam, he is author of three collections of poetry, a book of short stories, and a short study of Patrick Kavanagh. In a fanciful but rather appropriate turn of phrase, Barry calls O'Loughlin a 'highly confident swordsman', an image that recalls ironically the figure of his most well-known poem, 'Cuchulain'. This sword-bearer is an opponent of traditional Irish pieties and values, and seems to take up his weapon in the name of the rained-upon concrete, the seedy quotidian of contemporary Dublin poverty that appears un-picturesquely in his poems. He is an example of what Barry calls 'the first uncluttered generation' in modern Ireland – by which is meant free of the so-called clutter of nationalist values that pervade the work of the Revivalists, or free of the need to find some illumination in the shadow of the Revival. This notion of 'uncluttered generation' may seem appealing, but finally it raises more questions than it answers. It conveys an impression of clarity of thought and feeling, of free innovation untrammelled by ancestral piety. It might be argued that having the freedom to visualise bottoms instead of meditating on the eternal essence of nationhood, or feeling free to debunk the Cuchulain myth does express a certain liberation, but those debunkers may themselves be 'cluttered' by other kinds of modern things, such as the need to appear uncluttered, the need to demythologise, the need to debunk the nationalist past. One can hardly escape 'clutter' if it is defined as the concerns, values and struggles that are integral to consciousness itself. Perhaps O'Loughlin's image of a hero-free Ireland is a vision of an 'uncluttered' state, in which the natives 'have pushed a burning ship, an ark, and emigrant ship, out to sea. Perhaps on board, is the body of the last Irish hero.'[29]

This image plays with the notion that many of Ireland's unsung heroes (including Frank Ryan, the subject of one of his essays), were exiles, hence ignored by Irish history. He is critical of Ireland's failure, as he sees it, to treat its emigrés with the respect it showed to the indigenous population. The image also suggests there may come a day when Ireland no longer needs a pantheon of heroes, as if this reverence for the dead of 1916 has been ideologically counter-productive. As Declan Kiberd once wrote, citing Brecht's *Galileo*: 'Unhappy the land that is in need of heroes.'[30] Again, a society that does not heroise its dead may be uncluttered in one respect, but one imagines clutter will always return in some form, since it is, after all, another word for anxiety.

For O'Loughlin, the cultural memory is skewed to promote the official, state-sponsored story of a dominant nationalism (often rural in focus), which inevitably marginalises the poor, the female and the urban. His own satiric poetic differs from Durcan's in that it lacks humour and the touches of surreal vision that make Durcan's work so startling, surprising and fresh, but it has a notable candour and (sometimes) bitterness. His attitude to Irish language writing may be gauged by his poem 'Irish History Lesson', in which he articulates a muted rage against those arguments for cultural nationalism that actually bear some resemblance to what Thomas Kinsella has had to say elsewhere. 'The Irish History Lesson' is written in the rather brash, snappy, careless, iconoclastic tone that is characteristic of O'Loughlin (and which perhaps shows the influence of Kavanagh). The speaker in the poem (not necessarily to be confused with the poet) simply hates the Irish language, conveying a sense that it has been violently imposed upon him. The ditty he uses as epigraph is like some colonial English children's rhyme, cited ironically (or is it?). He did not care to learn Irish, even if it did mean he 'was cutting myself off/from a part of the nation's heritage'. He 'didn't want to know their nation's heritage/it wasn't mine'. However, a richer and more nuanced approach to the Gaelic tradition may be found in his poem 'On hearing Michael Hartnett read his poetry in Irish'. Here, the speaker skilfully portrays the history of English in Ireland, from the first conquests ('a handful of brutal monosyllables') to the present ('the fluent spread of the demotic suburbs'). Yet it is only through hearing Irish spoken that finally, in a chilling epiphany, he can hear 'the snow falling through moonlight/ Onto the empty fields.'[31]

The teleological, nationalist story of Ireland as a tale of manifest destiny, leading ineluctably from bondage to freedom, bothers O'Loughlin a good deal, and it creeps repeatedly into his prose writings. His hero (if you will), Frank Ryan, fought for republican socialism in Spain, 'to fight for a political culture which had not taken root in Ireland'.[32] It had not taken root, as O'Loughlin sees it, since it was a culture dominated by the glorious story of Irish nationalism. Neutrality cut Ireland off from 'the mainstream of European culture', which did not help matters. The Dublin he depicts is obsessed with the past and its indigenous heroes, and insular in outlook, hence Catholic and conservative.

This story of Irish destiny is by its nature exclusive, hegemonic:

> All narratives have their beginnings as a kind of justification and explanation of the society which produces them. At this stage, the Irish narrative can not be reduced to a simple tale with a beginning and end, recognisable heroes and villains, closed in between the covers of a green book with the title stamped in gold . . . These kind [sic] of narratives create borders which are no longer acceptable.[33]

In response, O'Loughlin seeks to represent areas of the national landscape that the founding myths have ignored or silenced.[34] His poem about Cuchulain is a clear illustration of the kind of thing Kiberd had in mind when he wrote that 'it became fashionable to rewrite the key documents of Irish nationalism in bitter acts of dismissive parody.'[35] Yet the poem is also an illustration of the poet's heartfelt concern to write about nationhood that matches the experience of contemporary Irish people, whose lives are obscured by the shadow of the dominant imagery of the state. Un-readable to the present, Cuchulain has no meaning:

> If I lived in this place for a thousand years
> I could never construe you, Cuchulainn.
> Your name is a fossil, a petrified tree
> Your name means less than nothing.[36]

The poem is written in the plain style which typifies his work. It is candid, prosaic, and direct to the point of blunt. It has a disillusioned but determined tone, the air of a youthful speaker who is decisively finished with a member of the older generation. However, no rebel without a cause, this speaker is rejecting the past in the name of the urban poor who are surrounded by the patriarchal symbolism of revolution but who remain poor.

> Your name means less than nothing
> To the housewife adrift in the Shopping Centre
> At eleven-fifteen on a Tuesday morning

It could be argued that the poem is 'traditional' in that it uses as subject matter that most traditional subject, Cuchulain, yet it does so in order to stress an innovative break with the past. It embraces modernity by invoking a traditional icon and claims, in tones of bewilderment, if not of near-contempt, that the icon is redundant. The poem is based on a moment of encounter between traditional and innovative, and as such it illustrates the kind of point Carra made, that the two can only operate dialectically, by responding to each other. The innovative is always post-traditional, suggesting that it has one eye on tradition, if only to debunk it. But it must recognise it in order to debunk it.

The poem's rhetoric relies upon a humorous extremism ('A thousand years') to convey the effect of complete estrangement from this figure and the nationalist world that produced him. The reference to the fossil implies a glance in the direction of Heaney territory, marking alignment with Samuel Beckett's famous remark that modern Irish poets were mere antiquarians, and establishing important critical distance between the poetic of the demythologised urban quotidian and the sacred landscapes of the Revival. This distance is also emphasised by the catalogue of brand-names ('Librium, Burton's Biscuits') and the reference to the precise time ('11.15 on a Tuesday morning'), stubbornly asserting a refusal to transcend the world of the supermarket clock in the name of some mythology. The poet expresses sympathy with the hard-pressed housewife, surrounded as she is by the heroic names of a revolution fought half a century before, and which is felt to have no meaning for her. The poet introduces a note of excess in the phrase 'less than nothing', as if he is fighting a battle with the past, not merely casually noting its redundancy, hence resorting to over-statement and strategic exaggeration.

Declan Kiberd has said of Nuala Ní Dhomhnaill that she 'taught her generation that the best way to protect a tradition is to attack and subvert it', which suggests a form of appropriation and revision – a branching off from, yet also a continuation of a particular tradition.[37] This is more or less the ambition of Eavan Boland, who has stressed in essays and interviews that her intentions are to reform the conventions of Irish poetry, particularly where the representation of female experience is concerned. Hence, in Kiberd's words: 'updating rather than a repudiation of the idea of the nation ... made her the logical laureate of Mary

Robinson's presidency'.[38] While she has never been dubbed an official laureate, of course, writing commissioned poems for state occasions and so on, the fact that the former President of the Irish Republic has on at least one occasion read her work in a public forum shows the civic dimension of her poetry, founded upon the overlap in many of her lyrics between cultural/national memory and personal argument. There is a brooding consistency to her writing, which makes her collections tightly knit and self-referential. She returns to the same themes time and again – domestic life, interiors, *objets d'art*, photographs and paintings, especially portraits of women. She is much exercised by history, memory, the limitations of art and narrative. Her language is pellucid and evocative and, while not being predictable, is sure enough of itself to be unafraid of fruitful repetition. Her favourite words include 'past', 'history', 'scar', 'language', 'wound', 'stars'; pastoral words like 'trees', 'flowers', 'pears', 'spring', and so on. Her meditative tone sometimes fades into the elegiac, since so much of her work revolves around loss.

Boland has written eloquently of her anxious relationship to Irish poetic traditions, which she finds troublingly male-dominated. She is insistent that literary tradition is not something she wishes to radically dismiss or destroy, but rather to subvert: 'my own discourse must be subversive. In other words, that I must be vigilant to write of my own womanhood – whether it was revealed to me in the shape of a child or a woman from Achill – in such a way that I never colluded with the simplified images of women in Irish poetry.'[39] Currently Professor of Poetry at Stanford University, her work sells well and has been very well received in the US, where her combination of national and feminist concerns has been much appreciated. Furthermore, an audience which enjoys the work of Adrienne Rich was ripe for Boland, despite her insistence that she is not a 'feminist' poet. Rich's much-anthologised lyric, 'Diving Into the Wreck', might be a gloss on Boland's own meditations on Irish culture and its own system of exclusions and silent suppressions, which is to say that it could be regarded as an influence on her work and, indeed, her view of culture. Rich is a diver-explorer:

> carrying a knife, a camera
> a book of myths
> in which
> our names do not appear.[40]

Boland is widely admired for producing an accessible, short-lined, meditative lyric, in which the Irish patriarchal book of myths is interrogated, and in which she gives an alternative reading of history and women's role in it. Again, her impatience with traditional depictions of Ireland as female, or with women 'as icons and figments', led her to produce portraits of real women in quotidian settings, or in other ways undermine the convention of depicting women as symbolic, iconic, passive.[41]

In 'Achill Woman', for instance, she offers a portrait of an old woman, which is turned into a salutary lesson in life for the young woman the speaker once was ('I was all talk, raw from college'). The poem turns on the contrast between the contemporary speaker and the youthful ingenue she once was when, as an undergraduate at Trinity College Dublin, she visited a friend in the West and met an old woman who regaled her with stories of the local region during the famine.[42] The first several stanzas focus on the Achill woman as she fills a bucket of water from a well. The author takes pains to show her actively working: 'She came up the hill carrying water.' Her physical appearance in all its ordinariness is carefully described – 'a half-buttoned wool cardigan', her hair falling into her eyes, and 'the cold rosiness of her hands'.[43]

The poet carried with her a copy of the 'Court Poets of the Silver Age', writers whose polished harmonies are significantly juxtaposed against the unpolished realities associated with the old woman and her world (we note she has tied around her waist a rag, marked with the words 'Glass Cloth' – there is no doubt what kind of polishing she does). The poem is written in short, irregular stanzas with casual, irregular rhymes, and notable for its felicitous aural and visual imagery ('the zinc-music of the handle on the rim'; 'a stream was/a fluid sunset'). However, the emotional crux can be found in the closing third of the poem, when the speaker turns indoors, and 'failed to comprehend//the harmonies of servitude' expressed in the Court poets, as if the world of rural poverty, recognised as part of her own history, casts such a shadow over that of the English court poets (and their effort to transform experience into a graceful music) that the latter becomes incomprehensible. Her mature, retrospective vision allows her to see the night sky, the spring moon, and to hear those poems – all of which she was oblivious to at the time – so impressed, somehow, is she by her acquaintance with the woman. If the tension between poetry and national history (embodied by the woman with her memories of the famine) seemed to involve mutually exclusive factors, at the time, the example of the Boland lyric demonstrates a way forward from the impasse: a way of resolving her attachment to worlds that seem mutually uncomprehending. This is what Boland often seems to do, or attempt to do, in her poetry: to synthesise the national, the historical, the personal and aesthetic in a coherent lyric form. Cultural memory is preserved in tandem with the personal.

Songs and poems are for Boland in a sense risky ventures which both record and remember, represent and express, and also falsify, distort. They can be 'a safe inventory of pain' (suggesting an aestheticised realm whose very safeness undermines its expressive capacity), and also vehicles of hegemonic Englishness. In 'The Emigrant Irish', what is called 'all the old songs' articulate a communal memory preserved in the New World by long-suffering travellers, whose example and whose lives the poet almost reveres: 'what they survived we could not even live'. Here is that 'heroising' stance to which Crotty refers and which links Boland – despite her mastery of the quotidian description, and her distrust of traditional mythologies – to those other poets who construct a tradition deeply indebted to a brilliant past. In 'Mise Eire', Ireland 's traditional songs tend to 'bandage up the history' – suggesting, again, the power of song to assuage grief by aestheticising and distorting experience. The poem opens with a dramatic, dogmatic pronouncement – 'I won't go back to it' – implying rigid resistance to the past, or perhaps a particular vision of the past, a distorting representation of it – 'my nation displaced/into old dactyls'. The patriotic tone of ownership of nation here, and the speaker's feeling that it's being maligned, 'displaced' by virtue of its being portrayed in a particular manner, conveys a note that is consonant with the Nationalistic associations of the title.[44] The speaker will not return to a country that uses words 'that make a rhythm of the crime//where time is time past'. Again, the focus is on aestheticising a crime (that of original colonisation perhaps, or of rebellion?). The pastness of the time indicates an exasperation with the nostalgic backward look.

The speaker portrays herself, in ironic tribute to the traditional personifications of the nation as female, as a prostitute and an emigrant with child. The poet at once deconstructs the myth of female purity ('she practices/the quick frictions,/the rictus of delight'), and humanises the myth of noble suffering with the image of mother and child:

> mingling the emigrant
> guttural with the vowels
> of homesickness who neither
> knows nor cares that
>
> a new language is a kind of scar . . . (78)

If the reference to 'guttural' and 'vowels' recalls the language poems of early Heaney, the stanza also recalls the image of the homesick child portrayed by Boland in some of her semi-autobiographical exile poems, such as 'Fond Memory', 'An Irish Childhood: 1951', and 'In Exile'. The woman in 'Mise Eire' recalls quasi-mythic voyages of generations of emigrants who left indigenous poverty to find deracinated urban poverty elsewhere. The familiar Boland trope of the scar re-surfaces here, to convey the idea that Ireland has lost its language. Boland's poetic allows for the recall of the memory of loss, combined with the knowledge that such loss can never be regained or paid for. The elegiac matter of the poem leads to a refusal to go back (heroic gesture that that is), yet the poem finally delivers less vigour than it promises, in its resigned and deflated final gesture of acceptance and regret. In the act of refusing memory, memories are awakened, and will not easily be appeased. The self-personifications of the poem revive the memory of nationalist patriarchal representations, only to undermine such traditions and to render moribund the comfort and potency such representations aspire to.

In recent years, critics have tended to find in modern literary history opposing tendencies in Irish poetics, between those who focus on or continually construct the past in certain ways, and those who ironise, repudiate or radically revise it. The former category includes poets and editors like Kinsella who wish to revive the Gaelic inheritance as a gesture of counter-hegemony and an act of cultural survival. Heaney is a poet who, in the early 1970s, took such an admonition very seriously indeed, and saw in the process of preservation an opportunity for self-definition, political unification and fulfilment. However, many younger writers regard such constructions of cultural memory with suspicion, seeing them as at best irrelevant, at worst limiting, incarcerating and atavistic. Durcan's poignant and melancholy bathos, his anti-fascist satires and demythologising monologues all contribute to this antithetical voice. O'Loughlin's disillusionment, and his uptight, politically correct revisionism offers a bracing challenge to the project of preservation, conservation and revival. If the Literary Revival was energising for the cultural nationalists of the revolutionary period, has it been enervating for the post-revolutionary republic? Does conservation collapse into conservatism with a capital 'c' – into a bog of regrets and an archaic self-image, tied to the past? These seem to be the kinds of question underlying the antithetical aesthetic. The words of Richard Kearney in the closing moments of his essay on mythology and motherlands encapsulate the problem:

Myth is a two-way street. It can lead to perversion . . . or to liberation . . . If we need to demythologize, we also need to remythologize. And this double process requires a discrimination between authentic and inauthentic uses of myth. For if myths of motherland are often responses to repression, they can also become repressive in their own right. That is why it is necessary to see how myth emancipates and how it incarcerates, how it operates as an empowering symbol of identity and how it degenerates into a reactionary idol. At best, myth invites us to reimagine our past in a way which challenges the present status quo and opens up alternative possibilities of thinking. At worst, it provides a community with a strait-jacket of fixed identity, drawing a cordon sanitaire around this identity which excludes dialogue with all that is other than itself.[45]

For Boland, inherited mythology tends to be synonomous with patri-archal nationalism, a conjunction of two narratives which – like the story of Ireland that O'Loughlin abhors – exclude and repress more than they liberate. And yet her tempered aesthetic of historical invocation, combined with reform and revision of the key terms in the narratives, offers a powerful lesson combined integrally with coherent aesthetic solutions to a complex of cultural and political problems. Above all, she shows how the political problems are indeed cultural, thus embedded in story-telling, in memory and national memory.

Notes

1 Edna Longley, *Poetry in the Wars* (Newcastle: Bloodaxe, 1986), p. 9.
2 Richard Kearney, *Transitions: Narratives in Modern Irish Culture* (Manchester: Manchester University Press 1988), p. 10.
3 Maurice Harmon, *Irish Poetry After Yeats* (Dublin: Wolfhound, 1987), p. 29.
4 *Changing States: Transformations in Modern Irish Writing* (London & New York: Routledge, 1993), p. 7.
5 Patrick Crotty, *Modern Irish Poetry: An Anthology* (Belfast: Blackstaff Press, 1995).
6 Robert F. Garratt. *Modern Irish Poetry: Tradition and Continuity from Yeats to Heaney* (London: University of California Press, 1986). Dillon Johnston, *Irish Poetry After Joyce* (Notre Dame: Notre Dame University Press, 1985).
7 The notion of European influence is reiterated by Brendan Kennelly in the preface to the second edition (1981) of his *Penguin Book of Irish Verse*: contemporary Irish poetry shows 'an increasing awareness of European and other cultures' (p. 41).
8 Paul Muldoon, *Faber Book of Contemporary Irish Poetry* (London: Faber, 1986).
9 Neil Corcoran, *The Chosen Ground: Essays on the Contemporary Poetry of Northern Ireland* (Bridgend: Seren, 1992), p. 8.

10 Higgins seems indebted to a version of Revivalism steeped in Irish-Ireland philosophy, often associated with the writer D. P. Moran. Gearoid O'Tuathaigh lists cultural nativism, anglophobia, and exaggeration of Irish achievements among the qualities of the Irish-Ireland idea. See 'The Irish-Ireland Idea: Rationale and Relevance', in Edna Longley (ed.), *Culture in Ireland: Division or Diversity?* (Belfast: Institute of Irish Studies, 1991), pp. 54–71. Higgins's outlook also resembles in some respects the views of Padraic Colum, as outlined in his introduction to his *An Anthology of Irish Verse* (New York: Liveright, 1922, 1948), pp. 3–20, in which he spoke repeatedly of the 'racial character' and the 'Gaelic spirit' of Irish poetry.

11 In a similar vein, in his introduction to the *Penguin Book of Irish Verse* (1970), Brendan Kennelly wrote: 'I am in fact talking about two traditions in poetry; the early native Gaelic and the later Anglo-Irish ... but I personally believe that both Gaelic and Anglo-Irish combine to create a distinctive Irish tradition' (p. 26). As Eavan Boland recently remarked: 'After all, the Irish poetic world – this is of course a figurative way of describing it – grieved for one language and wrote in another. Therefore it was in fact a place with two pasts.' 'The Veil Over the Future's Face', in *Profession 1997* (New York: MLA, 1997), p. 14.

12 Thomas Kinsella, *The Dual Tradition* (Manchester: Carcanet, 1995), p. 4.

13 'Wormwood,' in Thomas Kinsella, *Nightwalker and Other Poems* (New York: Knopf, 1968), p. 25.

14 Seamus Heaney, 'Bogland,' in *Door into the Dark* (London: Faber, 1969), p. 55.

15 In 'Feeling Into Words' he wrote: 'I had a tentative unrealized need to make a congruence between memory and bogland and, for the want of a better word, our national consciousness. And it all released itself after "We have no prairies..." – but we have bogs.' *Preoccupations: Selected Prose 1968–1978* (New York: Farrar Straus and Giroux, 1980), pp. 54–5.

16 Richard Kearney, *Transitions*, p. 101.

17 Jonathan Allison, 'Beyond Gentility: A Note on Seamus Heaney and American Poetry', *Critical Survey*, 8/2 (Spring 1996), pp. 178–85.

18 Louis Simpson, 'American Poetry,' in A. Poulin, Jr., (ed.), *Contemporary American Poetry* (sixth edition, Boston: Houghton Mifflin, 1996), p. 523.

19 Kearney, *Postnationalist Ireland: Politics, Culture, Philosophy* (London: Routledge, 1997), p. 132.

20 Anthony Thwaite, *Poetry Today: Critical Guide to British Poetry, 1960–1995* (London and New York: Longman, 1996), pp. 110–11.

21 Neil Corcoran, *After Yeats and Joyce: Reading Modern Irish Literature* (Oxford: Oxford University Press, 1997), p. 120.

22 Paul Durcan, 'Fjord,' in *Daddy, Daddy* (Belfast: Blackstaff, 1990), p. 106.

23 Durcan, *Daddy, Daddy*, p. 20.

24 Caroline Tisdall, 'Foreword', in Massimo Carra, *Metaphysical Art* (New York: Praeger, 1971), p. 15.

25 Carlo Carra, cited in Tisdall, p. 15.

26 Fintan O'Toole, 'Introduction. Ireland in the Eighties', in *A Mass for Jesse James: A Journey through 1980s Ireland* (Dublin: Raven Arts, 1990), p. 13.

27 Declan Kiberd, *Inventing Ireland* (Cambridge, MA: Harvard University Press, 1995), p. 609.

28 Sebastian Barry, 'Introduction'. *The Inherited Boundaries: Younger Poets of the Republic of Ireland* (Dublin: Dolmen, 1986), p. 27.
29 Michael O'Loughlin, 'Frank Ryan: Journey to the Centre', Dermot Bolger (ed.), *Letters from the New Island* (Dublin: Raven Arts, 1991), p. 72.
30 Declan Kiberd, 'The Perils of Nostalgia: A Critique of the Revival', in Peter Connolly, (ed.), *Literature and the Changing Ireland* (Gerrards Cross: Colin Smythe, 1982), p. 24.
31 Michael O'Loughlin, 'On hearing Michael Hartnett read his poetry in Irish.' In Seamus Deane (gen. ed.), *Field Day Anthology of Irish Writing*, vol. 3 (Derry: Field Day, 1991), p. 1429.
32 O'Loughlin, 'Frank Ryan', p. 59.
33 Ibid., p. 71.
34 In a thoughtful piece about Glasnevin, he mourns the forgotten dead, whose lives are not recorded on any headstones. There were many headstones in the cemetery – and again he has recourse to the story of Ireland – 'Here was the official story of Ireland laid out in sentences and paragraphs of stone...' Dermot Bolger (ed.), *Invisible Dublin: A Journey Through Dublin's Suburbs* (Dublin: Raven Arts Press, 1991), p. 71. Beyond this official story is the untold story of those whose graves are unmarked. In my view, the epiphany he achieves in prose here is the equal of, if not superior to, anything he has done in poetry.
35 Declan Kiberd, *Inventing Ireland*, p. 609.
36 Michael O'Loughlin, 'Cuchulainn', in Sebastian Barry, *The Inherited Boundaries*, p. 122.
37 Kiberd, *Inventing Ireland*, p. 605.
38 Ibid., p. 607.
39 Eavan Boland, 'A Kind of Scar', in Katie Donovan, A. N. Jeffares, Brendan Kennelly (eds.), *Ireland's Women* (Dublin: Gill and Macmillan, 1994), p. 241.
40 Adrienne Rich, 'Diving into the Wreck', in *Diving into the Wreck: Poems 1971–1972* (New York: Norton, 1973), pp. 22–5.
41 Boland, 'A Kind of Scar,' p. 242.
42 Helen Dunmore writes: 'Eavan Boland speaks of her meeting with the Achill Woman who appears in this collection in the poem of the same name. This west coast island woman talked to Boland of the Famine of 1847, of the people abandoning their cottages and eating seaweed against inevitable starvation. The nineteen-year-old Boland listened, and then '"went in to study the cadences of the Elizabethan court", turning her back on "a powerful, private world".' Helen Dunmore, 'A Civil Tongue', *Poetry Review*, 81 2 (Summer, 1991).
43 Eavan Boland, *Outside History: Selected Poems 1980–1990* (New York: Norton, 1990).
44 The title refers not only to Sean O'Riada's stirring 1966 musical commemoration of 1916, but also to Pearse's poem 'I am Ireland', in which the nation speaks as an old woman, mother of heroes. See P. H. Pearse, *Selected Poems: Rogha Danta*, ed. Dermot Bolger (Dublin: New Island Books, 1993), pp. 46–7.
45 Kearney, *Postnationalist Ireland*, p. 121.

3
'Something's Missing': Theatre and the Republic of Ireland Act

Chris Morash

We are bored. No, don't protest, we are bored to death, there's no denying it.[1]

Act I: Politics and Performance
Scene: The Debating Chamber

Throughout the autumn and into the winter of 1948, the sporadic and for the most part underwhelming debate which accompanied the passing of the Republic of Ireland Act slowly wound itself into a strange knot of contradictions. The Taoiseach of the day, John A. Costello, told *The Irish Times* that the establishment of an Irish Republic would mark 'the ending of an epoch and beginning what he hoped would be a new and brighter epoch for the people of this country',[2] while in the Dáil the Tánaiste, William Norton, announced that the Republic of Ireland Act would 'express before the world the ideals and aspirations of our people today, just as it represented the ambition of every Irish nationalist movement in the past'.[3] At the same time, Costello, Norton and the rest of the Coalition had spent much of their time during the previous three months convincing anyone who would listen that this landmark Bill – the culmination of Irish nationalist history – would in fact have no impact whatsoever on the economy, trade, citizenship, relations with Britain, relations with the Commonwealth, or, indeed, much of anything else. In opposition, Eamon de Valera put an even more metaphysical spin on the debate. Magnanimously declaring that his only regret was that he had not introduced the Bill himself, he told the Dáil on November 24: 'We are not to-day proclaiming a Republic anew; we are not establishing a new State: we are simply giving a name to what exists.'[4] De Valera took particular exception to Sean MacBride's claim that since 1922, Ireland 'was a republic and was not a republic'. 'We were a republic', even prior to the passing of the Act, de Valera declared in the Dáil on 2 December, 1948: 'no doubt whatever about it'.[5] The Sinn Féin President, Margaret Buckley, took this line of reasoning a step further when she told her party's Ard Fheis that it was impossible for the coalition government to declare a republic, because 'the Republic was proclaimed in 1916, established in 1919, and it never had been disestablished'.[6] With impeccable logic, she argued that you could not create something which already exists, while at the same time insisting that declaring a 26-county Republic would constitute a tacit acceptance, and hence a perpetuation, of Partition. In the end, it was left to Myles na gCopaleen, writing in his 'Cruiskeen Lawn' column in the *Irish Times*, to come up with a sensible suggestion, when he noted with his customary erudition:

> The Latin term *res publica* (which means 'commonwealth') is not always found written in full among the best authors. Cicero in particular . . . It is usually shortened simply to *res* and the equivalent English abbreviation for Republic would be Re. . . . When the republic is proclaimed here would it be an idea to signify the change openly by calling the country just plain RE? . . . RE is the last half of EIRE and its use, until the 'reintegration of the national territory', would be a permanent reminder that the country, like the word, was partitioned.[7]

If the year in which Ireland finally became a republic was rich in potential material for a satirist such as Brian O'Nolan's alter ego, Myles na gCopaleen, it is usually considered to have been the nadir of the modern Irish theatre, a trough between the giddy intensity of the years of Yeats, Lady Gregory and Synge in the early decades of the century and the emergence in the 1960s of Tom Murphy, Brian Friel and the generation of playwrights who continue to dominate the Irish theatre. Even a critic as sympathetic as Christopher Murray, who departs from recent practice by finding room in his *Twentieth-Century Irish Drama* for playwrights such as George Shiels, Louis D'Alton and M. J. Molloy, warns his readers that 'for the most part, Irish plays of the 1940s and 1950s are now of interest predominantly as cultural documents'.[8] Attempts to diagnose this theatrical malaise usually begin (and often end) with the 26-year reign of Ernest Blythe at the Abbey, a former Minister of Finance who was put in charge of the National Theatre in 1941, and who, although he managed to keep the theatre afloat after its premises burned in 1951, is remembered by Hugh Leonard as a man who 'regarded the performing arts as so much bunkum. The main function of the Abbey, he believed, was to revive the Irish language.'[9] Nor is Leonard alone in his dislike of Blythe; Peter Kavanagh's 1950 history of the Abbey seethes with anger and resentment, alleging that after Blythe's appointment 'the Abbey Theatre board of directors was now packed against the forces of intellect, taste, imagination, and poetry'. 'The Abbey Theatre was a dream in the mind of Yeats,' Kavanagh concludes. 'He had made it a reality during his life, but when he died the reality returned to the dream and passed away with its creator.'[10]

A closer reading of the theatre criticism of the period – and of the plays with which it treats – reveals that while contemporaries such as Leonard and Kavanagh recognised that Blythe was no Yeats (to say the least), all of those aspects of Blythe's management which were most disparaged were usually understood in terms of the opposition with which Kavanagh's *The Story of the Abbey Theatre* concludes: 'the dream' and 'a reality'. Perhaps because he was just outside the range of Blythe's personal abrasiveness, W. Bridge-Adams, a regular contributor to the London-based *Drama*, took a less personalised view of the problems faced by the Abbey in a 1958 article entitled 'A National Drama'. 'Under British dominion there were large-hearted plays sounding the note of resistance,' wrote Bridge-Adams. 'To write large-hearted plays about Partition may not be so easy.'[11] This sense of belatedness – of living in a time after all the great dreams have been dreamed – runs through the cultural criticism of the period in journals such as *The Bell*, *Studies* and *Hibernia*. 'The two pillars upon which the achievement of the Abbey Theatre rested were the dramatic treatment of legend and of contemporary life,' wrote the UCD lecturer Roger McHugh in 1951. 'The former was popular enough when people could identify the legends somehow with our struggle against England; after the heroes had appeared on both sides in the Civil War, they became suspect.'[12] In the same vein, a character in one Abbey play of 1957 describes the Republic as the home to 'a race of idealists who haven't had an ideal since 1922. . . . A race of Romantics with the lowest marriage rate in the world.'[13] In short, Irish cultural debate in the 1950s seems to have been trapped within the terms of one of the oldest binary oppositions in Western thought, the ideal (or 'dream', to use the Yeatsian term) and the reality, both, in this case, equally unattractive.

These are, of course, also the terms which give the debate that accompanied the passing and implementation of the Republic of Ireland Act in the winter of 1948–9 its curious mixture of incoherence and detumescent exhaustion. The dream of a nation which derives its sovereignty from its people – a nation which has always existed, which blazed into existence in 1916 (or 1798), which is now (in 1948) being born, and which awaits its incarnation, pending reunification – could never be satisfactorily reconciled with a state struggling to master the mundane, but none the less very real, problems of unemployment, emigration, political division and Partition. 'You live on', says an old I.R.A. veteran in Walter Macken's 1955 Abbey play, *Twilight of the Warrior*:

> You have won what you fought for; your vision is on fire; you have the indelible picture in your mind of what it will be like when the sweat and dirt and bleeding and hunger is over. You have won. So, what happens? It's not the same. . . . It could be, but it isn't. Because of necessity the patriot becomes a politician. There's the tragedy. The dream is watered down.[14]

While this friction between the dream of the nation and the reality of the state in post-Independence Ireland has often been noted, and continues to trouble many postcolonial histories, the passing of the Republic of Ireland Act acted as an extra irritant. De Valera's claims that Ireland had always been a republic notwithstanding, prior to 1948 the dream of the republic which had yet to be declared was the one remnant of a forward-looking republicanism which projected itself upon an open future – 'pending the reunification of the national territory.' 'Our version of history,' as the Bishop of Clonfert remarked in 1957, 'has tended to make us think of freedom as an end in itself and of independent government – like marriage in a fairy story – as the solution of all ills.'[15] To announce that the dream of the Republic was now a reality, while at the same time admitting that its realisation would have no tangible effect on people's lives, as the coalition government did in 1948, was to acknowledge the deconstructive kernel of the dream/reality binarism upon which the relationship between nation and state rested. If nothing changed in the state when the national dream became reality, the entire structure of the opposition is threatened with implosion, or, at the very least, incoherence.

There are at least two possible responses here. One is a retreat into an ideological metaphysics which would assert the reality of the republican ideal by continuing to defer it into the realm of the yet-to-be, much in the manner of a millenarian prophet, who, finding the world not disposed to end in 1666 or 2000, simply recomputes the figures and thereby maintains the yearning for the end. This was the Sinn Féin and, to a lesser extent, Fianna Fáil position in 1948, just as it was the position of those Northern nationalists of the time who doggedly referred to the 'Free State' long after such an entity had ceased to exist in law. The other response was the apostate's, the denial, in the name of realism, of the dream itself – sometimes, even, the denial of the validity of any form of idealism. This type of public discourse begins to take form as early as the mid-1920s in the plays of Seán O'Casey, for instance, particularly the resonant cry at the end of *Juno and the Paycock*: 'Sacred Heart o' Jesus, take away our hearts o' stone, and give us hearts o' flesh!' We find it again in *The Bell*'s statement of intent in 1940, that it would stand for 'life before any abstraction, in whatever magnificent words it may clothe itself. For we eschew abstractions, and will have nothing to do with generalisations that are not capable of proof by concrete experience.'[16]

If this troubled relationship between ideals and their realisation forms one of the basic structures of public debate in Ireland in the 1940s and 1950s, it helps to explain some of the difficulties faced by the Irish theatre in the period, over and above the shortcomings of individuals in the management of the Abbey. When a play is being acted on the stage, as any director or actor will attest, the relationship between the ideal and the real is not necessarily one in which the ideal pre-exists the moment of its realisation in performance. In performance, the possibility of a way of existing other than that which exists is created by the theatrical event itself. We can make this idea more tangible by returning to the basics of performance: a performance takes place in a real space, in the present time, with real human beings as performers. At the same time, this real space occupied by real human beings is transformed by performance into a parallel fictional time, in which a period of two or three hours can become months, decades or seconds of consciousness; places change with the drop of a curtain or the dimming of a light; and – most volatile of all – a living being, already transformed by the role she is playing, enacts the mutability of the individual human subject, capable of magical – although not necessarily supernatural – instantaneous transformation. In short, at every instant the play in performance is ripe with the potential to be other than what it is.

By testifying to human mutability, the theatre thus opens a gate from reality (in the sense of 'that which is') to its alternatives: 'that which is not', or, more powerfully, 'not yet'. In other words, the basic structures of the theatrical performance serve a utopian function, in the sense in which Ernest Bloch uses the term, to gesture toward something which is not present, but which can none the less be imagined through its absence. It is, writes Bloch, the 'decisive incentive toward utopia that is the meaning of Brecht's short sentence, "Something's missing."'... What is this "something"? If it is not allowed to be cast in a picture, then shall I portray it as in the process of being [*seiend*].' On the stage, writes Bloch, 'life as it happens is voided of its restrictions that it often gets into'; this, for Bloch, defines what theatre can do at its best, making it for him a paradigmatic utopian institution. Great theatre, he argues, is theatre which offers a glimpse of 'that which has *never entirely* happened *anywhere*, but which is *to come as a human event and which defines the task.*'[17] 'The theatre,' notes Peter Brook in a similar vein, 'is the last forum where idealism is still an open question'.[18] That which has never happened anywhere, the absent 'something', can never be presented on the stage as a fixed, permanent object (in such a case it would have 'happened' and would not be 'missing'); it can only be gestured towards by the process of performance in which transformation opens up the utopian possibility for future transformation and forces the audience to recognise that the present can be other than what it is. In short, the theatre is founded upon that profoundly utopian longing Brecht celebrates in his *Short Organum for the Theatre* as 'the possibilities of change in all things'.[19]

Not all theatrical performances activate this transformational utopian promise to the same degree. Yeats's *Cathleen Ni Houlihan*, for instance – 'that play of mine [and, of course, Lady Gregory's]' which 'sent out/ Certain men the English shot' – does so to an extraordinary degree. The play stages the sudden, magical transformation of Michael, from a quiet, passive young man into a warrior with his eyes locked on an unseen vision. His transformation in turn is played out in the context of the famous, and equally magical, transformation of the tired old woman who is the embodiment of Ireland into 'a young girl, and she had the walk of a queen', a line for which Arthur Griffith would later claim credit. Beyond this again, the audience of *Cathleen Ni Houlihan* also share (at least for the duration of the performance) the experience of listening to the songs and stories of sudden, millenarian change in the familiar stage context of a family kitchen, only to be driven by the logic of the narrative to reject that context and its values for something which the stage cannot show them. There are few purer instances of utopian theatre in any repertoire.

Cathleen Ni Houlihan is far from unique in the Irish theatre of the early decades of the twentieth century. Indeed, it is a part of what might be considered a genre of such plays, including Lady Gregory's *The Gaol Gate* (1906), Pádraig Pearse's *The Singer* (1915) and Thomas

MacDonagh's *When the Dawn is Come* (1908), all of which end with sudden, magical transformations. Even a relatively late and apparently non-political piece, such as Yeats' *The Cat and the Moon* of 1926 (the same year as O'Casey's anti-utopian *The Plough and the Stars*), has the same effect of challenging its audience's perceptions of reality by holding out the promise of sudden and complete change. 'How can I dance,' asks the Lame Man in *The Cat and the Moon*. 'Ain't I a lame man?' 'Aren't you blessed,' asks the First Musician, speaking the words of the saint. 'I am, Holy Man,' replies the Lame Man. 'Then dance,' is the reply, 'and that'll be a miracle' – which he does 'at first clumsily, moving about with his stick, and then he throws away the stick and dances more and more quickly':

> Minnaloushe creeps through the grass
> Alone, important and wise,
> And lifts to the changing moon
> His changing eyes.[20]

Act II: Pádraig Pearse and the Missing Bicycle Lamp
Scene: A Kitchen

This is not to say, of course, that the Irish theatre of the first two and a half decades of the twentieth century was exclusively transformational, utopian and 'poetic' (as O'Casey's early work should make clear); nor that the theatre of the middle decades of the century was the opposite of all these things. No history, much less theatre history, is quite so clear-cut. The repertoire of the early Abbey introduced genres that would become its staple in later years, including political satires such as William Boyle's *The Eloquent Dempsey* (1906) and Frederick Ryan's *The Laying of the Foundations* (1902), peasant comedies along the lines of Lady Gregory's *Spreading the News* (1904), and rural dramas, of which Padraic Colum's *The Land* (1905) is the best example. Conversely, earlier utopian plays such as Pearse's *The Singer* and an Irish-language version of Yeats' *Cathleen Ni Houlihan* would reappear on the Abbey stage as late as 1942 and 1946, respectively. To complicate matters even more, although the focus here is on the Abbey as Ireland's National Theatre, it needs to be remembered that throughout the 1940s and 1950s the Gate theatre was staging plays from the mainstream of European modernism – Strindberg's *The Father*, (staged in 1949), for instance, or Pirandello's deeply unsettling parable of the mutability of identity, *Henry IV* (performed in 1955) – which presented audiences with radical, and often frightening, moments of transformation. Indeed, the Abbey's smaller experimental theatre, the Peacock, was presenting a double bill of Gerard de Nerval's *Nicholas Flamel* and Yeats' *The Dreaming of the Bones* in late November of 1948, as the Republic of Ireland Act was being debated in the Dáil.

However, as a broad rule (with the significant exceptions noted above), the Abbey in the years immediately before and after Ireland became a Republic seemed determined to stage plays which resisted, in varying ways, the utopian possibilities of the theatre. To call such a theatre 'realistic' risks confusion with such a plethora of aesthetic doctrines as to be almost worthless as a working term. On the other hand, if the utopian, as T. W. Adorno once remarked in a debate with Bloch, is 'the determined negation of that which merely is',[21] the term 'post-utopian' (not simply anti-utopian, and not to be confused with the dystopian) is a better description of the theatre, and by extension, the culture, of Ireland in the 1940s and 1950s. If we can agree on this term, we must ask: how do you write plays for a culture which no longer trusts the utopian, which in some respects believes itself to have passed beyond utopia? 'The Irish theatre lacks vision,' wrote Gabriel Fallon in *Studies* in 1955, 'because we, its audiences, lack vision.'[22]

If there is no one answer to the question of how to create a theatre for a post-utopian culture, it can be said that there are few Irish plays written in the years after Independence in which there is not some form of mourning for the loss of a utopian future, and fewer again after the Republic of Ireland Act. Although that future is mourned before it has arrived in early plays like Frederick Ryan's *The Laying of the Foundations* in 1902, the trend first becomes glaringly obvious with the overwhelming popularity of the plays in O'Casey's Dublin trilogy, which between them made up three of the top four most frequently performed works at the Abbey between 1925 and 1948. It was also evident in less obvious ways, such as when in January of 1936 the Abbey mounted a production of Shakespeare's *Coriolanus*, in which the warrior finds that there is no place for him in the state he has helped to create. Similarly, when the Republic of Ireland Act took effect on Easter Monday, 1949, the National Theatre was staging a play which offered an eloquently contradictory critique of the tradition of physical force which had brought the state into being: Bryan MacMahon's *The Bugle in the Blood*, which opened at the Abbey on 14 March, 1949.

The Bugle in the Blood is set in the kitchen of a small lodging house in 'a country town in Southern Ireland', and like Seamus Byrne's *Design for a Headstone* (first produced at the Abbey in 1950), and a non-Abbey play, *Hunger-Strike* by Marin Cregan, it deals with the effects of a hunger strike. MacMahon's play follows the fairly mundane lives of the unseen hunger-striker's family, his parents Maroya and Joseph, and his brother, Andy. In the play's final act, his funeral cortège proceeds through the town, past the kitchen window, and the younger son, Andy, is suddenly transformed, seized with a hitherto unheralded desire to fight, and is changed from a schoolboy into an adult. Taking up his older brother's gun, he goes out to shoot a policeman, Tim O'Sullivan, and is himself killed, leaving his ageing mother to ask, in the manner of the O'Casey heroines who provide the play's obvious models, 'are we to go on, generation after generation, with black diamonds on our sleeves [in this] . . . green lunatic land where every child is born with a bugle in the blood?'.[23] At its most obvious, in other words, *The Bugle in the Blood* is like Byrne's *Design for a Headstone*, which its author claimed in the *Irish Times* 'preached the moral' of 'the futility of minority war against the State, . . . [and] the stupid wastefulness of political martyrdom'.[24] This, of course, was a message being widely preached at the time. 'We must adjust ourselves to present realities,' Alfred O'Rahilly was to write in *Hibernia* a few years later, 'practising co-operation for common interests, giving an example of toleration and liberty, renouncing physical force, abandoning even irritating propaganda which merely results in mutual denigration.'[25]

In *The Bugle in the Blood*, MacMahon makes this case through the characters of Joseph Trimble and Botany Connell, who are sober versions of Captain Boyle and Joxer in O'Casey's *Juno and the Paycock*, adding further weight to Christopher Murray's point – which is surely correct – that O'Casey is the most influential Irish dramatist of the century. Joseph, the father of the young hunger-striker, firmly believes that Irish society has moved beyond its need for heroes. 'When Pádraig Pearse was alive and speechifin' out of him he was a great hero entirely,' he says to Botany at one point. 'But people like you forget that if he had lived to be the first President of the Irish Republic he'd have to prosecute you and me for gaffing a salmon illegally or for riding at night without a light on our bicycles. The short and long of it is that there's no substitute for law and order.' The image of Pádraig Pearse pursuing poachers on improperly lighted bicycles may be funny, but it also indicates just how easily a conservative critique could end up cutting off the branch on which the state was perched.

The staging of one scene in *The Bugle in the Blood* indicates just how volatile such apparently orthodox sentiments could become in the late

1940s and 1950s. As his son's funeral passes by his house, Joseph speaks to Tim O'Sullivan, the detective and former I.R.A. man:

> I was thinking, Tim, and do you know what it is I'm thinking. I'm thinking that it was a misfortunate day for the mothers of Ireland, the day that Pádraig Pearse spoke at the grave of O'Donovan Rossa. (*Pause.*) Do you know what he did that day? He renewed the lease of idealism in this country. And because of what he said that day the youngsters will be giving their white lives, – ay, their lovely white lives . . .

There then follows a passage which has been struck out in the Abbey's prompt copy, and which did not appear in the performance of the play on stage. While scripts were often amended in rehearsal for the obvious dramatic reasons – trimming long speeches, or eliding redundant actions – in the case of *The Bugle in the Blood*, there is no aesthetic reason for the following speech by Joseph to have been cut:

> Right is a thing that is never still. It swings from day to day, from hour to hour and even from minute to minute. No man has a hold of it altogether. If a young man thinks he should die for an ideal who is there that can signal him to stop? And if a father or a Government should chastise a child or restrain a subject who can say who has the right or the wrong of things? And why should I blame my son? (*Loudly*). Or why should I blame you, Tim, or those you represent? I'm a father myself and many and many's [*sic*] the time I had to correct my children. (*smiles sadly, then falls into a reverie*)[26]

The reverie-inducing muddle in which Joe finds himself here as the Republic of Ireland Act goes into effect is not far removed from that which had taken up Dáil time the previous autumn. If it is right to declare an Irish Republic, surely (it could be argued) it must be right to continue to fight for the extension of such a republic? The none too subtly allusive names of the hunger-striker's parents in the play, Maroya (Mary) and Joseph, leave this possibility open. Later, hearing a shot fired at the funeral, Botany wonders (in a speech which was included in the final performance) if the struggle to make ideals into realities will ever end. 'I'm just wondering', he muses, 'just wondering, when we get our sweet tight united 32-County Irish Republic will we keep on fighting for the gas of it – whether it's going to be a Workers' Republic or a Christian Republic or a Socialist Republic or a Corporate Republic or a God alone knows what class of Republic.' In short, *The Bugle in the Blood* poses what is perhaps the key question of the whole period: what should be the limit of a revolution? Did the declaration of a 26-country Republic constitute – as Sinn Féin argued – an admission that the revolution was over, and Partition permanent? Or did it reaffirm the republican ideal in terms which gave new life to the campaign to end Partition by whatever means necessary?

What makes this play particularly interesting is not simply that it asks this question in a form which basically endorses what was an increasingly conservative government policy of suppressing continuing armed struggle, while leaving open the possibility that such struggle is Christlike; nor, indeed, that this is a play which openly denounces idealism, while staging a moment of miraculous change with the transformation through violence of the hunger-striker's younger brother in the final act. It not only does both of these things, it does them in the context of the family drama played out in a farmhouse kitchen: a set which had become so much the norm at the Abbey that Ernest Blythe felt compelled to defend it in 1963 by arguing that 'most people in Ireland are habituées of farmhouse kitchens, city tenements or middle-class sitting-rooms'.[27] The importance of this deliberately limited setting of *The Bugle in the Blood* – as, indeed, of most Abbey plays of the period – can be put in the context of a remark concerning the nature of utopian thought made by Jürgen Habermas in a recent interview. 'People do not fight *for* abstractions', he comments, 'but *with* images. Banners, symbols and images, rhetorical speech, allegorical speech, utopia-inspired speech, in which concrete goals are conjured up before people's eyes, are indeed necessary constituents of movements which have any effect on history at all.'[28] The Abbey kitchen set of the 1940s and 1950s did not present audiences with an image of what could be; it showed them only what was. As such, it may have presented them with an illusion of reality in the sense that such a set mimicked reality; but it did not offer an illusion in the sense in which Bloch speaks of illusion as an 'anticipatory illumination'. On the stage, he argues, 'despite a separating perimeter', the techniques of stage illusion can transform such an 'anticipatory illumination' into a moment of 'real experience'.[29]

'Anticipatory illumination' is precisely the term for Yeats' theatre, for instance, which uses the visual magic of the stage for some of its most powerful moments, such as the Lame Man's dance in *The Cat and the Moon*, or the reappearance of the ghostly figure in the window in *Purgatory*. It is possible to argue that the deliberate austerity of the visual aspect of production at the Abbey during the 1940s and 1950s (which so many commentators remark upon, comparing it unfavourably with Hilton Edwards' wonderfully baroque creations at the Gate) is part of a deliberate counter-revolutionary strategy, aimed at limiting the development of republican idealism by deliberately limiting what could be imagined of the future. Blythe 'would spot at once anything overdone or too theatrical', Tomás MacAnna would later recall. 'His attitude was that our work [Mac Anna joined the Abbey in 1947] must reflect life as it was; our stage had to reflect its natural image and never exaggerate it; indeed it was preferable to diminish it.'[30]

Act III: Intense Unrealism
Scene: A Kitchen (again)

Post-utopian 'realism', and not visionary illusion, was to be the aesthetic of a National Theatre which Blythe enlisted in a double-edged campaign waged in the cultural sphere both to defeat the I.R.A. and to end Partition. Although, as a handbill published while the Irish Boundary Commission were doing their work in 1925 reminded voters, Blythe had said in 1921 that 'the man who agrees to partition is a traitor and should be treated as such', in an influential memo of August 9 1922 Blythe had argued 'there is no prospect of bringing about the unification of Ireland within any reasonable period of time by attacking the North-East, its forces, or Government', arguing instead that the government of the Free State must apply 'psychological pressure'.[31] Forty years later, in the early 1960s, Blythe was still rejecting what he saw as 'the intense unrealism in which nearly everything relating to the Border had to be discussed', arguing in a privately printed pamphlet initially distributed to 'prominent Churchmen, to Members of Parliament and to other representative Catholic citizens in the Six Counties' that 'the problem of ending Partition, if it is ever to be ended, is neither more nor less than the problem of converting, say, a third of the Protestants of the North to Irish Nationalism'. This could be done, he argued, by removing the debate from the political sphere altogether, so that 'all work for the abolition of Partition should, for a minimum of a dozen years ahead, be kept outside the sphere of electioneering politics. During that period Nationalist patriotic endeavour should be directed wholly to the urgent task of reinforcing and developing a distinctive Irish sentiment and outlook in all sections of the population and towards enriching Irish cultural Nationality, particularly in the North'.[32]

In Blythe's 1963 defence of the Abbey, the theatre's role in this campaign to develop 'Irish cultural Nationality' becomes clear. 'It is sometimes asked,' Blythe writes, 'if in the future the Abbey will be able, in any way, to match the service it gave to the nation in former days when it helped to raise the fighting spirit of the people and so contributed toward making possible the hard military and political effort which secured the establishment of a sovereign Irish State.' He then goes on to cite Yeats's '*Kathleen Ní Houlihan* [*sic*]', Thomas MacDonagh's *When the Dawn is Come*, and Lady Gregory's *The Gaol Gate* as evidence of the Abbey's role in the revolutionary phase of Irish republicanism. Now, in its counter-revolutionary phase, he sees a new role for the National Theatre:

> There is a prospect that the Abbey, operating along different lines, because the problems of today are different from those of sixty years ago, will in future have a constructive influence on public affairs even greater than it ever exercised before.... Some of the satirical commentary which in very recent times helped to reduce the over-tense feeling that had previously frustrated all attempts to examine the problem of Partition coolly and with an eye to the future, got its best publicity in popular plays produced at the Abbey. Those who saw and laughed at Louis D'Alton's *This Other Eden*, John O'Donovan's *The Less We are Together* and John McDonnell's *All the King's Horses* will not again come under the influence of the doctrinaire views which used to impede, if not prevent, full consideration of the practical issues arising from the existence of the Border.[33]

In short, the post-utopianism which Blythe advocated in his pamphlet on Partition was to be created, in part, by the plays staged in the Abbey, plays which avoided radical magical transformations of the physical world of the stage, or of the characters on that stage. Instead of activating the utopian potential of the theatre, the Abbey in the age of a 26-county Republic was to perform its social function by defusing utopias, and this could only be done by creating a theatrical style which eschewed theatricality.

Blythe might have added a number of other plays to this list, most notably Walter Macken's tragedies, *Twilight of the Warrior* (1955) and *Home is the Hero* (1952) and Donal Giltinan's *The Flying Wheel* (1957), and it could be further extended to such non-Abbey plays as Maurice Meldon's remarkable *Aislinn* (1953) or to works from the burgeoning amateur circuit, such as D. C. Maher's farce, *Partition*, in which a man avoids the bailiffs in two jurisdictions by building a house on the border and shifting his furniture back and forth out of the reach of whoever happens to be at the door. Indeed, *Partition* is a particularly interesting case, for while it enjoyed a vogue with amateur companies in the 1950s, it was originally staged at the Abbey on November 15, 1916 – a full five years before Partition became a political reality. The play ends with a stage-trashing brawl between bailiffs and subsheriffs from the two states, while a cornet plays 'A Nation Once Again' and the main character comments: 'Begobs the Siamese twins will be kilt and buried in the wan coffin'. This list alone suggests that there is something amiss with Clare O'Halloran's claim that there is 'insufficient literary evidence for any major sense of public trauma over partition'.[34] Even if we limit ourselves to those plays which Blythe himself singles out as aiding in a 'cool' examination of Partition in the wake of the Republic of Ireland Act, we find a remarkably coherent set of strategies, in that they are all comic – either farces or satires – and they all make use of a single interior set, thereby limiting the visual element of theatrical presentation: D'Alton's *This Other Eden* (1953), which was made into a 1959 film, takes place in a public room in a hotel; O'Donovan's *The Less We Are Together* (1957) confines itself to a Taoiseach's office, and McDonnell's *All the King's Horses* (1961) has consciously subversive fun with that favourite Abbey setting, a farmhouse kitchen.

This Other Eden deals more generally with Anglo–Irish relations than with Partition as such. At the same time, using a form which echoes and develops Shaw's *John Bull's Other Island*, it defines with ironic clarity through the character of an Englishman, Crispin, who is purchasing Irish property, the Irish difficulty with idealism in the wake of Ireland becoming a Republic. Speaking to the character of Devereaux, who is described as 'an idealist . . . who has witnessed, as he believes, his country fall from grace', and Conor, an austere young visionary, Crispin tells them that it is his 'firm conviction that neither of you would know Zion if you saw it. You, Devereaux, would refuse to believe in it, and you, Conor, would insist it was still around the corner. Only I know that it is here and now, and that we must make the best of it.'[35] As Gabriel Fallon remarked of *This Other Eden* in *Hibernia*, 'there has been a marked tendency in the recent work of Abbey playwrights to suggest that things are anything but well with us'.[36]

The O'Donovan and McDonnell plays which Blythe mentions follow a similar line to *This Other Eden*, but tackle the question of Partition more directly. John O'Donovan's *The Less We Are Together*, which had a twelve-week run in 1957, is set in the future date of 1982 as the newly formed R.I.P. party have just gained power, largely on their leader's promise that they will end Partition within a year of taking office – a promise made against the advice of a canny Cork deputy, who warns the new Taoiseach, 'Let sleeping dogs lie. Nobody mentions the Border now except the English Sunday newspapers – in their Irish editions.'[37] Like the stage Taoiseach in Brian Friel's later play, *The Mundy Scheme* (1969), which resembles *The Less We Are Together* in many respects, O'Donovan's Felix Battersby needs a panacea, a miraculous solution to an intractable problem. 'Into the dustbin with all the dead ideals and the dead issues that our fathers and our grandfathers talked about but never did anything about', he declares, before announcing his great idea: 'Instead of asking the Six Counties to come in with us, we go in with the Six Counties.'

Needless to say, this stage Taoiseach encounters a few difficulties in creating his new state, with its proposed flag of 'six green stars and twenty-six orange stripes' . For one thing, the English Prime Minister, while enjoying the fishing in Galway, wants nothing to do with Ireland, South or North. In fact, he admits (in lines which still carry a satiric punch) that England 'may have to leave her own Commonwealth. She may even have to get out of the United Kingdom.' The play ends with the Ulster Unionists marching out of the negotiations to declare an independent Republic of Ulster. 'Take yourself and your ruddy British garrison to hell out of Ulster', bellows the Unionist leader, Sir Andrew M'Clusker. 'I'm going back to declare a Six-County republic, free and independent under the protection of UNO' – at which point the whole plan collapses. 'At this black moment Partition seems an insoluble problem', the stage Taoiseach tells the audience at the final curtain. 'But the long history of this country teaches one great lesson! – that the only problems we have ever solved were the insoluble ones.'[38]

As a fictional resolution to the problem of Partition, *The Less We Are Together* stages a moment of failure, as the plot collapses rather than concludes. However, as part of Blythe's larger project of discrediting 'unrealistic' dreams of dismantling the Border, it was written to order. The same is true of McDonnell's farce, *All the King's Horses*, in which two cousins, one an Orangeman from Belfast, the other a stout Republican farmer from the South, are forced to share a three-room cottage bequeathed to them by their allusively named aunt, Kate Houlihan, as a condition of her will. The plot settles into a comic stalemate after a lawyer – described in mock horror as 'a partitionist masquerading as an Irishman'[39] – prevents them from throttling each other by drawing a border through the middle of the cottage, so that one cousin has control of the electric light switch, and the other has the fireplace. By the play's end, the two men have developed a grudging respect for each other, but are still unable to live with each other, so they sell the cottage and drive off together in a taxi. 'All our history goes in that taxi,' comments their lawyer, in a line added during rehearsals.

Once again, in a manner even more explicit than was the case in *The Bugle in the Blood*, the Abbey kitchen set serves here as an image of the nation, making use of the visual restraint of the set and the highly codified conventions of the rural comedy to deny the possibility of any radical, revolutionary change; at the same time, the plot denies anything but the most hesitant solution to the problem of Partition which the play sets itself. Sitting in the audience in 1961, Desmond Fennell commented that *All the King's Horses* made it clear to him that 'the militant Republicans – and most of us – are aggrieved not by the Orangemen as people or as a cultural body, but by the Partition of Ireland as a political and maiming fact'.[40] The best *All the King's Horses* can offer, like *The Bugle in the Blood*, *The Less We Are Together* and Macken's *Twilight of the Warrior*, is an utter rejection of a past which is dangerously imbued with the possibility of utopia. In Macken's *Twilight of the Warrior*, the old I.R.A. man who is Ireland's past dies at the play's ending, mumbling incoherently. 'Want to know – are there marks for loving your country, scorched with love? Is it misapplied? The pain of frustration? Is that purgatory? And does it sit in balance against all the rest? . . . Yes. Oh yes, I am sorry; oh, I am heartily sorry – because – and I'm. . . .'[41] In *All the King's Horses*, the past drives off in a taxi, but the effect is the same.

Looking at the Abbey repertoire in the years immediately following 1949, it becomes clear that the theatre was being used to combat one possible response to the Republic of Ireland Act, a resurgence of political idealism directed towards the ending of Partition. Towards this end, the National Theatre had developed a comprehensive anti-utopian aesthetic which formed part of a concerted effort to contain 'intense unrealism' in the political sphere. 'As they have been realized,' comments T. W. Adorno in a discussion of utopia with Ernest Bloch, 'the dreams themselves have assumed a peculiar character of sobriety, of the spirit of positivism, and beyond that, of boredom.'[42] In short, what we are talking about in relation to the theatre at the time of the Republic of Ireland Act is an aesthetic of strategic boredom.[43] 'The nationalist impulses which led to the foundation of the Abbey Theatre are no longer with us,' wrote Gabriel Fallon in *Studies* in 1955, 'and seemingly we have nothing to take their place. In those days we knew what we wanted; to-day we seem not to know what we want, or to want things which are diametrically opposed to a flowering of great art in the theatre. . . . In the meantime,' he continues, 'we must suffer that theatre which we have made, that theatre with (to quote Yeats) "its continual restless mimicry of the surface of life"'.[44] This, of course, was the same year in which the Pike Theatre had an unexpected success with Beckett's *Waiting for Godot*, where Irish audiences perhaps recognised the aesthetic of boredom pushed to the point at which it became an auto-critique. 'We are bored,' exclaims Vladimir. 'No, don't protest, we are bored to death, there's no denying it.' Less than a decade later, plays such as Brian Friel's *Philadephia, Here I Come* and Tom Murphy's *A Crucial Week in the Life of a Grocer's Assistant* (rejected by Blythe at the Abbey) were to scratch at the 'surface of life' in the old kitchen set, becoming a part of the transformed attempts to re-imagine the Republic which were once again being born of the old utopian sense that 'something's missing'.

Notes

1   Samuel Beckett, *Waiting for Godot* (New York: Grove, 1954), p. 52.
2   'Taoiseach Speaks of New and Brighter Epoch'. *Irish Times* (25 Nov., 1948), p. 1.
3   *Dáil Éireann: Parliamentary Debates LXIII* (Dublin: Cahill, 1948), p. 961.
4   'Mr. de Valera Has Only One Regret', *Irish Times* (25 Nov., 1948), p. 1. For a good account of de Valera's responses to the Act, see John Bowman, *De Valera and the Ulster Question 1917–1973* (Oxford: Clarendon, 1982).
5   *Dáil Debates LXIII*, p. 926.
6   'A Perpetuation of Partition', *Irish Times* (22 Nov., 1948), p. 1.
7   Brian O Nolan [Myles na gCopaleen], 'Cruiskeen Lawn', *Irish Times* (19 Nov., 1948).
8   Christopher Murray, *Twentieth-Century Irish Drama: Mirror Up to Nation* (Manchester: Manchester University Press, 1997), p. 138.
9   Anthony Roche, *Contemporary Irish Drama: From Beckett to McGuinness* (Dublin: Gill and Macmillan, 1994), p. 39.
10 Peter Kavanagh, *The Story of the Abbey Theatre* ([1950] rpt. Orono, Maine: National Poetry Foundation, 1984), pp. 182, 184.
11 W. Bridges-Adams, 'A National Theatre', *Drama*, 51 (Winter 1958), p. 28.
12 Roger McHugh, 'Tradition and the Future of Irish Drama', *Studies*, 51 (Dec. 1951), p. 471.
13 John O' Donovan, *The Less We are Together* (1957, NLI Ms. 29, 423–4), pp. 423–9, 424.
14 Walter Macken, *Twilight of a Warrior: A Play* (London: Macmillan, 1956), pp. 57–9.
15 R. F. Foster, *Modern Ireland: 1600–1972* (Harmondsworth: Penguin, 1988), p. 569.
16 Seán O'Faolain, 'This is Your Magazine', *The Bell*, 1:1 (Oct., 1940), pp. 8–9.

17 Ernest Bloch, *The Utopian Function of Art and Literature: Selected Essays*, trans. Jack Zipes and Frank Mecklenburg (Cambridge, Mass.: MIT Press, 1988), pp. 14, 224, 244.
18 Peter Brook, *The Empty Space* (Harmondsworth: Penguin, 1968), p. 47.
19 Bertolt Brecht, *Brecht on Theatre*, trans. John Willet (New York: Hill and Wang, 1964), p. 202.
20 W. B Yeats, *Collected Plays* (London: Macmillan, 1982), pp. 471–2.
21 Bloch, *The Utopian Function of Art and Literature*, p. 12.
22 Gabriel Fallon, 'The Future of the Irish Theatre'. *Studies*, 44 (Spring 1955), p. 99.
23 Bryan MacMahon, *The Bugle in the Blood: A Tragedy in Three Acts*. 1949. NLI Ms. 29, 339, p.71.
24 'Shouts of Protest in Abbey Theatre', *Irish Times* (15 Apr., 1950), p. 1.
25 Alfred O'Rahilly, 'The Problem of North and South'. *Hibernia* (Jan. 1957), p. 6.
26 McMahon, *The Bugle in the Blood*, p. 52.
27 Ernest Blythe, *The Abbey Theatre* (Dublin: National Theatre Society, 1963), p. 21.
28 Jürgen Habermas, 'Conservative Politics, Work, Socialism and Utopia Today', in *Autonomy and Solidarity: Interviews with Jürgen Habermas* (London: Verso, 1992), p. 145.
29 Bloch, *The Utopian Function of Art and Literature*, p. 235.
30 Tómas MacAnna, 'Ernest Blythe and the Abbey'. *In The Abbey Theatre: Interviews and Recollections*, ed. E. H. Mikhail (Dublin: Gill Macmillan, 1988), p. 169.
31 Ernest Blythe, 'Policy in Regard to the North-East' (9 Aug. 1922), UCD Ms. Blythe Papers, p. 24/70.
32 Ernest Blythe, *A New Departure in Northern Policy: Appeal to The Leaders of Nationalist Opinion* (Dublin: Basil Clancy, 1959), pp. 3, 6, 30.
33 Blythe, *The National Theatre*, pp. 22–3.
34 Clare O' Halloran, *Partition and The Limits of Irish Nationalism* (Dublin: Gill and MacMillan, 1988), p. xiv.
35 Louis D'Alton, *This Other Eden* (Dublin: P. J. Bourke, 1954), pp. 8, 90.
36 Gabriel Fallon, 'Sitting at the Play', *Hibernia*, 17/7 (July 1953), p. 25.
37 John O Donovan, *The Less we are Together* (1957, NLI Ms 29, 423–4), p. 25.
38 Ibid., pp. 5, 25.
39 John McDonnell, *All the King's Horses* (1961, NLI Ms. 29, 323), p. 28.
40 Desmond Fennell, 'Partition: The Organisation Man', *Hibernia* (May 1961), p. 23.
41 Macken, *Twilight of the Warrior*, p. 90.
42 Bloch, *The Utopian Function of Art and Literature*, p. 1.
43 For a related argument, see Seamus Deane, *Strange Country: Modernity and Nationhood in Irish Writing Since 1790* (Oxford: Clarendon, 1997), pp. 164–72.
44 Gabriel Fallon, 'The Future of the Irish Theatre', *Studies*, 44 (Spring 1955), pp. 99–100.

4

The Republic and Ireland: Pluralism, Politics, and Narrative Form

Ray Ryan

State and Nation, Anthology and Ontology

As part of the revision of Irish history, the boundaries of the Irish nation have become almost indistinguishable from the 26-county state. Hence Tom Garvin can claim:

> Long before the island of Ireland was partitioned in 1920 . . . the areas that were to become the Irish Republic and Northern Ireland had shown clear signs of developing in different directions and of becoming different societies . . . Partition therefore accelerated or aggravated a process of divergence that had previously existed, and did not artificially instigate it for the first time.[1]

This is refreshingly frank, and 'artificial' is an intriguing term. As Joe Cleary notes, it swaps one mechanistic or deterministic conception of Irish history – the traditional nationalist claim of the island's organic unity – for another that moulds the Irish nation until it is congruent with state borders, thereby enabling the Republic to expunge any traces of the northern conflict from its collective memory.[2] But the impact of partition on the southern state, as Todd and Ruane explain, was profound, affecting almost every aspect of the new state and giving it a 'distinct spatial, economic, demographic, religious and political profile, shaping its culture, identity, institutions and sense of community'.[3] Cleary notes how Garvin seems to mechanistically ascribe national feeling or identity entirely to economic factors; but the states established by partition have experienced varying degrees of affiliation, legitimacy and cultural recognition since their foundation and what Garvin offers, throughout his work and in his contribution to this volume, is a political context for literary texts from the Republic. In what ways do the apparently inevitable processes of division he describes impact on these texts? How are they represented? What shape and personality, what social space, is the Republic as a cultural entity, a state, deemed to possess? Is there an aesthetic as well as a political division? What role does the aesthetic play in reflecting and enforcing division? In short, how does an entity such as the state, whose sole rational reason for existence is to ensure it continues to be, acquire the value-laden, inevitably selective ballast of cultural memory?

One of the most effective ways to naturalise a state in familiar and substantial language, to stir its national imagination, is through literature and, especially, the construction of a canon. The canon now emerging from the Republic, I want to argue, attempts to create the context in which its own work is understood. Because no pre-existing or inherited literary tradition has ever accounted for this experience, this new formation called the state, questions of identity, questions pertaining to the nation, are now subordinate to an examination of the structures of power, an investigation of the state. Colm Tóibín's introduction to *Soho Square*, an anthology of contemporary Irish writing, concludes with this ringing endorsement of the freedom the state makes possible:

> This book, then, is a sample of the reactions of forty writers ... to the sounds and the knowledge that inspired them. They have nothing in common except a beginning under the same sky, the same uncertain weather. And there is no collective consciousness, no conscience of our race, no responsibilities, no nation singing in unison. Instead diversity, the single mind and the imagination making themselves heard.[4]

This, then, is the Republic's liberal post-nationalism: only to the individual imagination is responsibility due. As in anthologies edited by Sebastian Barry and Dermot Bolger, Tóibín's identifies 1968, the year of the civil rights disturbances in Northern Ireland, as the founding moment for the contemporary southern imagination. After 1968, after the explosion of violence in the Northern state, Tóibín, Barry and Bolger claim that the inadequacy and irrelevance of the term 'Ireland' to the individual, southern imagination began to be acknowledged. The sceptical interrogation of the whole concept of 'Irish' writing is thus, at least in part, a response to the Northern troubles.

Dermot Bolger's work is the most sustained attempt to thematise the divisions of country and city in the Republic (a division that is not wholly new in Irish writing[5]) in order to reconfigure an ethnic Irish identity based on the idea of the island. A successful, innovative publisher first with The Raven Arts Press then New Island Press, Bolger favoured a demotic poetry and prose that addressed the often grim reality along north Dublin's suburban fringe. Here, a society without the consoling precedent of a literary tradition or historical identity began to find expression:

> This was neither country nor city – these streets possessed no place in the school books and poems we learnt at our wooden desks.[6]
>
> This aspect of Irish life, despite being an everyday reality for an increasingly large percentage of the population, was almost totally absent from Irish writing until recently . . . It is only in the post-1968 generation that the confidence to remain true to ordinary modern urban experiences around them finally begins to be displayed.[7]

Bolger formulates a tradition whose main feature is the lack of an underlying tradition. It is not a question of restoring dignity to what has been suppressed – for Seamus Deane, a liberating effect of nationalism – but of representing for the first time an entirely original Irish formation.[8]

This new context generates an incipient post-nationalism, one that emphasises the fragmenting, alienating experience of the city over pastoral values of wholeness and community. Irish nationalism's imagined community, Bolger claims, cannot incorporate the reality of sites that were 'neither country nor city', a fact which not only denaturalises the countryside as a locus of moral value, making it no longer an especially virtuous model for the Irish experience; it also excludes these sites from any concept which historicises their identity as part of any 'collective consciousness', anything remotely resembling a nationalist past.

Modern Irish canons are, of course, intensely contested and self-conscious constructs. For example, Seamus Deane's introduction to *The Field Day Anthology* claims 'there is a metanarrative here, a story of the island which can accommodate the competing micronarratives it hosts'.[9] This is the metanarrative of history, of the various groups who inhabited the island, the one stable signifier for Deane in Ireland's history of invasion and conquest. The Field Day metanarrative, setting aside its well-documented exclusions, subscribes to the principle of an immemorial historic identity comprised of any group historically resident on the island. It is elastic but systematic, inclusive but bound by a commitment to the idea of the nation and the notion that culture can co-operate with or even sponsor the patterns of political narratives. All writing is ideological, Seamus Deane claims in the introduction; all aesthetic terms are ultimately transposable with political terms in creating our individual and collective self-consciousness. The Irish are a written people as well as a risen people, and the fact and form of the latter are inescapably bound up with the former, whether the writing in question is ostensibly creative or political or religious.

In Bolger's anthology, *The Picador Book of Contemporary Irish Fiction*, the foundational text is Beckett's, whose language of exhaustion and abjection famously demystified the whole notion of identity and the concept of an indigenous tradition, while the introduction insists that we ditch such frameworks as post-colonialism in favour of an apparently untheorisable range of 'private, fictional, universes'.[10] Bolger's introduction praises *The Field Day Anthology* but, like Barry and Tóibín, he dispenses with the idea of a historic national identity, a notion aimed at a 'conservative American university audience'.[11] His writers overcome rather than incorporate history, offering instead a thrilling and, it has to be said, highly unlikely talent for self-generation unconnected to any collective entity called Ireland.

National identities, Anthony Smith claims, emerge from 'all those who feel they share certain symbolic codes, value systems and traditions of belief and ritual, including reference to a supra-empirical reality'.[12] Such identities are importantly negative, that is, formed and affirmed against an oppressive one elsewhere, so that once oppression is withdrawn, that identity is disowned. For Bolger, committed to transcending Field Day's obsessive opposition of Ireland and England, while still asserting the specificity of the Republic, some other 'supra-empirical reality' besides the historic nation is now necessary. This is why a critical framework such as post-colonialism, committed to an ethical evaluation of an historically oppressed Irish *national* identity, attracts concentrated fire. Instead, each writer's 'unique and private fictional universe' is acknowledged, and 'it is within the contexts of these private worlds that they [the anthologised writers] should be judged'.[13] Each private consciousness is deemed to constitute a closed space, and any representation of society as a totality must bring into coalition these sealed subjective worlds and their peculiar interaction. This decentring of the individual in relation to a totality, like the nation, Fredric Jameson describes as the essential spatial propensity of postmodernism, 'one that involves our insertion as individual subjects into a multidimensional set of radically discontinuous realities'.[14] Bolger repudiates the concept of a totality for the random and undecidable micropolitics these new urban sites contain. The notion of a totality, 'Ireland', seems to be rejected entirely by reference to the non-essential character of the links uniting the elements of the presumed totality.

But what is uniquely new about this abstract Irish space is its facility for being, as Henri Lefebvre describes it, simultaneously homogeneous and fragmented. The global expansion of industrial capital, Lefebvre claims, bred a remarkably complex relation to abstract space:

> The commodity is a thing: it is in space, and occupies a location... the commodity world brings in its wake certain attitudes towards space, certain actions on space, even a certain concept of space... each location, each link in a chain of commodities, is occupied by a thing whose particular traits become more marked once they become fixed... The space of the commodity may thus be defined as a homogeneity made up of specificities... Space thus understood is both *abstract* and *concrete*. This is a space, therefore, that is homogeneous yet at the same time broken up into fragments.[15]

The political equivalent of this spatial diffusion is, of course, pluralism. Bolger valorises difference for its own sake, envisaging no antagonistic relationship between different social constituencies. But the limits of pluralism are its inability to discriminate between differences that exist and should not, and those that do not but should.[16] Because liberty is the pre-eminent organising principle of Bolger's introduction, no confrontation occurs between the principles of equality and the individual's imaginative freedom. The artistic life, then, chooses the exact nature of its relationship to society, is not compelled to reflect the 'real' conditions surrounding it, any pre-existing 'supra-empirical reality', and is not compromised by its aversion towards history or tradition. Bolger's claim that each private universe is equally 'true' allows for no external ethical criteria by which to judge them, since 'truth' has no force unless there is some falsehood present. 'Truth' here seems to imply the writer's ability to evade the claims of any 'supra-empirical' term like the historic nation, and to claim 'truth' instead to be something linked entirely to the experience of each private fictional universe. In Bolger's terms, which resonate with Tóibín's introduction to his *Soho Square* anthology, this is

> a generation which is still in the process of forming itself; an antho-logy of writers... whose most remarkable characteristic is to share

almost nothing in common except originality; a body of writers who are all working from equally valid, equally true and yet equally different visions.[17]

The rhetoric of pluralism here erases the possibility of a collective cultural difference (and, it might be added, aesthetic discrimination: 'nothing in common except originality'), displacing even the category of Irishness in which we might expect an Irish anthology to invest. It also diminishes any claim for the 'truth' content of these universes, since truth-claims have to somehow measure one's experience against something else. Like Sebastian Barry's 1984 anthology *The Inherited Boundaries: Younger Poets from the Republic of Ireland*, Bolger's anthology inaugurates the tradition it seeks to reflect. But how does this anthology remain a whole if what characterises its constituent parts is an equal separateness, an inviolate individualism? What is the abstract term that links them, apart from Bolger's rhetoric of pure originality?

A literary canon is a hypothetical image of social diversity, a kind of mirror in which social groups do or do not see themselves.[18] But Bolger, Tóibín and Barry's anthologies are not interested in the pathos of admission or exclusion to an expanded canon of 'Irishness'. The object-ive is to banish the concept of an historical identity, any special theory of personality such as the nation or Ireland, and establish a canon that corresponds with Garvin's historiography of the state. And because the state is not partisan, because it has no rational purpose other than to exist, the fact that it sponsors this range of 'private fictional universes', these 'equally valid, equally true and yet equally different viewpoints and visions,' this is proof of its commitment to diversity, its funda-mental liberalism, its ability to sponsor an imagined community capable of incorporating new urban sites. In this incipient post-nationalism, the state begins to replace the island as the one stable signifier in Irish discourse.

Sebastian Barry's introduction to *The Inherited Boundaries*, however, reveals how an ostensibly liberal discourse can be deformed by the rigidity of its defensive postures, by its commitment to naturalise the state's jurisdiction. Barry's polemical aim to synthesise a counter-tradition drifts into utopian proclamations, where Irish identity, having first been banished as traditionalist, now reappears and finds both a ter-minus and new point of departure through writers from the Republic:

The poets assembled here ... they are Irish, the first Irish poets ever in a way, because that adjective has meant so many things in the past that it meant nothing . . . this is a first if fragmentary map of the country.[19]

Just as the state perceives itself to be the terminus of human development, with no horizon beyond its own existence, writers are admitted to this canon only when the artist has freely chosen to abdicate the right not to disobey or contravene the remit of the anthology. Hence the exclusion of writers who might thematise issues like Catholicism and nationalism, any history potentially hostile to the state formations, any writer for example, who subscribes to the ideal of Ireland as an historically definable collective entity.

Bolger's partitionism, along with his description of a 'seven-hundred-year occupation' by a 'foreign army', moved Edna Longley to lament his 'slide between two rhetorics', his 'schizoid separatism'.[20] Yet this rhetoric is consistent with a utopian element in both Barry and Bolger's anthologies. He claims that 1968 is the year when the Republic started to ditch Donoghue's 'premature meaning', a tradition that anchored writers to a socio-political context which they had no choice but to reflect. It is the year in which the Republic introduced free secondary education. By then, emigration had stopped and a generation emerged of 'writers and readers who had nothing to lose by taking apart that state to examine how it worked inside'.[21] This is typical of the relentlessly progressive dynamic of Bolger's introduction, and while it is obviously accurate within its own terms, nowhere does it register the festering civil rights agitation in the north that spawned the Provisional IRA and 25 years of armed conflict. Of course, the cataclysmic events of May '68 across Europe actually originated *in* the universities, as part of a general revolt against the sterility of political and cultural life the nation state sponsored. Inspired by May 1968, Foucault decoded the structures of power through which the state naturalised its authority over social space. If the rapturous political energies of '68 had one guiding theme, it was the challenge posed to all existing forms of political representation in order to liberate the individual into new, as yet unthought-of, forms of community.

Bolger's version of '68 is more modest. As outlined in the anthology, it is egalitarian and heterogeneous, homogeneous yet still fragmented, and implicitly it dissociates nationality from citizenship. The values contained in the social spaces it articulates are irretrievably organised around the idea of the state. With this symbolic opening, Bolger's anthology expunges the North from the Republic's collective memory. The state is enlisted as the guarantor of newly liberated imagination, and the traditional constraints of a national tradition no longer apply; the only meta-narrative these writers know is the silent, ever-present narrative of the state.[22]

But how different is this 'liberal' formation based on a neutral space like the state from the historically loaded narrative of the nation? Bolger's introduction focuses on the new socio-political structures represented, but has little to say about the aesthetic. Again and again he categorises writers according to the social constituencies they reflect – urban, gay, emigrant, women, etc. – terms which ultimately, of course, do not describe the writing but the society the writing describes. What is new and novel in Bolger's anthology is the *state*, the steady, relentless, Whiggish maturity of which the anthology describes, naturalises and elaborates. The only constant, premature order in Bolger's anthology is the state that permits a systematically random amalgamation of writers no longer gnarled by Irish/English, Catholic/Protestant dichotomies.

Bolger's anthology, his work as a publisher and his many edited collections sponsor and consciously create a youthful, liberally minded and enthusiastically European constituency. But the justification for the constituency is always made in terms which refer back to the idea of difference; it is just that the difference is no longer ethnic or national, but is instead difference from what has gone before, differences within and between the concept of 'the Irish' themselves. The reaction against an 'idea of nationhood which simply could not contain the Ireland of concrete and dual-carriageway (which is as Irish as turf and boreens) that was the reality before our eyes'[23] displaces colonial faultlines, the Anglo-Irish obsessions of Field Day, for the internal divisions of class and geography within the polity. There is still a systematic and elastic meta-narrative capable of containing competing micro-narratives; it is just that it is now the meta-narrative of the state. This is not a wholly unprecedented way of organising experience: it mirrors Field Day's much-criticised schema by retaining a totalising meta-narrative: all that differs is the stable signifier – nation or state – that makes possible meaning. And that, of course, if one concedes that the two differ, is ultimately a political, not an aesthetic choice.

The Marching Season

The political consequences of this kind of aesthetic distinction are, I want to argue, prominent and legible in Colm Tóibín's *Bad Blood: A Walk Along the Irish Border*,[24] a travel narrative which documents some of the most obstinately tangible realities of Irish history. Here is where

Tóibín's liberalism creaks under the weight of a sectarian history that refuses to end. The book enacts a belief that history can be reflected and recorded but not transformed, for it skirts along the perimeter of an area that the travel narrative deems to be irretrievably outwith history. Because the 'single mind and imagination' of Tóibín the traveller can never engage with the competing collective consciousnesses beyond the border, the southern intellectual disengages with the whole idea of the north as subject to change.

Mixing metaphysical exposition and sociological observation, *Bad Blood* details Tóibín's journey along the Northern Irish border in the summer of 1985, several months after the signing of the Anglo-Irish Agreement, a document which, by formally acknowledging the Republic's role in certain internal affairs of Northern Ireland, caused bitter resentment amongst Northern Unionists. The Republic as a state seemed willing to embroil itself in Irish nationalism, a strategy which offended many Irish liberals. Mary Robinson, for instance, resigned from the Irish Labour party in protest at its support for the agreement.[25]

In an important essay Joe Cleary has pointed to the 'discursive invisibility' of partition in Irish cultural discourse, the various modes of 'censorship, including self-censorship, [that] have generated elaborate circumlocutions or forms of doublespeak that express positions on the partition question even when they appear to side-step that uncomfortable topic altogether'.[26] *Bad Blood* aims to discover a discourse that is flexible and sufficiently ambiguous to manoeuvre between nationalism and unionism, Protestantism and Catholicism, revisionism and traditionalism. The journey cannot contest or transform territorial boundaries already established by the Boundary Commission formed in 1921. Tóibín's route has already been decided by history, so that complete volition or agency is neither possible nor necessary because the freedom to undertake this journey arises only when he accepts the limitations imposed upon him by both states. The book thus contains a psychology, a history and a politics: the journey's beginning, route and end are predicated on the notion that history is indelibly inscribed on the landscape and therefore exhausted as a dialectical process. The terrain cannot be transformed, and the only available challenge is to procure a form of words to endure the journey.

The only formal resource supporting Tóibín's trip is the Tyrone Guthrie Arts Centre in Annaghmakerrig, a centre set up by Sir Tyrone Guthrie to give artists and writers free board during projects. Other than this practical support, he is alone. The larger scheme of the book thus becomes: how can the category of the aesthetic and the category of the individual, as a discrete subject, survive in a sectarian landscape that recognises only the most polarised communal oppositions? The walk is full of moments which Mary Louise Pratt describes as 'contact zones': spaces in which peoples geographically and historically separate come into contact with each other and establish ongoing relationships.[27] Travel writing as a genre engages a narrator's individual consciousness with what is deemed to be alien, exotic or other, and in Ireland this has traditionally meant the West.[28] For Tóibín, the southern, secular post-nationalist intellectual, the north is culturally and constitutionally set apart from 'the South' (perhaps explaining Seamus Deane's pithy description of the book as 'futile').[29] Like Bolger and Barry's antholo-gies, the genre implicitly acknowledges a separate reality for the North.

This is how Tóibín's much-praised, simple, forensic prose style should be viewed. The tone is always non-judgemental, non-evaluative, for there is no possibility of Tóibín imagining ourselves as different from what we are. The kind of active virtue Yeats endorsed was part of the project of imagining a nation, an entity called Ireland; this passive acceptance of the current code is part of the project of naturalising the state, north and south. The style chronicles the inalienable separateness of both states. The facts, it would seem, speak for themselves, as the narrative naturalises the religious, cultural and ethnic divisions under observation and the political states that accord with them.[30] The separ-ate states become, as Cleary puts it, a symptom of a reality which is, *a priori*, irretrievably split along sectarian lines, and thus no further com-ment is necessary on differences incubated over centuries, no intrusive narrative evaluation need take place.[31] The solitary act of writing is thus analogous to the isolation of his journey. Writing provides a space that is somehow part of but removed from the complicated mesh of national boundaries and political borders he must physically inhabit. Tim Youngs' comments are suggestive here:

> This intense concentration on literary travel as an individual, imaginative and creative phenomenon is profoundly indicative of the 'postcolonial' shift towards a deceptively democratic form of peregrination. Writing one's way out of position becomes the very marker of one's place ... the concentration on writing as a process through which identity is realised may be a distraction from the political and cultural factors on which identity in fact depends.[32]

The state is a symptom, never a cause of the divisions he encounters, an inalienable element in the given order of things which his continually mobile, continually displaced status as a traveller cannot confront or change.

Such a methodology has deep ideological implications, for Brendan Bradshaw's primary criticism of revisionist history is of the myopia of its professionalism, its obsession with a value-free narrative that 'denies historians recourse to value judgements and, therefore, access to the kind of moral and emotional register necessary to respond to human tragedy'.[33] It lacks any tragic dimension, any capacity for registering the memory of loss, or, in Bradshaw's phrase, the catastrophic dimension to Irish history. As Carol Kaplan puts it, the 'nomad represents a subject position that offers an idealised model of movement based on perpetual displacement', a strategy that prematurely disallows the possibility of Tóibín becoming an agent in his own history.[34] His progress along the border is relentlessly progressive: there is a determined refusal to engage with or be side-tracked by any idealistic theory of the irrational, of imperialism, or of nationalism, those elements which fuel the history that actually created the border. The route taken possesses a gravitational, teleological pull that implies the solution to any problems encountered is known in advance; he rejects any narrative not insolubly linked to the local and the 'real' as they are encountered daily in the world, abdicating his right to enjoy a complete historical consciousness in order to act freely within the confines of an unchanging state.

The year 1985, the year of Tóibín's journey, also saw the Republic convulsed by a series of highly fractious referendums on divorce, and it is this context that surrounds the aesthetic.

> The result of the divorce referendum was made known the following Friday morning. It was clear and overwhelming: the country had voted no. I was in Monaghan, at Annaghmakerrig, the house which Sir Tyrone Guthrie had left to the Irish nation as a retreat for artists ... He specified in his will, when leaving the house to the nation, that the artists should eat together in the evening. The house was supported by the Arts Councils, North and South; people came from both sides of the border. The area around the house was still a mixed society, with thriving Church of Ireland, Presbyterian and Catholic congregations. (*BB*, p. 49)

The artist's immediate context is the oppressive Catholic legislation of the Republic; the Guthrie Centre provides a possible context, one in which religious difference is not synonymous with cultural and ethnic division. The Guthrie Centre is *of* history, but because it contains and sponsors the aesthetic, it is not destined to repeat history as politics: it does not funnel historic divisions into the present moment. Thus Culture is presented as an ostensibly autonomous zone, but the disinterested autonomy of the aesthetic, the mythic solution it opposes to the surrounding sectarianism, not only leaves the role of the state in all this unchallenged, it actively seals the Republic from contamination by a historical narrative in the North that shows no sign of ending.

The impact of the aesthetic is never fully explained, just glimpsed at irregular intervals when Tóibín has trouble with maps or travels down roads that end nowhere, have been abandoned, closed or in some way become redundant. The map that points the way towards feeling at home does not rely on the accumulation of empirical detail. The aesthetic is disinterested in any form of knowledge that is oppositional, as Tóibín's exchange with a British soldier demonstrates. For if topography is no longer an adequate or stable symbol for the contemporary Irish condition, as Tóibín, Barry and Bolger claim in their anthologies, cartography can no longer unproblematically reflect and represent that landscape. In other words, only the aesthetic can point the way towards feeling at home.

> I saw the soldiers straight ahead...He showed me his map...The map was incredibly detailed, every house, every field, every road, carefully denoted and described. It would be impossible to go wrong with such a map. Different colours made everything clear. He laughed when I explained my plight with maps. I showed him my Michelin and my Ordnance, and he shook his head in wonder at how out-of-date they were. His was the map I should have, he said. (*BB*, p. 163)

The militaristic facts and precision make everything cognitively clear but imaginatively opaque. The soldier's laughter stems from the epistemological, even ontological gulf between his and Tóibín's map.[35] Faced with roads closed or controlled by the British military or northern nationalism, Tóibín's map has to be created by transcending the immediate tangible realities of the conflict and trusting the aesthetic to ensure he *avoids* danger spots.

> None of the roads the soldier suggested was marked on my map...I had abandoned the Ordnance Survey map on the basis that it was

better to carry a map with a few roads marked than a map with too many, some of which didn't exist. (*BB*, p. 170)

The Guthrie Centre and the aesthetic thus offer the only realistic route through Irish history and politics. Tóibín has to map what Bolger called a 'private fictional universe' in order to negotiate this terrain. There is no possibility of changing the historical route he must take, just interpreting it as an inalienable element in the given order of things and avoiding any confrontation with it. The imagination that chronicles partition thus seals partition, finally accommodating its own segregation within inviolable state borders. For maps, as J. B. Hartley explains, are a major example of the interaction between a state polity and military technology.

> Military maps are a small but vital cog in the technical infrastructure of the army in the field ... Map knowledge allows the conduct of warfare by remote control so that, we may speculate, killing is more easily contemplated. Military maps not only facilitate the technical conduct of warfare, but also palliate the sense of guilt which arises from its conduct: the silent lines of the paper landscape foster the notion of a socially empty space.[36]

This 'socially empty space' (so similar to Lefebvre's view of the state as the space that flattens or crushes conflicts and contradictions in the social and cultural spheres) is given tacit assent by Tóibín's determination to adhere to already permanently inscribed, immutable borders between the northern and southern states. Tóibín appropriates the aesthetic to enable him to stick unerringly to the state's border, to a space whose only rational interest is in preserving its disinterest in everything except the present moment in which its own being is comprehended. This is the impoverished dialectical space Tóibín's aesthetic wilfully occupies. The cognitive map his aesthetic creates abdicates any possibility of a political agency that could deviate from this pre-programmed historical route. For as David Harvey notes, 'Mapping is a discursive activity that incorporates power. The power to map the world in one way rather than another is a crucial tool in political struggles. Power struggles over mapping ... are therefore fundamental moments in the production of discourses.'[37]

The passage on the Guthrie Centre occurs in the chapter entitled 'The Road to Darkley', scene of a sectarian massacre by the Irish National Liberation Army in 1985, and immediately afterwards in the narrative

Tóibín comes across Swift's entry in the guest book at an eighteenth-century guesthouse:

> Glaslough with rows of books upon its shelves
> written by the Leslies all about themselves. (*BB*, p. 165)

Swift is part of a cognitive map that enables Tóibín to confront and *evade* a militarised public space. Even on the road to Darkley, the aesthetic is glimpsed, inescapably caught up with politics but never necessarily political. For on both occasions, at the Guthrie Centre and this guesthouse, the aesthetic offers sanctuary from the route Tóibín negotiates. It is not the representation of place that determines whether the aesthetic comes into existence but the place that is being represented. The final effect of representing partition is the segregation of the imagination within the state that accords with its perceived originary moment. The last episode of 'The Road to Darkley' has Tóibín, and the pastor of the Darkley church where the massacre took place, point in opposite, completely incommensurate political and spiritual directions:

> When Bob Bain came out we walked around the hall until we faced north towards Armagh. I pointed to the Catholic Cathedral jutting up out of the town. 'Would you like to have a church as big as that?' I asked him. He wouldn't, he said; what he had here was stronger and better, he was sure of that. (*BB*, p. 182)

The implicit point of the exchange, which utilises the symbolic power of the Armagh Cathedral, home of the Catholic Primate of all Ireland, is that each belongs to fundamentally different, absolutely irreconcilable historical narratives.

A Public Sphere?

For Tóibín, Barry and Bolger, there is no common context or memory writers and individuals can be assumed to share. Bolger's urban space accords individual freedom priority over any public aspiration to the good: justice is construed as the absence of any impediment to the realisation of this private individuality. Throughout his novels, Bolger's characters are oppressed by any formulations of justice that are communal. By separating citizenship from nationality, the city provides a measure of anonymity and freedom; and the absence of public virtue is not, ultimately, a sufficient reason for Bolger to forego this inviolable privacy. Tóibín's travels along the border symbolically inscribe a narrow liberal space. Inaugurated and guaranteed by the existence of the state, this space is connected to but separate from the competing claims of nationalism and loyalism, Catholicism and Protestantism; and the present time of the state insulates Tóibín from these adversarial historical forces.

But are these public forces really in unrelenting opposition to a private individualism, as Tóibín, Barry and Bolger claim, and what form of liberalism is offered by these prominent proponents of a separate 'southern' culture? In *Liberalism and the Limits of Justice*, Michael J. Sandel touches on some of the issues at stake here, using language that has, in an Irish context, an additional resonance. Sandel comments on John Rawls' distinction between the right and the good, a distinction in which Rawls claims

> we are free and independent selves, unbound by antecedent moral ties, capable of choosing our ends for ourselves. This is the conception of the person that finds expression in the ideal of the state as a neutral framework. It is precisely because we are free and independent selves, capable of choosing our own ends, that we need a framework of rights that is neutral among ends. To base rights on some conception of the good would impose on some the values of others and so fail to respect each person's capacity to choose his or her own ends.[38]

Is the free and independent Republic a state in which the self retains some shared conception of the good? Does an adversarial past that is, as Tóibín's narrative demonstrates, still stubbornly visible in the present, disable any attempt to make the state something more than a neutral framework? And what role does the aesthetic play in this process? Tóibín disassociates the north from any possible conception of the good in the Republic, but the criticism here is not that Tóibín's diagnosis is wrong or that liberalism is structurally incapable of addressing the issues his work makes visible; Tóibín's is, of course, only one of the many varieties of liberalism, and his anti-nationalism is actually post-liberal. Rather, it is that the conscription of the aesthetic into his writing works to conceal the inadequacy of his political vision. In his writing, the aesthetic and the political are different aspects of the same things, braided together to avoid any possible contact with a history beyond the state's borders. Like Bolger, Tóibín seems to construe justice by its distance from any order that is antecedent to us. Neither allows for the possibility of a public culture in which the past has the potential to provide a shared fund of commonly recognised ideas. Tóibín, Bolger and Barry all posit disagreement on aims and goals as the reason for rejecting any philosophical underpinning that could provide aims or goals. The political life which their aesthetic describes leaves little room for the kind of public deliberation necessary to test the plausibility of contending moralities – to persuade others of the merits of nationalist or Catholic or Protestant ideals. It is not that Tóibín, Bolger and Barry are necessarily wrong that is the criticism levelled here: it is that they envisage a polis in which citizens may not introduce into political discourse their comprehensive moral and religious convictions, at least when debating matters of justice and rights, especially in the north.[39] The Republic is a space that should not invoke any philosophical foundations for the new liberal arrangements within the state, other than that they must remain distant from a nationalist past. If literary anthologies are hypothetical images of social diversity,[40] the variety of private fictional universes in Tóibín, Barry and Bolger's anthologies offers a form of pluralism that allows no substantive judgements on issues that might query the underlying assumptions of the role of the state, its potential for defining a justice that is not inalienably separated from the communal history of the nation. The fact of reasonable pluralism about the good is a form of postmodern relativism that establishes the priority of rights; there can be no social co-operation among these various adherents, except if they are co-operating to validate the state as a neutral space in which, to quote Tóibín's introduction to *Soho Square: New Writing from Ireland*, there are 'no responsibilities'. This affirmation of difference within the state is now the same as the affirmation of sameness with the nation: the very same conceptual framework of difference and sameness, opposition and affirmation, is replayed.

'Modern Irish politics', says Denis Donoghue, is 'a politics of the same, not a politics of difference'.

> Many Irish people have grown tired of being told that they are interesting beyond their numbers or that the trajectory from race through nation to state has made them distinguished among their European associates. They want to be the same as everyone else, the same as England to begin with and as the United States later on. It is their right.[41]

To claim the right to have 'no responsibilities', not even the responsibility to confront and evaluate Darkley, a slaughter which threatens the very basis of meaning and liberty, is to ensure that this brand of liberalism will never do more than facilitate two communities who point in incommensurate directions. Ireland will thus never be 'the same'; rather it will remain disfigured by differences which the state thinks it is its duty to genially accommodate. In Tóibín's presentation, the state will designate as an alien 'other' anyone who suggests its political duties exceed its territorial remit.

This form of liberal detachment is unduly severe. It affirms the virtues of political liberalism only for political purposes, for their role in supporting a constitutional regime, a state, that protects people's rights. But as Sandel notes, 'Whether and to what extent these virtues should figure in people's moral lives generally is a question political liberalism does not figure to answer.'[42] A liberalism that terminates the Republic's engagement with Darkley, with the north, with any theory of the 'irrational' that actually spawned the states we inhabit is not a liberalism worth having. It is abstract and decorous. In Ireland of all spaces, it is not possible to be neutral on every issue. Impartiality does not always serve justice; in certain instances it can simply mask oppression. In *Bad Blood*, when Colm Tóibín's 'liberalism' imaginatively insulates the state from the history of the nation from which it derives, this is an example of what Sandel calls the restrictive nature of liberal public reason: the belief that politics should avoid rather than express substantive moral judgements.

I think that Irish liberals like Tóibín should face this issue. Liberalism must offer some substantive and coherent conception of what is good, not withdraw to hermetic and private universes in defence of the right not to be assaulted by tradition and history. In Ireland, our conception of our selves as private citizens is not, after all, completely divorced from the public identity we establish through cultural practice. And it is not feasible for a claim to carry weight simply because it is made by us as private citizens. Fundamentalists rush in where liberals fear to tread, in the space between the incommensurate identities Tóibín's studiously non-judgemental prose describes but never evaluates.

Notes

1   Tom Garvin, 'The North and the Rest', in Charles Townshend (ed.), *Consensus in Ireland: Approaches and Recessions* (Oxford: Clarendon, 1988), pp. 95–109, p. 95.

2   Joe Cleary, 'Partition and the Politics of Form in Contemporary Narratives of Northern Ireland', *Ireland and Cultural Studies*, special issue of *The South Atlantic Quarterly*, 95:1 (Winter 1996), pp. 227–8. Cleary's essay provides important insights into the themes discussed here, and I am indebted to its general methodology as well as its local criticism.

3 See 'The Republic of Ireland and the Conflict in Northern Ireland', in Joseph Ruane and Jennifer Todd, *The Dynamics of Conflict in Northern Ireland* (Cambridge: Cambridge University Press, 1996), p. 249; more generally, see pp. 232–66.

4 Colm Tóibín (ed.), *Soho Square: New Writing from Ireland* (London: Bloomsbury, 1993), p. 9.

5 See Terence Brown, 'Dublin in Twentieth-Century Writing: Metaphor and Subject', in *Irish University Review*, 8, no. 1 (Spring 1978), pp. 1–19.

6 Dermot Bolger, *Invisible Dublin: A Journey Through Dublin's Suburbs* (Dublin: Raven Arts Press, 1991), p. 12.

7 Dermot Bolger, *The Picador Book of Contemporary Irish Fiction* (1993; revised and expanded edition, London: Picador, 1994), pp. xviii-xix.

8 See Seamus Deane, 'Heroic Styles: The Tradition of an Idea', in *Ireland's Field Day* (Notre Dame: University of Notre Dame Press, 1984), p. 47.

9 Seamus Deane, 'Introduction' in Seamus Deane (ed.), *The Field Day Anthology of Irish Writing*, Vol. I (Derry: Field Day, 1994).

10 Bolger, *The Picador Book of Contemporary Irish Fiction*, p. xxiii.

11 Ibid., p. xxii.

12 Anthony D. Smith, *National Identity* (Harmondsworth: Penguin, 1991), p. 6.

13 Bolger, *The Picador Book of Contemporary Irish Fiction*, p. xvi.

14 Fredric Jameson, 'Cognitive Mapping', in *Marxism and the Interpretation of Culture* (Basingstoke: Macmillan, 1988), p. 353.

15 Henri Lefebvre, *The Production of Space*, trans. Donald Nicholson-Smith (Oxford: Blackwell, 1991) p. 341. Emphasis in original.

16 On this point, see Chantal Mouffe, 'Democratic Politics Today', in Chantal Mouffe (ed.), *Dimensions of Radical Democracy: Pluralism, Citizenship, Community* (London: Verso, 1992), p. 13.

17 Bolger, 'Introduction', *The Picador Book of Contemporary Irish Fiction*, p. xxvii.

18 John Guillory, *Cultural Capital: The Problem of Literary Canon Formation* (Chicago: University of Chicago Press, 1993), p. 7.

19 Sebastian Barry, *The Inherited Boundaries: Younger Poets from the Republic of Ireland* (Dublin: Mercier Press, 1986), p. 17. The introduction is titled 'The History and Topography of Nowhere'.

20 Edna Longley, *The Living Stream: Literature and Revisionism in Ireland* (Newcastle-upon-Tyne: Bloodaxe, 1994), p. 48.

21 Bolger, *The Picador Book of Contemporary Irish Fiction*, p. x.

22 See 'Speaking with . . . Dermot Bolger', in *In Cognito*, 1 (1997). Interviewer: 'Do you think here is the foundation for a Dublin literary tradition?' Bolger: 'I don't think there's such a thing as a tradition' (p. 15).

23 Dermot Bolger (ed.), *The Bright Wave/ An Tonn Gheal: Poetry in Irish Now* (Dublin: Raven Arts Press, 1986), p. 10.

24 Colm Tóibín, *Bad Blood: A Walk Along the Irish Border* (1987; London: Vintage,1995). Hereafter referred to as *BB*, with all further page numbers bracketed within the text.

25 See Garret Fitzgerald, 'The Origins and Rationale of the Anglo-Irish Agreement of 1985', pp. 189–207, and Paul Arthur, 'The Anglo-Irish Agreement: A Device for Territorial Management', pp. 208–25, in Dermot Keogh and Michael H. Haltzel (eds.), *Northern Ireland and the Politics of Reconciliation* (Cambridge: Cambridge University Press, 1993).

26 Joe Cleary, 'Partition and the Politics of Form in Contemporary Narratives of Northern Ireland', pp. 227, 228.

27 Mary Louise Pratt, *Imperial Eyes: Travel Writing and Transculturation* (London: Routledge, 1992), pp. 1–10.

28 Barbara O' Connor and Michael Cronin (eds.), *Tourism in Ireland: A Cultural Analysis* (Cork: Cork University Press, 1992).

29 Dympna O'Callaghan, 'An Interview With Seamus Deane', *Social Text*, 38 (1994), p. 40.

30 See Thomas M. Wilson and Hastings Donnan, 'Nation, State and Identity at International Borders', in Thomas Wilson and Hastings Donnan (eds.), *Border Identities: Nation and State in International Frontiers* (Cambridge: Cambridge University Press, 1998), pp. 1–31.

31 Cleary, 'Partition and the Politics of Form in Contemporary Narratives of Northern Ireland', p. 267.

32 Tim Youngs, 'Punctuating Travel: Paul Theroux and Bruce Chatwin', *Literature and History*, 6, no. 2 (Autumn 1997), pp. 79–81. For an evocative and commendably sceptical view of contemporary Ireland through a travel narrative, see Rebecca Solnit, *A Book of Migrations: Some Passages in Ireland* (London: Verso, 1997).

33 Brendan Bradshaw, 'Nationalism and Historical Scholarship in Modern Ireland', in Brady (ed.), *Interpreting Irish History*, p. 204.

34 Quoted in Youngs, 'Punctuating Travel', p. 83.

35 See J. B. Hartley, 'Maps, Knowledge, Power', in Denis Cosgrove and Stephen Daniels (eds.), *The Iconography of Landscape* (Cambridge: Cambridge University Press, 1988), pp. 277–312.

36 Ibid., p. 284.

37 David Harvey, *Justice, Nature and the Geography of Difference* (Oxford: Blackwell, 1996), p. 112.

38 Michael J. Sandel, *Liberalism and the Limits of Justice* (2nd edition; Cambridge: Cambridge University Press, 1998), p. 187.

39 Ibid., p. 211.

40 John Guillory, *Cultural Capital: The Problem of Literary Canon Formation* (Chicago: University of Chicago Press, 1993), p. 7.

41 Denis Donoghue, *The Parnell Lecture 1997–1998: Ireland: Race, Nation, State* (Cambridge: Magdalene College Occasional Papers, 1998), p. 27.

42 Ibid., p. 195.

Part II
Culture

5
Modernization and Aesthetic Ideology in Contemporary Irish Culture

Joe Cleary

I

In Cathal Black's *Korea* (1996), a darkly lit and moody film set in rural Ireland in the summer of 1952, there is a scene in which the inhabitants of a small village assemble by lamplight for a ceremony to mark the turning on of the recently installed electricity. On a platform, surrounded by a knot of local notables sitting under a banner inscribed 'Rural Electrification', an elderly parish priest presides over the ceremony, scattering holy water and intoning a passage from Genesis about the creation of light 'which shines in the darkness and the darkness has not overcome it'. When the priest pulls the lever that is supposed to light up the village for the first time, however, nothing happens and the bemused villagers break into fatalistic laughter: 'Nothing works in this town', one guffaws; 'The electricity, how are yah!' another mocks. A moment later, though, there is a burst of illumination when the new streetlights suddenly flicker on, and the villagers erupt into excited applause. 'Rural electrification,' a local dignitary proudly proclaims, 'is more than an amenity. It is a revolution that will sweep away the inferiority complexes.' In the crowd, a disgruntled republican veteran of the War of Independence watching his Free State rival bask in satisfaction at this latest sign of the state's progress into modernity, grudgingly remarks: 'It wasn't for street lamps we fought.' By now, however, the villagers are belting out the national anthem, and the scene concludes with a shot of a magnificent summer moon evenly sliced between darkness and light.

For the political or constitutional historian, 1948 represents a landmark in modern Irish history, the moment when the Irish Free State severed its residual links with Britain to become a fully independent and sovereign Republic. For the economic historian, however, 1958 – the moment when Sean Lemass and T. K. Whittaker launched the First Programme for Economic Expansion that abandoned the protectionist policies of the previous generation and opened the country to foreign investment and multinational capital – will seem the more decisive watershed. The conjunction of the two events is suggestive. The establishment of an Irish Republic announced in 1948 was hailed at the time as a moment when the long struggle for southern Irish sovereignty finally attained its goal or end-point. A mere ten years later, a sceptic might argue, that vaunted sovereignty indeed reached its end – not as goal or fulfilment, however, but as terminus – when the strategy of autarkic development was jettisoned and the state embarked on an alternative strategy of dependent development. This strategy would see Ireland increasingly integrated into the global capitalist economy and into the European Union, a process that would entail a steady erosion of the political sovereignty that was supposed to have reached its apotheosis with the declaration of the Republic in 1948.

Though the strategy of dependent development pursued over the past four decades is nowadays generally considered much more successful than its autarkic predecessor, in reality both have been characterized from the start by recurrent, sometimes very severe, crises. During the period of autarkic development, the state's official policy was to build up domestic industry behind a protective wall of tariff barriers designed to stimulate Irish economic self-sufficiency and to reduce an inherited dependence on British markets. By the end of the 1940s, economic stagnation, continued dependence on Britain, and very high levels of emigration all seemed to confirm the ignominious failure of this particular modernization project. When the alternative strategy of dependent development was inaugurated in the late 1950s import restrictions were removed, and a whole variety of fiscal incentives was gradually put in place to court multinational capital, intended to supply the drive to economic development that domestic Irish efforts had failed to generate. From the 1970s until the mid-1990s, however, southern society suffered a severe and protracted recession that begged the question as to whether dependent development would prove any more successful than the abandoned autarky. Throughout this period Irish society struggled under a massive burden of international debt, continually escalating unemployment levels (in 1991 this exceeded the 20 per cent mark), and rates of emigration that had reached levels not witnessed since the 1950s.[1] Since the mid-1990s, however, the country has enjoyed a dramatic reversal of fortune, and has experienced unprecedented rates of economic growth, falling unemployment levels, dramatic urban revitalization and a steady inflow of return migration.

With the Irish Republic now widely hailed as the most rapidly growing economy in the European Union, the success of the 'Celtic Tiger' since the mid-1990s has inevitably been perceived as a triumphant, even if delayed, vindication of the strategy of dependent development. Moreover, for those disposed to see the essential conflict in Irish society as one between the backward forces of 'tradition' and the progressive forces of 'modernization', economic success seemed to bring with it a corresponding drive towards 'modernization' in the wider socio-political sphere as well. The success of the divorce referendum in 1995 represented a significant victory for the forces of liberal secularism over those of Catholic conservatism. When this was followed in 1998 by the overwhelming public endorsement of the Good Friday Agreement – which was expected to put an end to the 'armed struggle' in the North – the southern state's capacity to function as a 'normal' and prosperous liberal capitalist democracy unthreatened by war in its immediate vicinity seemed finally more assured.

The episode of rural electrification dramatized in Black's *Korea* can be read as a tightly compressed allegory of this wider history. The scene in which the electricity initially misfires but later bursts into illumination registers not only the sense of heightened expectation, but also the many false starts and attendant social tensions and misgivings that have characterized the course of Irish modernization in the latter half of this century. In several countries, including the United States and India, one of the quintessential icons of industrial modernization is the railway. In Ireland, rural electrification has served an equivalent function. The centrality of the motif suggests that in the Irish context there is a particularly acute stress on modernization not simply as a matter of technological or industrial development, but as a project which is expected to deliver cultural and psychological enlightenment as well: to serve as 'a revolution that will sweep away the inferiority complexes', as the dignitary in Black's film grandly declares. The shift from the age of De Valera to that of Lemass, or from autarky to dependent development, is commonly understood in precisely these terms: as a transition from the psychological insecurity and oppressive murk of an Irish 'dark age' into a self-confident and enlightened new era of economic, political and cultural progress.

While Black's film deploys this language, the awkward moment when the switch is tripped but the expected illumination fails to materialize suggests that the transition from a supposed social condition of prim-eval darkness to one of technological enlightenment is neither smooth nor assured. When a particular modernization strategy falters – as hap-pened in the 1940s and 50s, or again in the 1970s and 80s – doubts quicken and cynics readily step forward to assert that political and eco-nomic failure constitutes the predictable pattern of Irish history. In *Korea*, however, the electricity, despite the embarrassing glitch and nervous delay, does come on in the end and darkness does not overcome it. To this extent, it might be suggested, the film expresses a distinctively 1990s sense of confidence in the course of Irish modernization, the tra-vails of the previous quarter century notwithstanding. On the other hand, there is also the voice of the disgruntled republican who protests, amid the general chorus of approval, that 'we didn't fight for street lamps'. In Black's film that voice is inflected with a sense of *ressentiment* which undoubtedly undercuts its authority. None the less, it still strikes a discordant note, one that registers the anxiety that the path of contemporary Irish modernization might represent the dissolution of Irish sovereignty for which so much struggle and sacrifice had been expended. Closing as it does with that striking shot of the moon evenly segmented between light and darkness, the episode seems in the end to hesitate between confidence and doubt, to suggest a sense of tentative-ness about the course of Irish social development that will not easily resolve itself.

Why is it that contemporary Irish culture, even in the swinging 1990s, remains so obsessed with the decades of Irish autarkic develop-ment? What accounts for this fixation? To some extent the obsessive return to these decades at this remove suggests a sense of Irish history as trauma: it discloses a need to recreate a history in which an overwhelm-ing event could not be fully assimilated at the time of its occurrence, and which must therefore belatedly be compulsively re-possessed. In other ways, the recurrent return to that period, usually conceived as a grimly oppressive 'dark age', clearly acts as a negative validation of the present which, whatever else it might be, is understood as a lucky escape 'from all that'. Whatever the motives involved, and in the more interesting narratives they are usually mixed, there can be little doubt that contemporary Irish culture has constructed this period as *the* defin-itive zone of memory for an understanding of Irish society today. One of the tasks that I want to attempt in this essay, therefore, will be to examine the aesthetic ideologies and narrative codes through which that imagined past is constructed, and to consider the social functions that it serves for the present.

For a variety of reasons, the conception of modernization that currently prevails in contemporary Irish society is a quite restricted and even impoverished one. When the Republic entered the EEC in 1972, the Labour Party led the campaign against integration; but in the period since then it has become one of the standard-bearers for increased integration and has also tacitly endorsed the strategy of dependent development. Since the late 1980s especially, ever-increasing levels of cross-party political consensus on economic policy have helped to smother debate where matters concerning the general nature and direction of Irish development are concerned. Secondly, the terms that structure contemporary Irish discourse, especially in some elements of academia and the media, are borrowed wholesale from post-war American modernization theories. Such theories are predicated on a dichotomy between two ideal social types: the 'traditional' society (which can also be called 'rural,' 'backward' or 'underdeveloped') and the 'modern' society (or 'urban,' 'developed' or 'industrial'). These modernization theories assume that so-called traditional societies can follow the same patterns of change undergone earlier by more developed nations; they seek, therefore, to explore the institutional arrangements, cultural values and other social variables that allow traditional societies to become modern as effectively as possible.[2] Given the one-sided and non-dialectical understanding encouraged by the sclerotic dichotomy between 'tradition' and 'modernity' that subtends these theories, modernization can only be conceived in wholly positive terms, and opposition to it, from whatever source, can always be dismissed as simply another manifestation of recalcitrant 'tradition'.[3]

It would be wrong to suggest, however, that the political and academic discourses described here totally monopolize the public sphere. Cultural practices have an important, though usually less well recognized, role to play in making sense of various processes of modernization and in shaping popular response to the dilemmas which they generate. Do contemporary Irish cultural discourses, then, express a more complex response to the process of modernization than the orthodox political and academic discourses described above? Or do they simply serve as artistic alibi to the more official discourses? These are questions that I will want to investigate in this essay. My study will be confined to literary and cinematic works, and, given the narrow limits of the survey, the answers sketched will remain tentative and provisional. I will want to suggest that, on the whole, contemporary Irish literature and cinema display more ambivalence about the direction of current modernization policy than we are likely to find in the prevailing political and intellectual discourses, but that the dominant aesthetic ideologies that shape contemporary Irish narrative tend nevertheless to stymie strong critique.

II

In *All That Is Solid Melts Into Air*, Marshall Berman argues that the works of some of the major writers of the nineteenth century – among them Goethe, Carlyle, Marx, Kierkegaard, Melville, Pushkin and Dostoyevsky – are distinguished by their capacity to grasp both sides of the contradictions of capitalist development. 'Our nineteenth-century thinkers,' Berman writes, 'were simultaneously enthusiasts and enemies of modern life, wrestling inexhaustibly with its ambiguities and contradictions; their self-ironies and inner tensions were a primary source of their creative power.' Their twentieth-century successors, however, Berman argues, 'have lurched far more toward rigid polarities and flat totalizations. Modernity is either embraced with a blind and uncritical enthusiasm, or else condemned with a neo-Olympian remoteness and contempt; in either case it is conceived as a closed monolith, incapable of being shaped or changed by modern men.'[4] For Berman, this drastic polarization in modern thought is exemplified by, on the one side, the rhapsodic modernolatory of Marinetti and the Italian Futurists, Le Corbusier and Marshall McLuhan and, on the other, the visions of modernity as catastrophe and decline that run, as he sees it, all the way from Weber to Spengler to Eliot and from Leavis to Marcuse. Berman's work rests on an untenable distinction between a nineteenth-century intelligentsia receptive to the dialectics of modernity and a twentieth-century one that is much less so. One doesn't need to accept his thesis in its entirety, however, to grasp the importance of the argument that blind and uncritical enthusiasms or outright condemnations of modernity represent no substitute for an attempt to experience it whole, to see it dialectically as a world where 'everything is pregnant with its contrary'.[5]

For all their differences, the rhapsodic and critical currents in early twentieth-century modernist art shared in common a deep dissatisfaction with bourgeois society (dismissed by both as the incarnation of philistine vulgarity, social alienation and spiritual anomie), and each current was, after its own fashion, dedicated to projects of social renewal and revitalization. The literature of the Irish Revival shared the anti-realist, anti-mimetic thrust and a good deal of the anti-bourgeois sentiment that characterized all of the main currents of European modernism, but on the whole, to borrow Berman's terms, it quite clearly tends towards the critical rather than the celebratory conception of modernity and modernization. If we compare Irish and Russian literature, for example, during the roughly contemporaneous revolutionary periods in each society, it is evident that in the Irish case there is little or none of the libidinal investment in fantasies of the machine, technology, urbanism or the masses that characterizes major elements of early twentieth-century Russian art. On the contrary, in the Irish Revival modernization tends to be identified with urban and industrial enervation, and revivalist literature turns not to the machine, the masses or the city but to the primitive and the pre-modern, to restore a dimension of vital experience that modernity threatens to cancel. Many European modernists would also look to the pre-modern and the primitive for inspiration, but the writers of the Revival, as Seamus Deane has observed, were unusual perhaps in that that they looked for such sources not in the far-off non-West but in Ireland itself.[6] The Revival's characteristic nostalgia for versions of an imagined past is usually conceived nowadays as a regressive and reactionary rejection of the modern industrial world. Like European romanticism in general, however, the romanticism of the Revival seems a complex phenomenon with variegated strands, some more conservative or radical than others. In some cases at least, the characteristic romantic nostalgia for some sort of pre-capitalist golden age passes through a passionate rejection of present capitalist and industrialist society which amounts to more than simply a rejection of modernity. The nostalgia for the past does not disappear, but it is projected toward a post-capitalist future.[7]

Literary historians seem generally agreed that in the period since the southern state was established Irish narrative literature has been increasingly dominated by a sense of disenchantment with the romantic version of Ireland cultivated by the Literary Revival and later institutionalized by the state. Where the revivalists celebrated the country – or, more precisely, idealized versions of the West – the general thrust of later twentieth-century narrative has been to debunk such idealizations by insisting on the social and spiritual meanness and, above all, the sexual repression and the consequent neuroses and pathologies of rural and small-town Irish society. Literary visions of rural arcadia, that is, give way to visions of rural anomie. Patrick Kavanagh's *The Great Hunger* (1942) is not so much an inaugural as a seminal text in this respect, perhaps, one that consolidated this counter-revivalist conception of Irish society as the newly ascendant literary ideology, and in doing so prepared the way for a succeeding generation of writers who would develop this aesthetic. Several of the senior reputations in contemporary southern Irish writing – including William Trevor, John McGahern and Eugene McCabe to mention but a few – have worked largely within the literary mode of disenchanted romanticism and social realism which had already come to the fore by the 1940s.

In broad and schematic terms, the displacement of revivalist romanticism by a newly ascendant social realism roughly coincides with, or even anticipates, the collapse of economic autarky and the adoption of the new state policy of dependent development. Like its revivalist predecessor, the new social realist aesthetic has, of course, co-existed alongside several other rival literary modes, especially the fantastic and the modernist (a mode perhaps best exemplified in recent times by the work of John Banville and Aidan Higgins). Nevertheless, just as revivalist romanticism attained supremacy in the early decades of the century, the social realist aesthetic has enjoyed a comparable supremacy in recent decades.

The real difficulty, it seems to me, is how best to characterize the kind of realism that attained this supremacy. On the whole, though, its dominant character or ethos seems essentially a naturalistic one. Naturalism shares with classical and critical realism an emphasis on exact observation and description of the contemporary social world. What distinguishes it, however, is its tendency to present the world in terms of diminished individuals who are dwarfed by the vast and impersonal forces that confront them. Essentially an aesthetic of disillusion, naturalism insists on the monotony and omnipotence of capitalist society at the expense of any real appreciation of either its contradictory or its dynamic nature. For this reason, it allows little scope for active human change. Despite its hostility to capitalist modernity, then, the aesthetic communicates a sense of pessimism or pained resignation that tends to smother or cancel that critique.[8]

The kind of realism that has dominated Irish writing for several decades now meets this description. Its consistent emphasis is the social and political bleakness, the sexual repression and cultural poverty of Irish society. That Irish society in this period was indeed impoverished and repressive in all sorts of ways is not at all in question. What is questionable, though, is the conception, rehearsed in much of this fiction, of that society as a frozen monolith without either a history that would explain it or wider human resources within it that would combat the prevailing ethos in any meaningful way. From Kavanagh's Paddy Maguire to the narrators of McGahern's early novels such as *The Dark* (1965) through to Brian Friel's Mundy sisters in *Dancing at Lughnasa* (1990) or

Patrick McCabe's demented Francie Brady in *The Butcher Boy* (1992) or Dermot Healy's alcoholic Jack Ferris in *A Goat's Song* (1994), the protagonists in these fictions are typically passive victims of history. They are all acted upon rather than active social agents themselves, all injured and isolate, utterly unable to identify or to connect with any social forces outside of themselves that might allow them to combat the conditions that crush them.

For some time now the literary critical establishment, at home and abroad, has accorded this kind of writing a positive reception. The standard critical response is to applaud its realism as a necessary antidote to revivalist romanticism. To counterpoint the 'pastoralism' of the revivalist version of rural Ireland to the 'realism' of writers such as Kavanagh, Trevor or McGahern, however, is to underline the aesthetic ideology that shapes the revivalist vision while overlooking the fact that the counter-revivalist response does not represent a shift from idealization to demystified actuality but rather the displacement of one aesthetic by another. Moreover, even if we allow that Irish naturalism in its inception possessed a dissident charge, it seems clear that it has long since accommodated the new modernizing philosophy embraced by a southern Irish elite that had already acquired power with Lemass and which, in the decades since then, has consolidated its position. The stress on the social meanness, sexual repression and cultural and spiritual anomie of Irish society that characterizes naturalism is easily enough reconciled with a modernizing ideology which holds that Ireland can only become authentically 'modern' (essentially meaning urban, liberal and industrial along Anglo-American lines) when 'backward' or 'traditional' social forces – typically identified with Catholic conservatism, rural Ireland, and republican nationalism – are finally shaken off.

Despite some real affinities, it is important not to overstate the degree to which Irish literary naturalism and modernizing social theory are compatible. The displacement of revivalist romanticism by naturalism does not after all – to return to Berman's terms – inaugurate a shift from a hostile or negative to some sort of rhapsodic conception of modernity. Nothing so drastic or interesting occurs. The displacement still leaves Irish literature firmly at what Berman would describe as the critical rather than the celebratory end of the spectrum of responses to capitalist modernity. The shift that occurs, then, is from a conservative (or, at best, romantic anti-capitalist) refusal of capitalist modernity in the revivalist aesthetic to a naturalism which debunks revivalist idealizations by insisting on the drabness of Irish society but which none the less remains, in its own way, as hostile to any positive celebration of capitalist modernity as the romanticism it displaces. The difference between the two is that where revivalist romanticism looked, vainly, for sources of resistance to a hated capitalist modernity from social agents that were deemed to belong to some exotic place 'outside' modernity, naturalism is more defeatist and accepts the inevitability of modernity while insisting on its grimness.

III

Modernity, as Saree Makdisi writes, 'can never exist in pure form or "as such"' since 'there can be no such thing as the modern unless there is an anti-modern against which it can be dialectically defined'. Modernization, then, must 'be seen as a process that is always in a state of *becoming*; or, rather, a process of becoming whose condition of possibility is the continual positing of its own limits – limits that it needs to transcend and then rediscover, re-posit, in other forms, or at greater distances'.[9] The preoccupation in Irish naturalism with a darkly repressive Ireland identified with the decades of autarkic development has served precisely this function: the period is repeatedly evoked because it serves as the definitive image of the anti-modern which a modernizing Ireland needed both to define itself against and to transcend. With the victories of liberalism over conservative Catholicism represented by the introduction of divorce in 1997, with the recovery from the long recession of previous decades represented by the economic boom, and with the apparent triumph of constitutional over militant nationalism represented by the Good Friday Agreement later in the same decade, one might have expected that the 'dark age' of autarkic development would no longer work so effectively as an anti-modern Other against which contemporary Ireland could continue to define itself. Given, in other words, the extent of the sweeping social changes that have occurred in recent times, one might have expected that the discourse of Irish modernization (or dependent development) would now be required, to use Makdisi's terms, to re-posit new limits to transcend, to discover some new means of self-definition.

As any survey of the 1990s will attest, however, Irish culture, despite the wider political and economic developments, has continued to be fixated on naturalistic representations of rural Ireland of an earlier generation. Most of the literary and cinematic works that have achieved major international and domestic success during the past decade demonstrate the entrenched nature of this preoccupation. Among novels, one thinks of John McGahern's *Amongst Women* (1990) and Patrick

McCabe's *The Butcher Boy* (1992); in theatre, of Brian Friel's *Dancing at Lughnasa* (1990); in cinema, of a whole series of films such as Jim Sheridan's *The Field* (1990), Cathal Black's *Korea* (1996), Neil Jordan's *The Butcher Boy* (1998), Pat O'Connor's *Dancing at Lughnasa* (1998), and many others. In the same decade several highly successful memoirs and autobiographies, including Frank McCourt's Pulitzer Prize-winning *Angela's Ashes* (1996) – the publishing sensation of the decade, and also screened for the cinema – take the same period as their topic. In 1998, RTE screened major national TV adaptations of John McGahern's *Amongst Women* and Deirdre Purcell's *Falling For a Dancer*. Both series explored the same social landscape that appears in the successful novels, plays and autobiographies mentioned above.[10]

The point here is neither to homogenize all of these works nor to subsume them all under a single formula. Nor is it to complain that they are not contemporary enough, to suggest that contemporary Irish narrative ought somehow to be obliged to take the Ireland of the 'Celtic Tiger' as its setting. As the earlier reference to Dermot Healy's *A Goat's Song* or the tremendous success of Martin McDonagh's *The Leenane Trilogy* should indicate, it is possible to update the setting to the 1960s or 70s without seriously disturbing the established narrative codes that have characterized this kind of writing. And only those shallow enough to believe that an upswing in Irish economic fortunes ought to be sufficient to dispel the many discontents that afflict modernity will demand of art a cheerier or more positive tone. That said, it still has to be asked whether the collective body of works just described, predicated as it is on an essentially naturalistic presentation of a world increasingly regarded by audiences as a foreign past, can really respond in interesting or challenging ways to the demands of the present. As the distance between the present and that past widens, the social ills that obsess these works – clerical dogmatism, domestic tyranny and oppression, sexual repression, poverty of opportunity or whatever – will themselves increasingly come to be identified with the past, with a particular time and not with a social system that subtends both past and present.

Some works, such as McCabe's *The Butcher Boy* or McDonagh's *The Leenane Trilogy*, obviously ironize the naturalistic representations of rural anomie they deploy. But while irony reveals the insufficiency of a given standpoint, it also discloses an inability or unwillingness to posit an alternative perspective. Even though the works mentioned earlier do vary in terms of genre and style and so on, therefore, they also display quite striking continuities not simply in their common preoccupation with a particular past but, more importantly, in the ways in which they construct that past – so much so that I would argue that they can be regarded as part of a wider structure of feeling. In order to tease out some of the recurrent patterns that connect these works, but also to signal the scope for individual variation within the shared pattern, I want to look in more detail at this point at three of the more accomplished of the works already mentioned: namely, Jim Sheridan's *The Field*, John McGahern's *Amongst Women* and Brian Friel's *Dancing at Lughnasa*. Limitations of space permit only a short overview of these works. The intention, however, is not to offer comprehensive readings of these texts, but simply to disclose the attitudes towards Irish modernization that they express.

Like many contemporary Irish narratives, *The Field*, *Amongst Women* and *Dancing at Lughnasa* all depict a crepuscular rural world about to be pulverized by the arrival of industrial modernity. Attitudes to the imminent arrival of the new order vary. The most common response, as in Pat O'Connor's *The Ballroom of Romance* (1982), a screen version of William Trevor's award-winning drama of the same title, is to see the arrival of the new order as a welcome redemption from the pervading social darkness of the old dispensation. In O'Connor's film, rural Ireland of the 1950s is depicted as a boorish and desperate world cursed with problems of social and sexual deprivation, emigration and male tyranny. One of the recurrent topics of conversation between the characters, however, is that 'The factory was coming to town' – an event that seems to promise a welcome end to the arthritic social order depicted in the film. Brian Friel's *Dancing at Lughnasa* is set at the close of the 1930s, but here again we are dealing with a social order at the end of its days. The play tells the story of the Mundy sisters living in straitened circumstances in a small Donegal townland at a moment when, as the narrator in the play tells the audience, 'The Industrial Revolution had finally caught up with Ballybeg.' For Friel, the belated arrival of this 'industrial revolution' carries none of the sense of redemption that it does in *The Ballroom of Romance*. Instead, it simply accelerates the dissolution of the Mundy family, making two of the sisters who earn their living by hand-knitting redundant and thus accelerating a narrative of decline already in evidence from the start. McGahern's *Amongst Women* depicts once again a narrow and oppressive social order on the brink of its ultimate demise. Set sometime in the middle decades of this century, the central part of the novel consists of an extended retrospect which tells the story of Moran, a small farmer and ex-guerrilla fighter in the War of Independence, and of how his second wife and his five children cope with his tormented and oppressive rule over the world of Great Meadow. This central narrative is framed by a short opening sequence, which describes the closing stages of Moran's life, and by a concluding one that deals with his death and funeral. At the end of the opening sequence, Rose, Moran's second wife, smuggles into the house the brown Franciscan habit in which her husband will be buried. Since the repressive world at the centre of the narrative proper, then, is framed by its own demise, the narrative strategy at work here is one that serves to enhance a sense of the pastness of Moran's world, to place it at a remove from the temporality of the reader. A similar narrative device operates in Friel's *Dancing at Lughnasa*, in which an adult narrator intervenes at moments to comment on the action which occurs at a time when he himself was still a small boy. In each case, the device establishes a sense of distance between narrative and audience that may arguably encourage a sense of critical detachment, but which also runs the risk of simply making the audience, to borrow a phrase from Roger Bromley, 'tourists in other people's reality'.[11]

Though more linear in shape and melodramatic in tone than the McGahern or Friel narratives, Jim Sheridan's *The Field* recreates a very similar temporality.[12] Modernization in this instance takes the form of a violent conflict between the Bull McCabe (Richard Harris) and 'the American' (Tom Berenger). The Bull has spent a lifetime struggling to improve 'the field', but the American is determined to have it concreted over in order to construct a hydroelectric power-station and a lime quarry that he will use to build 'highways all over Ireland.' The 'primi-tivist' setting established by the visual iconography in Sheridan's *The Field* establishes, like the narrative devices in Friel or McGahern discussed earlier, a sense of distance between the narrative told and the receiving audience: once again, the collapse of an old social order – the common theme in all these tales – is something that the audience contemplates from a remove, secure in the knowledge that its own temporality is, so to speak, somewhere on the other side of the crisis that occupies its attention.

'The moments we call crises,' Frank Kermode writes in *The Sense of an Ending*, 'are ends and beginnings.'[13] This may be so, but in the narrat-ives described here it is endings and not beginnings that monopolize attention. In other words, it is always the death rattle of old dispensa-tions, and not the birth of whatever it is that displaces the old, that compels narrative interest. Thus in *The Ballroom of Romance* or *Dancing at Lughnasa*, 'the factory' exists only as a topic of conversation; the world represented by the factory has no substantive presence in either narrative. In *Amongst Women*, the quarrel between Moran and the more worldly McQuaid, his former lieutenant during the War of Independence and now a cattle-dealer and a master of the art of buying and selling that eludes Moran himself, represents the superseding of an older military ethos by a new pragmatic commercialism in the post-revolutionary period. McQuaid – big-bellied, vulgar, driving a white Mercedes – is a conventional enough icon of the rural bourgeoisie that would come to dominate the southern state; but McQuaid's milieu, like that of the Dublin and London where Moran's children live their adult lives, has only a sketchy existence in the novel as a whole, where the real focus is always the determinedly insular and separate world of Great Meadow. Likewise, in *The Field* the audience listens to 'the American' describe his plans for quarries, power stations and highways, but the visual landscape of the film itself is a 'primitive' one where such things can scarcely be imagined.[14] Even if the superseding of an old rural world by a more modern industrial social order is always assured at the level of plot, then, the narratives themselves remain rooted in the sensorium of the old order. Though nominally victorious, the new social order, lacking its own distinctive sensorium, remains at the same time curiously eviscerated: too insubstantial, too much of a blank space, to command either the strong assent or rejection of the audience.

Of the works mentioned here, the one that most overtly expresses anxieties about the dilemmas of Irish modernization is *The Field*. In Sheridan's version, the conflict between the Bull McCabe and the American can be read as one between autarkic and dependent development. It would be reductive to read the film simply in terms of an external disturbance of a settled traditional social order, since it is clear that the Bull and the American are *both* aggressive modernizers, though of a different kind: whereas the Bull's project is one of agricultural improvement, the American's scheme is of a more industrial character. For the Bull, land is not reducible to its cash value. From his perspective, he has earned the right to inherit the widow's field because he and his family have expended so much hard labour in improving it. Since he and his family have had to wrest the field from a harsh and inhospitable nature and fight to recover it from the British, he feels duty-bound in the name of the sacrifices expended to pass on control of it to the next generation. In contrast to the Bull's fiercely personalized conception of the land, the American's conviction that it is simply a commodity to be purchased on the open market by the highest bidder seems impersonal and abstract. Nevertheless, while his plans undoubtedly spell ruin for the Bull's dreams for the field, the American's project also has its positive side since it will, he asserts, bring employment and prosperity to the region as a whole. Moreover, while the Bull's claim to the field on the basis of ancestral struggles waged against the elements, against the Famine, and against the British are registered with some passion in the film, that claim is not sentimentalized. The Bull's almost fanatic devotion to the improvement of his land involves heroic investments of personal toil and struggle, but it also goes hand in hand with a good deal of aggressive machismo and with a contemptuous disdain for all those who have lost their grip on the land (emigrants and the Travellers). At one point in the narrative, the Bull recalls that when his mother had died in the field, he and his father had worked on to ensure that the hay would be saved, and only stopped to go for the priest when the task was completed. The anecdote suggests that the relentless struggle required to dominate external nature requires a suppression of internal nature that is in the end extraordinarily costly and even, in human terms, self-defeating.

While the Bull attempts to secure public support by representing the conflict between himself and the American as one between local and foreigner, the narrative demonstrates the situation to be more complex. The American is not simply an 'outsider' but the son of an Irish emigrant, and his plans to industrialize the countryside will, he suggests, provide the employment that will spare others his father's fate. Finally, the Bull's passionate commitment to maintaining his family's grip on the land is shadowed from the outset by an undisclosed trauma that has destroyed the bond between himself and his wife and between himself and his son. The emotional climax of the film is reached when the source of that trauma is revealed: driven by the Bull's constant insistence that the family farm could support only one of his two sons, and that the other would have no option but to emigrate, Shamie, the elder son, had taken his own life. Consequently, the Catholic Church had refused to allow him burial in consecrated ground. Where the film had earlier critiqued, in the voice of the Bull, a dehistoricized and dehumanized conception of the land as abstract commodity, this disclosure works in an opposite direction: it serves to indict sacralizations – whether religious or nationalist – of the land that prove no less alienating in human terms than the logic of commodification. On the one hand, then, the ascendancy of market value is dehumanizing since it strips the land of all intense human association by reducing it to an abstract commodity. On the other hand, however, religious and nationalistic inscriptions of the land with absolute symbolic importance prove no less alienating, because once the land is converted into a fetish it also takes priority over human needs.

The Field, then, sets in motion a conflict between autarkic modernization (represented here as bullishly independent and nationalistic but also as oppressively patriarchal and domineering in spirit) and dependent development (characterized as energetic and enterprising but recognizing no values beyond the cash nexus). In the end, however, it is unable to endorse the values associated with either side in that conflict. For much of the time the audience's sympathies are tilted in favour of the Bull, but the disclosure of his culpability for his son's suicide and the grimly maintained silence of his wife throughout the narrative suggests that the project with which he is identified is fatally flawed: the level of human sacrifice demanded in its name is too high and the sense of rugged independence which constitutes its most positive feature is in any case compromised by the shame of emigration. Since the values represented by the Bull and the American seem in the end equally alienating, the clash between the two lacks the consequential quality of authentic tragic collision. The American is killed off, but the Bull's victory is a Pyrrhic one, and the fact that he dies, Cuchulain-like, in a demented struggle to drive back the tide suggests an impossible battle against irreversible forces.

A somewhat similar sense of ambivalence about Irish modernity can be detected in McGahern's *Amongst Women*.[15] Moran, the central protagonist in the novel, is an insecure and cantankerous domestic tyrant who none the less commands the loyalty of all but one of his children. Though Moran is a product of the heroic phase of Irish nationalism, the novel is set in a time when that period is long past and when neither the values that the national struggle represented nor its political accomplishments compel much admiration. When Moran's daughters attempt to restore their father's declining spirits by reviving Monaghan Day, with its memories of republican heroics during the War of Independence, that attempt is shown to be miscalculated and futile. 'Monaghan Day revived nothing but a weak fanciful ghost of what had been' (*Amongst Women*, p. 5). Moran himself thwarts his daughters' project by disowning any heroic conception of the revolutionary period, sourly dismissing it 'as a bad business' that achieved nothing of any real substance: 'What did we get for it? A country, if you'd believe them. Some of our own johnnies in the top jobs instead of a few Englishmen. More than half my own family works in England. What was it all for? The whole thing was a cod' (*Amongst Women*, p. 5). Moran's derisive assessment of the post-independence period is not explicitly endorsed in the novel, and his attitude to the new state is clearly rooted in a sense of *ressentiment* that stems from his failure to retain in the post-war period the social status that he had enjoyed as a guerrilla commander. At the same time, there is no strong repudiation of Moran's assessment in the novel either, and the extended and harrowing depiction of Moran's crass and puritanical despotism over Great Meadow clearly registers an overwhelmingly negative impression of post-independence Irish society.

Moran and McQuaid represent the revolutionary nationalist generation in the novel. McQuaid is enterprising and aggressive and makes his way in the post-independence social order, but he is a vulgar philistine. Moran stubbornly insists that the new social order fails to measure up to the ideals of the independence struggle, but his rejectionist stance is productive of no alternative set of political values except for his desperate cult of the family which seems in part at least a form of compensation for his loss of authority in the wider public sphere. As observed earlier, however, the structure of the narrative establishes from the start that this generation has reached the end of its days. Will the next generation, then, the one represented by Moran's children, represent a more promising society than the one depicted in the novel?

There is little enough in the novel to suggest that it will. Mona, Sheila and Maggie, Moran's daughters, all settle in the world beyond Great Meadow, but, as Maria DiBattista observes, the girls 'always return to "Daddy" and the parental home to regain an identity imperilled in the cosmopolitan world of London or Dublin where they are no more than urban debris, "specks of froth"'.[16] Michael and Luke, Moran's sons, both rebel against paternal despotism, but Michael is soon reconciled with his father, and only Luke remains permanently alienated, the affective bonds that link him to his father and his siblings irreparably shattered. Yet although Luke's is the only outright and sustained rebellion against the values represented by his father and Great Meadow, his repudiation of Moran, like Moran's of the Irish state, generates no positive set of values in the novel. In his detachment and isolation, Luke seems emotionally crippled or stunted – 'Luke had always been slight of build and he hadn't filled out much with the years' (*Amongst Women*, p. 147). It is as though the tremendous effort required to break free had somehow incapacitated him, leaving him suspended in a condition of permanent emotional arrest that allows neither for reconciliation with the past nor for future growth and development.

This extraordinary novel, then, is constructed in terms of two refusals, each of which displays a certain integrity, but neither of which can offer any humanly satisfying alternative to the world that is refused. Moran's insistence that independent Ireland is a sorry travesty of the high ideals of the independence struggle is registered sympathetically, but the twisted cult of the family which is the only alternative that he himself can offer empties his rejectionist stance of positive content. Likewise, Luke's rejection of his father's domineering cult of the family is obviously conceived as valid, but his own life is so emotionally sterile that his rejectionist stance is also bleached of positive content. The indictments of the political shabbiness of post-independent Ireland, and of the narrow cult of the family which is represented as a twisted response to that wider poverty, are both allowed to stand, but what is clearly absent in the novel is anything that might amount to a positive alternative to those conditions which are indicted.

In a novel in which the thematics of family and home are central, Great Meadow is, then, a place of shocking trauma and terror, but one from which most of the younger generation none the less manage to draw strength, and the world of the city is conceived in contrast as a place of transcendental homelessness. Luke, significantly, studies accountancy in London and, we are told, 'had become friendly with a Cockney man... who had been a french polisher and who now sold reproduction furniture to antique shops from a van. He mentioned some plan they had of buying old houses and converting them into flats for sale' (*Amongst Women*, p. 67). Sheila's house in the Dublin suburbs is described as 'a low, detached bungalow in a new estate of a couple of hundred bungalows exactly the same, the front gardens still raw with concrete' (*Amongst Women*, p.151). The descriptions here are spare and noncommittal, but the urban houses are none the less sketched in terms that suggest transience, abstract commodification and mechanical reproduction: they are dwellings that somehow fall short of being homes. It is this failure of the city to provide a satisfying alternative to Great Meadow which is offered as explanation for the Moran sisters' constant return to the country in search of regeneration: 'The closeness [offered by Great Meadow] was as strong as the pull of their own lives; they lost the pain of individuality within its protection. In London or Dublin the girls would look back to the house for healing... Beneath all the differences was the belief that the whole house was essentially one. Together they were one world. Deprived of this sense they were nothing, scattered, individual things' (*Amongst Women*, pp. 85, 145). The vision of Irish modernity which informs *Amongst Women* is, it seems to me, more or less consistent with the conventional opposition between pre-modern *Gemeinschaft* (organic community) and modern *Gesellshaft* (corporative society) that structures the nineteenth-century sociology of Tonnies, Durkheim and Weber. Great Meadow displays the conventional negative and positive qualities of *Gemeinschaft*. It is rigidly patriarchal, illiberal and intolerant by modern standards, and governed by seasonal and ritualistic rather than progressive notions of time (the recital of the Rosary runs like a refrain across the novel); but its mode of authority, though despotic, is personalized and charismatic rather than contractual or bureaucratic. Likewise, the world outside of Great Meadow displays the usual qualities of the *Gesellschaft*. Sheila and Mona escape Great Meadow not by overt rebellion but through the state education system, which takes them into the civil service and the city. In other words, the tight communal world of Great Meadow is superseded by the educational and bureaucratic institutions of the state, and the younger generation abandons the country for the city, a place associated in the novel with the dissolution of natural kinship bonds and social atomization and alienation. The distinction here is not only between two different kinds of society, and their contrasting impact on the quality of human experience, but also on two historically successive stages of development within one and the same society: whatever the gains and losses, rural *Gemeinschaft* inevitably gives way to urban *Gesellschaft*, which represents the only future there is.

Whether deployed by sociologist or novelist, an element of nostalgia is perhaps unavoidable in this construction, but McGahern's novel seems quite determined to close off any sentimentalization of the past or regressive desire for its recovery. The world of Great Meadow is too grimly depicted to invite any sense of tragic loss, and restorationist attempts such as the revival of Monaghan Day are shown in any case to be useless. In both McGahern's novel and Sheridan's film, the dissolution of the period of Irish autarkic development is represented in terms of the demise of a charismatic but authoritarian patriarch. Whereas Sheridan's film works towards some sort of apocalyptic showdown between the old and the new, however, McGahern's novel represents the demise of the old social order represented by Moran in terms of the slow and natural passage of time. This is, I think, in keeping with the quietist and more evolutionary sensibility of McGahern's novel, a sensibility to which all strong forms of revolt seem somehow psychologically suspect. If the novel affirms anything, it is perhaps a pragmatic capacity for survival: a quality associated with the women who surround Moran and who without ever severing their allegiance to him still manage eventually to survive and even master him. At the close of the novel, it is the women who walk away from Moran's grave with an assured sense of their own power.

Of the three works discussed here, Friel's *Dancing at Lughnasa* seems, on first encounter at least, the one most steeped in nostalgia for pre-industrial community and most openly hostile to industrial modernity.[17] The narrative, in which the adult Michael summons to memory a moment from his childhood past, is wistful and elegiac in tone. Friel's Ballybeg, moreover, is a 'softer' landscape than Sheridan's or McGahern's, since it is identified not with aggressive patriarchal figures such as McCabe or Moran, but with a struggling but supportive community of women. Finally, when the Industrial Revolution arrives in Donegal it leads immediately to the redundancy of Aggie and Rose, and sets them on the road to destitution in England. All of this establishes an autumnal atmosphere, which inevitably tints the past in sepia and casts the new social order that displaces it in humanly destructive rather than redemptive terms.

Though this initial impression is not altogether misplaced, closer inspection will prove the play more complex. After all, the imagined Ireland of *Dancing at Lughnasa* is not some pristine pre-modern community offering a genuine alternative to modernity, but only the incompletely realized modernity of De Valera's Ireland of the late 1930s. The faltering radio, which starts intermittently into song only to stutter silent again throughout the action, is a metaphor for this condition of stumbling modernization. Friel's Ballybeg is imagined as a depressed society pressured between two different kinds of Dionysian energy that threaten to shatter it: that is, between 'pre-modern' pagan energies associated with Africa and the local wild people of the back hills, and 'modern' (or even 'post-modern') Dionysian energies identified with the mass culture dance tunes played over the radio. This affinity between the pre-modern and the modern is established in the opening lines of the play which begin with Michael's memory of his family's acquisition of 'our first wireless set' and of how Maggie 'wanted to call it Lugh after the old Celtic God of the Harvest' (*Dancing at Lughnasa*, p. 1). This peculiar complicity is reiterated when Michael recalls the pivotal dance at the centre of the play: 'I remember the kitchen throbbing with the beat of Irish dance music beamed to us all the way from Dublin, and my mother and her sisters suddenly catching hands and dancing a spontaneous step-dance and laughing – screaming! – like excited schoolgirls ... I had witnessed *Marconi's voodoo* derange those kind, sensible women and transform them into shrieking strangers' (*Dancing At Lughnasa*, p. 2). Audiences usually perceive this dance, which constitutes the centrepiece of the play, in wholly positive terms as a liberating outburst of repressed energy that expresses the pent-up protest of the sisters against the narrow constraints of De Valera's Ireland. It is this, of course, but Friel's script makes it clear that the dance is shot through with both positive *and* negative qualities; it has a dual quality which resembles that which Nietzsche associated with Dionysian ecstasy or intoxication. For Nietzsche, Dionysus might represent the positive instinctual energy associated with 'the approach of spring when the whole of nature is pervaded by lust for life', but in its unalloyed form the same energy could always degenerate into 'that repulsive mixture of lust and cruelty which has always struck me as the true "witches' brew"'.[18] In Friel's extended stage directions to the dance scene, both qualities are clearly involved: we are told that 'there is a sense of order being consciously subverted', and the word 'defiant' appears several times, but it is also stressed that there is a sense 'of near-hysteria being induced' and that 'the sound is too loud; and the beat is too fast, and the almost recognizable dance is made *grotesque*' (*Dancing at Lughnasa*, pp. 21, 22). The dance is a sensual frenzy, then, but its rapture is not a wholly positive one: there are suggestions of a disfiguring surrender to cruelty and pain as well. It is not insignificant in this regard that the play is set against the wider continental history of 1936, its action shadowed by the overthrow of the Spanish Republic and by Europe's imminent collapse into the maelstrom of the Second World War.

Friel's play turns on a dialectical opposition between primitive and modern civilization conventional to nineteenth-century romanticism and exoticism, but it de-energizes this opposition as well, hollowing it out yet none the less conserving it in weakened form. When set against the anomie and sexual repressiveness of Ballybeg, Father Jack's Rwanga appears to possess attractive qualities of primitive communal vitality and sexual tolerance. 'In Rwanga,' Father Jack tells us, 'women are eager to have love-children. The more love-children you have, the more fortunate your household is thought to be '(*Dancing At Lughnasa*, p. 41). But we are also reminded that Father Jack's Rwanga is a leper-colony, not some idealized edenic state. England's urban modernity too has positive qualities when compared to Ballybeg. Bernie O'Donnell, Maggie's childhood friend, leaves Ireland in disgust when she and her partner are cheated of victory by local judges in a dancing competition in a neighbouring parish. When she returns years later, married to a Swede, glamorous as 'a film star' (*Dancing At Lughnasa*, p. 19) and with two beautiful children, her success abroad sets off Maggie's homebound stasis and childlessness. Nevertheless, England is also the place where Agnes and Rose descend into despair and disaster; like Rwanga, it represents no wholly idealized alternative either.

The Ireland or Ballybeg of *Dancing at Lughnasa* is essentially conceived, then, as an unhappy limbo suspended somewhere in the slipstream between the worlds of Rwanga and London. It is too trapped in its prissy Catholic respectability (a quality exemplified by Kate, the eldest sister who is identified, like McCabe and Moran, with the national struggle for independence) to be able to respond to either London or Rwanga except in terms of scandalized disbelief. But since neither 'primitive' Africa nor 'modern' industrial England represents a wholly positive pole of value, there is little sense in Friel's work that there are any attractive historical choices open to Ballybeg. If England is where Aggie and Rose meet their tragic end, Father Jack's account of how the sisters might return with him to Rwanga and live as wives to one husband in a small commune is clearly the stuff of comic farce. For *Dancing at Lughnasa*, Ballybeg's course into modernity is inevitable but it is not emancipatory: what nostalgia there is for the past is activated not by a desire to resurrect that world but only to put into question a modernity to which the past itself patently represents no alternative. Unable to identify substantive historical options, the narrative consigns the sisters to their doom, settles for a kind of wistful post-modern playfulness (the music of 'Anything Goes' plays out the piece), and seeks no positive value outside art or the formal order of ceremony (one of the key words in the play).

IV

Different aesthetics sometimes fasten themselves with particular tenacity to specific historical moments or social groups. The Gothic aesthetic, for instance, attached itself, like the literary equivalent of creeping ivy, to the Anglo-Irish community in its long decline, and the social construction of emotion shaped by that aesthetic continues to exert a decisive force on popular conceptions of that decline. In a similar way, a naturalistic aesthetic has claimed the decades of Irish autarkic development as its own, to such an extent indeed that our reflex responses to that period probably owe more to the codes of naturalism than to any serious historical comprehension of the forces that shaped it.

As the world of 'De Valera's Ireland' or the decades of autarkic development recede into the past, either a more apologetic or a more complex understanding may well emerge to contest the condescension towards that period that conventional naturalistic representations invite. What needs to be stressed, however, is that it is not the past that needs to be rescued or redeemed, but the future. The fact that contemporary Irish society continues to rely so heavily on invocations of the darkness of the past to validate its sense of its own enlightenment is not very reassuring. Such a society equips itself neither with the imaginative resources nor the strategies required to meet the challenges of the future. And, in the works of Sheridan, McGahern and Friel examined here, it is ultimately not the depiction of the past, but the very limited expectation of the future that disturbs most.

Notes

1 Denis O'Hearn, *Inside The Celtic Tiger: The Irish Economy and The Asian Model*, (London and Sterling, Virginia: Pluto Press, 1998); John Kurt Jacobsen, *Chasing Progress in the Irish Republic: Ideology, Democracy and Dependent Development* (Cambridge: Cambridge University Press, 1994).

2 Jorge Larrain, *Theories of Development: Capitalism, Colonialism and Dependency* (Oxford: Polity Press, 1989).

3 What one misses most in contemporary Irish discourse is any real assimilation of the rich heritage of Marxist critical theory which – at its best – has developed an altogether less one-sided and much more dialectical conception of modernity, one which attempts to sort out the matrix of oppressive and emancipatory forces involved. Following the lead of Marx and Engels in *The Communist Manifesto*, but also incorporating elements from other great thinkers of modernity such as Weber, Nietzsche and others, marxian critical theory starts from the assumption that the process of capitalist development is both progressive – dissolving precapitalist social hierarchies, creating new connections, possibilities and so forth – and destructive – creating a world subject to recurrent economic crises and dependent upon the exploitation and alienation of the working classes. For Marx, capitalist modernity is compelled, by sheer economic necessity, to continual and ceaseless innovation: the capitalist bourgeoisie 'cannot exist without constantly revolutionising the instruments of production, and thereby the relations of production, and with them the whole relations of society.' Consequently, 'constant revolutionising of production, uninterrupted disturbance of all social conditions, everlasting uncertainty and agitation distinguish the bourgeois epoch from all earlier ones. All fixed, fast-frozen relations, with their train of ancient and venerable prejudices and opinions, are swept away, all new-formed ones becoming antiquated before they can ossify' (Karl Marx and Friedrick Engels, *Manifesto of the Communist Party* (Beijing: Foreign Languages Press, 1990), pp. 36–7). On the positive side, this ceaseless transformation liberates the human capacity for continual change and renewal in all modes of life. On the negative side, it is destructive of all social stability, and creates an alienated and atomized society which has 'resolved personal worth into exchange value, and in place of the numberless indefeasible chartered freedoms, has set up that single, unconscionable freedom – Free Trade' (Marx, 36). Refusing either one-sided celebrations or equally one-sided rejections of capitalist modernity, then, marxian critical theory offers a systematic and comprehensive theory of the historical trajectory of modernity which offers critical diagnoses of its limitations, pathologies and destructive effects, but which also defends its more emancipatory elements. See Douglas Kellner, *Critical Theory: Marxism as Modernity* (Oxford: Polity Press, 1989), pp. 3–9.

4   Marshall Berman, *All That Is Solid Melts Into Air: The Experience of Modernity* (Harmondsworth: Penguin, 1988 [1982]), p. 24.

5   Karl Marx, cited in Berman, *All That Is Solid Melts Into Air*, pp. 35, 36.

6   Seamus Deane, *Celtic Revivals*, (Winston-Salem, N.C.: Wake Forest University Press, 1985), p. 57.

7   Whether one emphasizes the regressive or romantic anti-capitalist dimensions of the Revival, however, one of its more disabling legacies is that its critique of modernity is typically articulated in terms of a dichotomy which identifies the 'pre-modern' or 'non-modern' as the only authentic source of resistance to the 'modern'. In a characteristically exoticist vein, resistance to what are felt to be the more catastrophic dimensions of modernity is identified with some social agent supposedly exterior to the temporality and process of modernization – hence the valorization of imagined versions of the western peasantry or the Anglo-Irish aristocracy. It is this quest for a social agent of resistance 'outside' the space of modernity that most distinguishes revivalist romanticism from socialism. Simply put, where the revivalist vision conceives of the crisis of modernity in terms of an abstractly civilizational struggle between the 'modern' and the 'pre-modern', socialism constitutes the crisis as one in which capitalist modernity must be understood as tendentially a world system from the outset, one without an 'outside', then, but in which the main agents of resistance – namely, the exploited classes – emerge within the uneven space of modernity itself.

8   The account of naturalism presented here follows that developed by Georg Lukács (1950). For a supplementary commentary on Lukác's analysis of literary naturalism, see Stuart Sim, *Georg Lukács* (New York and London: Harvester Wheatsheaf, 1994), pp. 50–51.

9   Saree Makdisi, *Romantic Imperialism: Universal Empire and the Culture of Modernity* (Cambridge: Cambridge University Press, 1998), p. 190.

10 The only other major work in the south to achieve anything like the popular success and critical recognition attained by those mentioned above was Roddy Doyle's urban novel *Paddy Clarke Ha Ha Ha*, which won the Booker Prize in 1993. Doyle's success is usually taken to represent a major new departure in Irish writing: his work is deemed to have given voice to an Irish urban society rendered silent by a post-independence state ideology which insisted that Ireland was a rural and agricultural society and which could therefore find no place for the city in the national imagination. Nevertheless, Doyle's *Paddy Clarke*, like his earlier novels, is located in a more or less hermetically sealed Dublin ghetto milieu which is almost completely severed from the wider currents of middle- or upper-class Dublin life. Doyle's novels, in other words, detach the urban ghetto from the wider social totality of modern city life. His working-class characters are perceived anthropologically (as a distinct object of specialized curiosity) rather than in terms of that class's relationship to the wider social totality. In its own way, then, Doyle's imaginative world remains as distant from the social world of financial services centres, computer industries, comfortable middle-class suburbs or centre-city gay saunas – that is, from the Celtic Tiger Dublin of the 1990s, the Dublin with which Doyle's own success is usually considered synonymous – as Friel's *Dancing at Lughnasa* or McCourt's *Angela's Ashes*. The scope of this essay does not allow me to deal with the generation of 'new novelists', many of

whom experiment with literary modes quite different to those to which I confine my attention in this essay. It is questionable, however, whether the 'new' novelists', individually or collectively, have yet decisively reconfigured the landscape of Irish writing for either a wider popular audience or a smaller critical one.

11 Roger Bromley, *Lost Narratives: Popular Fictions, Politics and Recent History* (London and New York: Routledge, 1988) p. 10.

12 Jim Sheridan, *The Field*, Granada Film Production, in association with Sovereign Pictures, 1990.

13 Frank Kermode, *The Sense of an Ending: Studies in the Theory of Fiction* (Oxford: Oxford University Press, 1966), p. 96.

14 Of all of these narratives, *The Field* is perhaps the most instructive in this respect. Given its technological resources, cinema as a medium has a capacity which goes beyond that of either the theatre or of the novel to convey something of the sight, sound and lived sensation of the modern industrial world. But whereas John B. Keane's play, on which Sheridan's film is based, has a 'period feel' quite close to that of the moment of its initial staging in 1965, Sheridan goes to some trouble to set the narrative in some much more distant period. In Keane's play there are references to motorbikes, bingo-halls, hairdressing salons and telephones, and a distinctly contemporary boom in land prices precipitates the crisis that it depicts. In Sheridan's film – which appears some quarter of a century later than Keane's play – the setting is a remote 'primitivist' world where motorbikes or hair salons would have no place.

15 John McGahern, *Amongst Women* (London: Faber and Faber, 1990). All further references bracketed within the text.

16 Maria DiBattista, 'Joyce's Ghost: The Bogey of Realism in John McGahern's *Amongst Women*' in Karen R. Lawrence (ed.), *Transcultural Joyce* (Cambridge: Cambridge University Press, 1998), pp. 21–36, p. 25.

17 Brian Friel, *Dancing at Lughnasa* (London and Boston: Faber and Faber, 1990). All further references bracketed within the text.

18 Fredrick Nietzsche, *The Birth of Tragedy and Other Writings* (Cambridge: Cambridge University Press, 1999), pp. 17, 20.

6
Irish Film: Screening the Republic

Richard Haslam

I

One could argue that indigenous Irish film-making contributed to the 1948 Republic of Ireland Act. Liam O'Leary's election campaign film *Our Country* (1947), made for Sean Mac Bride's Clann na Poblachta, sharply detailed the alleged shortcomings of Fianna Fáil's sixteen years in office and was widely viewed throughout the Free State, its influence prompting alarmed government responses.[1] Ousted in February 1948, Fianna Fáil were replaced by a coalition government that included Clann na Poblachta, and Taoiseach John Costello announced within seven months his intention of declaring the Republic. In the subsequent five decades, Irish film has screened (and sometimes screened out) important dimensions of the Republic's social, political and religious ways of life.

I wish first to identify some milestones in the ongoing development of an indigenous film industry and then to examine the implications of narrative, genre and audience for the work of some leading Irish film-makers. I focus on fiction films, but Irish cinema in the opening decades of the Republic principally comprised documentaries and drama-documentaries. George Morrison's documentaries *Mise Éire* (1959) and *Saoirse?* (1961) use actuality footage, photographs, and an Irish-language soundtrack to delineate, commemorate, and largely celebrate the development of nationalism from 1900 to 1922. The Department of Health-funded drama-documentaries *Everybody's Business* (1951) and *Keep Your Teeth* (1951) promote food and dental hygiene, while *Voyage to Recovery* (1952) and *Stop Thief* (1953) describe the treatment of tuberculosis and dyptheria. Fiction films of the 1970s, 80s and 90s would find alternative cinematic methods to probe nationalism and the health of the nation.

Although Mícheál MacLiammóir and Hilton Edwards' Dublin Gate Theatre Productions company was responsible for two short films with supernatural themes, *Return to Glennascaul* (1951) and *From Time to Time* (1953), and Lord Killanin's Four Provinces company produced John Ford's *The Rising of the Moon* (1957) and The *Playboy of the Western World* (1962), Emmet Dalton was the major 'player' in Irish film in the late 1950s and early 1960s. He was a director of the company that created Ardmore Studios in 1958, and over the next four years his production company made eight feature films, six adapted from Abbey Theatre plays, with Abbey actors in supporting roles. *This Other Eden* (1959), based on Louis D'Alton's 1953 play, and the most absorbing of these productions, explores how mysteries and controversies surrounding the killing of an IRA commander during the War of Independence resurface in his home village two decades later. Although witty and multi-layered, the film, like George Bernard Shaw's play *John Bull's Other Island* (1904), initially subverts clichés of Irish and English national character, only to revert to type. The depiction of the fickle, violent Irish villagers *en masse* shares much with images of the quasi-organic mob in such exogenous productions as John Ford's *The Quiet Man* (1952) and David Lean's *Ryan's Daughter* (1970). *This Other Eden* thus participates in 'auto-exoticism', Joep Leerssen's term for the mode in which indigenous artists view their country in the light of exogenous expectations.[2]

During a hiatus in indigenous film output in the mid-1960s, Ardmore became principally a base for British productions, only some of which were set in Ireland.[3] When native Irish film-making recommenced, three works generated controversy. In Peter Lennon's documentary *The Rocky Road to Dublin* (1968), Irish commentators queried the legacy of independence; in the fiction film *I Can't, I Can't* (1969), the Catholic Church's attitude to contraception was addressed; and in *Paddy* (1969), adapted by the Irish writer Lee Dunne from his novel *Goodbye to the Hill* (1965), sexual promiscuity was a theme (leading to the film's banning in Ireland). These works, which to varying degrees challenged the Republic's political, religious and social structures, were followed in the mid and late 1970s by Irish films that actively critiqued inherited images and precepts.

Bob Quinn's *Caoineadh Airt Uí Laoire* (1975), like *This Other Eden*, used the encounter of an Englishman with an Irish community in order to interrogate the pressure of the past upon the present. However, Quinn's Irish language film, set in the Connemara Gaeltacht and depicting a modern-day amateur stage production of an eighteenth-century lament, is formally and thematically more complex than *This Other Eden*. By using deliberately unsettling cuts between the eighteenth- and twentieth-century narratives, Quinn allows each temporal perspective to challenge the presuppositions of the other, a technique previously utilized in Denis Johnston's play *The Old Lady Says 'No!'* (1929). Funded by Sinn Féin, the Workers' Party (formerly the Official IRA), *Caoineadh* was one of the first native Irish films to comment upon the post-1968 outbreak of armed conflict in Northern Ireland.[4] Quinn later described the film as an attempt 'to deconstruct a monolithic approach to Irish culture and the Irish language . . . to distinguish between Irish culture and language and its theological associations and its hijacking by particular religious clans . . . [and by] the respectable, middle-class, urban interpretation of Gaelic culture'.[5]

1975 also saw the release of Cathal Black's short film *Wheels* (based on a story by John McGahern), which follows a young man's rejection of patriarchy and his rural background for the comparative freedom of the city. The cameraperson on both Quinn and Black's films was Joe Comerford, who proceeded to direct *Down the Corner* (1977), a study of the daily lives of working-class teenage boys from the Dublin housing estate of Ballyfermot. Both Quinn and Black participated in Comerford's film, and the three were frequently involved with one another's later work. They sought to challenge exogenous conventions about the cinematic representation of Ireland and to reveal the lives of marginalized social groups. For example, Bob Quinn's Irish language film *Poitín* (1979) dissects the mythical, bucolic, rollicking west of Ireland propounded in *The Quiet Man*. Quinn's unquiet men, swayed by anomy and animus, cheat, threaten, and assault, until they are duped into drowning. Paraphrasing Leerssen, one could view *Poitín* as auto-destruct-exoticism. In his drama-documentary *Our Boys* (1981), Black incisively anatomizes the educational, psychological and social repercussions of the pedagogy of the Irish Christian Brothers. In his short film *Withdrawal* (1982), Comerford discloses the devastated lives of the insane and the drug-addicted. Amongst the other socially engaged independent films made during this period were Tommy McArdle's *The Kinkisha* (1977), which reveals how folklore beliefs intervene in the lives of a modern rural family, and *It's Handy When People Don't Die* (1980), which uses its setting of the 1798 Rising of the United Irishmen to comment obliquely upon the Northern Irish conflict. Kieran Hickey's *Exposure* (1978) and *Criminal Conversation* (1980) unveil the sexual insecurities and hypocrisies of middle-class Irish males.

Exposure was partly funded through the Arts Council Film Script Award for 1977. The Award programme, commencing in 1976 (when it was won by *Poitín*), helped to jump-start several independent films; further financial and technical assistance came from RTE (the national television company), the National Film Studios of Ireland (established at Ardmore in 1975) and the Arts Council of Northern Ireland. The Irish Film Board Act of December 1980 provided the sum of £200,000 (in the first year) for investment in 'the expression of national culture through the medium of film-making'.[6] However, this long-overdue commitment by the State to screening the Nation soon became enmeshed in controversy. In a resolution made when it was barely quorate, the Film Board allocated half of its 1981 budget to one film, Neil Jordan's *Angel* (1982); the resentment of independent film-makers was fuelled by Jordan's limited experience in film and the fact that Board member John Boorman, an English director resident in Ireland, was *Angel*'s executive producer. The subsequent protests led in the short term to the resignation of the Board's chairperson, John Heelin, and later of Boorman, and in the long term to rancour on all sides.[7]

Despite his relative inexperience, Jordan made an extremely accomplished film. *Angel* traces the quest of the saxophonist Danny to discover the identities of the paramilitaries who murdered both a girl he had befriended and the manager of his showband. In the process of exacting revenge, Danny becomes dehumanized into an angel of destruction. Jordan says he wished to 'make a film with the barest possible facts about Northern Ireland and concentrate on the most grotesque and simple of issues: what it means to kill another human being'.[8] However, this metaphysical approach alienated those critics who believed it imperative for an Irish film-maker utilizing this subject matter to provide an accurate political context and to eschew the stereotypes about violence proffered in many British and American representations of 'the Troubles'.[9]

Angel also received funding from Channel 4, a major British television company which was new at the time. The financial resources for Irish film provided by British and Irish television companies somewhat compensated for the disappointment arising from the putting into receivership of the National Film Studios in 1982.[10] Robert Wynne-Simmons' *The Outcasts* (1982), a haunting tale of wonderworking and scapegoating in nineteenth-century Ireland, which had won the Arts Council Film Script Award for 1981, also received funding from Channel Four. Joe Comerford's *Withdrawal* (like *Exposure, Poitín, Criminal Conversation, It's Handy When People Don't Die* and *Our Boys*) received funding from RTE, as did Pat Murphy's *Anne Devlin* (1984). Murphy had first gained recognition through writing and co-directing the British-funded *Maeve* (1981), which employs distancing, formalist devices to depict an emigrant's return from London to Belfast, where she reflects upon childhood influences (particularly her storytelling father) and debates with a former boyfriend about possible conflicts between feminism and Irish republicanism. While *Maeve* explicitly deals with allegiances in the modern Northern Irish 'Troubles', *Anne Devlin* approaches the same issues in a more latent but less formalist manner, through the story of a woman (based upon a real historical figure) who participates in the preparations for Robert Emmet's unsuccessful 1803 rebellion, undergoes imprisonment, and resists pressure to inform.[11] Murphy has described the film as 'a tribute to the women I know right now who do see themselves as feminists, but who are working within the Republican Movement'.[12]

While Murphy's politically committed films focused on the Northern 'Troubles', Cathal Black's *Pigs* (1984) engaged with some of the Republic's peripheralized individuals and communities, charting the agglomeration and disintegration of a group of squatters in inner-city Dublin and tackling the subjects of poverty, addiction, mental health and homosexuality. Bob Quinn's *Budawanny* (1987), based upon Pádraic Standún's novel *Súil le Breith* (1983), also explored the micropolitics of communal life, depicting the clash between priestly celibacy and desire on a western Irish island. The present and its expedient orthodoxies, filmed in colour and with synchronous sound, alternate with the past and its transient heterodoxies, filmed in black and white and with silent-cinema conventions. Joe Comerford, the second-unit cameraperson on *Budawanny*, had also used formalist devices in his earlier short film *Waterbag* (1984), whose production team included Black and Quinn. Some of the characters and *mise-en-scène* from *Waterbag* reappear in Comerford's less formalist, feature-length film *Reefer and the Model* (1987); like *Pigs* and *Budawanny*, *Reefer* uses marginalized groups to critique the established order. Set in Connemara in 1981, the film concerns the exploits of Reefer, an ex-IRA man, and the Model, an ex-addict, ex-prostitute, and expectant mother. As in *Pigs* and *Budawanny*, an unstable quasi-family emerges, comprising in this case the Model, Reefer, his mother, and Spider and Badger (his partners in a trawler business); as in *Pigs*, the narrative depicts class conflict and the difficulties attending the demonstration of homosexual desire.[13]

Peter Ormrod's *Eat the Peach* (1986), while less openly occupied with socio-political issues than the work of Murphy, Black, Quinn and Comerford, acknowledges the economic and psychological repercussions of unemployment. In a border region where hopes of European Community funding and extended multinational investment have evaporated, Vinnie Galvin is inspired by the Elvis Presley film *Roustabout*

(1964) to construct a motorcycle Wall of Death. However, frustrated by the absence of any clientele, Vinnie burns down the structure that he laboured so long to build. Like *Reefer*, *Eat the Peach* analyses what it means to linger in the residuum of idealism. For a study of failure, it was a considerable financial success.[14] The utilization of tax incentives for private investors by the production company Strongbow exhibited a degree of achievement markedly lacking from Vinnie's enterprise.

In a round of economic cuts made by the incoming Fianna Fáil government in 1987, the Film Board was dissolved. Although Irish film-makers resisted the urge to make Walls of Death, the disappearance of an important source for the seed money vital for script completion and initial investment doubtless led to the stifling of projects equally as worthy as Siobhán Twomey's *Boom Babies* (1987) and Fergus Tighe's *Clash of the Ash* (1987), which had both benefited from Board funding. However, students at the College of Commerce, Rathmines, and Dun Laoghaire School of Art and Design began to produce what has become a steady stream of short films, many of which, such as Kieron Walsh's *Goodbye Piccadilly* (1988) and Declan Recks' *Big Swinger* (1989), show considerable flair.[15]

Margo Harkin's *Hush-A-Bye Baby* (1989) was a welcome addition to the regrettably meagre catalogue of what could be termed *cinemná*: films by Irish women about Irish women.[16] Set principally in Derry, it focuses on 15-year-old Goretti, who becomes pregnant but hides it from her family and most of her friends. Goretti's plight is set in the wider context of the Republic's 1983 Abortion Referendum, which she hears being dis- cussed on the radio during her brief stay in the Donegal Gaeltacht. Based on interviews and drama workshops with local teenagers, the film is shot in a vividly realistic mode, except for its effectively expressionist opening credits and ending. During the latter, the recurrent imagery of the Virgin Mary reaches a nightmarish visual and aural climax, as Goretti gives birth.[17]

Released in the same year as *Hush-A-Bye Baby* was *My Left Foot*, directed and co-written by Jim Sheridan. It traces the real-life story of Christy Brown, who becomes an acclaimed writer and painter, despite suffering from cerebral palsy. The familiar theme of a triumph of the human spirit over adversity, combined with bravura performances, led to international exposure, BAFTA awards and Oscars for acting. In *The Field* (1990), Sheridan altered significant aspects of his source – John B. Keane's 1965 play – in order to construct a critique of Ford's *The Quiet Man* (as Quinn had done in *Poitín*). Sheridan's 'hard primitivist' repres- entation of rural Ireland may also have been a response to the 'soft primitivism' of his earlier screenplay for *Into the West*, which was directed in 1992 by Mike Newell.[18] Although *The Field* did not repeat the U.S. success of *My Left Foot*, Universal Pictures backed Sheridan's *In the Name of the Father* (1993); to the indignation of many British politicians and journalists, the film dramatized the experiences of Gerry Conlon, one of the 'Guildford Four', who all suffered a grave miscarriage of justice, on the evidence of false confessions extracted by physical and psychological torture. The film was the first in a trilogy of works by Sheridan and co-writer Terry George that scrutinized the 'Troubles' and contemporary Anglo-Irish relations. George's *Some Mother's Son* (1996) tackled the 1981 Hunger Strike by republican prisoners in pursuit of political status, while Sheridan's *The Boxer* (1997) negotiated the obstacles to the Northern Irish peace process.

While Sheridan and George confronted the conflict head-on, Joe Comerford's *High Boot Benny* (1993) adopted a more allegorical approach, charting a troubled teenager's eventual decision to join the IRA. The film explores the symbolic as well as practical consequences of crossing the Border between the Republic and Northern Ireland, as did Comerford's *Traveller* (1981), *Hush-A-Bye Baby*, Peter Yates' *The Run of the Country* (1995) and Tom Collins' *Bogwoman* (1997).[19] While Sheridan, George, Comerford, Harkin and Murphy concentrated on the North's Catholic and nationalist communities, Thaddeus O'Sullivan's *December Bride* (1990) featured Ulster Presbyterians, an extremely marginalized group (at least in terms of frequency of sympathetic cinematic portrayal). Adapted from Sam Hanna Bell's 1951 novel, the film is set in the early twentieth century, and concerns a *ménage à trois* that scandalizes a God-fearing congregation. O'Sullivan's early works *A Pint of Plain* (1977) and *On a Paving Stone Mounted* (1978) experimentally reconnoitred the experiences of Irish emigrants, another group under-depicted by indigenous film-makers.[20] O'Sullivan also worked as a cameraperson for Black, Comerford and Murphy, before directing *The Woman Who Married Clark Gable* (1985), a short based on a Sean O'Faolain story. In *Nothing Personal* (1995), adapted by Daniel Mornin from his novel *All Our Fault* (1991), O'Sullivan returned to a Northern, protestant locale, depicting the casual ties and casualties generated during the 1975 Loyalist and Republican paramilitary ceasefire.[21]

The resurrection of the Irish Film Board in 1993, and support from the European Script Fund and other European organizations, encouraged a host of new projects, including Paddy Breathnach's *Ailsa* (1994) and *I Went Down* (1997), Barry Devlin's *All Things Bright and Beautiful* (1994), Martin Duffy's *The Boy From Mercury* (1996), David Keating's *The*

Last of the High Kings (1996), and Gerry Stembridge's *Guiltrip* (1995).
There was also a gratifying number of films by Irish women, including
Trish McAdam's *Snakes and Ladders* (1996), Geraldine Creed's *The Sun, the
Moon and the Stars* (1996) and Mary McGuckian's *Words Upon the Window
Pane* (1994) and *This is the Sea* (1996). With this new talent, plus the tax
incentives for indigenous and exogenous film production in the country,
and the opening of the Irish Film Centre (with its archive of Irish film)
in 1992, the filter has never seemed rosier for Irish film culture.[22]

Two factors distinguish many of the films of this new generation from
their predecessors: firstly, a less explicit engagement with the socio-
political issues that mark the films of Black, Comerford, Harkin, Murphy
and Quinn; secondly, a more explicit involvement with the requirements
of the international film market. I want to explore the divergence
between politically and commercially engaged projects, and between
national and international markets, in terms of narrative, genre and
audience, and then to assess the implications for future screenings of
the Republic.

II

Traveller (1981), directed and edited by Joe Comerford from Neil Jordan's
screenplay, follows Angela and Michael, two young travellers who
undergo an arranged marriage, a smuggling trip to Northern Ireland, an
encounter with a dissident Republican, and involvement in a crash, a
robbery, and eventually a murder. Formalist in its use of editing and
sound, the film intermittently interweaves the personal and the political,
metaphorically linking Angela's childhood sexual abuse by her father
with the Northern 'Troubles' and republican ideology with Catholic
theology.[23] However, Jordan claimed that the finished film bore little
relation to his screenplay and that his resulting unhappiness impelled
him to direct 'because I wanted my scripts done correctly'.[24]

The quality that Jordan wished the filmed version of his scripts to
maintain can be inferred from his 1993 comment that much recent
Irish cinema lacked 'a strong narrative drive . . . narrative excitement'.[25]
Although he has referred somewhat dismissively to 'screenwriting man-
uals about dramatic structure [which refer to] . . . the first, second, and
third act (why only three?)', Jordan regularly channels the 'narrative
drive' of his work through three acts.[26] In a book that became a bible
for many aspiring screenwriters, Syd Field identified several esteemed
and successful mainstream Hollywood films that utilize a three-act structure and incorporate a 'midpoint' turn or twist in Act Two.[27] Whether

consciously or not, Jordan has frequently used this model, especially in his Oscar-winning screenplay for *The Crying Game* (1992): the first act is set in Ireland, the second in England, and the third commences with the reappearance of Fergus' IRA colleagues; the mid-point twist is the revelation concerning Dil's sex.[28] The second-act midpoint in *High Spirits* (1988) occurs when the real ghosts arrive; in *We're No Angels* (1989) – with its David Mamet screenplay – it occurs when the 'miracle' of the Weeping Virgin statue is explained naturally (although the statue simultaneously appears to channel miraculous aid for Neddy and Jimmy); in *The Miracle* (1991), the midpoint occurs when Renée is revealed as Jimmy's mother; in *Interview with the Vampire* (1994), when Lestat reappears from the (undead) dead; in *Michael Collins* (1996), when the War of Independence ends; and in *The Butcher Boy* (1997), when we learn that Francie's father is dead.[29] I am not classifying Jordan's films as formulaic, but indicating that they are attuned to a widespread and successful Hollywood model. Despite working within this model, Jordan none the less often achieves his declared goal of preventing the audience from guessing in the first five minutes what will happen in the last five.[30]

However, Jordan's mode of narrative drive differs from the approach of independent film-makers like Pat Murphy. Although divided into three acts, *Anne Devlin* charts what Murphy calls 'a series of false climaxes':

> The way in which you think that the climax of this woman's life is her rebellion and it's not; the same with the hanging, and it's not that either. The climax becomes about the whole release of her strength in the third act.[31]

The film's pacing is deliberately slow, as Murphy recreates an earlier mode of temporal process. The narrative incorporates what she calls '[t]hings that are not normally considered worthwhile to be filmed but that are fundamental to life'.[32] This can be compared with Joe Comerford's treatment of Jordan's *Traveller* screenplay: it became (in Ciaran Carty's words) 'a working framework . . . subordinated to the promptings of actuality . . . found on location with the travellers'.[33] *Traveller*'s formalist editing style also countered Jordan's narrative drive. In Comerford's *Reefer and the Model*, the first half of the film moves at a completely different pace to the second. As Kevin Rockett notes, this has genre implications: *Reefer*'s first half 'has the feel and resonance of a European art film but much of the rest is informed by Hollywood chase movies'.[34] Like Murphy and Quinn, Comerford is uninterested in the generic and narrative concerns of mainstream cinema, as his comment on *High Boot Benny* reveals:

> When you try to make a film and you approach various agencies for funding, they ask you what 'genre' the picture is. I never filled that in, and if I was asked, I explained that I refuse to say what genre it is, because I don't know. You see, when you start a film, I think it's vital that you know what direction you are going in, but it's vital also that you don't have a pre-decided structure of the film, or of what's going to come out of it at the other end.[35]

While this experimental approach undoubtedly has merits, its dangers are all too visible in the meandering plot and somnambulistic pace of *High Boot Benny*.

Jordan's attitude to genre has its dangers too. As the thriller conventions in *Angel*, *Mona Lisa* and *The Crying Game* indicate, he is (unlike Comerford) happy to start with genre, although he likes 'a certain tension between the genre in which one is working and what one is doing to it, and also between the film and the audience expectations of the genre'.[36] *Michael Collins* splices the genres (or sub-genres) of historical epic, 1930s biopic, 1930s gangster, 1970s gangster, film noir, spy and thriller. 'You look like a gangster' – Collins' words to Boland upon the latter's return to Dublin from America – encapsulate the visual style of numerous sequences in the film. Jordan's diary obliquely acknowledges Francis Ford Coppola's *Godfather* films and admits that 'in their period suits the actors are in danger of seeming to be in 1920s Chicago'.[37] Luke Gibbons argues that one reason the film drew fire from certain historians is because its representation of 'the War of Independence through the optic of the gangster genre' suggests that 'the foundations of the state may itself rest on terror'.[38] He claims, however, that there is 'a striking difference in the moral sensibility' of *Collins* and that of the 1958 IRA gangster genre film *Shake Hands with the Devil* (starring James Cagney):

> Cagney's character is drawn from the psychotic personality which stalked his later gangster films, such as *White Heat* (1949), and is identified with the 'die-hard' republican element which refused to accept the Treaty; by contrast, Liam Neeson's playing of Michael Collins is of a character on the side of 'reason', and is more akin to the sympathetic figure of Michael Corleone, including his tragic flaws. By reworking the image of the gangster in the light of both recent developments in the genre, and the aura surrounding Collins, Jordan's

film has, in effect, lifted the crude, sinister associations off the stereotype of the 'Godfather', thereby depriving revisionist demonology of one of its favourite tropes. It is this, perhaps, more than any other factor, which accounts for the extraordinary animus directed against the film in the British press, and by revisionist critics and historians in Ireland.[39]

The force of this argument depends to some extent upon whether one is persuaded that Michael Corleone is a 'sympathetic figure' (after all, in *Godfather II* [1974], he has his brother killed, and his wife despises him so much that she aborts their child). Gibbons' thesis is also challenged by his previous paragraph, which describes how *Collins* 'draws a set of uncomfortable analogies' between the War of Independence and 'the present conflict in Northern Ireland':

> The fact that the implementation of a criminalisation policy towards republican prisoners in the North in the mid-1970s coincided with the vogue enjoyed by the Godfather films handed the British authorities a valuable rhetorical weapon in their propaganda war against republicans. From then on, the leaders of Sinn Fein could be denigrated simply as 'Godfathers', and political violence similarly dismissed as 'organised crime', perpetrated by the mindless thugs of the republican mafia produced by the nationalist ghettoes. By extending the rhetorical range of the metaphor into the foundations of the Irish state, Jordan's film issues a powerful rejoinder to such simplistic readings of political violence.[40]

If one accepts that the film advances this subversive reading, then one must also accept that Jordan's generic strategy reinforced rather than rebutted British and Ulster unionist suspicions that twentieth-century Irish republicanism *in extenso* is a form of gangsterism.[41] Those critics who were hostile to what they perceived as a pro-(Provisional) IRA slant in Collins' representation of the War of Independence seized upon the scene in which four Belfast detectives are blown up by a car bomb (anachronistic in 1920, but not in the 1970–1990s).[42] Jordan's later defence of the scene highlights the dangers of screening history through the anamorphic lens of genre:

> [A] scene in my film, in which a Belfast detective is blown up in Dublin Castle, was being seen as a direct and conscious reference to the Troubles, a calculated insult to the North's unionist population.

The scene, of course, is nothing of the kind. Its purpose is to show the escalation of the guerrilla war ... The scene as I shot it relates, if it relates to anything, to the kind of cinematic shorthand audiences are used to from gangster movies.

I can be accused of aesthetic misjudgement in using the cinematic language of crime drama for the depiction of Collins' war with the British administration. That might portray him – as Lloyd George saw him – as a criminal. But I was not making any reference to any party in the current Troubles.[43]

Genre jeopardy also occurs in both Sheridan's *In the Name of the Father*, where the screening of *The Godfather* during an IRA prisoner's brutal attack on a guard reinforces the 'republican mafia' propaganda to which Gibbons refers, and in O'Sullivan's *Nothing Personal*, whose U.K. video cassette classifies it as a 'thriller', and bears the tag 'The Deadliest Gangsters Are Those With A Cause'.[44]

Genre is one way in which a film situates its audience, and I want briefly to consider the audience question. After a preview of what was intended to be the final cut of *Michael Collins*, Jordan realized that an American audience (his primary market) would probably be unaware and possibly be disappointed that Collins dies at the end. He therefore shot five new scenes, including a prelude preparing the international audience for Collins' fate.[45] Jim Sheridan has commented that his agenda for *In the Name of the Father* 'was to take this story out of England and Ireland and universalise it, take it to a wider audience' – it was, of course, a Universal picture.[46] On the other hand, Margo Harkin stresses that in *Hush-A-Bye Baby*, the film-makers 'were trying to engage with people on this island. It was not meant for consumption in Britain.'[47] And Bob Quinn does not care whether his films are shown abroad or not: 'I'm only concerned that they're shown in this country ... I think there are not sufficient film-makers interested in the idea of showing their films in and around this country.'[48]

Do Comerford, Harkin, Murphy and Quinn embody a national Irish cinema, while Jordan, Sheridan, and Pat O'Connor represent an internationalized (or denationalized) notional Irish cinema? Not necessarily. Andrew Higson has suggested that concepts of national cinema should move from 'the analysis of film texts as vehicles for the articulation of nationalist sentiment and the interpellation of the implied national spectator, to an analysis of how actual audiences construct their cultural identity in relation to the various products of the national and international film and television industries, and the conditions under which this is achieved . . . For what is a national cinema if it doesn't have a national audience?'[49]

Whatever the flaws generated by a lack of fit between its historical material and its three-act structure and gangster genre, *Michael Collins* certainly had a national audience, which engaged in intense debate about the uses to which the film could be put. The box-office success of Jordan's film in Ireland complicates any binary division between national and international cinema. Almost any feature film now made in Ireland, whether by independents or major studios, relies on some form of international financing, whether from Europe, America or Japan. While the auto-exoticist *High Spirits* demonstrated the dangers of working within the Hollywood system, Jordan skilfully used the international success of *The Crying Game* and *Interview with the Vampire* to secure major studio backing for two films about Ireland that sought to balance the demands of the local market with the global. While his aim was only partially achieved in *Michael Collins*, it was fulfilled in *The Butcher Boy*, which uses all the technical resources provided by a multi-million dollar budget to confront questions previously addressed in the 1970s and 1980s by independent Irish film-makers. Jordan's adaptation of Patrick McCabe's 1992 novel seizes upon issues such as social marginalization, mental illness, institutional abuse, the legacy of independence and the impinging of American genres upon Irish culture, but defamiliarizes and reinvigorates them through an oneiric perspective.[50]

The Butcher Boy demonstrates that it is possible to make a film that is both stylistically innovative and revelatory about the nuances of Irish experience, a film that can engage with the imagination and intellect of national and international audiences. It is an exemplar for the present generation of Irish film-makers, who, in the wake of overwhelming assent to the 1998 Good Friday Agreement, face a new artistic challenge – as Fintan O'Toole has observed, 'in return for peace the people of both parts of Ireland will have to give up a comfort that most Europeans take for granted: a fixed sense of where their nation begins and ends'.[51] Consequently, future screenings of the Republic will require new forms of narrative and new interpretations of genre for a new kind of audience.

Notes

1   Kevin Rockett, 'History, Politics and Irish Cinema' ['HPIC'], in Rockett, Luke Gibbons, and John Hill's *Cinema and Ireland* (London: Routledge, 1988), pp. 3–144 (pp. 76–80). Further information on Irish documentaries and drama-documentaries of the 1950s and 60s can be found in this essay and in Rockett's *The Irish Filmography: Fiction Films 1896–1996* (Dublin: Red Mountain

Media, 1996). I have drawn upon these two invaluable sources throughout this essay.

2 Joep Leerssen, *Remembrance and Imagination: Patterns in the Historical and Literary Representation of Ireland in the Nineteenth Century* (Cork: Cork University Press, 1996), pp. 35–38.

3 See Rockett, 'HPIC', pp. 111–14. Amongst the Irish-set British productions that used Ardmore were *Shake Hands with the Devil* (1959), *A Terrible Beauty* (1960), and *The Violent Enemy* (1969). These films about the IRA had themes and plots similar to earlier British-made, IRA films such as *Odd Man Out* (1947) and *The Gentle Gunman* (1952). In his cogent essay 'Images of Violence', *Cinema and Ireland*, pp. 147–93, John Hill provides an astringent critique of all five films (pp. 152–71).

4 In 'HPIC', Kevin Rockett argues that the Workers' Party's reading of *Caoineadh* as a critique of romantic nationalism is not necessarily borne out by the film's representation of social class and generation of pathos (p. 138).

5 'Interview with Bob Quinn', in Brian McIlroy, *World Cinema 4: Ireland [WC4: I]* (Trowbridge: Flicks Books, 1989), pp. 142–46 (p.143).

6 Rockett, 'HPIC', p. 118. On pp. 114–22, Rockett analyses the mechanisms that produced the Board and the machinations that accompanied its first two years.

7 See Rockett, 'HPIC', pp. 118–19. In 'Celtic Dreamer', an interview by Marina Burke in *Film Ireland* (April/May, 1993): 16–21 (21), Jordan gives his side of the affair, as does Boorman in 'General Boorman: The Interview', by Ted Sheehy, *Film Ireland* (June/July, 1998): 16–19 (17–19).

8 McIlroy, *WC4: I*, 'Interview with Neil Jordan', pp. 114–18 (p. 115).

9 See Hill's indictment in 'Images of Violence', pp. 178–81, 184. Richard Kearney, in *Transitions: Narratives in Modern Irish Culture* (Manchester: Manchester University Press, 1988), pp. 175–83, defends Jordan's depiction of political violence. Later in this essay I discuss Jordan's subsequent work.

10 However, as Kevin Rockett notes in 'HPIC', the Ardmore/National Film Studios contributed little to native Irish film culture, since (prior to the Film Board) state policy was rooted in the mistaken belief that incentives to attract foreign film-makers to Ireland would have an epiphenomenal effect upon indigenous production (pp. 95–114). On television funding of cinema in an Irish context, see John Hill and Martin McLoone, (eds.), *Big Picture, Small Screen: The Relations between Film and Television* (Luton: John Libbey Media, 1996), especially pp. 118–32, 205–9, and 210–14.

11 In *Transformations in Irish Culture* (Cork: Cork University Press, 1996), Luke Gibbons perceptively analyses both *Maeve* (pp. 117–27) and *Anne Devlin* (pp. 107–16).

12 David Will, 'An Interview with Pat Murphy', *Framework* 26/27 (1985): 132–6 (136).

13 See Lance Pettitt, 'Pigs and Provos, Prostitutes and Prejudice: Gay Representation in Irish Film, 1984–1995', in Éibhear Walshe (ed.) *Sex, Nation and Dissent in Irish Writing* (Cork: Cork University Press, 1997), pp. 252–84.

14 However, Luke Gibbons, in 'Romanticism, Realism and Irish Cinema' ['RRIC'], in Rockett, Gibbons and Hill's *Cinema and Ireland*, pp. 194–257, accuses the film of being 'a flat, one-dimensional . . . pastiche' of 'the traditional stereotype of the imaginative, impractical Celt' (pp. 242–3). Contrariwise, in *Critical*

Regionalism and Cultural Studies: From Ireland to the American Mid-West (Gainesville: University Press of Florida, 1996), Cheryl Temple Herr argues that the film accurately diagnoses 'the Irish experience of uneven industrial development, of economic marginalization, and of incredible potential perversely thwarted by multinational and governmental interventions' (p. 194).

15 On the importance of short films for Irish film culture, see Guiney, 'Film and Television in Ireland', in *Big Picture, Small Screen* (pp. 210–14).

16 Besides Pat Murphy's work, one could include Orla Walsh's short *The Visit* (1992) and (although British-funded) Aisling Walsh's *Joyriders* (1988), which explores the odyssey of an abused wife, who is driven first to abandon and then to reclaim her children. More recent examples are given later in the main text.

17 Information about and analysis of the film can be found in Megan Sullivan, 'From Nationalism to "Baby X": An Interview with Northern Irish Filmmaker Margo Harkin', *Éire-Ireland* 32/2 and 3 (Summer/Fall, 1997): 40–51 and Elizabeth Butler Cullingford, 'Seamus and Sinéad: From "Limbo" to *Saturday Night Live* by way of *Hush-A-Bye Baby*', *Colby Quarterly* 30/1 (March, 1994): 43–62.

18 Erwin Panofsky's differentiation between 'soft' and 'hard primitivism' in pastoral is deftly adapted by Luke Gibbons, in 'RRIC', for the analysis of cinematic representations of Irishness (pp. 197–203). For an astute reading of *Into the West's* rejection of capitalist modernity, see Joe Cleary, 'Into Which West?: Irish Modernity and the Maternal Supernatural', in Brian Cosgrove (ed.), *Literature and the Supernatural* (Blackrock: The Columba Press, 1995), pp. 147–73.

19 *Eat the Peach* features Border crossings in the form of smuggling, as does the British-funded *The Playboys* (1992), which, like *The Run of the Country*, is written by Shane Connaughton. Other British-funded films in which the Border is a significant plot element include *I See A Dark Stranger* (1946) and *The Gentle Gunman*. *Border Crossing: Film in Ireland, Britain and Europe* (Belfast: Institute of Irish Studies, 1994), edited by John Hill *et al.*, investigates some of the practical aspects of cross-border film financing.

20 However, Irish emigrant experience has been a staple of American cinema: see Kevin Rockett, 'The Irish migrant and film', in Patrick O'Sullivan (ed.) *The Creative Migrant* (Leicester: Leicester University Press, 1994), pp. 170–91.

21 On the screening (out) of Northern protestants, unionists and loyalists, see Brian McIlroy, 'The Repression of Communities: Visual Representations of Northern Ireland during the Thatcher Years', in Lester Friedman (ed.), *British Cinema and Thatcherism: Fires were Started,* (London: UCL Press, 1993), pp. 92–108, and 'When the Ulster Protestant and Unionist Looks: Spectatorship in (Northern) Irish Cinema', *Irish University Review*, 26:1 (Spring/Summer, 1996): 143–54.

22 I use the words 'filter' and 'seemed' advisedly, since the film business is notoriously unpredictable. For an independent Irish film producer's overview of the various funding sources currently available and the need for RTE to become more substantially involved, see Guiney, 'Film and Television in Ireland'.

23 For two differing interpretations of *Traveller's* political allusions, see Kevin Rockett's 'Like an Expedition . . . ', *IFT News* V. 2 (Feb., 1982): 4–6 and Kevin

Barry's 'Discarded Images: Narrative and the Cinema', *The Crane Bag* 6. 1 (1982): 45–52. *Traveller*, like *The Field*, *Into the West* and *Trojan Eddie* (1996), uses the often hostile relationship between the travellers and settled communities in order to chart the inclusion and exclusion zones of Irish society. Paul Rotha's British-funded film *No Resting Place* (1951), adapted from a novel set in Cumberland, could be seen as a precursor to this quasi-genre.

24 McIlroy, *WC4: I*, p. 114.

25 Burke, 20–1. However, his example – *Joyriders* – is not a product of independent Irish cinema.

26 'Introduction to The Crying Game', in *A Neil Jordan Reader* (New York: Vintage Books, 1993), pp. xi–xiii (pp. xi–xii).

27 *The Screenwriter's Workbook* (New York: Dell, 1984), pp. 121–45. The book follows Field's *Screenplay* (New York: Delta, 1979), where the three-act thesis is first advanced. John Badham's American comedy-thriller *The Hard Way* (1991) amusingly acknowledges the three-act structure's stranglehold on recent Hollywood output.

28 Jordan may also have been inspired by earlier three-act Irish plays like Synge's *The Playboy of the Western World* (1907), whose midpoint is the 'resurrection' of Old Mahon, and O'Casey's *Juno and the Paycock* (1924), whose midpoint is Johnny's offstage vision of the ghost of Robbie Tancred.

29 Lack of space precludes for the present a detailed exposition of this hypothesis. Regarding the earlier films, the major twist of the transitional *Mona Lisa* (1986) – that Simone is a lesbian – occurs towards the close rather than at the midpoint (where a minor twist reveals that Mortwell and Anderson are conspirators). *Mona Lisa's* search motif echoes *Angel* and (partly) *The Company of Wolves* (1984), where a quest circles back to its origin. This motif also links *Angel* to John Boorman's *Point Blank* (1967): introducing the *Angel* screenplay (London: Faber and Faber, 1989), pp. vii–ix, Boorman notes that its 'style and structure (not its story content) were partly inspired' by *Point Blank* (p. viii). However, both films also share the story content of revenge. For further observations on Jordan's plot construction, see my 'Neil Jordan and the ABC of Narratology', *New Hibernia Review*, 3:2 (Summer 1999): 36–55.

30 Burke, 20.

31 Will, 'Interview with Pat Murphy', 133.

32 Ciaran Carty, *Confessions of a Sewer Rat: A Personal History of Censorship and the Irish Cinema* (Dublin: New Island Books, 1995), p. 150. This description could also be applied to *Maeve*. However, while the plot of Anne Devlin is chronological, the storyline of *Maeve* is deliberately fragmented.

33 Carty, p. 136.

34 Kevin Rockett, 'Ireland', in Ginette Vincendeauld (ed.), *Encyclopedia of European Cinema*, (London: BFI, 1995), pp. 217–19 (pp. 218–19).

35 Laoise Mac Reamoinn, 'Crossing the Border' [Interview with Joe Comerford], *Film Ireland* (Oct./Nov., 1994): 10–11 (11).

36 McIlroy, *WC4: I*, p. 115.

37 Neil Jordan, *Michael Collins: Film Diary and Screenplay* (London: Vintage, 1996), p. 9. Two montage sequences (depicting 'Bloody Sunday' and Collins' death) allude to the famous intercutting between baptism and assassination in *The Godfather* (1972).

38   'Framing History: Neil Jordan's *Michael Collins*', *History Ireland* 5.1 (Spring, 1997): 47–51 (51).
39   Ibid., 51.
40   Ibid.
41   See, for example, Glen Newey, 'Both gangster and Gandhi', *TLS* (Nov. 15, 1996): 20; Quentin Falk, 'Movie Reviews', *Sunday Mirror* (Nov. 10, 1996): 44; Tom Shone, 'Patriot Games', *The Sunday Times, Review* (Nov. 10, 1996): 6–7.
42   See, for example, Paul Bew, 'History it ain't', *The Daily Telegraph* (Oct. 14, 1996): 20; and 'Truth died when Jordan shot Collins', *The Sunday Times, News Review* (Nov. 10, 1996): 6. While Kevin Myers (on the basis of the published screenplay) was initially one of the film's harshest critics (see 'Kitty get your gun', *The Irish Times, Weekend* [Oct. 12, 1996]: 12), he changed his mind upon seeing the film (see 'An Irishman's Diary', *The Irish Times* [Nov. 16, 1996]: 15).
43   'Truths we must tell', *The Guardian, Friday Review* (Oct. 25, 1996): 2–3, 19 (19). Keith Hopper's '"Cat-Calls from the Cheap Seats": The Third Meaning of Neil Jordan's *Michael Collins*', *The Irish Review*, 21 (Autumn/Winter, 1997): 1–28, includes some astute readings of scenes in the film, but fails to consider the political implications of Jordan's use of genre (see Hopper 7).
44   On the other hand, the apolitical use of the gangster genre in *I Went Down* helped to sell the picture to American audiences: see, for example, Steven Rea's review, 'Here's a gangster flick with charm and an Irish lilt', *The Philadelphia Inquirer, Reviews* (July 3, 1998).
45   Jordan, *Michael Collins: Film Diary and Screenplay*, pp. 62–4. The other scenes were a coda after Collins' death, plus 'two additional scenes to deepen the love-triangle' (p. 63), and the scene in which Kiernan learns of Collins' death. Concerning the inclusion of the latter, Jordan remarks that for an American audience, emotion must be 'presented'; the previous cut relied upon 'the great European tradition' of implication (p. 62).
46   Quoted in Ronan Bennett, 'The big screen trial of the Guildford Four', *The Observer*, Arts, (6 Feb. 1994): 2–3 (3). The production notes for *Some Mother's Son* and *The Boxer* also emphasize the 'universal' dimension of their stories.
47   Untitled address, in Martin McLoone (ed.), *Culture, Identity and Broadcasting in Ireland: Local Issues, Global Perspectives*, (Belfast: Institute of Irish Studies, 1991), pp. 110–16 (p. 113).
48   McIlroy, *WC4: I*, p. 144.
49   'The Concept of National Cinema', *Screen*, 30 (1989): 36–46 (45–6); see also Higson's *Waving the Flag: Constructing a National Cinema in Britain* (Oxford: Clarendon Press, 1995), pp. 1–25 and 272–9.
50   However, Jordan once again demonstrated his inability or unwillingness to depict on film complex female characters.
51   'The Meanings of Union', *The New Yorker* (May 4, 1998): 54–62 (54). Declan Kiberd, in 'Romantic Ireland's dead and gone', *TLS* (June 12, 1998): 12–14, notes that the Agreement 'offers a postcolonial version of overlapping identities of a kind for which no legal language yet exists' (14).

7
Legal Texts as Cultural Documents: Interpreting the Irish Constitution

Patrick Hanafin

> It is the text that establishes our social identity and institutional place, it is the text that provides us with our jurisdiction or right of speech, it is the text in which we are born and in which we die.[1]

Introduction

After over sixty years in existence, does the Irish Constitution of 1937 represent the Ireland of today or are its core values no longer representative of cultural reality? This question involves analysing the conception of Ireland which influenced the framers of the 1937 Constitution and the extent to which that conception has changed in the intervening years. Looking at the themes of collective and individual identity, this essay attempts to analyse the constitutional text in the light of sixty years of interpretation and amendment. Can the Constitution be defined as an evolving narrative in that it is gradually adapting to the unfolding story of Irish society, or is it firmly rooted in an imagined past forcing citizens to play the roles which the Constitution's framers conceived for them? This essay tries to recuperate the voices of those groups who have been lost in the interstices of constitutional discourse in Ireland. Looking at the way in which the issues of gender, family and territory have been visualised in cultural and legal discourse, it identifies the ways in which the Constitution may be interpreted to provide a less restrictive model of Irish society.

The transformations in Irish society during the period since the introduction of the Constitution have demonstrated that there is no such thing as a monolithic Irish identity. Rather, Irish selfhood is fragmented into many diverse pieces, all of which have a role to play in constituting the whole. The Constitution should act as an enabling mechanism for the development of Irish identities rather than as a means, as it has done in the past, of constricting a more inclusive idea of citizenship.

Announcing the Nation

The writing of a constitution is an act which founds a nation. However, the term 'foundational document' is laden with complexity. A foundational document such as a constitution is usually given to the people by themselves. But by what authority do the people give themselves this new nation which is inscribed in the constitutional document? Strictly speaking, the people do not exist at the moment of founding. It is the founding document which gives them legal effect. Therefore in order to exist the people must found themselves. This is the puzzle which Derrida has written of when he speaks of the signature of the people authorising itself to sign.[2] The inauguration of the constitutional text preceded the establishment of a *de jure* Irish Republic by twelve years. Thus the foundational document of the new polity pre-empted Ireland's status as a republic. In this sense it mirrors Derrida's notion of the performative nature of such foundational documents. Referring to the American Declaration of Independence, Derrida notes that the act of writing a constitutional document paradoxically creates that which gives it authority. In other words, the national entity which empowers the inauguration of the Constitution can only exist with the signing into law of the Constitution. The people cannot decide as a result whether it is constating that the people already constitute an independent republic or whether it is performing the act which makes the people independent. As Derrida notes:

> The total unity of a nation is not identified for the first time except by a contract – formal or not, written or not – which institutes some fundamental law. Now this contract is never actually signed, except by supposed representatives of the nation which is supposed to be 'entire'. This fundamental law cannot, either in law or in fact, simply precede that which at once institutes it and nevertheless supposes it: projecting and reflecting it. It can in no way precede this extraordinary performative by which a signature authorises itself to sign, in a word, legalises itself on its own without the guarantee of a pre-existing law.[3]

Moreover, the Constitution is not a petrified document. Writing a constitution or inscribing a collective identity is just the beginning of an unending dialectic between text and people. As Norton notes:

Acknowledgement of the Constitution's authority, coupled with recognition of the Constitution's author, must persuade one of the dialectical relation between the people and the text. Consideration of this relation reveals that the dialectic must continue while the text retains its constitutional character. There is no end to it. The process of transubstantiation that the writing of the Constitution inaugurates is not simply one from flesh to word and word to flesh. It reiterates a series of earlier transformations from a collective to an individual condition, from an unconscious to a conscious state. This greater dialectic marks a fundamental difference in human constitution. Rather than a state of being, of uniformity and constancy in the constitution of the species and its individual members, humanity is characterised by a condition of inconstancy, a state not of being but of becoming.[4]

The Constitution and the notion of national identity encapsulated therein is not fixed or stable. It is always in a state of becoming, never complete, with no definitive construction of identity gaining permanency. The so-called monolithic notion of Irishness which it is assumed is captured in the text is not the end of the constitutional story. The notion of identity contained within the text of the Constitution is always open to disruption, always open to the presence of contrary notions of 'Irishness'. National identity is as fluid as individual identity, ever changing and reforming in a reflexive reaction to societal transformations. As Mellor has observed: 'self-identity is . . . subject to the pervasive reflexivity of high modernity, so that it is created and maintained through the continual reflexive reordering of self-narratives.'[5] As the narratives of the individuals who make up the nation are reordered, so too is the narrative of the nation.

The Constitution is an example of the attempted writing of a national identity. It is an attempt to pass from the imagined idea of Irishness to the realised state of Ireland. The writing of the nation cannot found the nation; the nation, to paraphrase Derrida, is always in the future (*avenir*), always to come (*a venir*). The foundational legal document attempts to posit a definitive national identity. However, this notion of Irishness is only posited against difference, against the 'other', the marginalised, whether that be the foreigner in the case of Articles 2 and 3 or women in the case of Article 41. The national self is always already constructed in opposition to otherness. As De Silva has noted in the case of the Sri Lankan Constitution of 1972 but which is equally the case in relation to the Irish Constitution:

[the Other] succeeds in breaching the boundary and distorting the outline ... of the Constitution's self identity as a projection of the desires of the majority ... The boundary (i.e. the external limit) of the Constitution's self-identity confronts its limit, what it can never fully be, as it finds itself tethered to the 'excess' that is the ... 'Other'. This internal limit prevents the Constitution from achieving a full identity with itself. Simultaneous to a failure of a full identity is the ultimate failure of exclusion ... The 'Other' is ever-present even if in a marginalised space that is never quite outside but never quite inside either.[6]

The Constitution purported to be a definitive narrative of Irish identity. However, this narrative could not erase the other stories of Irishness against which it was composed. Within its very framework it contained the seeds of its revision. As Brannigan has pointed out: 'At the heart of the writing of national identity, is also its contradiction, its frustration, its impossibility, and waiting within these aporetic spaces, the other.'[7] The original text of the Irish Constitution portrayed a particular model of Irish societal identity. However, through reinterpretation or the dialectic between text and reader this model of identity has been transformed, mirroring changes in Irish culture. The dialectic between text and people is an ongoing one, facilitative of change in societal identity rather than restricting such change. Thus, the very notion of a founding document is riven with complexity. What de Valera was doing, in effect, was founding an Ireland of the imagination, an Ireland in which certain values were to prevail and others were to be excluded. However, the permanence of this project was to be stymied by the constitutional text's own inherent contradictions. The mingling of dominant and subordinate ideologies in the constitutional text was to lead to its transformation through the medium of textual exegesis.

The Constitution of Community

The Irish Constitution of 1937 encapsulated a conception of Irishness which was traditional and irredentist. The Constitution of 1937 was not the first attempt to announce a new nation. The Declaration of 1916, the Dail Constitution of 1919 and the Irish Free State Constitution of 1922 all preceded this so-called foundational document. The aim of the Constitution's primary framer, Eamon de Valera, was to create a more authentic notion of Ireland than that contained within the text of the 1922 Constitution. In this sense, the Constitution of 1937 acted as a belated means of enunciating the elite's notion of a separate Irish polity. The Constitution is a text in which two very different notions of Irish selfhood have existed side by side in an uneasy relationship. The Constitution is heavily indebted to the Thomist Natural Law tradition but also acknowledges notions of liberal constitutionalism. The framers of the Constitution attempted to reconcile their theocratic aspirations with their republican ideals. This was an impossible task, as the divine and the secular are twin faiths which cannot live in harmony. The divine is constantly disrupted by the liberal in constitutional interpretation. In combining these two strands in the constitutional text, the framers created a legal fiction which recalls the mythico-religious fiction upon which the postcolonial state was founded. The Natural Law content of the Constitution signifies in constitutional discourse the myth of the monotheistic, monocultural Irish state. Natural Law theory formed the basis of the dominant strand in the Constitution as envisioned by its framers. This strand in constitutional discourse reflects in turn what Prager adverts to as the Gaelic Romantic tradition in Irish political thought. The Gaelic Romantic tradition constructed a version of Irishness in which, as Prager has put it:

> the nation ought to strive to re-create its past and resist those changes that seemed to challenge the basic meaning of Ireland as embodied in its traditions ... Ireland was to be celebrated as a pre-industrial nation; its identity was to be found in its rural character. The sanctity of the family was to be preserved, the [Roman Catholic] Church was to remain a central social institution second only to the family, and the farm was to serve as the backbone of a healthy, thriving society.[8]

The Preamble announces the transcendental origins of the Constitution. The Constitution is given to the people by themselves 'in the name of the Most Holy Trinity'. This model of the Constitution as being endowed by a divine source complicates the notion of self identity which is contained within the document. It links the notion of Irishness with Roman Catholicism and as a result Irish values become coextensive with the values of the Roman Catholic Church. To paraphrase Prager:

> The people of Ireland, in acting for God, were establishing a holy nation where decisions were providentially legitimated. This constituted an absolutist conception of a political community whose

actions were not determined by an emergent and indeterminate collectivity, but were telelogically justified.[9]

The original understanding of the Irish Constitution configures with the textualisation of the social form of community. This social form, to paraphrase Post, 'attempts to organise social life based on the principle that persons are socially embedded and dependent'.[10] The notion of community as applied to the postcolonial Irish context exhibits a state which is insular, autocratic, agrarian and imbued with a set of values which reflected such notions of social formation. However, the Constitution also contained elements of what Prager has referred to as the Irish Enlightenment tradition in political thought. These elements were included in the text of the Constitution as a sop to those groups in Irish society who did not adhere to the Gaelic Romantic view. Prager defines the Irish Enlightenment model in the following terms: 'the objective was to construct a social order characterised by autonomous individuals and independent spheres of social life in which the Irish citizen could rationally influence the course of Irish affairs'.[11]

The discourse of individuality encapsulated in the Irish Enlightenment tradition configures with Post's notion of 'responsive democracy', which he defines in the following terms: 'Responsive democracy begins with the premise of independent citizens who desire to fashion the social order in a manner that reflects their values and commitments . . . [it] posits persons with autonomous selves . . . [and] strives to open up the field of social choice.'[12] The liberal notion of personal rights contained in the Constitution was in large part derived from the Irish Enlightenment model. Thus, the 1937 Constitution incorporated both traditions, but initially the Irish Enlightenment model was occluded by the Gaelic Romantic model. The Irish Enlightenment model could thus be seen as a textual liminar, in an intermediate phase on its way towards becoming part of Irish selfhood. It was in effect a 'minor literature' in the territory of Irish constitutional literature, to put it in Deleuzo-Guattarian terms.[13]

By 1949, with the *de jure* creation of the Republic of Ireland, the Constitution had not been subjected to judicial interpretation which challenged the originary notion of national identity contained within its four corners. Its function was symbolic, creating an imagined idea of Ireland, rather than acting as a document which reflected and in some cases provoked societal change. The development of a more activist phase in the Supreme Court's jurisprudence in the 1960s led to a questioning of Irish identity as constitutionally posited. It was not until the emergence of this more activist Supreme Court that the consequences of mingling within a foundational legal text such antithetical philosophies as those represented by the Gaelic Romantic and Irish Enlightenment traditions were to emerge. How were the courts to reconcile the Thomist Natural Law influences with more liberal notions of personal rights?

The Constitution as originally understood was an inward-looking narrative of Irish identity, constricting individual autonomy in favour of a more community-oriented model. However, the Constitution was open to alternative readings which were to emerge in the 1960s. In this sense the Constitution configures to Deleuze and Guattari's notion of a rhizomatic document. In other words, it is a text which is open rather than closed and homogeneous.[14] The recognition of the Constitution as a rhizomatic text was instantiated by interpreting the document to create a more heterogeneous notion of Irish identity. The interpretation of the Constitution in this period can be likened to the process of creating or recreating a work of art or, as Deleuze would have it, the reforming of the work.[15] Like the process of painting, the task of interpretation involves the deforming and the subsequent reforming of a figure from the same raw materials.

For the purposes of this essay I will concentrate on a number of tropes in Irish constitutional discourse and examine how they have been revised in the wake of shifting societal perceptions. The tropes I will analyse are encapsulated in the phrase 'Motherland'. This phrase encompasses the importance of particular notions of gender, territory and the family as politico-cultural symbols of nationhood. The way in which these tropes were defined in constitutional terms reflected the Gaelic Romantic allegiances of its framers. However, in the reality of a fractured postcolonial Ireland these symbols have lost their currency and, as a result, the way in which they are represented in constitutional discourse has changed.

The Constitutional Landscape: Motherland

'Motherland', the bond between word, flesh and land, encapsulates key themes in Irish constitutional discourse. The land is personified as female in opposition to the previous male-identified coloniser in an antithetical attempt at averting the connotations of colonial rule. Hibernia, both mother and home, is further linked to the way in which woman is constitutionally identified as both mother and homemaker. The word became flesh and recolonised the female citizen. The historical struggle for the land is emphasised both in the original Articles 2 and 3, the aspirational Gaelic Romantic element of the Constitution, and in the more explicit protection given to private property in Article 43, an article which combines both the Gaelic-Romantic and Irish Enlightenment strains in Irish cultural thinking. The continuing presence of these articles revealed hidden yet deep-seated notions of Irishness based on ties of blood, soil and word. These are arguably the key examples of how the constitutional text encapsulated a perceived notion of Irishness. The persistence of some of these articles is by no means a sign that Ireland remains trapped in an imagined past. However, neither does it mean that Ireland has entered fully into the age of late modernity. These themes in Irish constitutional discourse create spaces both imagined and real within which the physical and intellectual boundaries of the nation are delimited. Taken in conjunction with the influence of Roman Catholic social teaching on constitutional discourse, one is enabled to study in microcosm the principal tenets of traditional Irish constitutional doctrine. The Constitution is, in effect, a powerful instrument for conveying a homogeneous narrative of Irish citizenship. The traditional narrative of citizenship is being slowly reinterpreted in the light of wider social transformations. This is, in turn, reflected in the notion of identity represented in constitutional discourse. As Alexander has noted, these narratives are 'shaped by underlying political visions, that is, belief structures about how society is and ought to be organised'.[16]

The myths told by the founding fathers of the postcolonial state infiltrated legal discourse, giving these myths a sense of reality in the political domain. Yet at the same time these notions of nationhood created what Deane has called a 'really unreal' Ireland.[17] It was an Ireland which fell back on myths of origin to recreate a state which never existed. In writing the word of the revolution in the foundational text of the postcolonial Irish polity, the founding father of modern Ireland, Eamon de Valera, instituted a performative which gave effect to the new nation. In so doing de Valera was not merely instantiating a neutral legal document which would form the basis for the governance of the new state. Rather, he was textualising the mythico-religious violence of the anti-colonial struggle. The creation of an authentic past and of an authentic national tradition was therefore necessary. As Zizek has noted:

national identity constitutes itself through resistance to its oppression – the fight for national revival is therefore a defence of something

which comes to be only through being experienced as lost or endan-
gered. The nationalist ideology endeavours to elude this vicious circle
by constructing a myth of origins – of an epoch preceding oppression and exploitation when the nation was *already there* ... the past is
trans-coded as Nation that already existed and to which we are
supposed to return through a liberation struggle.[18]

This new state was in a very real sense unreal, a *mélange* of myths and
stories projected onto the *de jure* reality of the 26-county state. Thus as
Deane has put it: 'The fake nation with its inflated rhetoric of origin
and authenticity, had given way to the fake state, with its deflated rhetoric of bureaucratic dinginess. In the passage from the fantasy of one to
the realism of the other, the entity called Ireland had failed to appear.'[19]

Yet paradoxically this projection of mythical rhetoric led to the
instantiation of a political reality which was to reflect the values of this
imagined Gaelic Romantic notion of Ireland. This new state was indeed
fake, yet for its citizens it was only too real in its narrow-minded, craven
'bureaucratic dinginess'. This use of rhetoric by the elite reflects Threadgold's thesis that the telling of stories by elites can lead to the creation
of particular institutional realities:

> The telling of stories at all levels in a social system becomes a huge
> machinery for the construction of social realities, social and cultural
> institutions and the people ... who inhabit them and make them in
> their turn. For they are made, not given ... and the law is but one of
> the factors involved in this making ... This begins to explain how
> apparently just, impartial and 'truthful' institutions like law 'make'
> the worlds they think they merely represent – and do it in talk and in
> writing – in discourse as social process.[20]

The law, and in particular the Constitution, became the canon which
contained these traditional tales of Irishness. However, as in literary
practice, the canon can be challenged by other stories, other voices
which reflect alternative notions of reality and identity. Constitutional
discourse as social process is evidenced in the manner in which the
foundational themes of Irish identity have been subject to reinterpretation and amendment in recent years. Thus the core themes of territory,
gender, family and religion have been opened to interrogation and
revision. In this sense the canon that is the Constitution has been challenged by the 'minor literatures' which exist within the space of constitutional discourse.

Familial Fallacies

The conception of the family as understood in constitutional discourse has until recently been that of the heteropatriarchal family unit bound by marriage. The family was seen as a key unit in society, an exemplar of the utopian vision of a traditional Roman Catholic Ireland. In a state which for most of its existence outlawed the sale of contraceptives and prohibited divorce and abortion, the family was more of a prison than an ideal type of social unit. The family of Irish law reflected and reinforced the conception of the national family, inward-looking and subject to the rule of a weak patriarchal figure. The law thus enabled the entrenchment of a patriarchal social order based on the family unit. Subsequent interpretation and amendment of the Constitution reflected a transformation in the nature of Irish society, moving from the valorisation of the heteropatriarchal family unit to more disparate notions of family and social partnerships. The centrality of the heteropatriarchal family unit in Irish legal discourse enshrined liminality in the Constitution, drawing heavily on the national narrative of familialism which was a residue of nineteenth-century notions of Irishness.[21] In so doing it created a hierarchy within the family and between the family and other social bondings. A disproportionate amount of power was ceded to the father figure within this model. In Ireland, the father figure was a weak figure who as Kiberd notes, exemplified the notion of patriarchy: 'Patriarchal values exist in societies where men, lacking true authority, settle for mere power ... Patriarchy is, rather, the tyranny wrought by weak men, the protective shell which guards and nurtures their weakness.'[22]

The metaphor of the ideal family in its double sense, that of the Irish family as essentialised group identity and as the formal legal arrangement based on marriage, exposed an intolerance of difference. Thus, the family served as a keyword for exclusion. This familial fallacy shrouded the reality of liminality in Irish society, and in recent years it has been challenged at many levels. One indication that this attitude to the family no longer endures is the recent introduction of divorce legislation in the form of *The Family Law (Divorce) Act 1996*, after a majority of the electorate voted in favour of an amendment to Article 41.3.2 of the Constitution in 1995. The constitutional referendum on divorce reflects the change in the status of the family in contemporary Irish society. To paraphrase Stychin: 'The family as public/national institution has become a site with no essential role or obvious conditions of membership.'[23]

The (M)other in Law

The construction of woman in Irish constitutional discourse reflects the construction of woman in patriarchal nationalist discourse. The conflation of nationhood with gender was a residue of the Irish experience of colonialism, where Ireland was gendered female in opposition to the representation of the coloniser as a male figure. As Kearney has pointed out:

> In the historical evolution of Irish religious ideology, we witness a shift away from the early Irish Church which was quite liberal in sexual matters and assigned an important role to women, to a more puritanical religion which idealised women as other-worldly creatures of sublime innocence. And it is perhaps no accident that this shift coincided in some measure with the colonisation of Ireland. The more dispossessed the people became in reality the more they sought to repossess a sense of identity in the imaginary. Since the women of colonised Ireland had become, in James Connolly's words, the 'slaves of slaves', they were in a socio-political sense at least, the perfect candidates for compensatory elevation in the order of mystique... Women became as sexually intangible as the ideal of national sovereignty became politically. Both became imaginary, aspirational, elusive.[24]

The representation of the country as female did not end on the gaining of independence. Indeed, the patriarchal nature of Irish society was reinforced in the postcolonial period. The rhetorical strategy of the double woman expressed the desire on the part of patriarchal Irish nationalism to harness the symbolic power of Ireland as woman to their own ends. As Valente has pointed out, this strategy of the double woman allowed for the bifurcation of:

> the mythic personification of Irish society into an avowedly symbolic woman and a plainly literal woman, a symbolic figure representing what Lacan calls *the* Woman who authorises the (founding) father's law, and a literal figure representing the individual women who remain subject to it, in short the legitimating and the excluded other of a patriarchal nationalism.[25]

This opposition between the phallic mother, the symbolic Mother Ireland of nationalist discourse and the woman as phallus, the literal women of Ireland who continued to suffer under male tyranny is textualised in the Constitution of 1937. Thus, in constitutional discourse it is implicit in the text that the value placed in women in postcolonial society lies almost completely in their reproductive function. Woman's social role as mother is cherished more than any notion of individual female autonomy. A woman's value, as constitutionally predicated, lay only in what she could contribute to the greater good by her role as mother. The Constitution in this regard reflected the extant cultural construction of women by including in Article 41.2 the following provisions in relation to the role of women in society:

> In particular, the State recognises that by her life within the home, woman gives to the state a support without which the common good cannot be achieved.

> The State shall, therefore, endeavour to ensure that mothers shall not be obliged by economic necessity to engage in labour to the neglect of their duties in the home.

These provisions represent an outmoded and patriarchal view of societal organisation. It is at the symbolic, rather than at the strictly legal, level that such provisions are of importance. As Casey has noted, these provisions:

> do not bind the State to a philosophy that a woman's place is in the home. Nor would they provide any foundation for legislative restrictions on married women entering the labour market ... Indeed the only legal effect of the [provision] would seem to be to oblige the State to ensure that mothers do not have to work outside the home.[26]

It is therefore in the symbolic sphere that such provisions are important, in that the very persistence of such provisions in the Constitution lend tacit support to the notion of patriarchy. This constitutional fiction (in that it no longer reflects the current social consensus on gender roles) defies the notion of female autonomy. The reality of contemporary Irish attitudes to gender does not reflect the conception of woman as mother and homemaker contained in the constitutional text. This dichotomy reflects a tendency in Irish society to accommodate simultaneously antithetical views on gender. As Whelan has noted in this regard:

> a conservative approach to many aspects of women's position sits side by side with the Irish electorate's claim to have been the first

country in the world to elect a feminist . . . as head of state. In the legal field, strong support in statute and constitutional law for the 'traditional' family has coexisted with decisive moves away from traditional legal concepts in order to accommodate to new patterns of behaviour in family life.[27]

Territorial Aspirations and Fictional Identities

The legal fiction which was the claim to Northern Ireland was integral to the Gaelic-Romantic mode of thinking. That it was little more than rhetoric can be evidenced in the former Article 3's deferral of the claim to the six counties 'pending reintegration of the national territory'. None the less, the importance of the constitutional claim to Northern Ireland lay in its symbolic power to unite nationalist opinion in the Republic. Thus, the constitutional construction of Irish identity was exclusivist. It created an essentialised Irish type, a *fior Gael*, who was Catholic and nationalist, as the dominant subject of Irish law. The northern Protestant population as a result was not seen by the new elite as part of the postcolonial Irish family. In this sense, the northern Protestant became, to paraphrase Norton, the 'territorial liminar [who was] identified with the adjacent, usually hostile, nation'.[28] The writing into being of the republic also included by necessity the writing out of the northern unionists as an entity. The erasure of the unionist population of Northern Ireland constituted them as Other in opposition to the nationalist, Roman Catholic self of Irish nationhood. However Article 3 confirmed the non-completion of the Irish nation: it is yet to come, to be realised. This impossibility of an homogeneous Irish state is therefore marked in the basic text of national identity. We the people are not whole: this depends, in nationalist rhetoric, on the reintegration of the six counties. However, on reintegration a substantial number of the population will not be defined as part of the nation as constitutionally posited, but rather as 'Other', thus leading to their treatment as marginals, or, if integrated, dispelling the myth of homogeneity. As Brannigan has noted in this regard:

> The constitution marks out a destination, the 'reintegration of the national territory' as Article 3 refers to it. In the rhetoric that sustains this claim, a future united Ireland that 'finally' establishes a correlation between the idea of the nation and its completion, what is conveniently forgotten is the difference that is posited by the language of unity, integration. To unite, one must first have

differences. To unite, one cannot be the 'same people'. To achieve this completion of the project of national identity, then, one must unite with the other, a task that requires us firstly to recognise the other as other, and also to recognise then the impossibility of sameness, the impossibility of saying 'we'. 'We, the people of Eire', it is written in the constitution, 'give to ourselves this constitution'. In this, there is no guarantee of sameness, not even that the 'We' that begins the sentence is the same as the 'ourselves' later on. But also here is the impossible contradiction of national identity.[29]

At the level of judicial interpretation of Articles 2 and 3 of the Constitution, the courts perpetrated the fallacy of a homogeneous territorial identity. The courts initially adopted two competing models in interpreting Articles 2 and 3. The aspirational model as enunciated in the case of *Re Article 26 and The Criminal Law (Jurisdiction) Bill 1975* ([1977] IR 129) provides that the national claim to Northern Ireland existed in the political rather than the legal order. In this sense it was purely aspirational and did not form a claim of legal right. However, under this model the political entity of the nation possesses rights which, even though not recognised by law, are anterior to law. The competing model is the legal claim model which was enunciated in the case of *Russell v. Fanning.* ([1988] IR 505) This model was described in this case in the following terms: '[t]he reunification of the national territory is by the provisions of the Preamble of the Constitution and Article 3 . . . a constitutional imperative and not one the pursuit or non-pursuit of which is within the discretion of the government or any other organ of state.' ([1988] IR 505, 537)

In the case of *McGimpsey v. Ireland* ([1990] 1 IR 110) the Supreme Court adopted the legal claim model as the correct interpretive model in cases concerning Articles 2 and 3. The Supreme Court's decision in *McGimpsey* is important in that it confirmed that Article 2 was to be interpreted as being a declaration of the extent of the national territory as a claim of legal right. The reintegration of the national territory was accordingly to be seen as a constitutional imperative. Article 3 was interpreted as prohibiting the enactment of laws with any greater area of application or extra-territorial effect than the laws of the Irish Free State, pending the reintegration of the national territory. Moreover, the restriction imposed by Article 3 pending the reintegration of the national territory in no way derogates from the claim as a legal right to the entire national territory.

Notwithstanding the Supreme Court's interpretation of Articles 2 and 3 of the Constitution, it would seem that the irredentist ethos of the Constitution no longer sits comfortably with the current Irish societal paradigm. It is now at least arguable as to whether the national claim to Northern Ireland is reflective of the Irish population's attitude to Northern Ireland. The clause in the Belfast Agreement of 10 April 1998 which speaks of the willingness on the part of the Irish Government to amend Articles 2 and 3, pending a constitutional referendum, reflects this new ethos in Irish political culture. Thus, the period since the introduction of the Constitution has seen Ireland's imagined community becoming less cohesive and less willing to adhere to the old certainties of motherland and church. As Longley has put it: 'cultural change and changing awareness of culture, in the Republic and even in the North, have already exposed political Irishness (the ethos on which the independence movement was built) as now more a prison than a liberation'.[30] If opinion polls are to be seen as an indicator of the national mood in the Republic of Ireland, then the post-nationalist thesis may have a claim to validity. In a recent *Guardian-Irish Times* poll only 30 per cent of those polled in the Republic were in favour of an United Ireland, with 29 per cent of the poll in favour of a federal solution.[31] The latest developments in the Northern Irish peace process reveal the political will on the part of the Irish government to revise the wording of Articles 2 and 3. The very fact that this sacred cow of Irish nationalist discourse was revised by the people in a referendum in the summer of 1998 is a sign of a transformed society. At the level of writing a national identity, the constitutional claim itself gives the lie to the notion of a 'united Ireland'. The unity of the territory will not bring with it the founding or the completion of an overarching sense of Irish national identity: instead, what it reveals is the impossibility of homogeneity and the presence of difference. In effect the reality of non-identity and the impossible project of founding a nation of sameness. Only by accepting the nation as difference can the aporia of territorial conflict be settled.

The Death of the Transcendental Textual Author

The writing of the Constitution tried to establish an homogeneous Irish state. Instead, however, all it created was the reality of difference and the frustration of the impossibility of identity. The extent to which this has been realised in constitutional terms has been underlined by the Supreme Court's decision to strike down Thomist Natural Law as the basis of its interpretative strategy in the case of *Re Article 26 and the*

Regulation of Information (Services Outside the State for Termination of Pregnancies) Bill 1995 ([1995] 1 ILRM 8). By rejecting the Thomist model the Court is also rejecting the Gaelic Romantic model which it underpins. This constitutes a means of reading the Constitution, and, as a corollory, the notion of national identity, otherwise. It is but one tangible example of how the Constitution of national identity has been read otherwise as an opening to the other, to difference, and as an instance of the nation to come. The impossibility of sameness results in the reality of difference, constituting a clear break with traditionalist conceptions of Irish constitutional identity. The Gaelic Romantic tradition of the Constitution has now become the 'minor literature' of the Irish constitutional space. The dominant discourse has now been identified as the Irish Enlightenment tradition. There has been a move, in Post's terms, from the constitution of community to the constitution of democracy. This deliberative democratic model allows the voices of the varied individuals who make up Irish society to be heard above the clamour of the previously dominant official discourse, allowing for their recognition as individuals within a democratic society rather than as passive recipients of the wisdom of the elite. The Constitution now stands, ironically, as a site of resistance to that ethos upon which it was founded.

The tension between the Gaelic Romantic strand of the Constitution and the Irish Enlightenment strand in effect holds the Constitution together. The idea that this tension is amenable to some form of definitive resolution is somewhat over-optimistic, because as an attempt to express national identity the Constitution faces an impossible task. What the framers of the Constitution were attempting to do in inserting a notion of identity into the constitutional text was in effect trying to postpone what McNeil has adverted to as the 'real trauma of non-identity'.[32] In instantiating a notion of Irishness the framers were trying to bring together the diverse groupings that formed the postcolonial nation to create a false notion of united nationhood. In so doing they denied the existence of difference within what was and continues to be a highly fragmented society. The fissures which began to appear in this notion of constitutional identity when the Constitution was used as a means of contesting traditional notions of national identity exposed the futility of trying to impose a homogeneous idea of the nation. This more indeterminate notion of nationhood exposes the notion of a monolithic Irishness to question and opens the way to the recognition of difference. Any attempt to write a national identity will be defeated by its own inherent contradictions. In this sense, to paraphrase Zizek,

Irishness 'becomes an "internal limit", an unattainable point which prevents empirical [Irish people] from achieving full identity-with-themselves.'[33]

Notes

1 Peter Goodrich, 'Introduction: Psychoanalysis and Law', in Peter Goodrich, (ed.), *Law and the Unconscious: A Legendre Reader* (Basingstoke: Macmilllan, 1997), pp. 1–36, p. 4.

2 Jacques Derrida, 'Declarations of Independence', *New Political Science*, 15 (1986) pp. 7–15. Jacques Derrida, 'The Laws of Reflection: Nelson Mandela in Admiration', in Jacques Derrida and Mustafa Tlili, (eds.), *For Nelson Mandela* (New York: Seaver Books, 1987), pp. 11–42. Jacques Derrida, 'Force of Law: The Mystical Foundation of Authority', in Drucilla Cornell, Michel Rosenfeld and David Gray Carlson, (eds.), *Deconstruction and the Possibility of Justice* (New York: Routledge, 1992), pp. 3–67.

3 Derrida, 'The Laws of Reflection', p. 20

4 Anne Norton, 'Transubstantiation: The Dialectic of Constitutional Authority', *The University of Chicago Law Review*, 55 (1988), pp. 458–72, p. 468.

5 Phillip Mellor, 'Death in High Modernity: The Contemporary Presence and Absence of Death', in David Clark (ed.), *Sociology of Death* (Oxford: Blackwell, 1993), pp. 12–29, p. 19.

6 Roshan De Silva, 'Ambivalence, Contingency and the Failure of Exclusion: The Ontological Schema of the 1972 Constitution of the Republic of Sri Lanka', *Social and Legal Studies*, 5 (1996) pp. 365–81, p. 372.

7 John Brannigan, 'Writing DeTermiNation: Reading Death in(to) Irish National Identity', in John Brannigan, Ruth Robbins and Julian Wolfreys (eds.), *Applying: To Derrida* (Basingstoke: Macmillan, 1996), pp. 55–70, p. 69.

8 Jeffrey Prager, *Building Democracy in Ireland: Political Order and Cultural Integration in a Newly Independent Nation* (Cambridge: Cambridge University Press, 1986), p. 42.

9 Prager, *Building Democracy in Ireland*, p. 79

10 Robert Post, *Constitutional Domains: Democracy, Community, Management* (Cambridge, Mass.: Harvard University Press, 1995), p. 179.

11 Prager, *Building Democracy in Ireland*, p. 16.

12 Post, *Constitutional Domains*, p. 188.

13 Giles Deleuze and Felix Guattari, *Kafka: Toward A Minor Literature* (Minneapolis: University of Minnesota Press, 1986).

14 Giles Deleuze and Felix Guattari, *A Thousand Plateaus: Capitalism and Schizophrenia*, ii (London: Athlone Press, 1988).

15 Giles Deleuze, *Francis Bacon: The Logic of Sensation, Volume 1* (Boston: MIT Press, 1993).

16 Geoffrey Alexander, 'Takings, Narratives, and Power', *Columbia Law Review*, 88, (1988) pp. 1752–73.

17 Seamus Deane, *Strange Country: Modernity and Nationhood in Irish Writing since 1790* (Oxford: Clarendon Press, 1997), p. 149.

18 Slavoj Zizek, *For They Know Not What They Do: Enjoyment as a Political Factor* (London: Verso, 1991), pp. 213–14.

19   Deane, *Strange Country*, p.162.
20   Terry Threadgold, *Feminist Poetics: Poiesis, Performance, Histories* (London: Routledge, 1997), p. 148.
21   Joseph Valente, *James Joyce and the Problem of Justice: Negotiating Sexual and Colonial Difference* (Cambridge: Cambridge University Press, 1995), pp. 198–9.
22   Declan Kiberd, *Inventing Ireland: The Literature of The Modern Nation* (London: Jonathan Cape, 1995), p. 391.
23   Carl Stychin, 'Queer Nations: Nationalism, Sexuality and the Discourse of Rights in Quebec', *Feminist Legal Studies*, 5 (1997) pp. 3–34, p. 25.
24   Richard Kearney, *Postnationalist Ireland: Politics, Culture, Philosophy*, (London: Routledge, 1997), p. 119.
25   Joseph Valente, 'The Myth of Sovereignty: Gender in the Literature of Irish Nationalism', *English Literary History*, 61 (1994), pp. 189–210, pp. 198–9.
26   James Casey, *Constitutional Law in Ireland* (London: Sweet and Maxwell, 1992), p. 522.
27   Christopher Whelan, (ed.) *Values and Social Change in Ireland* (Dublin: Gill and Macmillan, 1994), pp. 46–7.
28   Anne Norton, *Reflections on Political Identity* (Baltimore: Johns Hopkins University Press, 1988), p. 55.
29   Brannigan, 'Writing DeTermiNation', p. 69.
30   Edna Longley, *The Living Stream: Literature and Revisionism in Ireland* (Newcastle-upon-Tyne: Bloodaxe Books, 1994), p. 180.
31   Michael Linton, 'Most Catholics in North Reject United Ireland', *The Guardian*, 28 February, (1996), p. 5.
32   William McNeil, 'Enjoy your Rights/Three Cases from the Postcolonial Commonwealth', *Public Culture*, 9 (1997), pp. 377–93, p. 391.
33   Zizek, *For They Know Not What They Do*, p. 110.

8

From Gombeen to Gubeen: Tourism, Identity and Class in Ireland, 1949–99

Michael Cronin and Barbara O'Connor

Only two years after the establishment of the Irish Free State, Daniel Corkery published a book that became an instant classic. *The Hidden Ireland* was hailed for its depiction of Gaelic Ireland in the eighteenth century, a depiction that subsequently, of course, was the object of much scholarly critique and controversy.[1] Corkery's work deliberately sets out to celebrate the culture outside the Big House, a culture of poetry and poverty, the sacralisation of hardship resonant with the grim asceticism of the new State. Sixty-four years later another publication appeared with the same title, *The Hidden Ireland*. The subtitle, however, marked a radical difference in emphasis, 'Accommodation in Private Heritage Homes'. George Gossip in the preface to the brochure describes the heritage homes:

> Some are great houses, at the centre of large estates. They may have been designed by famous architects and lived in or visited by famous people. Others are smaller but no less beautiful or interesting. Most are surrounded by their own tree-studded parks or by gardens, often internationally renowned. They are all in beautiful or historic parts of the country. Some have belonged to the family for generations.[2]

The Hidden Ireland is no longer the Ireland of the cottier and the spalpeen but that of the Big House and the Landlord. If Corkery's text was ideologically important in providing a genealogy for national frugality and self-sufficiency, there is a sense in which the *Hidden Ireland* brochure with its expensive and exclusive accommodation articulates the values of a new Ireland whose self-image is crucially mediated by tourism. Rather than being an extraneous reality foisted on Irish life, tourism has in fact been central to the Irish experience of modernisation and continues to inform not only how we represent ourselves to others but, equally importantly, how we represent ourselves to each other and to ourselves.

In this chapter we pursue the trajectory of tourist discourse by tracing shifts in tourist practice, policy and representation since the establishment of the Republic in 1949. Tourist representations will be analysed as a cultural barometer of the way certain dominant groups have sought and continue to seek to represent Ireland for touristic consumption. In exploring how we represent ourselves to others outside the Republic, we will see how as a society we have set ourselves up for tourist consumption. One of the key players in the process is the state, which has sought to win popular support for tourism development by casting this development as part of the production of modernisation. It is not possible to include all the other players in our discussion since there is a relative dearth of information on the relationship between the state and other groups engaged in tourist development. Despite the importance of tourism to Irish economy and society there is a chronic need for more detailed ethnographic research on tourism, particularly at regional and local level, that would illuminate the often complex and contradictory interaction between different groups and interests. Such research would allow tourism studies to move beyond the narrow, quantitative economism and footlose textual criticism that often limit the interpretive purchase of analyses of Irish tourism.

Here we shall argue that the rhetoric of modernity has dominated tourist discourse from the foundation of the state. As in the past, this rhetoric continues to embody inherent contradictions in relation to tourist policy, practice and representation in the Republic. The theme of modernisation was central to the rhetoric of Bord Fáilte, the state body founded in 1952, for the promotion of tourist development. We get some indication of the variety of perceived benefits to the nation in Bord Fáilte's annual report for 1956, in which the following rationale is advanced for tourism development:

> While based upon the Transport, Hotel and Catering and Entertainment industries, Tourism enters all branches of Social, Cultural and Sporting Activities; and operating as it does, over a wide and varied range of interests it plays a major part in the country's development and progress.[3]

In an unpublished Bord Fáilte document entitled 'History of Irish Tourism' references are made to the organisation of Tidy Town, Roadside Garden and Lock-Keepers' competitions. Under the heading 'Social Significance' the social and cultural benefits of tourism are explicitly underlined:

> As well as the obvious economic benefits, tourism contributes substantially to the social and cultural life of the national community. Examples of this range from the obviously tangible benefits to local communities from the provision of facilities for tourists such as swimming pools, roads, promenades and so on, to the equally important concepts of revitalising our cultural heritage (such as through Siamsa) and improving international understanding.[4]

In a Bord Fáilte publication from 1983, *The Welcome Industry*, we are told 'not all the benefits of tourism can be assessed in money terms'. Among the other benefits are:

> The amenities and attractions which are developed for visitors from tourism funds are there to be enjoyed by Irish people. Improved roads, scenic drives, golf courses, entertainment complexes, forest parks, angling and equestrian centres, festivals and cultural events of many kinds have all been created with tourism in mind, but the main users and beneficiaries are our own people.[5]

However, the economy has not been forgotten, and we read on:

> Neat and tidy towns have attracted industry, local crafts have been revived, existing businesses expanded, all creating more employment and adding to the prosperity and well-being of the community. A pleasant environment or relaxed way of life and a country which still holds to traditional values all add up to a strong inducement for businessmen to look favourably on Ireland as a possible base for new enterprises.[6]

The implication of these policy statements is that the traditional classification of tourism as an industry among others is in fact mistaken, and that there is a confusion of logical categories. Tourism here is not a subset of the set 'industry', but rather 'industry' becomes a subset of the set 'tourism', a set that includes other subsets such as 'culture', 'environment' and 'lifestyle'. In this respect, the rhetoric of modernisation informing Irish tourism since the establishment of the Republic pre-figures later discourses of de-differentiation normally associated with postmodernity.[7] Indeed, it is arguably a source of confusion in debates on tourism that the word, terminologically speaking, is used as both a superordinate and hyponym. The result is that the full extent of its impact on national culture is minimised if a narrow sectoral reading of the activity is the only one that is advanced.

However, the developmentally holistic rhetoric of the newly estab-lished national tourist board failed to materialise into an effective and systematic development of tourism.[8] A combination of *laissez-faire*, ambivalent, and at times, contradictory attitudes by government departments impeded substantial and coherent development within the tourism sector. In their study of tourism policy, Deegan and Dineen outline the prevalent Government attitudes of the time,[9] suggesting that tourism development was seen as peripheral to real economic development in sectors such as agriculture and manufacturing. The evidence also points to the feeling among policy-makers that Ireland's reputation as a country of beautiful scenery and friendly and hospitable people was sufficient to ensure the survival of the tourist industry. In addition, they claim that even the lip service paid to tourism develop-ment was the result of external pressure, notably the strong pressure from the U.S. government (as part of Marshall Aid in Europe following the Second World War) to put more effort into the sector.

The fact that the reality of tourism development fell well behind the rhetoric at this juncture was not due solely to state neglect, but, we would suggest, was also influenced by an active resistance to tourism which was expressed through various public discourses. For instance, an article in the *Irish Independent* newspaper of 1 May, 1946 referring to the dramatic increase in British tourists visiting Ireland immediately follow-ing the Second World War mixes a hostility to strangers with the political philosophy of self-reliance:

> There is not enough accommodation for our own people. Yet, the government intends to permit visitors from other countries to encroach on that accommodation. The *Irish* people should have the first claim on the food and board in this country.[10]

There was also a fear that the services provided for tourists could be a source of moral contamination. This was evidenced in a Dáil debate on the licensing laws proposed in the Tourism Traffic Act (1952) in which one deputy, Desmond, recounts his own observations and opinions:

It was before 12 . . . but even so, we had the misery of seeing young girls drinking in a bar attached to the hotel. My opinion is that if you are going to cater for tourists – including those from our own country – and if we are prepared to stoop to such a low level it will be a bad day for our country.[11]

This is the obverse of Bord Fáilte's arguments for tourism; rather than enhancing the quality of life for Irish society, tourist facilities are seen to be a positive danger particularly to what were perceived to be the weaker, more vulnerable, and perhaps more impressionable sectors of that society. While the antipathy towards British tourists may be understood in the light of prior historico-political relations with the British,[12] available evidence indicates that internal tourists were also targets for expressions of hostility and resentment. In her analysis of representations of tourists in the literature of the West Kerry Gaeltacht from the 1920s to the 1980s, Nic Eoin vividly captures the negative stereotypes and, at times, scorn which were heaped upon the unwitting visitors and Gaeilgeoirí – attitudes generated by a combination of social class, and other subcultural (including linguistic) differences between host and visitor.[13] These observations are indicative, at the very least, that Bord Fáilte's enthusiasm for tourism development was not shared unanimously by all sectors of Irish society in the early decades of the Republic. What is apparent here is the association of the project of modernisation with that of modernity expressed in the fear that by materialising the material infrastucture there would be an inevitable and irreversible transformation of values and decline in moral standards.

Tourism and holiday travel are themselves both a reaction to, and an index of, modernity, according to MacCannell.[14] By this he means that it is only in modern urban societies that people become so alienated that they feel the need to seek meaning and authenticity elsewhere, usually in more 'simple' societies. The Ireland of the 1950s was not a 'modern' society on this count, since the vast majority of people did not take holidays. This is not unexpected in a largely agricultural society with a predominantly rural population and a relatively small urban middle class. It is hardly surprising, therefore, that many Irish people failed to express enthusiasm for an activity in which they did not and could not participate. However, the rise in standards of living in the 1960s saw a broadening of the class base for internal tourism. Heuston[15] writes about the increase in the numbers of skilled working-class families at this time taking holidays at the resort of Kilkee, which until then had been the preserve of middle-income groups, while Gillmor[16] documents the beginnings of the charter flight and package holidays abroad in the 1960s which also began with young, urban and single groups.

Some of the paradoxes of modernisation may also be witnessed in the tourist representations of Ireland of the 1950s, paradoxes which still persist today. The tourist normally expects a combination of familiarity and difference/exoticism in her/his holiday destination.[17] It is imperative that the place to be visited must offer something which is not encountered in everyday life. But simultaneously it must also be a 'home from home' – not too much out of place. In marketing terms, Bord Fáilte was charged with the task of representing Ireland as simultaneously premodern and modern; on the one hand providing a culture and a people who are easygoing, convivial, garrulous and curious, and on the other capable of providing a clean, comfortable and efficient accommodation of tourist needs.

Ireland of the Welcomes, Bord Fáilte's marketing publication established in 1952, provides an interesting case study of the management of these tensions. Throughout its pages we see a division between the advertising and feature articles both in terms of visual iconography and in terms of language and discourse. It is the advertisements which foreground the 'modern' aspects of Ireland. They repeatedly use the adjectives 'comfort', 'ease', 'convenience', even 'luxury' in relation to accommodation and travel facilities as well as emphasising the regularity of the public and private transport service. Cheek by jowl with these advertisments for comfort, reliability, economy and safety – characteristics of a 'modern' service provision – are feature articles which represent the pre-modern Ireland. These articles show evidence of a kind of salvage ethnography referring to the primitive and the exotic and carrying titles such as 'Life at Europe's Edge' (2/4, 1953). Even when we were not being represented as remote from western civilization, and modernity, we were still portrayed as a romantic place and people, where one might wonder whom we hired to provide the regular bus and coach services among such a relaxed population. These feature articles were given extra authenticity and literary value by the fact that they were written by well-known and respected literary figures of the era such as Paddy Kavanagh, Maurice Walsh, Benedict Kiely, and Walter Macken.

From (national) Modernity to (global) Post-Modernity?

The last decade has seen a phenomenal growth in Irish tourism, the rate of growth between 1986 and 1995 being twice the OECD average

Table 8.1.   Tourism growth in OECD countries, 1986–94

	Tourists 1994 (M)	Tourists[a]	Hotel Nights[b]	All Accommodation[a]
Canada	16.0	102	–	93
Mexico	17.0	120[b]	–	–
USA	45.5	185	–	–
Australia	3.4	235	184	237
Japan	3.4	163	–	–
New Zealand	1.3	180	–	155
Austria	–	–	108	108
Belgium	5.3	–	144	133
Denmark	–	–	136	–
Finland	–	–	141	–
France	61.3	170	156	152
Germany	–	–	112	125
Greece	11.3	159	120	114
Iceland	0.2	157	–	–
Ireland	3.7	202 (258)[c]	212	220
Italy	51.8	97	116	101
Netherlands	–	–	122	127
Norway	–	–	152	135
Portugal	9.2	169	131	123
Spain	21.7	129	111	–
Sweden	–	–	100	94
Switzerland	12.2	106	100	–
Turkey	6.7	279	206	258
UK	21.0	151	–	–

Notes:
[a] 1994 Index (1986 = 100).
[b] Mexico (1988 = 100).
[c] 1996 Index for Ireland: 258.
Source: OECD Tourism Policy and International Tourism in OECD Countries, 1993–1994, Paris 1996.

(see Table 8.1). The total number of overseas tourists increased in that period by 121 per cent. Income from tourism had risen from £436m in 1986 to £1,451m in 1996.

In addition to overall growth there has also been a shift in the origin and the type of tourist. The most notable feature in terms of tourist origin has been the increase in tourist numbers from continental Europe. Political difficulties arising out of conflict in the North meant the stagnation of the British market from the late 1960s onwards. The American 'roots' market was always under threat from the age-profile, but was severely affected by fears of international terrorist violence at the end of the 1980s. As Bord Fáilte put it rather coyly in 1983, 'The diversification of source markets, a conscious achievement of Bord Fáilte, ensures greater independence for Irish tourism from specific economic recessions or political uncertainties within any market area.'[18] The result was that one of the markets specifically targeted was the continental European market in the 1980s, and the results were impressive, as can be seen from the Table 8.2. Tourist numbers from mainland Europe increased from 408,000 in 1988 to 1,177,000 in 1996. This threefold increase in tourist arrivals from continental Europe reflected a positive growth in almost all the European source markets.

The change in type of tourist was most clearly articulated by Marie O'Donnell in a collection entitled *Tourism on the Farm*. O'Donnell,

Table 8.2   Tourism numbers and revenue 1996

Number (000s)	1988	1993	1994	1995	1996
Britain	1,508	1,857	2,038	2,285	2,590
Mainland Europe	408	945	988	1,101	1,177
Germany	113	265	269	319	339
France	111	242	231	234	262
Italy	21	116	121	112	119
Netherlands	38	69	80	94	109
Spain	34	57	59	67	66
Switzerland	24	40	62	62	62
Belgium/Lux	20	41	41	53	60
Norway/Sweden	12	32	33	46	55
Denmark	14	17	19	22	23
Other Europe	21	66	73	93	83
North America:	419	422	494	641	729
USA	385	377	449	587	660
Canada	34	45	45	54	69
Rest of World:	90	124	159	204	186
Australa/New Zealand	46	56	68	89	88
Japan	na	18	22	30	33
Other Overseas	44	50	69	85	65
Total Overseas	2,425	3,348	3,679	4,231	4,682
Northern Ireland	582	540	630	590	600
Total Out-of-State	3,007	3,888	4,309	4,821	5,282
Domestic Trips	4,161	7,660	7,244	6,924	6,170

Source: Bord Fáilte/Irish Tourist Board, Tourism Facts 1996.
• Domestic trips in 1988 are not comparable due to changes in survey methodology
• Domestic trips 1993–5 revised in 1996 due to changes to the 'other trip' category

appointed by Bord Fáilte to promote rural tourism, describes the new breed of tourist that emerged in the 1980s:

> He *(sic)* is interested in culture and heritage, the environment, health. He demands high quality standards in accommodation. He seeks ease of accessibility to a range of activities and special interests.[19]

This new tourist is younger, better-educated and increasingly a member of the rapidly expanding tertiary sector in Western economies. Drawing on the work of Bourdieu,[20] Urry outlines how the cultural consumption of the new tourist is marked by an 'ascetic aestheticism' and includes preferences for 'natural' cultural symbols and practices, including leisure activities which involve an engagement with nature such as walking, hillwalking, horse-trekking, swimming and canoeing. This also applies to culinary taste, and is evidenced in the dramatic increase in restaurants offering what are described as prime quality natural products. Craft goods now range from the explicit kitsch of leprechauns to the stylish understatement of the Mulcahy lampshade. The cheese board moves from the processed hegemony of Calvita to the organic diversity of Gubeen and Milleens. The nature of accommodation changes with the appearance of the *Blue Book*, *The Hidden Ireland* and the *Friendly Homes of Ireland* brochures. There is a dramatic increase in the number of museums and heritage centres (148 heritage-based attractions alone were reported for 1997)[21] and more and more houses and gardens are open to the general public. One of the reasons for these developments is that the bulk of tourist spending is on items other than accommodation. Barrett observes that:

> The breakdown of tourist spending ... shows that 76 per cent of it is spent in sectors not traditionally regarded as tourism such as shopping, internal transport, food and drink, and sightseeing and entertainment. In these sectors, tourism demand mingles with the demand from residents.[22]

Barrett's conclusions are based on the figures in Table 8.3. If we compare the percentage breakdown of tourist spending with the average weekly household expenditure for 1987 and 1994–95 detailed in Table 8.4, there are indeed remarkable similarities between the consumption patterns of tourists and residents.

Table 8.3. Distribution of tourism expenditure

	per cent
Bed and board	24
Other food and drink	30
Sightseeing/entertainment	7
Transport in Ireland	12
Shopping	18
Miscellaneous	9

Source: Irish Tourist Board, Tourism Facts 1995

Table 8.4. Average weekly household expenditure, 1987 and 1994–5

Main Commodity Groups	1987		1994–5		% increase in Expenditure 1987 to 1994–5
	£	%	£	%	
Food	56.26	25.2	70.75	22.7	+25.8
Drink and tobacco	17.81	8.0	23.85	7.7	+33.9
Clothing and footwear	15.04	6.7	19.92	6.4	+32.4
Fuel and light	14.00	6.3	15.48	4.9	+10.6
Housing	19.66	8.8	30.56	9.8	+55.4
Household non-durables	4.64	2.1	7.26	2.3	+56.5
Household durables	8.75	3.9	11.28	3.6	+28.9
Miscellaneous goods	7.75	3.5	11.89	3.8	+53.4
Transport	30.30	13.6	44.73	14.4	+47.6
Services and other expenditure	48.87	21.9	76.01	24.4	+55.5
Total expenditure	223.08	100.0	311.73	100.0	+39.7

Source: Central Statistics Office, Household Budget Survey 1995

In common with many other countries in the developed world, Ireland has seen a dramatic expansion in its services sector over the last decade. Much of the impetus for the economic recovery of Ireland in the 1990s came from strong growth in the services sector. As can be seen from Table 8.5, though agriculture, forestry, fishing and manufacturing still employ large numbers of people, there is sizeable growth in all the private-sector service categories.

Like their European counterparts, the Irish have also been going on foreign holidays as opposed to staying with relatives and friends or holidaying in Ireland. This trend towards increased holidaying by the Irish has been commented on by Peillon[23] and has been borne out by

Table 8.5.   Labour force in the Republic of Ireland 1992–7 (estimated persons)

Category at work per sector (thousands)	1992	1993	1994	1995	1996	1997
Agriculture, Forestry and Fishing	154	144	142	143	138	134
Mining, quarrying, turf production	6	5	5	6	5	6
Manufacturing	226	225	236	248	250	271
Building and construction	74	71	78	83	87	97
Electricity, gas, water	13	11	14	13	14	12
Commerce, insurance, finance	234	244	245	262	275	281
Transport, communication and storage	68	70	73	76	81	84
Public administration and defence	70	67	68	73	77	74
Other non-agriculture economic activity	300	314	327	345	371	379
Total at work	1,145	1,152	1,188	1,248	1,297	1,338
Total Unemployment	217	230	219	192	191	179
Total Labour Force	1,362	1,382	1,407	1,439	1,488	1,517
Not in Labour Force	1,262	1,275	1,280	1,284	1,278	1,298
Population 15 years and over	2,624	2,657	2,687	2,723	2,766	2,815

Note: 'Total unemployment' are those people who are available for employment but who cannot find work. 'Not in Labour Force' are those people who are not available for work (primarily children and old people).
Source: Central Statistics Office.

recent statistical evidence. In 1997 the number of Irish visitors going abroad was 2,397,000 for the year to September, compared with 2,158,000 for the same period in 1996, an increase of 11.1 per cent (Central Statistics Office 1998). The growth in the indigenous service class, increased personal exposure to holidaying practices and similarities in patterns of consumption outlined above signal changes in the Irish experience of tourism. The former antithesis between sedentary native and transient newcomer begins to break down as the members of the new Irish service class become tourists in their own land. No longer tied to the once-a-year holiday on the family farm, they now compare 'bed and board' on an international level with a range of competing destinations, including Ireland itself. As with foreign visitors, they will visit the same design-conscious craft shops, park outside the same heritage centres and dine in the same restaurants listed in foreign good food guides and in the in-house journal of the new service class, *The Irish Times*, as foreign visitors. One of the paradoxes of contemporary tourism is that, as tourists come to Ireland in pursuit of difference, the Irish themselves increasingly come to resemble the tourists in terms of life-style and cultural practices. Young Europeans find that Europe's Edge is peopled with other aspiring Young Europeans.

There are two further aspects to tourism development that need to be mentioned in the present context. The first is the contribution of tourism not so much to the modernist project of industrial development as to the post-modernist project of post-industrial development. Lash and Urry argue that:

> the increased mobility of people means that the ability of a locality to attract temporary visitors may play a crucial role in its economic development. Indeed, there are considerable interconnections between tourism, services and economic development strategies. In Britain, there is scarcely a free-standing town or city that does not have the encouragement of tourism, that is tourist-related services, as one of the central planks of its economic development strategy.[24]

At one level, this development can be seen as a classic example of post-modern de-differentiation, where work and leisure are seen as a seam-less continuum rather than as polar opposites, a development that is epitomised in the advertising for drinks of the young service classes, 'Work Hard. Play Hard.' The blurring of boundaries between tourism and other leisure activities that is evident in the triple portfolio of the minister responsible, namely, Tourism, Sport and Recreation, not only suggests that tourism is a practice that informs our lives all the year round, but also that choices of economic location for the producer/consumer service class will be dictated by the pleasures of tourist con-sumption (clean environment, access to leisure facilities, good restau-rants, cultural infrastructure including clubs, theatres and cinemas, and heritage attractions).

Post-industrial production and consumption have further implications for tourism development in Ireland. In common with contemporary modes of self-reflexive production and consumption, tourism is design- and knowledge-intensive, as are the culture industries that have come to the fore in recent decades in the Republic, such as cinema, television, multimedia and music. Mr Michael Kenna, marketing manager for

An Bord Tráchtála, explicitly linked Irish tourism and new Irish music at the International Record Music Publishing and Video Music Market held in Cannes in January 1998. He argued that music provided large amounts of invisible earnings for the Irish economy and that musical culture works as a tourist magnet:

> Studies carried out by Bord Fáilte and the National Economic and Social Council show that up to 80 per cent of tourists who visit Ireland cite our music as one of the main reasons why they come here – whether that be people coming over to see where U2 record their albums in Dublin or people who are attracted by live traditional music in pubs all over the country.[25]

A central part of Bord Fáilte's European strategy in 1998 was to capitalise on Riverdance's European tour, and the continuing success of the show in the US was also exploited: 'With Irish bands and theatre continuing to take America by storm, Bord Fáilte's sponsorship of the television screening of *Riverdance – the Show* on PBS stations in every major US market, was seen as a natural publicity partnership.'[26] Tourism was an important element in the funding rationale of the *Imaginaire irlandais* festival in France and the 'Ireland and its Diaspora' stand at the Frankfurt Book Fair. The association between tourism and the culture industries is not simply one of straightforward incorporation where a Cranberries song ghosts a video-clip, however, but relates more fundamentally to a post-industrial mode of production where symbol-processing of various kinds is at a premium. In this sense, U2 songs and Neil Jordan films become so many tourism advertisements for Ireland, just as stylish tourist video promotions become advertisements for Ireland's culture industries. Here again, we see evidence of de-differentiation between tourism and other culture industries such as music, dance, film and literature, where tourism becomes one culture industry among others.

Drowning the Shamrock?

Economic developments at a European and global level over the last decades have resulted in a rolling-back of the hegemonic and centralising role of the state in constructing tourist imagery and, indeed, policy. This is manifest in the shift in tourist funding from the national government to Europe. The emphasis is now on 'Europe of the Regions', and much tourist funding is distributed through the Leader programmes, structural funds and other projects largely financed by European monies. The phenomenal growth in heritage centres and golf clubs, for example, is due mainly to the availability of European funding. The declining hegemony of the state's role in tourism is also manifest in the recent controversy surrounding the changes proposed for marketing logos. The Shamrock motif has long been popular as a logo among a number of state companies including, *inter alia*, Bord Fáilte. Plans to update the logo initiated in 1996 were the result of a joint effort on the part of Bord Fáilte and the Northern Ireland Tourist Board (NITB) to develop a new all-Ireland marketing strategy. The aim, according to Robin Wilson in an *Irish Times* article of 20 November 1997, 'was to market Ireland as a single destination building on its clean, green and "emotional" image', and the strategy was to include an international television advertising campaign and an internet site in addition to a new logo. The shamrock was no longer the main visual feature of the new logo, which consisted instead of a somewhat abstract representation of two dancers, arms outstretched, forming a circular gesture of embrace and included a tiny image of a shamrock in the corner. When the new logo was presented to the minister for Tourism, Sport and Recreation, Dr James McDaid, he was unhappy with it and requested that it be changed back to the original. A public debate ensued between the minister and the representatives of the design company which had produced it. The main argument used by McDaid for the retention of the old logo was in terms of the familiarity of its appeal over the years, how people had developed a sense of emotional attachment to it and how it had come to be identified with Ireland and Irishness over a long period of time. The appeal of the new logo, according to the design company, was that it was based on market research and that it would appeal to an international market. Furthermore, the NITB were happy with the new logo. And indeed, any fears that the NITB might have had about the political association of the shamrock with only one cultural tradition in the North of Ireland were justified in the light of the comments of the Ulster Unionist leader, David Trimble. Speaking at a meeting of the Institute of Directors in Dublin in May 1996 he roundly attacked the idea of a joint tourism authority and objected in no uncertain terms to the use of 'Gaelic' imagery:

> It is important to unionists that an all-Ireland, essentially Gaelic image of shamrocks, Irish music and Guinness is not slowly imposed on Northern Ireland, which has a range of different traditions.[27]

But it was not just sections of unionist opinion which were critical of the shamrock imagery. It was described by a design consultant as 'deeply religious and backward-looking'. And Brian Boylan, chair of the London-based consultancy, Wolff Olins, compared it to the Union flag, and suggested that both stood for a country 'more of the past than of the future'.[28]

This debate over the symbolism of the shamrock generated a number of oppositional categories: between the 'old-fashioned' and the 'modern', between the 'past' and the 'future', between the 'national' and the 'anti-national', between the 'national' and 'international' and between the 'religious' and the 'secular'. The clash between the minister McDaid and the other participants in the debate could be seen as symptomatic of a broader clash between the desire to maintain the role of the state in the construction of national symbols and the desire to change symbols in accordance with the market; or in other words is expressive of the tensions between the national and the global. What we are witnessing is the start of an era where the state is no longer the key player in the construction of national imagery, and one in which the 'free market' is taking precedence. This shift must also be understood in terms of the shift in the profile of tourists visiting Ireland over the last two decades; the relative decline in the 'returning emigrant' market and the relative increase in the 'global' but particularly the European and other new markets, for whom the shamrock symbol will not have the same 'national' emotional resonance.

Real Irelands

Tourism, as we have argued, is a powerful vector of modernisation in the Republic of Ireland. As Graburn notes about tourism generally:

> The very success of the tourist industry brings with it a way of life – work schedules, pay rates and promotions, literacy and electronic skill, bureaucracy and attitudes – which are imported along with the tourists.[29]

The recent success of the tourist industry in an Irish context highlights the conflict between tourist expectations of appropriate host behaviour and the changing cultural values and practices of the host population. The recent debate in the national press about the demise of hospitality, until now one of the key factors in Ireland's tourist allure, provides an interesting example of just such a conflict. Traditionally Ireland has been a tourist destination in which engagement with the people was one of the main ingredients in the tourist package. Indeed, the title of

Bord Fáilte's trade magazine 'Ireland of the Welcomes' makes this promise to tourists and the content, too, places emphasis on the hospitality afforded to tourists. 'If you want to know Galway,' says Walter Macken in the May–June issue of 1953, 'meet its people.' In the same issue a letter from a recent tourist from France marvels at the hospitality received during a family visit the previous season. The reasons for the highlighting of hospitality as a tourist expectation have been addressed elsewhere.[30] David Rose, an English journalist and long-time visitor to Ireland, writes in an *Irish Times* article of 13 September 1997[31] of the problems associated with the growth of modernity on a family visit to Co. Clare the previous summer.

> We love the music, the mountains, the food, the Murphy's. And we also love the people: their unsolicited interest and hospitality; their warmth, culture and charm. For a long time, we've thought they enjoyed seeing us. But for the first time, this summer, we found ourselves wondering if that was the case: and whether the intangible qualities which made Ireland different from anywhere else we've visited were vanishing before our eyes.

He recounts some of the changes following on the economic boom which he and his family have noticed:

> In little towns like Corofin, where there used to be one shop open if you were lucky, there's now a bustling High Street, and daily deliveries of items such as fresh French bread. The boom in Ballyvaughan has turned old bars into bijou eateries where you can wash down oysters with Cabernet supplied by the Australian wine-exporting commission next door.

Rose welcomes these improvements in quality of food and other tourist services but feels that the economic boom also has its downside. He goes on:

> It's difficult to be specific about a feeling like this, difficult to identify incidents whose cumulative effect amounts to a change in atmosphere. But one of the things I did notice this summer, in hamlets as much as bigger towns, was that the people who serve in shops and restaurants have become just like their counterparts in London: not quite rude, but almost; brusque; businesslike; pressed for time; keen to get on to the next customer.

In effect Rose is registering one of the fundamental paradoxes of contemporary tourism; namely that the desire to escape the pressure of modern living generates those selfsame pressures in the host destination.

Tourism has occupied an unusually important place in the development of economic and cultural identity in the Republic of Ireland. The sector continually presented itself internally as a driving force behind the modernising project of the State in the age of high modernity, and has latterly been a key element in the emergence of new class identities in the post-Fordist era of late twentieth-century Ireland. The project of modernity was not uncontested, as we saw, and a certain ambivalence characterised Irish responses to tourism development in the early years of the Republic. More recently, the debate surrounding the symbolism of the shamrock evidences a tension between an older State-driven and nationally defined notion of identity and a newer, globalised, market-driven idea of what constitutes iconic identity in the post-modern world. Uncertainty over market representation is not the only difficulty, however, facing Irish tourism. The tourism sector in Ireland may paradoxically become a victim of the very project of modernisation that it has so ardently espoused. In a country with an uncertain climate, the personal contact element that is a standard feature of tourism becomes even more crucial than elsewhere. If you spend your day lying out on a beach, surly, unwelcoming natives may be nothing more than a mild irritation. However, if low temperatures and driving rain mean you spend a lot of time indoors, then indifferent or unfriendly hosts can be a major source of dissatisfaction. Whether the 'Welcome Industry' will survive the distancing effect and instrumentalisation of human relations that is frequently a feature of modernity is an open question that has been asked by David Rose among others in this article. There is, in addition, the problem of 'spatial polarisation' where tourists tend to congregate in a limited number of areas thus destroying the initial desirability of these areas. Getting Away from It All for the independent traveller usually entails Getting Away from Them All, but this is increasingly problematic when everyone wants to escape to the same few places.

The process of de-differentiation that we have described as operating in Irish society means that tourist practices have invaded all areas of Irish life. Distinctions between host and guest become more and more unstable, and the symbolic capital of the dominant sections of the Irish middle class is increasingly (though not exclusively) based on the cultivation of a lifestyle that was formerly associated with the tourist on holiday: conspicuous consumption in expensive restaurants, four-wheel-drive cars (adventure holidays), an increased frequency of foreign holidays, ethnic cooking, foreign theme bars such as 'Pravda' and 'Zanzibar' in Dublin, a dramatic growth in wine drinking and supermarket shelves in affluent inner and outer suburbs laden with exotic produce. In a society that places a greater value on consumption than hitherto as a marker of identity, tourism has emerged as a crucial paradigm for the lifestyle of the new identity-makers in the Republic of Ireland. In an article on Westport whose title was taken from a postcards series called 'The Real Ireland', Kathy Sheridan spoke of the regeneration of Westport in County Mayo. The introductory section tells the reader that Westport has 'a thriving, cosmopolitan air, yet its character remains intact'.[32] The local Teachta Dála (Member of Parliament), Michael Ring, is quoted approvingly on the cosmopolitan air, 'Sure, all you've got to do is to stand in Bridge Street any evening and you might be in New York or Amsterdam. You'll hear more languages than in both put together.' Keva Lawlor, a Dublin-born restaurateur, came to the Mayo town in the belief that 'Westport was ripe for kangaroo, wild boar, enormous field mushrooms, old Irish bread recipes and dishes from her travels in the Far East.' Another American resident claims, 'It's like walking through Temple Bar without Dublin around it.' The analogy with another urban area in Ireland that targets both tourists and native consumers of the culture industries is significant. The sobriquet generally given to Dublin's cultural quarter is 'Dublin's Left Bank', the cosmopolitan tag a guarantor of the forward-looking modernity of the capital's cultural precinct. So, the Real Ireland is no longer the polychrome Eden of turf-gatherers and elderly cyclists, but a land of gourmets and espresso drinkers, where identity is a nomadic as opposed to a fixed construct. None the less, the Hidden Ireland remains, and it is more like Daniel Corkery's than George Gossip's, an Ireland of urban deprivation and vastly restricted social mobility, where long-term unemployment and poverty mean that the benefits of modernisation, including the prospect of tourist travel, remain as remote a possibility as they were at the inception of the Republic over fifty years ago.

Notes

1   Daniel Corkery, *The Hidden Ireland* (rpt.; Dublin: Gill and Macmillan, 1979).
2   *The Hidden Ireland: Accommodation in Private Heritage Homes* (Dublin, 1998), p. 4.
3   Bord Fáilte, *Annual Report and Accounts. Year ended 31 March 1956* (Dublin: Bord Fáilte, 1956), p. 5.

4   Bord Fáilte, 'History of Irish Tourism' (unpublished and undated document, c.1980), p. 5.
5   Bord Fáilte, *Tourism: The Welcome Industry* (Dublin: Bord Fáilte, 1983), p. 8.
6   Ibid.
7   David Harvey, *The Condition of Postmodernity* (Oxford: Blackwell, 1989).
8   This represented no more than a continuation of the status quo since independence. The Irish Tourist Association, a voluntary group, had been established in 1925 shortly after the foundation of the state under pressure of the Ministry of Industry and Commerce, but after its establishment tourism was effectively left in its hands by government.
9   J. Deegan and D. Dineen, *Tourism Policy and Performance: The Irish Experience* (London/Boston: International Thomson Business Press, 1997).
10 Ibid., p. 14.
11 Ibid., p. 22.
12 Barbara O'Connor, 'Tourist Images and National Identity', in Barbara O'Connor and Michael Cronin (eds.), *Tourism in Ireland: A Critical Analysis* (Cork: Cork University Press, 1993).
13 M. Nic Eoin, 'The Native Gaze: literary perceptions of tourist in the West Kerry Gaeltacht', paper presented at Dublin City University/St. Patrick's College, Drumcondra, Joint Faculty of Humanities Conference, 20–1 February 1998.
14 D. MacCannell, *The Tourist: A New Theory of the Leisure Class* (New York, Schocken, 1976/1989).
15 J. Heuston, 'Kilkee – The Origins and Development of a West Coast Resort', in O'Connor and Cronin (eds.), *Tourism in Ireland*, p. 24.
16 D. Gillmor, 'Irish Holidays Abroad: The Growth and Destinations of Chartered Inclusive Tours', *Irish Geography*, 6/5 (1973).
17 J. Urry, *The Tourist Gaze: Leisure and Travel in Contemporary Societies* (London, Sage, 1990).
18 Bord Fáilte, *Tourism: The Welcome Industry*, p. 5.
19 Marie O'Donnell, 'The Role of Bord Fáilte in Rural Tourism', pp. 33–40 in J. Feehan (ed.), *Tourism on the Farm* (Dublin: UCD Environmental Institute, 1992), p. 34.
20 P. Bourdieu, *Distinction: A Social Critique of the Judgement of Taste* (London: Routledge and Kegan Paul, 1986); Urry, *The Tourist Gaze*.
21 E. Sheerin, 'Heritage Centres', in Michel Peillon and Eamonn Slater (eds.), *Encounters with Modern Ireland* (Dublin: Insitute of Public Administration, 1998), pp. 39–48.
22 S. D. Barrett, 'Policy Changes, Output Growth and Investment in Irish Tourism 1986–96', *Irish Banking Review* (Autumn 1997), pp. 39–48, p. 42.
23 M. Peillon, 'The Irish on Holidays: Practice and Symbolism', in O'Connor and Cronin (eds.), *Tourism in Ireland*, pp. 258–71.
24 S. Lash and J. Urry, *Economies of Signs and Space* (London: Sage, 1994), pp. 214–15.
25 Brian Boyd, 'Cannes' Mediterranean marketplace of music', *The Irish Times*, 23 January 1998.
26 Bord Fáilte, *Annual Review* (Dublin, Bord Fáilte, 1997).
27 Robin Wilson, 'Political slow learners are reflected clearly in Ireland's tale of two logos', *The Irish Times*, 20 November, 1997, p. 16.
28 Ibid.

29   N. H. H. Graburn, 'Tourism, Modernity and Nostalgia', in Ahmed and Shore (eds.), *The Future of Anthropology* (London: Athlone Press, 1995), p. 171.

30   Barbara O'Connor, 'Tourist Images and National Identity', in O'Connor and Cronin (eds.), *Tourism in Ireland*.

31   David Rose, 'Drive for big bucks could leave Irish hospitality in the ha'penny place', *The Irish Times*, 13 September 1997.

32   Kathy Sheridan, 'The Real Ireland', *The Irish Times*, 4 July 1998.

Part III
Politics

9

A Quiet Revolution: The Remaking of Irish Political Culture

Tom Garvin

Faith, Fatherland, Fianna Fáil

In 1949 independent Ireland declared itself a republic and left the British Commonwealth. With a simple one-sentence Act of the Irish Parliament, the issue over which a bitter little civil war had been fought a generation previously was resolved. Younger people often wondered what the fuss had been all about. Republican status did not change people's lives in any magical way; the 1950s were to be a depressing decade economically and psychologically. Having weathered the Second World War with a precarious non-belligerency, Ireland proceeded to miss out on the first half of a generation-long world economic boom, partly because of continuing loyalty to outdated nostrums concerning self-sufficiency and Anglophobia.

1950s Ireland was a quiet place, both North and South. The revolution of 1913–23 had burned out, despite a half-hearted IRA campaign against Northern Ireland mounted from the South by a handful of young men loyal to older ways of thinking. There was a sullen but quiet acquiescence in the partition settlement that had emerged between 1920 and 1925. De Valera, the iconic hero of the 1916 Rising and leader of Fianna Fáil, the natural governing party of the Republic, became Taoiseach (prime minister) for the last time in 1957. He had been leader of the country for most of the period between 1932 and 1954, and was to retire finally from active politics in 1959, a date that marks a turning-point in the history of independent Ireland. His last cabinet consisted substantially of the same group of old comrades who had sided with him in the split of 1922 and who had formed his first cabinet in 1932. De Valera, the firebrand radical of the Twenties, had become the grey-haired leader of a nationalist and republican gerontocracy by 1957. Old hatreds from the civil war period dominated the minds of many of Ireland's leaders, and revolutionary fanaticism prevented some of them from thinking constructively about the post-imperial and post-British future.

Politics and culture intersected in peculiar ways in this small, peripheral, ingrown and post-revolutionary polity. Fianna Fáil in particular presented itself as a party that was the true and loyal heir of the heroic tradition of 1916, and cultivated a cult of the martyrs of the Rising. The party had provided the Constitution of 1937, and refused to accept the partition settlement, insisting on Ireland's right to an all-island independence. The party also represented itself as being the true defender of the Catholic faith of the great majority of the people on the island. Irish people were pious and literal-minded believers in the tenets of the Catholic faith. The priests of the Catholic Church had immense social, cultural and political power. Authoritarian clerics enforced their own view of what should be done in many areas of cultural, intellectual and social life. Priests taught sociology and politics; priests ordered doctors and nursing staff to avoid certain operations; priests were feared and obeyed even by senior figures in government, the universities and the newspapers. Fianna Fáil represented itself as the true defender not only of Irish republicanism, but also of the Catholic faith of the ordinary people. Foreign newspapers, films and books were subjected to a draconian and profoundly anti-intellectual censorship. This combination of fundamentalist Catholicism and purist, all-Ireland 'republicanism' formed a 'blended ideology', to use the term of Robert Dahl, of great political power; Fianna Fáil was nearly always in power on its own, and was, in the minds of many, identified with the nation itself.

Thus, a national Catholic tradition of cultural defence was ensconced in power in both state and church. This tradition defended itself energetically against real and imagined enemies, both internal and external, by using the instruments of state against all comers.[1] Religious traditionalism, a rural nostalgia dressed up as a political programme and cultural isolationism attempted to preserve themselves against the perceived menaces of liberalism, cosmopolitanism and non-Catholic, commonly British, freethinking. Battles were won and lost in the democratic arena of Irish politics; occasionally Fianna Fáil even lost an election, but underneath there existed a continuous politics of cultural defence which certainly dated back a century. In many ways that battle was still being waged in the late 1990s, but the cultural defenders have now suffered a series of decisive defeats.

I would like to outline the process by which this popular nationalist alliance between fundamentalist Catholicism and post-revolutionary republicanism gradually disintegrated in the generation after de Valera's retirement in 1959. I wish to suggest that it has been replaced by a general Irish civic patriotism which does not need to attach itself to a religious or tribal identity. Unfortunately, this new secular identity is one that is little understood in Northern Ireland, Britain or parts of Irish America. It is little understood in parts of the Republic itself, or if it is so understood, it is disliked and feared by older and more tradition-ally minded people. Fianna Fáil has been at the centre of this process of change, adjusting itself reluctantly and slowly to changes forced on it from outside, and rarely regaining the psychological initiative which it had enjoyed in its halcyon days of 1932–48.

This politics of cultural defence is not one that is peculiar to Ireland, although it has taken a particularly well-articulated and persistent form there. In the United States, for example, movements of cultural defence have reacted to social change much as they have in Ireland over the last hundred years. The populism of William Jennings Bryan in the 1890s was echoed in many ways by the nationalist alliance of Faith and Fath-erland offered to the Irish by de Valera after 1922. Again, Prohibition in the United States between 1920 and 1933 was to a considerable extent a nativist reaction to the growth of great cities and of non-Protestant and somehow un-American communities with social values derived from recent European experience.[2] The difference, of course, was that Ireland, as an independent nation-state, was reacting to social and cultural forces transmitted to her in apparently almost irresistible form from England and, to a lesser extent, from America and mainland Europe.

Ireland has seen a succession of waves of reaction to secularism and other by-products of modernisation and economic development in the last hundred years; the continuity between the politics of modernisa-tion since 1957 and the politics of the previous two generations is strik-ing. Catholicism and nationalism had repeatedly interacted to produce a series of moralistic popular political movements often of impressive organisational effectiveness, intellectual forcefulness and political soph-istication.

A National Church and a Democratic Caesar

Ireland was seen in the official ideology as a Catholic nation, bravely resisting the modern tide of liberalism and unbelief. The people of Ire-land were a democratic community, but a loyally Catholic community as well, faithful to faith and fatherland. The symbolism was one of the Green Island, washed by the pure waters of Ocean, innocent, virginal and unpolluted by the modern and secular world of the Enlightenment. The ideology also argued that Ireland needed to be defended by Catholic intellectual patriots; censorship and a closed society were the devices used by the Church–State alliance of the time. There were other versions of Irish separatist nationalism: secular, socialist, liberal and individualist. However, all were to lose out for a generation after 1922 to the essentially religious version proposed by Catholic ideologues. A German scholar, writing in the late 1950s, summarised de Valera's version of this essentially Victorian ideal as reflected in the policies put forward by the Fianna Fáil party during its rise to power in the late 1920s.

> The [Fianna Fáil] programme was well-calculated to appeal to the smaller Irish farmers: a frugal, Gaelic Ireland, as little despoiled as possible by the forces of civilisation, especially English civilisation . . . a state in which there would be no rich and no poor, but rather a countryside scattered with small farmers and small industries.[3]

Such a Jeffersonian programme, he might have added, tied in well with the ambitions of the Catholic Church. Ireland was seen as a source of priests and nuns; in the early twentieth century Ireland produced more priests, brothers and nuns than any other country in the western world. Ireland, in the eyes of international Catholicism, was a beachhead in the English-speaking, Protestant world, a world which was powerful beyond measure and not faithful to the Church of Christ. Irish young men and women were to be the collective vehicle by which the British Empire and the United States would be converted to the true faith. Even demographically, Ireland was bent to Catholic purposes by the social engineering of the Church. The huge rates of clerical vocations were related to the post-Famine social structure of rural Ireland, which enforced high rates of celibacy on non-inheriting young people. Clerical control of schools ensured easy propagandising in favour of the religious life. Ireland was a highly religious country, and also a popularly religious country; authoritarian Catholicism and populist democracy had a firm alliance with each other. The main menaces to this putatively happy condition were the outside world and any tendency toward dynamic economic development which was uncontrollable by the public authorities or their political allies.

Cultural Defence

From the 1880s through to the 1960s, over a period of three generations, nationalist, nativist and religious themes were used to erect ideological and organisational defences against the cultural and political
assaults seen to be emanating from the Anglo-Saxon world and elsewhere. Sometimes these influences were seen as being in the main
literary and cultural, sometimes as being engineered by secretive organisations dedicated to liberalism, atheism, communism or freemasonry.
Sometimes they were seen as emanating from traitors within the ranks:
local artists, writers, sceptics, anti-clerics or radicals. In particular the
fear of secular individualism, seen as threatening Irish communal
values, was often associated with a fear of the modern and an imper-
fectly camouflaged hatred of, and contempt for, Protestant liberal
culture. To be fair, this hatred was returned with interest by the more
anti-Catholic Irish and British power-holders and voters inside the old
two-island United Kingdom.

Catholic antisecularism dates from the French Revolution and was
immeasurably strengthened by the experience of the Italian Risorgi-
mento, inspired as it was by French ideas and hostile as it was to the
papal territorial claim to central Italy. A series of *Kulturkaempfe* occurred
in Ireland over clerical control of education between 1812 and 1850.
The churches in Ireland succeeded in acquiring control over primary
and secondary education, to the virtual exclusion of secular education
of any kind. A further struggle over tertiary education resulted in a stalemate which effectively denied university education of an acceptable
kind to Catholics until the early twentieth century. A sixty-year-long,
bishop-led boycott of Protestant and secular institutions was partially
lifted only in 1908. In that year the nominally secular but substantially
Catholic National University of Ireland was founded, while Queen's
University Belfast made concessions to Catholic sensibilities. The other
tertiary-level college, Dublin's Protestant Trinity College, remained
under ecclesiastical ban until the second half of the twentieth century.

This extraordinary assault on higher education by the priests had
incalculable but huge impact on the general mentality of lay Catholic
political leadership in Ireland in the first half of this century. Among
these effects was an intellectual subordination of many lay leaders to
ecclesiastical direction, combined with a general acceptance of Catholic
social and cultural ideas. The ideology of cultural defence, combined
with an intense nationalism of the Faith and Fatherland type, was
disseminated with great enthusiasm by the priests, brothers, nuns and

subordinated national schoolteachers who dominated the education, limited as it was, of the bulk of the population. The ideology was accepted to varying extents by the young men and women who were to become the ruling elites of independent Ireland. Through the national schools and the Christian Brothers it became the ruling ideology of a large proportion of the general population.

The achievement of independence in 1922 meant also the triumph of the Catholic lay and clerical forces which adhered to this blended ideology of Catholicism, cultural defence and nativism. The ideology, now with a state behind it, pitted the stereotypical puritan, heroic and clean-living Irish nationalist against both the equally stereotyped effete and corrupt aristocratic world of the British and Anglo-Irish establishments and the vulgar, drunken and anglicised proletarian Irish of the towns.[4]

C. S. Andrews has given us an extraordinary and unselfconscious sketch of his own group of young, proto- Fianna Fáil republican activists on the eve of their coming to power in 1932. They were products of the Christian Brothers schools, the Gaelic League and its programme of cultural and moral rearmament, Sinn Féin and the IRA of 1913–23. They had been close together from early boyhood, and they were 'dyed-in-the-wool republicans'. They didn't drink and knew nothing about women. They hated ostentation, formal clothes, evening or morning dress and above all silk hats. They disliked horse racing, gambling, golf, tennis and the 'plus fours and white flannels that went with them'. They disapproved of people who were interested in fine food. Eating was for living, not for enjoying. They disliked elaborate wedding ceremonies and women wearing jewellery or makeup.[5]

Driven by attitudes such as these, an elaborate apparatus of legal and extra-legal cultural and political censorship was set up after independence. The censorship of books was particularly vicious. In 1954 the list of books whose sale was illegal in the Republic of Ireland included books by the British Government (*Report* of the Royal Commission on Population), James Branch Cabell, Truman Capote, Joyce Cary, the Church of England (*Threshold of Marriage*), Simone de Beauvoir, John Dos Passos, Theodore Dreiser, William Faulkner, F. Scott Fitzgerald, C. S. Forester, Anatole France, Sigmund Freud, Oliver St. John Gogarty, Henry Green, Graham Greene, Ernest Hemingway, Aldous Huxley, James Joyce, Arthur Koestler, W. Somerset Maugham, Bryan Merriman (*Cúirt an Mheán-Oichdhe* in English translation by Frank O'Connor; it was legal in Irish, the first national language under de Valera's 1937 Constitution, and bits of it were on the Leaving Certificate curriculum for schools), Kate O'Brien, Sean O'Casey, George Orwell (*Nineteen Eighty-Four*), J. D. Salinger, George Bernard Shaw, John Steinbeck, H. G. Wells and Herman Wouk (*The Caine Mutiny*).[6] Film was subjected to a similarly stringent system of censorship.

At an informal level, the discouragement or suppression of 'foreign' or heterodox ideas was carried to further and sometimes grotesque extremes. The Catholic Church and its political allies in Fianna Fáil, Fine Gael and the Labour Party denounced and intimidated individuals who had stepped out of line and expressed ideas or behaved in ways disliked by the post-revolutionary establishment. Education for most was controlled, directly or indirectly, by priests and their allies. A static and unchanging, mainly rural economy underpinned a democracy and public policy which attempted to prevent cultural change from occurring. However, as many observant people within the elite realised, the alliance between ageing patriots and young priests was behaving rather like a collective King Canute.

The End of the Revolution in Power

Sometime in the period between 1945 and 1960 something snapped. Relations between church and state were intimate and friendly; considerable governmental power in effect rested in the hands of ecclesiastics. The Mother and Child incident of 1951 appeared to demonstrate that the Catholic bishops had a veto on government public health policy. However, the incident generated considerable *sotto voce* resentment in middle-class and working-class circles. A common remark of the period was 'this time the bishops have gone too far'.

This was a period of economic stagnation compared to the booming postwar economies of Britain and northern Europe. The old men were still in power and were increasingly seen as having outlived their time. The social forces that were eventually to liquidate most of the extraordinary system of social control that had been built up since 1850 were complex. Many commentators have pointed to increased education for lay people, to increased prosperity and therefore increased mental independence and have also acknowledged the significance of the ideological thaw that occurred internationally in the Catholic Church after the Second Vatican Council. Fundamentalism and antimodernism were assaulted from both outside and inside the Irish church.

There was, however, a deeper reason for the disintegration: the fragility of the old alliance between priests and politics. The two sides of the nationalist establishment had ceased to see eye to eye, and the alliance had begun to decay. The nationalist and developmentalist component of the alliance came increasingly into open conflict with the puritan, culturally defensive and quietist component. By the late 1950s the conflict was becoming open. The patriots had come to the conclusion that economic protectionism would have to be abandoned in favour of free trade, that multinational capital would have to be used to supplement local capital, that cultural protectionism was stultifying and that education for pious citizenship would have to be replaced by education and training for economic growth.

The nationalists, political children as they were of Arthur Griffith's Sinn Féin, wanted to create a strong, modern nation with industries, cities, a growing population and a place among the nations of the earth, as the old slogan had promised an earlier generation. Spreading what little wealth there was around equally in a stagnant rural and small-town, protected local economy was not going to work any more. Educating young men for the priesthood and little else was a recipe for cultural stagnation and sterility. Furthermore, ideas were badly needed in the prevailing atmosphere of intellectual and political bankruptcy; baiting the intellectuals and the unorthodox did not impress the newly educated young on whom the younger nationalist leaders in Fine Gael and Fianna Fáil increasingly had to count. Puritans and priests wished to preserve and reproduce a certain social type, pious, familial, loyal to the native acres, culturally ingrown and obedient to clerical authority in matters moral and intellectual. By the Fifties this latter project could be, and increasingly was, accused of being a threat to the nationalist one, and was increasingly seen as such even by some younger priests.

An undercurrent of doubt about the sociocultural policies espoused by the clerical and lay puritans had always existed in the nationalist tradition, many-stranded as it was. This undercurrent went back to Griffith's own doubts about the rural and conformist arcadias beloved of so many early Sinn Féiners and Gaelic Leaguers before 1912. As early as 1903, Griffith wrote that a 'cocky disparagement of the work of modern thinkers was characteristic of the "shoddy side" of the nationalist cultural and political movements in Ireland'. Young men praised an imaginary mediaeval Ireland and then wondered why Ireland was decaying around them. While the world outside had intellectual vitality and economic growth, Ireland preserved her picturesque ignorance. 'Ireland's clever young men,' he continued, 'while knowing better in private, announced in public that Ireland's innocence was more sacred than "the wisdom of an infidel world" and Ireland emigrates.' More than anything, Ireland needed free thought.[7]

Many writers and artists, in particular perhaps the Bell writers of the 1940s, led by Seán Ó Faoláin and Peadar O'Donnell, echoed this plea for mental freedom throughout the first generation after independence. Modernisers who had made explicit connections between mental freedom, innovation and economic and cultural progress had always existed in the movement, but had been shunted aside in the 1930s by those who, in effect, espoused a pious stasis and who got their way because of the depression and the isolation imposed by the Second World War.

Concern about this situation was also expressed, more loudly and without fear, by sympathetic outsiders whose views seem to have influenced establishment opinion more effectively than those of internal commentators; the latter's criticisms were too easily dismissed as treason in the ranks. In 1954 an Irish American priest, Fr. John A. O'Brien, edited a much-discussed collection of essays entitled, rather alarmingly, *The Vanishing Irish.*[8] The title alone was enough to get a public reaction in Ireland. The contributors launched what amounted to a sustained and devastating attack on the intellectual assumptions of Irish political and ecclesiastical leaders.

Michael Sheehy, in a book entitled *Divided We Stand*, offered a calm critique of the official position on partition for a newly attentive younger generation, an argument which even now looks advanced. The doublethink of official anti-partitionism, combined with the imprisonment of IRA men who were obeying something suspiciously like the official line, was made evident to many. In 1957 J. V. Kelleher, a well-known Irish-American, wrote in *Foreign Affairs* that a lack of intellectualism among Irish leaders, combined with an emigration-generated apathy among the general population, was almost literally killing the country. A hatred of intellectual and psychological freedom was finally coming to be recognised as a real threat to the entire nationalist project.[9]

Even the Irish Catholic Church was not impervious to criticisms coming from sources such as these. One famed defender of orthodoxy and an authoritarian 'moderniser' of sorts, was John Charles McQuaid, Archbishop of Dublin 1919–72, friend of de Valera and controller of the school systems attended by over a quarter of the population. In 1962 he retained an American Jesuit sociologist to study the attitudes of Dublin Catholics towards religion and clerical authority by survey.[10]

The picture that emerged was rather startling, and, from the Church's point of view both reassuring and alarming. Attitudes to the Catholic Church and its priests varied little by class, sex or age. Almost 90 per cent of the sample agreed, for example, that the Church was the greatest force for good in Ireland. Priests were accepted willingly as the natural social, cultural and political leaders of society. This was accompanied with a contempt for lay politicians, even those in the democratically elected Irish Parliament. Cynicism about lay attempts at political or social leadership were widespread. The post-Famine church had done its work well, and ensured that it was difficult for any non-priest to aspire to leadership without explicit ecclesiastical support. When asked what side they would take in the event of a clash between church and state, an astounding 87 per cent said that they would back their church.[11]

This was scarcely more than a decade after a spectacular political crisis in which the bishops had successfully vetoed a welfare scheme designed to assist expectant women in health matters. The politicians were helpless in the face of such a political climate, and sensitive legislation was routinely cleared secretly with the bishops in advance of Dáil ratification.[12] The formally democratic Irish political process was heavily tinged with a democratic theocracy. However, future change was also predicted by the evidence. Those few who had completed secondary school were more willing to question the system and formed an isolated group, denied political power both by the clergy and by the mass of their fellow citizens. Whereas 88 per cent of the sample endorsed the proposition that the church was the greatest source for good in the country, an almost equally massive 83 per cent of the educated group disagreed with it.[13]

Clerical fears of educated lay people were demonstrated to be well-founded. There was a solid core of what we may call the intellectual elite, who resented clerical power and denied the church's right to rule.[14] Rather like the communist regimes of Eastern Europe, the Catholic Church in 1950s Ireland had begun to educate itself out of power; her own secondary schools were hatcheries of sceptics and anti-clericals. An undercurrent of anti-clericalism ran through the steadily growing educated stratum of a relatively under-educated nation. It may be that in its high-handed approach to health and social issues, the church had already swept aside a nascent lay Christian Democratic tendency in Irish society and killed any prospect of a powerful intellectual lay Catholicism which was loyal to, if often critical of, the Catholic Church. Certainly, in 1962, the church was bitterly resented by its own most favoured sons and daughters. The researcher commented that the Irish priest was caught in a dilemma; he was confronted by a slowly growing educated future ruling class which required more sophisticated answers

Table 9.1. Average annual GNP growth rates, various periods

	1953–60	1960–77	1979–86	1985–95	1993–7
per cent	1.8	3.1	0.3	5.0	7.0

than the platitudes which had satisfied its elders. On the other hand, 'he was confronted also by the suspicious gaze' of many people, poorer or more rural, who were hostile to leadership which was not clerically approved.[15] The researcher concluded that the church had estranged the educated class and had deprived herself and the country of the intellectual energy they both needed by forcing young people of energy and mental independence to find a living in other countries.[16]

Faced with evidence of this kind from friendly commentators, the will to continue the full campaign of cultural defence weakened in the 1950s and 1960s as the people in power in church and state themselves ceased to believe in its desirability or efficacy. Some commentators have argued recently that the defeat of the official faith-and-fatherland ideology had actually been quite easy.[17] However, this is not the way it felt at the time.

Culture Shift

Certainly, independent Ireland has changed more since 1960 than it did in the era between the end of the Civil War in 1923 and the retirement of de Valera in 1959. Social change is notoriously difficult to measure and assess, but useful indicator variables are offered by such aggregate and crude measures of change as Gross National Product (GNP) and indicators of educational levels.

Table 9.1 gives estimates of the economic growth of the Republic since 1953.[18] It should be remembered that economic growth between 1923 and 1959 was low; GNP in 1959 was somewhat higher than it had been in 1923, perhaps as much as 50 per cent higher, but the aftermath of independence, the Great Depression and the World War had contributed to a general climate of stagnation in which state enterprise attempted to fill the gap made by the weakness of private enterprise. The 1960s was a boom period, and certainly modern Irish change was kick-started at that time. Despite a depression in the early 1980s, Irish economic development has not slowed down. The last ten years have seen an extraordinary surge in the country's economic fortunes, one which economists seem to be at a loss to explain. There are many

Table 9.2.   Enrolment in tertiary education, as a proportion of age cohort, selected years

	1960	1980	1994
per cent	9	18	34

factors involved, one certainly being a revolution in mass education, another being the foresight of government agencies in betting on key emergent economic sectors, in particular food processing, electronics, software and pharmaceuticals.

Another measure, Gross Domestic Product, would give an even more favourable picture of the country's economic progress. A 1997 OECD report claimed that Ireland's GDP per head is now possibly higher than that of Britain, for the first time in over two centuries, and perhaps for the first time since the barbarian invasions of 1100 years ago. GNP growth figures for the 1997–2000 period have averaged 8 per cent, an OECD record. GNP has probably doubled in the last decade. Ireland's historically persistent image as the poor sister in the north European family of developed nations looks like needing some revision.

Educational levels have also been raised considerably. Education, as a monopoly of religious organisations, was neglected by the state, deferential as it was to clerical claims to jurisdiction. However, government intervention increased in the 1960s, and in 1967 fees for secondary education were abolished. The infamous 'ban' of Archbishop McQuaid, which prohibited Catholics of the Dublin diocese from attending Trinity College, Dublin, was abolished and competition between the two major Dublin universities became the norm. Expansion of educational opportunities has had an indirect but pervasive impact on power relationships in Irish society. The old peasant deference to clerical authority, partly derived from a sense that the priest was an educated and powerful man who could be trusted because he was on your side, faded away.

Wealth and education have not only accompanied the growth of a new, large middle class, they have also had the usual sociological consequences of spreading 'middle-class' values beyond the traditional middle class. A relative secularism, tolerance of diversity and a tendency to follow one's own conscience in moral and civic matters as distinct from taking the advice of moral mentors such as priests characterise this new social type. Relative wealth means personal independence and a lack of need for powerful protectors or patrons. Older patron–client relationships have weakened in number and strength. Opinion surveys and referendum votes since the late 1960s have clearly indicated a steady increase in the post-Catholic and 'à la carte' Catholic segments of the population. This growth follows a class and urban rural divide, and also shows an age dimension.

A parallel shift in attitudes toward the perennial 'national question' has also occurred; Fatherland has followed Faith. The island was divided into the entities now known as Northern Ireland (NI) and the Republic of Ireland (RI) in 1920. Echoes of the violence of that time have shaped the internal politics of both Irish states ever since. In NI, the Protestant two-thirds majority successfully resisted incorporation into the south, and domineered over the Catholic nationalist minority.

Somewhat similarly, in the Republic the nationalist Faith and Fatherland official ideology had reached extraordinary heights for a time after independence, lasting as long as the revolutionary generation of leaders; as they retired from office in the 1950s and 1960s, the ideology became increasingly muted and seen as *passé*. In parallel to this, attitudes to Northern Ireland and to Britain gradually changed. Whereas loyalty to the idea of a united independent Ireland persisted, the idea that the local majority in NI could somehow be coerced or manoeuvred into such a union against its wishes weakened, although some doublethink about this is still detectable. Here, television has been crucial. The sight of the bodies of children killed by IRA murder bombs being shovelled into body bags, and the relentless reportage of IRA and loyalist murderousness north and south, has led to a general acceptance of the proposition that the worldview of traditional physical-force republicanism is moribund. The collapse of the Soviet Union further undermined the insurrectionists; their traditionalism was coloured by a vaguely internationalist socialism. Also, the USSR and its European and Arab allies had been important suppliers of arms and explosives. The parallel conversion of Irish America from a sentimental republicanism by Dublin diplomacy has dried up support for the Provo campaign.

The signing of a new and historic British–Irish agreement between the representatives of the Northern Ireland parties and the Dublin and London governments on 10 April 1998 echoes this new flexibility in the culture. The old inability to move from entrenched positions, combined with a quasi-religious propensity to confuse a political position with some divine ordinance, has faded. This quasi-religious Faith and Fatherland cult has been a real casualty of the modernisation of Irish political culture. Concomitantly, the old alliance of Church and State, or Drumcondra and Leinster House, is virtually extinct. The Second

Vatican Council of the early sixties officially declared an end to the Counter-Reformation, thereby discomfiting one of the most Counter-Reformist of all national Catholic churches. Irish bishops publicly welcomed the changes brought in by the Council, but their welcoming voices sounded distinctly hollow.

The IRA campaign in the North, involving the killing of Irish people in the name of an imaginary all-Ireland republic, had the ironic effect of demilitarising the existing Republic. The IRA encouraged an increasingly noisy revisionism in the Republic and even engendered a growing crypto-partitionism. Of course, the IRA blamed everybody but itself for this sea change.

Time is another cause of change. The Republic has forgotten British rule; British soldiers marched out of Dublin and Cork three generations ago, and sailed out of the Treaty ports two generations ago. In the Republic, Britain is history. The Empire is dead, and Irish anti-imperialism has died with it, despite attempts to convert itself into a tradition of neutralism and 'America-bashing'. The Republic increasingly sees itself as a smaller European democracy which happens to have extremely close cultural and familial links with the North and with Britain.

Money shifts cultural gears as well. Independent Ireland is now perhaps four times as rich as it was at the time of independence. In 1922 it was a peasant country, with a large proportion of its population living at subsistence level; it is now a country which is relatively rich, approaching in standard of living the old imperial master, and, most crucially, it is clearly out of the economic trap in which it had languished for three centuries. Membership of the European Union has clearly ended the old dominance of the British economy; trade with mainland Europe and the rest of the world now dwarfs the British trade, important though that remains. At the time of independence, nearly 60 per cent of the population worked directly in farming, and 100 per cent of exports went to the United Kingdom; the proportion in farming now is about 10 per cent, and well over half of foreign trade is with mainland Europe and the rest of the world. Furthermore, subsistence farming has been substantially replaced by commercial farming. In effect the Republic has skipped the heavy-industry stage of the classic development sequence and has gone directly from pre-industrial to post-industrial economic activity.

Information is another major force for change. Ireland fifty years ago was a society of many secrets. Newspapers and individuals feared to print stories about powerful people in politics or about religious organisations. However, over the past thirty years there has been increasing pressure on public figures to defend themselves in public and to submit to increasingly rigorous questioning and criticism. This has particularly hurt the Catholic Church; an apparently endless stream of scandals involving misconduct on the part of brothers, priests and bishops has hit the media. A bishop was found to have fathered a son and to have laundered diocesan funds to pay for his education; a well-known television priest who defended conservative lines was found to have fathered two children by his housekeeper and to have forced her to have one of them adopted; the psychiatrist who defended the woman when she went public was taken to task by a Catholic-dominated medical board of inquiry until the public uproar became too great. Again, a paedophile priest was found to have been sheltered by ecclesiastical authority for decades and given continued access to children under clerical care until he was finally exposed and imprisoned; this incident toppled an entire government. Weekly mass attendance rates have plunged from 91 per cent in 1973 to 77 per cent in 1994 and to 60 per cent in 1998 in the wake of the recent clerical scandals. Confession is now mainly a practice confined to older people.[19] The rebellion against the obligation to go to confession dates back to the prohibition on artificial birth control by the Catholic church in 1968; women had already discovered the contraceptive pill and were not going to give it up at the behest of elderly and officially celibate men. The growing independence of women has been a conspicuous feature of the Irish long revolution.

Synergy seems to have been part of the quiet revolution in Ireland. Sensible economic policies, expansion in education, the parallel discrediting of certain traditional political stances in the political and religious fields, the discrediting of both extreme left and right and investment by both multinational and Irish companies have transformed the situation. A prominent Irish economist, Professor Brendan Walsh of University College, Dublin, no booster of official Ireland, answering a question as to how recent economic success has changed Irish society, comments:

> [It has] made it richer. Made it richer, bigger, more populous; there are more people added to the labour force and to the population since 1987 than there was in all the years since independence. It's just amazing.[20]

Envoi

The Irish are still rather proud of themselves, and it was, perhaps, the humiliations of Irish history which impelled them to go through a phase of exaggerated national and religious collective piety. They are still a religious people, but in a less triumphalist and exhibitionist way than formerly, and they are still quite nationalistic. However, the authoritarianism, moralism and anti-individualism of former times have faded, giving rise to a somewhat laid-back but problem-solving approach toward political and economic problems. A secular patriotism, which does not lean on tribal or religious identities, has evolved in Ireland in recent decades. This relative secularism has made *rapprochement* between North and South, Britain and Ireland, not only feasible, but inevitable and obvious. The process is by no means complete, but it seems that the Irish, a politically rather able people, are well up to completing it in their own good time. Some would see these changes as decadent; others see it as a long-overdue return to normal.

On Good Friday, 1998, these changes reached a climax of sorts. An agreement was signed in Belfast between the Dublin and London governments and the main Northern Ireland parties to share power and provide for North–South and British–Irish representative bodies. In return, the Republic was to delete clauses in its Constitution which could be regarded as making a claim to the territory of Northern Ireland. The agreement was ratified by enormous majorities in both parts of Ireland on 22 May, 1998. The Irish electorate, voting island-wide for the first time since 1918, have agreed to live in peace, and have effectively agreed also to dismantle de Valera's enshrinement of Faith-and-Fatherland values in his 1937 Constitution.

Notes

1   I have aired, in earlier forms, some of the ideas in this essay elsewhere over the last ten years; possibly what is mainly good news bears repetition. See for example my 'The Politics of Denial and Cultural Defence: the Referendums of 1985 and 1986 in Context,' 11 *Irish Review*, 3 (1988), 17 and, my 'Hibernian Endgame? Nationalism in a Divided Ireland,' in Richard Caplan and John Pfeffer (eds.), *Europe's New Nationalisms* (New York and Oxford: Oxford University Press, 1996), pp. 184–94. See generally Terence Brown, *Ireland: A Social and Cultural History, 1922–79* (London, Fontana, 1981); Paul Blanshard, *The Irish and Catholic Power* (London: Derek Verschoyle, 1954); Tom Garvin, *Nationalist Revolutionaries in Ireland, 1858–1927* (Oxford: Clarendon, 1987), particularly pp. 56–77.
2   S. M. Lipset and E. Raab, *The Politics of Unreason* (London: Heinemann, 1971), pp. 78–80 and *passim*.
3   E. Rumpf, *Nationalism and Socialism in Twentieth Century Ireland* (Liverpool: University Press, 1977), p. 103.
4   Garvin, *Nationalist Revolutionaries in Ireland*, pp. 56–77.
5   C. S. Andrews, *Man of no Property* (Dublin and Cork: Mercier, 1982), p. 29.

6   Blanshard, *The Irish and Catholic Power*, pp. 89–121.
7   *United Irishman*, 25 July, 1903.
8   J. A. O'Brien, *The Vanishing Irish* (London: Allen and Unwin, 1954).
9   Michael Sheehy, *Divided We Stand* (London: Faber, 1955); J. V. Kelleher, 'Ireland... And Where Does She Stand?' *Foreign Affairs* (1957), 48–95; Brown, *Ireland: A Social and Cultural History*, pp. 29–43.
10 B. F. Beiver, *Religion, Culture and Values* (New York: Arno Press, 1976).
11 Ibid., pp. 270–1, 306.
12 Ibid., p. 397.
13 Ibid., pp. 226–7.
14 Ibid., p. 227.
15 Ibid., p. 278.
16 Ibid., pp. 497, 503.
17 Fintan O'Toole, *The Ex-Isle of Erin* (Dublin: New Island, 1996), p. 110.
18 Sources for economic figures: World Development Report, appropriate years; Kieran A. Kennedy *et al.*, *The Economic Development of Ireland in the Twentieth Century* (London: Routledge, 1988); *Irish Times*, 23 December 1997; *Daily Telegraph*, March 17 1998. In general, see *The Economist* (May 17–23 1997), 15–16, 23–9.
19 Sources for religious attendance: *Irish Times*, 4 and 7 February 1998.
20 *Magill* (May 1998), p. 47.

10
'A Miserable Failure of a State'[1]: Unionist Intellectuals and the Irish Republic

Colin Coulter

Introduction

Observers of Northern Irish political life have often come to regard Ulster unionism as a curious anachronism. This common characterisation is, of course, entirely understandable. Many members of the unionist community continue, after all, to be moved by sentiments and ambitions that would seem to have ceased to animate the residents of other Western societies. Moreover, the discourse of contemporary unionism habitually draws upon a political lexicon that would appear to belong to a century other than our own. The unionist tradition cannot, however, be reduced merely to the antediluvian rantings of men in dog collars. While there are many elements of the unionist disposition that are evidently anti-quated, there are at the same time others that are clearly 'modern' in a particular sense of that most troublesome of terms. Indeed, the cadre of unionist intellectuals that has emerged in recent times has typically mobilised ideas and distinctions that are the hallmark of those discurs-ive formations that would seem to have assumed hegemonic status throughout the Western world.[2] Contemporary unionism may perhaps be best understood as a localised variant of that voracious ideological programme usually designated as 'modernisation theory'. It is largely this particular philosophical inclination that has rendered unionists unable to understand or appreciate those with whom they happen to share the island.

The Meaning of Modernity

'Modernisation theory' represents a generic classification that accommodates a complex cluster of diverse ideological impulses. While modernisation theorists may differ on a range of issues they tend to share an understanding that the process of social evolution entails a profound moment of rupture.[3] The essential watershed that chronicles the progress of every social formation is that which marks the transition from 'tradition' to 'modernity'. The genuinely 'modern' society is considered to possess numerous admirable characteristics. Rapid economic development ensures that an increasingly substantial swathe of citizens come to enjoy material security and ultimately, indeed, affluence. Those political institutions that herald and enable the arrival of modernity tend to be concerned to underwrite the interests not of the collective but of the individual. The principles that guide the liberal democratic state are primarily those of right and law. The extensive protection that modern social formations offer their citizens enables individuals to transcend communal identities and enmities in order to assemble their own complex biographies out of the fulsome literal and figurative resources of everyday life.

The glowing representation of 'modernity' that modernisation theorists advance inevitably finds its mirror image in their understanding of the nature of 'tradition'. The traditional society is considered to exist in a perennial state of economic stagnation that condemns the overwhelming majority of inhabitants to precarious and often miserable living conditions. Those political institutions that are the hallmark of tradition invariably choose to privilege the rights of the group over those of the individual. The legal and normative structures that exist within traditional social formations seek to enshrine and enforce the strictures of collective morality. Individual social actors are compelled to live out an essentially stunted and conservative existence that departs little from that of their predecessors.

The ideological formation of modernisation theory rests, therefore, upon a particular intimate sequence of oppositions.[4] The fundamental distinction between 'modernity' and 'tradition' gives rise to a whole stream of others such as those between 'development' and 'underdevelopment', 'civilised' and 'primitive', 'democratic' and 'autocratic', 'first world' and 'third world' and so on. The familiar series of oppositions that define the modernisation approach provides a great deal of the substance of contemporary unionist thought. From the perspective of unionism the political divisions that exist within the island articulate two mutually exclusive understandings of the meaning of the good society. In the minds of unionist intellectuals, the Irish border represents nothing less than a boundary between a society that is modern/ progressive/civilised and another that is traditional/regressive/primitive.

The United Kingdom and the Irish Republic

The unionist community in Northern Ireland has often appeared prone to ideological indolence. For long periods of the recent conflict unionists proved either unwilling or unable to articulate their beliefs and ambitions beyond the confines of the laager. The acceleration of the Anglo-Irish process during the mid-1980s, however, rudely awakened many unionists from their philosophical slumber. The introduction of the Hillsborough Accord in the winter of 1985 led elements within the unionist fold to realise the importance of bringing their views and concerns to a rather wider audience than hitherto. In the emotional aftermath of the Anglo-Irish Agreement a stream of articles, pamphlets and ultimately books appeared seeking to state the unionist case. The scores of publications that were produced during the late eighties and early nineties often advanced arguments that could have been drawn from various earlier periods in the development of Ulster unionism. An especially familiar feature of the work of the cadre of unionist intellectuals that emerged in the wake of the Hillsborough Accord was a systematic attempt to contrast the two states that exist on the archipelago.

In those writings that are designed to advance the cause of unionism the United Kingdom inevitably emerges as a veritable acme of modernity. A central article of faith among contemporary unionist intellectuals is an insistence that the United Kingdom does not represent a single homogeneous community of descent. The influential unionist thinker Arthur Aughey[5] has consistently and vigorously contested that there is no British nation, only the British state. The status of the United Kingdom as a multicultural society ensures that public institutions are unable to garner legitimacy through appeals to particularistic identities such as ethnicity, religion or race.[6] In order to engage the allegiance of all of its diverse peoples, the British state must acknowledge those universal principles that find expression through the ideal of citizenship and the rule of law. Accordingly, the United Kingdom has assiduously assembled an extensive framework of legal protection that both underwrites the liberties of the individual and establishes an environment in which a diversity of ethnic and religious expression can flourish.[7]

In the minds of unionist intellectuals, therefore, the United Kingdom represents a political association that embraces and nurtures the cherished modern ideals of liberalism and pluralism. British citizens are entitled and enabled both to express their own cultural identities and to experience those of others. The unionist perspective considers the cultural life of the United Kingdom to be not only diverse but genuinely great. In the writings of numerous unionist thinkers, the British state is portrayed as the site of one of the foremost civilisations that humanity has produced. The literary critic John Wilson Foster,[8] for instance, has likened the Union to a 'causeway' that allows the individual access to the finest artistic and intellectual traditions.

The proponents of unionism insist that the rich and diverse indigenous cultural life of the United Kingdom has not encouraged those forms of introversion that foster chauvinism. In recent unionist texts the British are portrayed as a singularly cosmopolitan people. The distinctive writings of Arthur Green[9] have frequently rehearsed the view that modern technological innovations have facilitated forms of social communication that increasingly transcend regional and national boundaries. According to Green, the United Kingdom represents one of the principal gateways to the transnational cultural community presently taking shape. The pivotal role that Britons are considered to play in the exchanges of the 'global village' is held to find reflection in the status of English as the dominant mode of communication in various fields of science and the arts. It would seem that for Arthur Green, therefore, to be a British citizen is to be a resident of one of the planet's cultural superpowers.

The unionist perspective considers that the cultural vitality of the United Kingdom finds echoes in the economic life of the state. The current band of unionist intellectuals has consistently declared that the Union binds the people of Northern Ireland to one of the world's most developed economies. The material wealth of the United Kingdom has allowed the construction of a welfare state assumed to be the envy of other countries. Unionists are keen to point out that the articulation of welfarist principles through the agencies of the British state has conferred particular advantage upon the residents of the Six Counties. The anxiety of central government to redistribute income throughout the regions is assumed to have prompted the metropolis to provide increasingly substantial financial transfers to the province over the past quarter of a century.[10] At present the British exchequer subsidises the Northern Irish economy to the tune of around £4 billion per annum. The magnitude of the annual 'subvention' from Westminster is invariably cited by unionists as irrefutable evidence that citizenship of the United Kingdom represents materially the most advantageous constitutional status available to the people of the province.[11]

The writings of unionist intellectuals, therefore, tender an entirely favourable understanding of the United Kingdom. The representation that unionists provide of the other state that exists on these islands turns out, of course, to be rather less flattering. Ulster unionists argue that the evolution of the Irish Republic – and its predecessor, the Irish Free State – has infringed those noble principles of liberalism and pluralism to which they proclaim devotion. The architects of southern Irish society are considered to have assumed that there exists within the 26 Counties one 'people' united in their commitment to a common ethno-religious heritage.[12] For northern unionists, the sectarian nature of the Irish Republic has assumed numerous forms. The Roman Catholic church has traditionally exercised an authoritarian and thoroughly baleful influence within southern Irish society. Clerical figures have routinely intervened in the political life of the 26 Counties and controlled the provision of essential public services, like health and education, that are properly the preserve of the state. Furthermore, the legal and normative codes that operate within the Irish Republic draw heavily upon the doctrine of Catholicism. The constitutional ban on divorce that lasted for almost sixty years has often been cited by unionists as damning evidence of the moral authoritarianism that pervades life south of the border.

The ideological formation of unionism contests that the narrow sectarianism that blights the Republic of Ireland has oppressed and alienated various elements within southern society. The moral orthodoxy that has reigned within the 26 Counties has allowed little room for freedom of expression. Those individuals who have refused to subscribe to the tenets of conservative Catholicism have invariably been shunted to the margins of political and cultural life.[13] The stifling moral authoritarianism that shrouds the Irish Republic further discriminates against those social collectivities that exhibit cultural traits different to those of the hegemonic ethno-religious tradition. The unionist reading of history promotes the belief that Protestants living in the 26 Counties have fared badly since the introduction of partition.[14] The demographic decline of the southern minority provides many Ulster unionists with compelling evidence of the cultural intolerance of the Irish Republic. As Arthur Aughey[15] has observed, the apparent plight of the Protestant community within the 26 Counties remains indelibly inscribed in the 'folk memory' of their co-religionists living north of the border.

In the unionist mind, the social, order that has emerged within the Irish Republic has been fashioned in the image of a nation assumed to be not only wholly Catholic but exclusively Gaelic as well. The course that the 26 Counties have followed since partition has been that of cultural autarky. Proximity to the United Kingdom has continually offered the citizens of the Irish Republic the opportunity to inhabit an intellectual and artistic environment that transcends the merely local. The counsel of national vanity, however, has ensured the triumph of cultural introspection within the 26 Counties. Ulster unionists contend that the southern Irish have invariably chosen to move within the profoundly constricted intellectual orbit of 'small town hibernianism'. The essential parochialism of the Irish Republic has, Arthur Green[16] argues, ensured that public life south of the border has assumed the form of a relentless 'gaelic cultural tyranny'.

The unionist perspective insists, therefore, that the institutions of state established within the 26 Counties enshrine the exclusive interests of the principal ethno-religious tradition on the island. For the Ulster unionist, the quintessential particularism of the Irish Republic finds confirmation in the specific manner in which Dublin has sought to intervene in the affairs of Northern Ireland. According to Arthur Aughey[17] the conduct of the Irish government throughout the recent conflict has been guided by the belief that it holds 'an abiding responsibility for its people who happen to be under the rule of a foreign power'. Those administrations formed in Dublin during the troubles have, however, been faced with two rather different – and, indeed, ultimately contradictory – interpretations of the identity of the Irish 'people'. The first definition assumes that everyone living within the Six Counties, regardless of political or ethno-religious affiliation, belongs to the imagined community of the Irish nation. The entire population of the province, Catholic and Protestant alike, is therefore the legitimate concern of the Irish government. The second definition that has gained currency claims that only Northern Irish Catholics are genuinely members of the national community. The obligations of the southern Irish state, therefore, extend solely to the nationalist minority that resides within the province.

Arthur Aughey notes that it is the latter – essentially exclusive and sectarian – definition of peoplehood that has proved most persuasive to the southern Irish political establishment. From the outset of the Anglo-Irish process in the early 1980s the Dublin government has sought to establish itself as the guarantor of the rights and interests solely of those Catholics living in the Six Counties. This particular role was of course formalised with the signing of the Anglo-Irish Agreement in November 1985. For Arthur Aughey,[18] the terms of the Hillsborough Accord merely served to confirm the status of the Irish Republic as a sectarian state:

> The significance of the Anglo-Irish Agreement lies in its confirmation that Irish nationalism is nothing other than the political expression of catholicism with the prime minister of the Republic cast in the role of political pontiff to the Ulster flock and the foreign minister as his nuncio.

The political settlement finalised at Stormont on Good Friday 1998 heralds the dissolution of the Anglo-Irish Agreement so reviled within the unionist community. The Hillsborough Accord is to be replaced, however, with alternative arrangements between the two sovereign governments. The role that the new British-Irish Agreement will afford to the Republic of Ireland will remain that of representing the concerns of northern nationalists. The dramatic political developments that have overtaken the province in recent times are unlikely, therefore, to disarm the seasoned unionist criticism that the participation of Dublin in the Anglo-Irish Process reflects an ambition to advance particular sectarian interests.

Ulster unionists have conventionally held to the view that the backwardness they believe defines the Republic of Ireland finds especially vivid illustration within the realm of the economic. As Paul Bew and Henry Patterson[19] have observed, the ideological formation of unionism has from its inception centred upon a particular understanding of the scale and origins of 'Ireland's uneven development'. Unionist intellectuals and others have perennially sought to draw a 'contrast between bustling progressive industrial Ulster and "backward", "stagnant", peasant southern Ireland'. In seeking to capture the purported economic retardation of the Irish Republic unionists have inevitably drawn upon one of the fundamental artefacts and emblems of modernity – that of the road. The unionist perspective has traditionally contested that the essential economic fragility of southern Ireland has been mercilessly exposed by the poverty of the infrastructure within the 26 Counties. Unionists who travel to the Irish Republic often feel moved to comment that crossing the border involves a noticeable deterioration in the quality of the roads.

The apparent unionist preoccupation with the state of the island's highways is clearly revealed in an election poster drawn from the period in which Basil Brooke held the position of Northern Irish Prime Minister (1943–63) which features on the cover of Dennis Kennedy's book *The Widening Gulf.*[20] The illustration in question sets out the constitutional alternatives available to the people of the Six Counties. The viewer is located at a crossroads and presented with a signpost pointing in opposite directions. The path south towards a united Ireland is inevitably portrayed as leading to economic ruin. An evidently dejected Eamonn De Valera is depicted slumped at the side of a road that is unmarked and poorly maintained. The alternative route available appears altogether more attractive. The path that enables Northern Ireland to remain within the United Kingdom is considered to offer to the people of the province the prospect of sustained material prosperity. A distinctly dapper Basil Brooke is shown ushering prospective voters along a road northwards that is impeccably lined and bounded.

The significance that the road has traditionally had within the figurative system of Ulster unionism would appear to have persisted into the present day. In the spring of 1998 the coterie of unionist intellectuals that operates under the *nom de guerre* of *The Cadogan Group* published a collection of quite disparate readings of those recent political developments that culminated in the formulation of the Good Friday Agreement. One of the essays that appears in *Rough Trade*[21] offers the criticism that the direction that the Anglo-Irish process has taken over the last few years has primarily reflected the interests and aspirations of northern nationalists. Interestingly, the anonymous author chooses to characterise the drift towards a united Ireland supposedly currently afoot as a movement along an 'unapproved road'.

Ulster Unionism and Irish Nationalism

From the ideological vantage-point of Ulster unionism, therefore, the Irish border marks the frontier between two rather different forms of social order. In the myriad writings of unionist intellectuals the United Kingdom emerges as the prototype of the good society. The Republic of Ireland, in contrast, is portrayed as profoundly dystopian. The divergent representations that unionists provide of the British and Irish states respectively clearly inform their understanding of the nature of the two principal ideological traditions that coexist uneasily within the island.

Ulster unionists would seem to regard themselves as the bearers of a distinctly noble philosophical creed. Sympathetic intellectuals have argued with growing frequency over recent years that the ideological impulses that guide unionism are not those that arise out of exclusive substantive identities. The constitutional preferences of the Ulster unionist are informed not by a desire to be close to those who share the same cultural traits, but rather by an ambition to live in an ontologically diverse society that cherishes the liberties of the individual.[22] The appropriate concept through which to understand the unionist mind, therefore, is the universal ideal of citizenship rather than the exclusive notion of nationalism.[23]

In the eyes of its adherents, the unionist tradition further articulates a longing for cultural and intellectual breadth. The political allegiances of the unionist are considered to reflect an ambition to move within a figurative community that promises to enrich both the mind and the spirit in a manner that the merely local simply cannot. British citizenship bestows upon the individual the artistic and scientific wealth of one of the wellsprings of human civilisation. An insatiable appetite for cultural and intellectual enrichment ensures that the unionist possesses a field of vision that extends far beyond the narrow ground of the Six Counties. In the words of John Wilson Foster,[24] the force that animates Ulster unionism is that of a 'centrifugal energy'.

Ulster unionists consider themselves to be above all else the heirs of a version of reason that has held sway since the Enlightenment. The spring of 1995 saw the publication of one of the fullest expositions of the unionist perspective to have emerged thus far. Perhaps the dominant theme that embroiders the diverse essays that appear between the covers of *The Idea of the Union* is that the arguments that unionists advance are eminently rational.[25] Many contributors to the collection assert that the ideological tradition of unionism speaks not to emotion but rather to reason. The political outlook of the unionist is held to reflect the rational calculation, *inter alia*, of the respective economic benefits of the various constitutional alternatives that are available. In part unionists wish to continue to live within the United Kingdom because British citizenship offers optimal standards of living. The ideological disposition of unionism would therefore appear to accommodate that instrumental variant of reason that Max Weber[26] characterised as 'zweckrational'.

In their writings, unionist intellectuals portray the ideological programme to which they lend their name as admirably liberal and rational; but the understanding of Irish nationalism that unionists advance inevitably turns out to be rather less flattering. The unionist perspective suggests that over the past couple of centuries the peoples of these islands have been afforded the opportunity to live in a state – that of the

United Kingdom – that is singularly pluralist and prosperous. Irish nationalists, however, have chosen to chart an alternative course. As a result, most of the people of Ireland either live or aspire to live beyond the environs of the Union. The political direction that Irish nationalism has pursued simply perplexes unionists. From the viewpoint of unionism, in following the path of independence nationalists have decided to belong to a state that has inevitably transpired to be both politically and economically retarded. The ideological formation of Irish nationalism exists, therefore, beyond the pale of the rational.[27] Indeed, within the minds of Ulster unionists the actual existence of the Republic of Ireland proves emblematic of the triumph of emotion over reason.[28]

The interpretations advanced by contemporary unionist thinkers denounce Irish nationalism as an essentially irrational version of idealism.[29] In seeking to characterise the wilfully romantic nature of nationalism, unionists inevitably draw upon a familiar metaphor common to zones of colonial engagement. Unionist intellectuals and others are wont to liken Irish nationalists to children. The propensity of unionists to 'infantilise' the nationalist tradition was dramatically revealed in a controversial pamphlet written by the academic economists Esmond Birnie and Paddy Roche. In choosing to entitle their essay *An Economics Lesson For Irish Nationalists and Republicans* (1985), Birnie and Roche clearly cast those with whom unionists share the island in the role of errant schoolchildren. The strategy of 'infantilisation' that unionists have adopted reveals an ambition to establish moral and ideological authority over Irish nationalism. While children are frequently cherished within society, they are at the same time denied those essential rights that are the entitlement of the bona fide citizen. Considered to lack the maturity that enables responsible conduct, most of the decisions that affect the lives of the young are, of course, taken by individuals other than themselves. The role that unionist intellectuals seek to appropriate is the ideological equivalent of that of the parent. The view among unionists would seem to be that nationalism lacks those powers of reason that promote responsible political judgement. One of the tasks of the unionist intellectual, therefore, is to offer Irish nationalists ideological salvation.[30] Only the patient, rational counsel of Ulster unionism holds the promise that nationalists can ultimately be saved from themselves.[31]

The image of the child that appears within contemporary unionist discourse encodes perhaps not only condescension but violence as well. Children are often considered immune to the power of rational persuasion. The insouciance that the young seem to exhibit towards reason ensures that their lives are subjected to multiple and often unaccountable forms of authority. The sanctions that are employed to regulate the behaviour of children are sometimes, of course, physical. Regarded against this particular backdrop, the infantilisation of Irish nationalism begins to suggest an inclination towards violence among unionist intellectuals. The belief that nationalists are unwilling or unable to listen to reason has at times encouraged even the most liberal unionists to consider the necessity of rather cruder forms of persuasion. While unionists have in the main opposed the unofficial violence of loyalist paramilitarism they have found themselves able to justify the draconian excesses of the British state.[32] The questionable maxim that to spare the rod is to run the risk of spoiling the child would appear to be one that exercises a resonance within the unionist mind.[33]

Members of the unionist community frequently dismiss nationalism as the ideological creed of the helplessly romantic.[34] Irish nationalists are regularly perceived to be betrothed to notions as fanciful as those that periodically flit through the minds of children. The alleged indifference of nationalism to reason is also considered to assume other rather more unsavoury forms. Ulster unionists regard the nationalist aspiration to live outside the United Kingdom as mere folly. The ambition of nationalists to ensure that unionists join them as citizens of an independent Irish state, however, is believed to be purely malicious. From the standpoint of unionism, the proclivity of nationalism towards malice assumes various guises.[35] Unionists are prone to regard their own attempts to win nationalists to the ideal of the Union as exercises in moral and civic responsibility. The parallel efforts of Irish nationalism to attract converts, however, are roundly denounced as invasive and aggressive.[36] The discursive practices of nationalist intellectuals are invariably regarded as the veiled entrapments of accomplished sophists. The persistent endeavours of public figures like John Hume to persuade unionists of the veracity of the nationalist cause are experienced as purposeful 'harassment'.[37]

For unionists, the essential malevolence of Irish nationalism is institutionalised within the southern state. The sense of besiegement that unionists famously emanate stems largely from the conviction that Dublin harbours improper designs upon the region of the United Kingdom in which they choose to reside. The judgement of unionism has conventionally been that the Republic of Ireland constitutes a state driven by an irrational compulsion to 'conquer and subdue its neighbour'.[38] Until very recently, of course, the ambition to assimilate the Six Counties was enshrined within the principal source of legal authority that exists within the 26 Counties. Over the last sixty years unionists have consistently cited the second and third articles of the 1937 Constitution as evidence of the irredentism that corrupts the southern Irish state.[39] In the minds of unionists, the constitutional claim to jurisdiction over Northern Ireland has served to underline the belief that nationalists are prepared, given the opportunity, to ride roughshod over their aspirations and interests. More importantly still, unionism tends to the view that the existence of Articles 2 and 3 prompted and sustained the horrific violence that has consumed the Six Counties over the last three decades.

Ulster unionists have frequently contested that the provisions of the Irish Constitution have offered encouragement and succour to the campaign of republican insurgence that has unfolded within Northern Ireland since the late 1960s.[40] In seeking to terminate British jurisdiction over the Six Counties through force of arms, the present generation of republicans, unionists insist, has merely acted out the constitutional imperatives of the southern Irish state. Among the unionist community there exists an understanding that republican violence represents a considered strategy intended to prosecute certain political objectives. The actions of the Provisional IRA and their fellow travellers are also frequently interpreted, of course, as the expressions of an insatiable bloodlust.[41] Some unionists have asserted that there exists within the nationalist community a 'cult of violence' that will survive even the most equitable political settlement.[42] The unionist conviction that at the heart of Irish nationalism there lies a fundamental pathology was captured in an illustration curiously chosen to appear on the cover of a essay written by Arthur Aughey.[43] The cartoon under consideration seeks to represent the relationship of nationalism to unionism as one of irrational violence. A demonic elfin figure wearing hobnail boots and a peaked cap embroidered with a telling shamrock is shown attempting to trample a dove in the process of taking flight and clutching in its beak the Union flag.

New Times

The wave of unionist literature that appeared in the initial decade after the Hillsborough Accord, therefore, offered an entirely familiar understanding of the nature of southern Irish society. The relentlessly dystopian vision of the Republic of Ireland that unionist intellectuals advanced during the period frequently strained the credulity of the dispassionate viewer/reader/listener. There were none the less some elements of the unionist reading that possessed at least a kernel of truth. Certainly, were one to go back to the late 1980s, the contention that the Republic of Ireland represents an economic casualty would appear reasonably persuasive. The limited credibility that traditional unionist perceptions of the 26 Counties may have had at that stage, however, has been all but eroded by the sequence of developments that has unfolded since.

Over the last decade the Republic of Ireland has undergone a remarkable process of social change. The 26 Counties have come increasingly to exhibit the essential hallmarks of a secular and liberal society. The spate of scandals concerning the clerical abuse of children that has broken over recent years has both heralded and accelerated the decline of the power of the Catholic church. As the moral authority of organised religion has waned, individuals have begun to explore more fully alternative ways of being in the world. The current of pluralism that flows through contemporary southern Irish society has come to be acknowledged by the institutions of state. In the last few years the Irish government has introduced a range of social legislation that promises to underwrite certain indispensable personal freedoms. Homosexuality has been legalised, contraceptives have become more freely available and the constitutional ban on divorce has been lifted. As the century turns, it has become difficult to name a single substantial civil liberty that the citizens of the United Kingdom enjoy that is denied to their counterparts in the Republic of Ireland.

The shifts that have occurred within the political culture of the Irish Republic have, significantly, entailed changes in attitudes towards the 'national question'. The nineties would seem to have marked a dilution of certain versions of nationalist feeling within the 26 Counties. It would be premature, of course, to pronounce the demise of orthodox nationalism within the Republic of Ireland. The ideal of Irish unification continues to exercise enormous appeal south of the border. None the less, there have been signs over recent years that the citizens of the Irish Republic have come to adopt a rather less dogmatic approach towards Northern Ireland than was often the case hitherto. The growing pragmatism of people living in the 26 Counties has found expression in a distinct enthusiasm for the 'peace process' that has gathered pace over the last decade.

On 22 May 1998 the electorate of the Irish Republic voted overwhelmingly in support of political arrangements that had been agreed at Stormont six weeks earlier. The unequivocal endorsement offered to the Belfast Agreement signals a readiness among the people of southern

Ireland to critically re-evaluate and indeed discard certain essential tenets of nationalist orthodoxy. The terms of the political settlement finalised on Good Friday 1998 envisage fundamental revision of the controversial second and third articles of the Irish constitution. The proposals which the Irish government subsequently advanced for public approval advocated that the existing constitutional claim that each of the 32 Counties belongs to the same national territory should be replaced with a statement that all of the peoples who live on the island share a common identity. The referendum on the Good Friday Agreement, therefore, offered to the southern Irish electorate two rather different interpretations of 'the nation'. In choosing to vote overwhelmingly 'yes', the residents of the 26 Counties would appear to have decided to discard a traditional version of nationalism that demands the integration of land for another, more contemporary form, that privileges the assimilation of peoples.

The evolution of the peace process has marked a further, related shift within the discourse of contemporary southern Irish nationalism. The provisions of the Belfast Agreement insist that the constitutional status of Northern Ireland will be decided solely by the people who happen to live there. Given the prevailing balance of ethno-political forces within the Six Counties, it is likely, of course, that the province will remain a region of the United Kingdom for quite some time to come. The emphatic endorsement that the Good Friday Agreement received south of the border would seem, therefore, to represent an acknowledgement that a united Ireland exists beyond the realm of the possible at least in the foreseeable future. The outcome of the referendum would appear to indicate, in other words, that the residents of the 26 Counties are rather more concerned to end violence than to end partition.

The nineties have witnessed a burgeoning cultural vitality within the Irish Republic that acknowledges, in part, a growing willingness to look beyond the boundaries of the state. The residents of the 26 Counties are increasingly enthusiastic participants in a figurative community that bears the inscription of the complex process of globalisation. In recent years numerous southern Irish authors, filmmakers and popular musicians have secured international renown. Moreover, the everyday lives of people in the Republic of Ireland increasingly centre upon ideas and artifacts drawn from well beyond these islands. The enormous popularity of 'piped' television throughout the 26 Counties would seem to underscore the assertion that the southern Irish are increasingly citizens of the global society of the spectacle.

Perhaps the most significant developments that have overtaken contemporary southern Irish society are those that have taken place within the economic field. A decade ago the Republic of Ireland appeared arrested in an especially dependent form of underdevelopment. The citizens of the 26 Counties were burdened with proportionately greater public debt than those of any other state. The abiding frailty of the southern Irish economy, moreover, was indexed in the haemorrhage of mass emigration. The present decade, however, would seem to have recorded a dramatic revival of the economic fortunes of the 26 Counties. Over the last few years the Irish Republic has registered formal rates of economic growth that have clearly exceeded those of every other western European state. The seemingly phenomenal recent expansion of the southern Irish economy has, of course, inspired the formulation of the ubiquitous and increasingly tiresome metaphor of the 'Celtic Tiger'.[44]

Clinging to the Other

The direction that the Irish Republic has taken in the course of the last decade has undermined still further orthodox unionist constructions of the 26 Counties. The literature that has appeared over the last five or six years would suggest that the recent transformation of southern Irish society has drawn two rather different responses from unionist intellectuals. The first of these would seem to be the more prevalent. Those pamphlets and articles that have appeared in the latter half of the nineties indicate that there are elements within the unionist community that are currently in denial.[45] Unionist intellectuals and others often appear unwilling and unable to acknowledge the scale and significance of the changes that have occurred south of the border during the past decade. The anxiety of many unionists to cling to conventional readings of the Irish Republic has become especially apparent within contemporary economic debate.

The recent apparent revival of the southern Irish economy has inevitably offered encouragement to the nationalist cause. Nationalists have counselled that the advent of the 'Celtic Tiger' enhances further the prospect that a 32-County state would be financially viable. The contention that the economic conditions necessary for the unification of Ireland are currently materialising has, of course, invoked the ire of unionist intellectuals. Economists with unionist sympathies have begun to challenge vigorously the characterisation of the Irish Republic as the 'Celtic Tiger'.[46] In a trenchant and somewhat idiosyncratic pamphlet that appeared in 1997 the unionist academic and activist Esmond Birnie argued that the growth rates that have been declared within the 26 Counties over the last few years have been inflated by the Machiavellian practices of multinational corporations. The actual performance of the southern Irish economy, Birnie insists, lags considerably behind that suggested by the relevant official statistics. Rather than having undergone an 'economic miracle', the Irish Republic remains relatively under-developed and unable to keep the British citizens of Northern Ireland in the manner to which they have become accustomed. The material circumstances that would facilitate the unification of Ireland, therefore, still simply do not exist. The enterprise of Irish nationalism is 'bad politics' guided by 'dubious economics'.[47]

The interrogation of the 'Celtic Tiger' that Birnie proffers often makes a good deal of sense. Indeed, elements of his critique can be found in the work of other economic commentators who are overtly hostile to the unionist project.[48] The rational formalism of Birnie's prose cannot, however, conceal the particularism that informs his disposition. The purpose of a pamphlet such as *Without Profit or Prophets* is, of course, not merely to ascertain 'the truth' but also to advance specific ideological interests. It is difficult to imagine that if the United Kingdom were to register growth rates comparable to those that have recently become the norm in the Irish Republic a conservative like Esmond Birnie would subject the British economy to an equally radical critique.

The writings of unionist intellectuals further reveal an unwillingness to recognise the seismic shifts that have occurred within the cultural and political life of the 26 Counties over the last decade. In the minds of many unionists, the Republic of Ireland continues to represent an essentially exclusive and authoritarian society.[49] According to one member of the Cadogan Group,[50] the Gaelic Catholic orthodoxy that reigned after partition has been 'modified only slightly' in recent times. For many within the unionist community, the immutable nature of the Republic of Ireland finds especially insidious expression in the unflinching irredentism of the southern state. The seemingly substantial reformulation of nationalism that has taken place within the 26 Counties over the last few years is often dismissed by unionists as purely cosmetic.[51] The explicit acknowledgement of the principle of 'consent' by successive Dublin administrations, and the overwhelming support of the people of southern Ireland for the rewording of Articles 2 and 3 of the Constitution, are interpreted merely as astute strategic revisions. While the form of Irish republicanism may have altered, its substance remains unchanged. The ambition of the southern state to dominate and ultimately assimilate the Six Counties is unsated and, indeed, 'insatiable'.[52]

The marked unwillingness among unionist intellectuals to acknowledge the developments that have unfolded within southern Irish society over the previous generation clearly undermines their claim to be the custodians of an entirely dispassionate and rational ideological tradition. Advocates of the Union have often claimed that their political allegiances are the outcome purely of objective calculation of the relative merits of the various constitutional arrangements that are available. Unionist thinkers suggest that their opposition to the unification of Ireland simply reflects an aversion to living in a society that is sectarian and intolerant. The vision of the Irish Republic that has traditionally existed within the political imagination of Ulster unionism has always been somewhat tendentious. The representation of southern Ireland advanced by the present generation of unionist intellectuals, however, simply bears little resemblance to the realities of life today in the 26 Counties. The construction of the 'other' within contemporary unionism would seem, therefore, to be the reflex of epistemological procedures rather different to those that would be conventionally understood as the exercise of 'reason'. To have depicted the Republic of Ireland as an underdeveloped and authoritarian society two decades or even one decade ago would have had some credence. To rehearse the same argument today is merely to parade one's ignorance and prejudice for public perusal.

The second unionist response to the recent trajectory of southern Irish society reveals a rather greater openness of mind. Over the last few years some unionists have come to an understanding of the processes of revision at work south of the border. In an essay commissioned by the Forum for Peace and Reconciliation the leading unionist theorist Arthur Aughey delineates some of the liberal and secular currents that are presently redefining the 26 Counties.[53] Aughey observes that the progressive trends that may be discerned within contemporary southern Irish society are welcome in themselves. He moves on to contest that it would be naive, however, to expect that the liberal course that the 26 Counties have followed of late will have any real bearing upon the ideological disposition of the unionist community. The argument that Aughey advances suggests that unionists are opposed to the nationalist enterprise not necessarily because they consider the Irish Republic to be culturally odious but rather because they regard it as culturally *different*. The island of Ireland simply does not constitute the site of the principal community to which members of the unionist tradition imagine themselves to belong. The particular path of development that the Irish Republic may pursue in the years to come will inevitably be unable, therefore, to convince unionists that their future lies outside the Union. Even the emergence within the 26 Counties of a genuinely pluralist social formation that offered optimal civil liberties would be insufficient to persuade the unionist community to regard a united Ireland as 'home'.

The essay that Arthur Aughey contributed to *Building Trust in Ireland* perhaps reveals an important change of direction among the present generation of unionist intellectuals. Proponents of the unionist cause, as we have seen, have frequently argued that their constitutional preferences are simply an expression of rational calculation of interest. The unionist ambition to remain within the United Kingdom has been portrayed as being motivated primarily by a desire to live in a state that offers both enviable material prosperity and generous personal freedom. In the more recent writings of aligned intellectuals, however, we encounter an altogether less instrumental reading of the unionist mind. Those polemics that have appeared over the last five or six years have begun to advance an understanding of the unionist disposition as not only cerebral but, significantly, emotional also. The likes of Arthur Aughey and John Wilson Foster have persisted with the view that unionism represents a pristine and dispassionate philosophical enterprise that orbits around the sacred and ultimately abstract ideal of citizenship. The recent work of these prominent figures, however, has come to reveal an appreciation that unionists are also animated by those substantive identities that give rise to feelings of kinship. The ideological project of unionism is held to rest not only upon a conviction that Westminster constitutes the birthplace of democracy but also upon a belief that the history of the Six Counties merely represents a subtext of the broader narrative of the United Kingdom.[54] The constitutional affiliations of Ulster unionists are considered to articulate not only a sense that their fellow British citizens share an equally fervent devotion to the principles of liberal pluralism, but also a feeling that they share a common lineage with the peoples of England, Scotland and Wales. The inflection of contemporary unionist thought would appear, therefore, to be changing in subtle though significant ways. The most recent writings of certain sympathetic thinkers portray unionism less as an esoteric philosophical doctrine than a grounded way of being in the world. It would seem, in other words, that unionist intellectuals are finally coming to terms with their own real status as the bearers of a version of British nationalism.[55]

The shifts that have occurred recently within unionist discourse may be further read as a strategic response to the direction that southern Irish nationalism has taken over the last fifteen years. The increasingly voluminous writings of unionist intellectuals evidently represent an attempt to secure ideological hegemony. The particular constructions that certain academics have advanced have clearly marked an ambition to establish unionism in a position of moral authority that would brook no challenge from Irish nationalism. Ironically, however, the counsel of the present generation of unionist intellectuals would often seem to have had precisely the opposite impact upon the nationalist tradition. Many within the nationalist fold have, of course, dismissed as mere cant the notion that unionism represents an abstract philosophical programme that centres upon the ideal of citizenship. Others would seem, however, to have taken rather more seriously the musings of thinkers committed to the unionist cause.

Elements within the 26 Counties would appear to have believed for some time that the commitment of unionists to partition reflects an anxiety that the Republic of Ireland offers relatively few rights to the individual citizen. The creation of a unitary state on the island would therefore require the removal of those aspects of life south of the border that are offensive to the unionist conscience. This reformist zeal, of course, provided the inspiration for the ill-starred 'constitutional crusade' of the 1980s. In the last decade, the ambition to render the Irish Republic more amenable to the unionist tradition has provided one of the multiple strands of the 'peace process'. The recent endeavours of southern Irish nationalism to court the other principal ideological tradition on the island have encouraged unionism to change tack somewhat. Intellectuals and others have insisted that the revisions that are unfolding within the 26 Counties are admirable, but have no influence upon the political allegiance or ontological state of the unionist community. Unionists will remain opposed to a united Ireland – even a liberal pluralist one – precisely because it is a place that does not accord with their sense of historical or cultural self.[56] Regardless of the renovations that are carried out, the Irish Republic remains somewhere that the Ulster unionist will never truly regard as 'home'.

Conclusion

The constructions of the Republic of Ireland that unionists provide mercilessly expose the weakness of the ideological enterprise which they seek to advance. Intellectuals and others within the unionist community have consistently claimed that their aversion to the 26 Counties has arisen out of a process of sober and reasonable reflection. The manner in which unionists have responded to the changes presently at work within southern Irish society, however, has revealed these claims to be distinctly threadbare. The inability of most unionist thinkers to come to terms with the liberal course that the Irish Republic has charted over the last generation suggests that they are animated by concerns that exist beyond the realm of pure reason. The shortcomings which it exhibits frequently moves commentators to regard unionism as an antediluvian ideological formation. An alternative reading, however, suggests itself. Those who seek to promote the unionist cause frequently employ a discourse that emphasises the rational and universal in order to advance interests that are thoroughly unreasonable and particular. In so doing, unionists declare themselves the bearers of an ideological programme that is genuinely 'modern'.

Notes

1 The characterisation of the Republic of Ireland as 'a miserable failure of a state' appeared in the fourth edition of *The Equal Citizen*, published in February 1986. The journal was produced by the Campaign for Equal Citizenship (CEC), whose demand that the British political parties should organise in Northern Ireland proved persuasive to many unionists in the aftermath of the Anglo-Irish Agreement. At the time of the edition cited the CEC was controlled by the Stalinist splinter-group, the British & Irish Communist Organisation (B & ICO).

2 G. McLennan, 'Fin de Sociologie? The Dilemmas of Multidimensional Social Theory', *New Left Review*, 230 (July/August 1998), pp. 58–90, p. 77.

3 Luke Gibbons, 'Coming Out of Hibernation? The Myth of Modernisation in Irish Culture', in *Transformations in Irish Culture* (Cork: Cork University Press, 1996), pp. 82–94.

4 A. So, *Social Change and Development: Modernisation, Dependency and World System Theories* (London: Sage, 1990), pp. 17–59.

5 Arthur Aughey, 'Political Progress: Substance and Shadow', *The Equal Citizen* 2(2) (1988), pp. 3–5; Arthur Aughey, *Under Siege: Ulster Unionism and the Anglo-Irish Agreement*, (Belfast: Blackstaff, 1989); Arthur Aughey, 'The Idea of the Union', in J. W. Foster (ed.), *The Idea of the Union: Statements and Critiques In Favour of the Union of Great Britain and Northern Ireland* (Vancouver: Belcouver, 1995), pp. 8–19.

6 B. Clifford, *Parliamentary Sovereignty and Northern Ireland: A Review of the Party System in the British Constitution With Relation to the Anglo-Irish Agreement* (Belfast: Athol Books, 1985); B. Clifford, *Parliamentary Despotism: John Hume's Aspiration*, (Belfast: Athol Books, 1986).

7 Arthur Aughey, 'Ethnic Mending', pp. 9–11 in D. Smyth (ed.), *Conflict and Community*, Supplement to *Fortnight* 311 November, 1992; J. W. Foster, 'Why I Am A Unionist', in Foster (ed.), *The Idea of the Union*, pp. 59–64, p. 59.

8 J. W. Foster, 'The Task For Unionists', in Foster (ed.), *The Idea of the Union*, pp. 69–78, p. 71.

9 Arthur Green, 'Unionist Horizons', *Irish Review*, 4 (Spring 1988), pp. 27–32; 'Conservatism Meets "Cultural Traditions"', *Fortnight*, 280 January 1990; 'The British Isles: A Cliché For Rediscovery', in Foster (ed.), *The Idea of the Union*, pp. 20–27.

10 G. Gudgin, 'The Economics of the Union', in Foster (ed.), *The Idea of the Union*, pp. 75–89.

11 E. Birnie, 'Economic Consequences of the Peace', in Foster (ed.), *The Idea of the Union*, pp. 107–20; The Cadogan Group, *Northern Limits: Boundaries of the Attainable in Northern Ireland Politics* (Belfast, 1992).

12 Robert McCartney, *Liberty and Authority in Ireland* (Derry: Field Day, 1985).

13 Robert McCartney, 'Sovereignty and Seduction', in Foster (ed.), *The Idea of the Union*, pp. 91–2.

14 Richard English, 'The Unionists', in Foster (ed.), *The Idea of the Union*, p. 44.

15 Arthur Aughey, 'Obstacles to Reconciliation in the South', in *Building Trust in Ireland: Studies Commissioned by the Forum for Peace and Reconciliation* (Dublin, 1996), pp. 1–52, p. 23.

16 Green, 'The British Isles: A Cliché for Rediscovering', in Foster (ed.), *The Idea of the Union*, pp. 24–6.

17 Aughey, *Under Siege*, p. 42.

18 Aughey, *Under Siege*, p. 43.

19 Paul Bew and Henry Patterson, *The British State and the Ulster Crisis: From Wilson to Thatcher* (London: Verso, 1985), p. 3.

20 Dennis Kennedy, *The Widening Gulf: Northern Attitudes to the Independent Irish State 1919–49* (Belfast: Blackstaff, 1988).

21 The Cadogan Group, *Rough Trade: Negotiating a Northern Ireland Settlement* (Belfast, 1998).

22 Robert McCartney, *We Have a Vision* (Belfast: Campaign for Equal Citizenship, 1986); *What Must Be Done: A Programme for Normalising Politics in Northern Ireland* (Belfast: Athol Books, 1986); Aughey, *Under Siege*; 'Unionism and Self-Determination', in Roche and Barton (eds.), *The Northern Ireland Question*.

23 N. Porter, *Rethinking Unionism: An Alternative Vision for Northern Ireland*, (Belfast: Blackstaff., 1996); P. Roche, 1995, 'Northern Ireland and Irish Nationalism', in Foster (ed.), *The Idea of the Union*, pp. 128–34.

24 Foster, 'Why I am a Unionist', in Foster (ed.), *The Idea of the Union*, p. 60.

25 J. W. Foster, 'Introduction', in Foster (ed.), *The Idea of the Union*, pp. 4–7.

26 Max Weber, *Economy and Society* (New York: Bedminster, 1968).

27 E. Birnie, *Without Profit or Prophets: A Response to Businessmen and Bishops* (Belfast: Ulster Review Publications, 1997), p. 7; The Cadogan Group, *Northern Limits*, p. 1; E. Birnie and P. Roche, 'Irish Nationalism and Government Policy: Appeasing the Insatiable', *Times Change* (Summer/Autumn 1997), pp. 10–12.

28 English, 'Unionism and Nationalism', in Foster (ed.), *The Idea of the Union*, p. 135.

29 The Cadogan Group, *Rough Trade*, p. 21.

30 Foster, 'The Task for Unionists', in Foster (ed.), *The Idea of the Union*, p. 73.

31 J. W. Foster, 'Strains in Irish Intellectual Life', in L. O'Dowd (ed.), *On Intellectuals and Intellectual Life in Ireland: International, Comparative and Historical*

Contexts (Belfast/Dublin: Institute of Irish Studies/Royal Irish Academy, 1996), pp. 71–97, p. 96.

32 John McGarry and Brendan O'Leary, *Explaining Northern Ireland: Broken Images* (London: Blackwell, 1995), pp. 122–5.

33 P. Roche and E. Birnie, *An Economics Lesson for Irish Nationalists and Republicans* (Belfast: Ulster Unionist Information Institute, 1995), p. 12.

34 A. Aughey, 'The Idea of the Union', in Foster (ed.), *The Idea of the Union*, pp. 8–19; G. Gudgin, 'The Economics of the Union', in Foster (ed.), *The Idea of the Union*, pp. 77–9, 87–8.

35 Robert McCartney, *The McCartney Report on Consent* (Belfast, 1997), p. 18.

36 Robert McCartney, 'Priests, Politics and Pluralism', in Foster (ed.), *The Idea of the Union*, p. 98.

37 Foster, 'Why I am A Unionist', in Foster (ed.), *The Idea of The Union*, p. 63.

38 *The Equal Citizen*, 4 (1986), p. 4.

39 McGarry and O'Leary, *Explaining Northern Ireland*, pp. 95–6.

40 McCartney, *The McCartney Report on Consent*, p. 16.

41 The Cadogan Group, *Decommissioning: A Discussion Paper* (Belfast, 1996).

42 The Cadogan Group, *Rough Trade*, p. 30.

43 Arthur Aughey, *Irish Kulturkampf* (Belfast: Ulster Young Unionist Council, 1995).

44 P. Sweeney, *The Celtic Tiger: Ireland's Economic Miracle Explained* (Dublin: Oak Tree, 1998).

45 Porter, *Rethinking Unionism*, pp. 34–41.

46 *The McCartney Report on the Framework Documents*, p. 5; Robert McCartney, *The McCartney Report on Consent*, p. 18.

47 Birnie, *Without Profit or Prophets*, p. v.

48 D. O'Hearn , 'The Celtic Tiger: The Role of the Multinationals', in E. Crowley and J. MacLaughlin (eds.), *Under the Belly of the Tiger: Class, Race, Identity and Culture in the Global Ireland* (Dublin: Irish Reporter, 1997), pp. 21–39; *Inside the Celtic Tiger: The Irish Economy and the Asian Model* (London: Pluto, 1998).

49 Foster, 'The Task for Unionists', in Foster (ed.), *The Idea of the Union*, p. 62.

50 The Cadogan Group, *Rough Trade*, p. 38.

51 D. Kennedy, 'A Peace Built on Rewriting History', *The Irish Times*, 5 Oct. 1988, p. 14.

52 E. Birnie and P. Roche, 'Irish Nationalism and Government Policy: Appeasing the Insatiable', *Times Change* (Summer/Autumn 1997), pp. 10–12.

53 Arthur Augley, 'Obstacles to Reconstruction in the South', pp. 15, 29.

54 Foster, ' The Task for Unionists', in Foster (ed.), *The Idea of the Union*, p. 64.

55 McGarry and O'Leary, *Explaining Northern Ireland*, pp. 92, 366.

56 J. Ruane and J. Todd, *The Dynamics of Conflict in Northern Ireland: Power, Conflict and Emancipation* (Cambridge: Cambridge University Press, 1996).

11

The Profession of History: The Public and the Past

Tony Canavan

'Our own history has been hard on lives young and old,' said Mary McAleese on the day of her inauguration as President of Ireland in November 1997. It was a particularly poignant remark not just because of its truthfulness but also because it highlights the close relationship between history and public life in Ireland and because the course of the election campaign, which ultimately saw her elected by the largest margin of victory since the office was established in 1937, raised many of the concerns regarding history as expressed in the debate over Revisionism. For Irish history – the writing and teaching of it – has had an interesting history since the foundation of the Irish Free State and more so since the outbreak of the Troubles in Northern Ireland in 1968. At times it has seemed that there was open hostility between the academy and the people over the interpretation of Ireland's past. In politics, the rhetoric of the parties often echoed the opposing views of Irish historians. What apparently began as an argument among academic historians became a public argument fought out in the media, the hustings and even the classroom. Revisionism, which claimed to be a discipline without emotionalism, aroused passions and became itself shorthand for a whole series of political assumptions and values, which were perceived to be opposed to traditional Irish nationalism and sympathetic to unionism. I want here to look at the debate over Irish history as it affected popular perceptions of the past through two key interfaces between the academy and the people: the curriculum and the media.

Revisionism may have achieved prominence in recent years, but its origins lie in the 1930s. Many historians were concerned at the direction the popular perception of history was taking in the decade after the Civil War. There seemed to be a developing cult of the gunman and glorification of political violence which they believed was antithetical to democracy, which in the 26 Counties did not seem so stable then as it does now. History in school and in popular publications portrayed a simplistic view characterised by the epic struggles of the Irish against the Invader with a pantheon of heroes and martyrs from Brain Boru to Patrick Pearse. The electoral success in 1927 of the 'slightly constitutional' republican party, Fianna Fáil, seemed to confirm these fears. A new alternative view of history emerged primarily

> with three young historians, all very able people at the time, Robin Dudley Edwards, T. W. Moody and David Quinn, being trained in the Institute of Historical Research in London. On their return to Ireland, they attempted to establish the practice of history here on the same basis. Part of this tradition was the notion of 'Revisionism;' that history up to that point had been going along a wrong track and the whole record needed to be re-written in a detached, objective way.[1]

That these historians saw it as their mission to convert the Irish people away from the nationalist version of history to the more scientific approach is evidenced in the setting up of the journal, *Irish Historical Studies*, which was intended to have a wide readership and to influence the research and writing of Irish history.

To the founders of the Free State, history in the classroom was seen as crucial in anchoring the new state and in fostering 'a sense of national identity, pride and self respect . . . by demonstrating that the Irish race had fulfilled a great mission in the advancement of civilisation'.[2] At both primary and secondary level Irish history with little or no reference to Britain was prescribed. The curriculum originated in a programme for teaching history instigated by the Irish National Teachers Organisation in 1920 and duly adopted by the first Free State government. Although at secondary level the history curriculum was more complex and did involve study of other European countries, the emphasis was still very much Irish-nationalist. The overall role of history in schools was seen as a key factor in promoting a national Irish culture which would be Gaelic (it was felt that the teaching of the history of Irish civilisation would lead to a revival of the language) and, as the Church had an all-pervasive role in the educational system, Catholic. With the coming of Fianna Fáil to power in 1932, espousing an even more entrenched attitude towards history, and its subsequent dominance of government until after the Second World War, the nationalist tone of history teaching was consolidated despite the emergence of the Revisionist school in the academy.

In this it reflected the majority consensus regarding Ireland's story as a nation. In the printed media, newspapers lined up behind whichever party they supported – the Press group supporting Fianna Fáil, Independent Newspapers Fine Gael – while popular publications, such as the not-to-be-underestimated Ireland's Own or the Capuchin Annual, endorsed the Gaelic Catholic Nationalist interpretation of the nation's history. Bearing this in mind, the post-war coalition government's formal declaration of an Irish Republic in 1949 can be viewed as bowing to popular sentiment while trying to outflank Fianna Fáil on the national question.

If the closeness of the War of Independence and the Civil War had added immediacy to historical argument at the popular level and in politics during the 1920s and 1930s, these were remote in the period after 1945, as economic and social problems seemed more pressing, and while talk of the 'Evils of Partition' or 'The Twin National Aspirations' featured in electoral rhetoric they had little concrete meaning in either the classroom or the media. Indeed, if Revisionism is to be defined as a less nationalist and more pro-British attitude, then it almost succeeded by default in the 1940s and 1950s. This period has been characterised as one in which the Republic was enveloped in a 'Paper Wall' that prevented any wider outlook and filtered foreign influences, while foreign news-gathering at Radio Éireann, the former editor of *The Irish Times*, Douglas Gageby, tells us, 'meant, for one thing, good shorthand for the taking down of BBC bulletins; and as there is no copyright in fact, Irish radio got away with two decades of piracy.'[3] This meant that the public's perception of the outside world was to a large degree a British one. Likewise in the classroom there was stagnation. If the Revisionist school was gaining ground in the universities, it had yet to impact on education at a national level. Changes in the curriculum in this period marked a drift away from earlier aspirations of nation-building towards, on the one hand, the religious, moral and cultural development of the child, and on the other the preparation of young people for the economic needs of the country;[4] but as yet the question of how history should be taught remained untouched.

Things might have continued thus had it not been for a number of significant events in the 1960s. The first of these was the celebration of the fiftieth anniversary of the 1916 Rising in 1966. With a Fianna Fáil government again in Leinster House and Eamon de Valera, the last surviving leader of the Rising, as President, there was confidence at an official public level in celebrating this event as the foundation of the modern state. The character of the celebrations throughout the country, including the North, and the reaction these provoked among Northern unionists – the UVF murdered two Catholics in Belfast – caused unease among those historians who were wary of nationalism. It was again feared that the cult of the gunman was coming to the fore and that a wrong interpretation of events was being promoted by the state. Such an attitude, however, was out of step with the popular mood. In his book, *Twentieth-Century Ireland: Nation and State*, Dermot Keogh comments that at the time of the 'fiftieth anniversary of the 1916 Rising simplification of the past by the official mind was thought necessary in order to rekindle a sense of lost patriotism'. Whatever misgivings there were about these celebrations were soon compounded by events in the North. The campaign by nationalists for civil rights, which began in 1968, had by 1969 resulted in widespread violence and gave rise to the re-emergence of the IRA as an armed organisation the following year.

Brendan Bradshaw, a prominent historian in the Revisionist debate, characterises the reaction of these historians thus:

> In the late '60s, a number of things exacerbated the mood of Revisionism, and its cynical approach to Irish history. First of all came the 50th anniversary celebration of the 1916 Rising. At that point, it hit the Irish intelligentsia how disillusioning the experience of political freedom had been. Added to the mood of disillusionment about what had been achieved was the more flourishing secular liberalism of the '60s which had the effect of melting the attachment to a sense of tradition. And then the final thing was the recrudescence of violence in the North. After the eulogistic and euphoric times of the late '60s and early '70s, a mood of shock set in as the IRA took up the cause of nationalism and you got these horrendous atrocities. Consequently there has been the feeling that the Irish had been fed a nationalist myth which has stoked the fires of militant nationalism and that the best antidote was an increasingly strident anti-nationalism. This feeling was expressed by a whole series of writers. You get it cautiously in the deep pessimism of F S L Lyons' last book, *Culture and Anarchy in Ireland*, and then represented much more stridently and unapologetically by a younger generation – Roy Foster, David Fitzpatrick, Ronan Fanning. They began to write in a very militant, aggressive, anti-traditional style.[5]

The violence which erupted in the North lasted over thirty years and claimed almost 3,500 lives. It had a profound influence on the Republic, affecting politics and the media as well as the writing and teaching of history. The generation of historians emerging at this time had two responses to the Troubles. The traditionalist attitude was that what was happening in the North was the culmination of an historical process and the proper reaction was not to blame nor seek to discredit the traditional view of history but rather to put the North in its proper historical context. The Revisionist response was to analyse what was happening in the North as the result of extremism fuelled by myths about the past. The Revisionists argued that a misrepresentation of history had created an atavistic hatred of all things British and promoted a cult of glorifying political violence. They said that not only was the popular myth of Ireland's heroic struggle for freedom incorrect, but that it was being perpetuated in the educational system. In particular the Catholic Church, especially the Christian Brothers, was blamed for engendering a Catholic nationalism which encouraged tacit support for the IRA South of the Border and recruited members for it North of the Border. As one historian has noted, in the early decades of the state only the Catholic Headteachers Association and the Christian Brothers were regularly consulted by the educational authorities.[6] Indeed, Séan Lemass, a Fianna Fáil Taoiseach, had reinforced this view when in 1953 he praised the Christian Brothers for their 'great work in sustaining and strengthening the spirit of Irish nationalism'.[7] Some felt that the Brothers had continued to play this role to the detriment of modern Irish society. For example, one historian, Tom Dunne, said recently that 'at the Christian Brothers school we were imbued with an intensely nationalist version of the [1798] rebellion, whose ballads were staples of our singing classes'.[8] The Revisionists argued that what was needed was a version of Irish history which was truthful and analytical. There is not the space here to consider the question of whether Revisionism in the universities had primed younger Irish historians to respond in this way to the Troubles or if the violence itself provoked such a reaction. However, that history was now being written in response to the Troubles is evidenced by Dermot Keogh's comment (in *Twentieth-Century Ireland: Nation and State*) that 'members of the historical profession looked at the past from the perspective of having to live at a time when paramilitary violence in Northern Ireland heaped atrocity upon atrocity'.

By this time, however, the latter view had become the majority one in academic history circles. Those in a position to do so felt that drastic changes had to be made to the history curriculum in schools, that it was time to move away from the nationalist version and towards a more objective view of the past which would not appear to justify republican violence. Elma Collins, author of a number of history textbooks such as

Conquest and Colonisation and *History in Context*, was one of these. 'The early Revisionism was beginning to reach a wider audience,' she has said. 'Most of the school text books before this had been written in the 1920s and '30s and were strongly influenced by a nationalist agenda. We were trying to write school-level history that would be, if not value-free, as near as being non-partisan as one could realistically get. Because of the civil rights movement...we were conscious of the Northern issue and the whole question of religion in politics.' And also, 'Nearly thirty years of trouble in the North has been at least as important as historical research in developing one's critical faculties.'[9] The process of curriculum reform has been an ongoing one since the late 1960s and the type of history taught in Irish schools from the 1970s onwards is dramatically different from that before.

For example, the series of books aimed at 16-year-olds, sponsored by the Teaching of History Trust, *Questions in Irish History* (published by Longmans), 'aims to deal directly with controversial questions and challenge bias and received points of view about Irish history'.[10] This series makes no bones about being influenced by events in Northern Ireland or that it is consciously promoting a Revisionist interpretation of history. For example, in writing a book in this series *Ireland and the Normans: Progress or Decline?* Brendan Smith 'was encouraged to give attention to Ulster'. The book itself reflects the new thinking on teaching history, setting the Normans in their European context and revising the traditional view that Dermot MacMurrough was a traitor for inviting Strongbow and his followers into Ireland. The picture drawn of the Normans in Ireland is not one of conquest and oppression of the native Irish but rather of an interaction between 'two nations' which was not inevitably destructive. Even so remote an era as the period of the Norman Invasion leads to a discussion on 'Catholic' and 'Protestant' surnames, provoking debate in the classroom with, for example, the following –

> Lenny Murphy was the leader of a gang called 'the Shankill Butchers' which murdered many Catholics in Belfast in the 1970s. Murphy has been described as 'a young man warped by bitter hatred of Catholics caused partly by ragging when he was a child because of his "Catholic surname"' (*Irish Times*, 3 August, 1989). Does the idea of a 'Catholic' or 'Protestant' surname make any sense?[11]

This in itself not only gives an indication that history was taught with an eye to what was happening in the North, but carries within it an unspoken analysis of why there was trouble there.

It would be dangerous, however, to over-emphasise the part of Revisionism in the motivation behind developments in the history curriculum in these years. In common with many other European countries in the 1960s, and more particularly the 1970s after entry into the European Economic Community, Ireland underwent a period of great change, and attitudes to all aspects of society were transforming. This was inevitably reflected in education also, and saw developments not just in subject content but in teaching methods. Indeed, the pace of change has barely let up until the present. The curriculum in schools has also evolved, and as this paper is being written further changes are being implemented. Under such circumstances the teaching of history was bound to develop and the traditional view challenged. One significant shift is away from 'passive' teaching methods to a system whereby pupils, at both primary and secondary level, are encouraged to be more proactive. In history this is seen in a greater emphasis on the study of first-hand sources and the encouragement of pupils, particularly at Leaving Certificate level, to think for themselves. *Field Studies in History: activity guides* (History Teachers' Association, Dublin Branch, 1995) is a good example of this aimed at Junior Certificate students. This book is designed to facilitate field trips to sites of historical significance such as Glendalough, medieval Kilkenny or the National Museum as a means of introducing students to original sources and how to use them. Such a different attitude to teaching from that when the Free State was first established was bound to lead to a radical rethinking of the past and a patently untraditionalist view of Ireland's history – similar things were happening to the curriculum in Britain, although with a different emphasis. So even without the input of Revisionism the teaching of history in the 1980s and 1990s would have been radically different in any case. Furthermore, it must be born in mind that a Revisionist curriculum does not always make a Revisionist teacher, and there was still enough leeway in the curriculum to allow for individual teachers to put their own personal stamp on the teaching of history.

For decades after the outbreak of the Troubles open debate in the Republic's media about the North was hampered by Section 31 of the Broadcasting Act, introduced in 1972, which barred any representative of the northern Republican movement, or apologists for it, from the airwaves. This followed the sacking of the entire RTÉ Authority after a member of the IRA was interviewed on television.[12] The advent of Irish television in 1961 had the long-term effect of blurring the divisions between academic history, the media and politics. Historians were frequently on television discussing their views (as in the 1966 series of lectures to mark the 1916 anniversary) occupying the same arena as politicians and journalists. This is illustrated by the career of the minister who introduced Section 31, Conor Cruise O'Brien, a politician, an historian and journalist as well as being a chief Revisionist. Lack of debate in the broadcast media did not prevent debate elsewhere. The Northern issue was dealt with directly or indirectly in newspapers, magazines and books. History books in particular were in demand by a public eager to have the origin of the Northern troubles explained. A book such as Roy Foster's *Modern Ireland 1600–1972* quickly became a bestseller, fuelling debate in the media and informing political analysis of what was happening in contemporary Ireland. Foster became a media personality and was seen by many to epitomise the Revisionist approach. The fact that Garret Fitzgerald, leader of Fine Gael, made no secret of his admiration for Foster's work only facilitated the cross-over from academic debate to politics. Revisionism, whatever its practitioners might have claimed, came to be defined as a political ideology closely associated with the anti-Fianna Fáil parties, such as Fine Gael and Labour, espousing a 'partitionist mentality' in the Republic. For example, in *Twentieth Century Ireland: Nation and State*, Dermot Keogh defines the nation as the 26-county state.

In this guise, Revisionism made headway in both the printed and broadcast media. *The Irish Times* in particular became associated with it, and Revisionist historians such as Foster regularly contributed opinion pieces or background articles to the *Times*, while columnists such as Fintan O'Toole and Kevin Meyers were widely viewed as pursuing a Revisionist agenda, albeit from different angles. In the state broadcasting agency, Radio Teilifís Éireann, it is now widely acknowledged that there were those, associated with the Workers Party, who were determined to ensure that the non-nationalist, Revisionist, view of modern and historical matters prevailed.[13] This is said to have had an influence on RTÉ's coverage of events in the North, such as, for example, the 1981 IRA Hunger Strikes and the election of Bobby Sands as a Westminster MP.[14] One person who was an RTÉ producer at this time, Eoghan Harris, states that his aim was 'to convert [the Workers Party] from republicanism to revisionism', and acknowledges that influence was brought to bear on RTÉ's programming.[15] Whether Harris or anyone else really had a profound effect on broadcasting may be debatable, but the fact that Harris happily describes his politics as Revisionism is a clear indication of what the term had come to stand for. That Revisionism was openly embraced by unionist historians in Northern Ireland, such as A. T. Q. Stewart,

Paul Bew or Brian Walker, reinforced the view that it was anti-nationalist and pro-unionist.

In 1990, in the first issue of *The Irish Review*, Roy Foster declared that 'we are all Revisionists now'. Indeed, it seemed to be the case that, throughout Ireland, university history departments were dominated by Revisionists. Four years earlier, in his satirical look at Irish politics, Breandán O hEithir jokingly described the Department of Modern History at University College Dublin as a 'Confraternity of Latter-Day Blueshirts' engaged on 'The Revision of Irish History'.[16] In society at large, however, Revisionism had only minority support. Politics continued to be dominated by Fianna Fáil which, with its unreconstructed nationalist rhetoric, had core support of over 40 per cent of the electorate (although support for Sinn Féin was negligible). At a local level, history societies and museums, even some of the newly emerging summer schools, continued to portray what Foster describes as 'the old "800-years-of-uninterrupted-struggle" view of Irish history'. In Wexford County Museum, for example, Father Murphy was still portrayed as the great hero and martyr of 1798. In local and county museums throughout the country, the epic version of history was replicated, focusing on traditional heroes such as O'Connell, Davitt or Pearse. In the music charts groups such as the Wolfe Tones featured with traditional patriotic ballads and newer 'anti-Brit' songs penned in response to events in Northern Ireland (such as 'The Men Behind the Wire' and 'The Ballad of Bobby Sands.'). If the Irish broadcast media shied away from engaging with Irish history, the British media was not so coy, and a series such as 'Ireland: a history' by Robert Kee was eagerly watched by viewers in the Republic. This series was so in keeping with popular Irish sentiment that a public row broke out between Foster and Kee over it, the former criticising it for being too nationalist. For whatever reason, the Revisonist view of Irish history failed to grasp the public imagination, and perhaps, in its pursuit of objectivity, appeared to question the validity of the nation itself. The public's view of Revisionism is neatly encapsulated in the anecdote of how one well-known historian went into a Dublin pub for a pint one evening and was approached by an irate member of the public: 'You so-and-so historians are all the same. One million people died in the Famine and you put it down to a case of mass-anorexia!'[17] A more intellectual, but no less typical, view is that 'the Revisionists were saying that not only were we actually responsible for our own colonisation but the sooner we confessed, the sooner our shriven souls could enter that promised land called Modern Ireland.'[18]

If excluded from the academy, non-Revisionists found other outlets of expression. A new magazine, *The Irish Reporter*, provided a forum for non-Revisionist historians and political commentators. The foundation of the Field Day Theatre Company and its staging of the plays of Brian Friel – such as *Making History* or *Translations* – were viewed as a direct challenge to the Revisionist establishment and proved more successful in striking a chord with society at large. *Translations*, for instance, has gained a great deal of credence and is accepted internationally not just as literature but as an historical record of British attempts to purge the Irish people of their cultural heritage by Anglicising the Irish landscape.[19] Field Day went on to produce an anthology of Irish writing which was seen as an anti-Revisionist manifesto and drew down the wrath of Revisionist academics. The long running dispute between Edna Longley of Queen's University, Belfast, and Séamus Deane, its editor, over the anthology is legendary in academic circles. It was also an example of how Revisionism was no longer seen as simply relating to history but to culture in general. Non-historians had also entered the debate. For example, *Revising the Rising*, another Field Day publication, had contributions not just from historians but literary critics and cultural commentators as well.[20] Whatever might have been the case within the academy, Revisionism was at odds with popular opinion. The launching of *The Irish Review*, like *Irish Historical Studies* sixty years before, might be seen as an admission that it had failed to strike a chord with the Irish public and that some proselytising was required. Yet if anything the arguments pro- and anti-Revisionism had opened up the debate among the general public and created a demand for a fresh approach to history, which was met with the launch in 1993 of another magazine, *History Ireland*, one which has made a significant contribution to public understanding of the issues involved.

If the Revisionists who emerged like Roy Foster, David Fitzpatrick or Ronan Fanning saw themselves as rebelling against, or at least departing from, an older-established view of history, then by the 1990s they themselves had become the establishment, and a newer generation of historians had begun to question what was increasingly seen as their simplistic, negative approach to the subject. Ironically, it was universities outside Ireland, such as Cambridge, that were home to those who espoused a different analysis of Irish history. Brendan Bradshaw, a leading anti-Revisionist, has been teaching at Cambridge for many years and has influenced a new generation of historians there. At Liverpool, for example, Christine Kinealy made significant contributions to the history of the Great Famine. In the universities of America and Australia, historians have challenged the Revisionist consensus, like James S. Donnelly at the University of Madison-Wisconsin or John Molony of the Australian Catholic University. A leading non-Revisionist, Christine Kinealy, has commented that 'Irish university history departments are dominated by Revisionists and those with dissenting views have to look to Britain or the US for jobs.'[21] From the late 1980s onwards, however, more voices were raised even within Ireland which challenged the Revisionist analysis. The opposition to Revisionism was not confined to academic books, journals and conferences, but the argument was carried on in front of the TV cameras, in popular publications and in the newspapers. Even within the pages of *The Irish Times*, the non-Revisionist case was heard from guest contributors, like Brendan Bradshaw or Brian Murphy, and even from its own columnists such as John Waters.[22] However, there was no simple swing back to the traditional patriotic story of Ireland's struggle for nationhood. This new history is characterised by a breakdown of the grand narrative and a closer examination of other aspects such as economic influences on social change, examining Ireland in an international context, women's history and local history. A good example of this approach is the collection of essays, *The United Irishmen: Republicanism, Radicalism and Rebellion* (David Dickson, Dáire Keogh, Kevin Whelan, eds.,1993), Cormac Ó Gráda's work on the Great Famine, or the more woman-centred approach of Margaret MacCurtain. In this respect, these historians do not see themselves as engaging in the pro/anti-Revisionism debate so much as moving beyond that into a new phase of historiography. Many of the best-known historians today would probably be happy to describe this phase as being post-Revisionist.

However, if, as Paul Bew claims, there is now a ceasefire within the academy,[23] this is not true at the popular level of culture, where some still feel that Revisionism is a potent force that needs to be challenged. In part this is because of the coincidence of a number of anniversaries in the 1990s and reactions to them. This decade, for example, witnesses the 200th anniversary of the founding of the United Irishmen, and subsequently of their Rebellion, likewise of the founding of the Orange Order, as well as the 150th anniversary of the Great Famine and the 75th anniversary of the 1916 Rising and the Battle of the Somme. All these were crucial events in Irish history each with its particular resonance for contemporary Ireland. The issue of how – indeed why – these anniversaries should be commemorated or celebrated brought the debate over Revisionism into the public arena once more. This decade has seen a reassessment by historians of all these events and a rehearsal in the media of the arguments that had been going on in the academy.

The Great Famine in particular raised again the question of who was responsible for the Famine and what culpability, if any, rested with the British Government. Not just in books or at conferences, but in the pages of daily and weekly newspapers, those who argued against the traditional view and promoted the idea of the Famine being a product of socio-economic circumstances with no-one in particular to blame came into conflict with those who emphasised the human tragedy and argued that the Famine, if not man-made, could certainly have been alleviated. As in other such arguments, political considerations played their part, with the recognised sub-text of the debate being attitudes to Irish nationalism. In this context, Prime Minister Tony Blair's acknowledgement in May 1997 that the British government of the day could have done more to prevent the Famine and to treat the Irish who suffered more fairly was widely accepted as being an apology by most in Ireland and criticised for being such by Revisionists. Again, the Revisionists would appear to have been out of step with popular sentiment.

In September 1997, a new body, the Ireland Institute, was established, among others, by Declan Kiberd, his brother Damien, Edna O'Brien, Robert Ballagh, and Thomas Kenneally, to 'nurture writing which tackles the Revisionist and anti-nationalist stance'. The perception among these people is that the academy and the media in Ireland are still dominated by Revisionists, that is, by those opposed to republicanism and nationalism. It seeks

> to invite speakers from inside and outside Ireland to discuss issues such as cultural policy in post-colonial countries. Through the medium of newsletters and pamphlets, it aims to provide a forum in which to offer critiques of current practices in print and mass media, particularly what it sees as 'pack journalism: the tendency of all journalists to ride together', particularly with reference to republicanism and nationalism.... It wishes to extend the debate on Ireland's history by moving beyond the schools of nationalism and Revisionism, to 'seek a fuller confrontation with the past.'[24]

Whatever the merits of the case, the foundation of the Ireland Institute is another clear example not only of the interaction between history, politics and the media, but also of how Revisionism is defined in political terms.

Much of what constituted the debate over Revisionism, and more particularly its influence on the Republic, came to a head in the campaign to elect Ireland's eighth president in 1997. While four of the five candidates were women, it was not gender but place of birth that became the issue as the arguments focused on the suitability of a Northern Ireland nationalist, Mary McAleese, as president. This is not the place to go into the details of the campaign or the validity of the various charges made against McAleese, but we can focus on those aspects which are relevant to this essay. From the outset, McAleese was viewed as a bad choice by some because it was felt that the election of a Northern nationalist would not only send out the wrong signals to unionists but would be seen as an endorsement of the view that the Irish nation was not the 26 Counties, but the whole island. The selective leaking of documents from the Department of Foreign Affairs further attempted to 'taint' her with assocation with Sinn Féin. Labels such as 'unreconstructed nationalist' and 'tribal time bomb' were applied to her, most often by people already identified as anti-nationalist. During the campaign the intervention of Eoghan Harris, the self-proclaimed Revisionist, in support of a particular candidate as the one most likely to scupper McAleese and his famous declaration that he would vote for Donald Duck for president rather than a northern nationalist crystallised the issue for everyone. On the other side, McAleese's main opponent, Fine Gael's Mary Banotti, was accused of having a 'Free State vision', and allusions were made to the antecedents of Fine Gael in the Blueshirts. Gerry Adams, leader of Sinn Féin, who was drawn into the controversy, referring to the anti-nationalists' agenda, commented, 'In the past censorship and Revisionism made their task a relatively easy one.'[25] It seemed as if the campaign was centring on the issues of partition and nationalism, rather than the individual merits of the candidates. The Sunday before polling day, one newspaper said that the election had been turned 'into a sort of plebiscite' in which the electorate were being asked 'to align [themselves] with a narrow, reactive Free State concept of Irishness'.[26]

On the day, McAleese got an unprecedented majority of votes cast. Her victory was viewed by many as a defeat for Revisionism. The extent to which the controversy over the Department of Foreign Affairs memos and the attempts to 'taint' McAleese with unreconstructed nationalism actually influenced the outcome of the election is open to debate. The concern expressed by many over a Revisionist agenda being pushed by some in politics and the media during the campaign may say more about their own sensitivities than reality. However, the fact that the controversy did arise shows quite clearly the position that Revisionism occupies in the popular imagination and that the term has come to define an outlook and a set of political values rather than simply a school of history. If, indeed, the McAleese victory represents the durability of traditional nationalism, then it illustrates how Revisionism still retains only minority support in the Irish Republic.

What is remarkable about the Revision of Irish History is not that it occurred but that the debate over it was conducted in public and carried into politics, the media and culture in Ireland. Revisionism is not unique to Ireland – the USA and Britain too have their Revisionists, such as Norman Stone or Andrew Roberts; but their writing does not influence the political agenda. On the other hand, neither is Ireland unique in having history play this role. In Germany, for example, history is seen as potentially destabilising – because of the circumstances of nineteenth-century unification, the Third Reich and the collapse of the Democratic Republic – and the teaching of history is carefully monitored in schools and universities. In France the 1989 bicentennial celebrations of the Revolution gave rise to a great deal of acrimonious public debate about the nature of the Revolution, the course of subsequent French history and even the legitimacy of the Republic. One television channel restaged the trial of Louis XVI with the viewers as the jury and, in a surprise result, they voted to acquit him. The Second World War is not just history to the French either, and it raises a number of questions about legitimacy, collaboration and responsibility that still cause problems today. In the former Yugoslavia, as Steve Bruce points out, 'Croats and Serbs exchange accusations over Ushtasi and Chetniks in the Second World War and the Albanians in the Kosovo province of Serbia probably hold the record for the longest-held ethnic grievance. Their claims for independence from Serbia rest on atrocities in the early part of the fourteenth century!'[27] Ireland, then, is not unique in finding the study of history problematical or political. Perhaps what is remarkable is that the debate over Revisionism has been conducted in such a public way over so many decades.

Revisionism had its origins in the 1930s and began as an attempt to promote a more scientific, value-free approach to the writing of history, in contrast to the patriotic, epic narrative of Ireland's 800-year struggle for nationhood that was not only being promoted in popular publications, but actually taught in schools. Revisionism did not have an immediate popular appeal, but it made steady progress in the academy. However, it was not until the 1960s that it made any significant headway, when changes in the history curriculum for schools began to move away from the traditional approach. The Troubles in the North accelerated and intensified the process. Revisionists readily admit that the Northern violence, particularly the IRA's campaign, influenced them.

As Dermot Keogh put it in *Twentieth Century Ireland: Nation and State*, 'The mystique of violence lost its appeal in the 1970s and 1980s as members of the historical profession looked at the past from the perspective of having to live at a time when paramilitary violence in Northern Ireland heaped atrocity upon atrocity.' By the 1980s the Revisionists had set the agenda for the history curriculum in both primary and secondary schools. Likewise in the media, the Revisionist view was becoming the accepted norm, and influenced not just reporting on the North but the analysis of politics in the Republic. However, it would be a mistake to imagine that this was a straightforward or simple process. Not until 1990 did Roy Foster feel it safe to declare that Revisionism was in control.

For a school whose aim was to remove emotion from history, it aroused a great deal of passion and always had its opponents. With the Northern Troubles as the backdrop, the debate between historians was conducted in public, and it soon became clear that popular sentiment was with the anti-Revisionists. In politics, Fianna Fáil remained the single biggest party, and in cultural terms – whether it be the republican ballads of the Wolf Tones or the theatrical and literary works of Field Day – it was the anti-Revisionists who struck a popular chord. Within the academy, the 1990s saw the Revisionist hegemony challenged and the emergence of a new generation of historians who were more post- than anti-Revisionist in outlook. Yet in politics and the media the old battlelines remained, and the 1997 presidential election campaign brought things to a head, with the controversy over Mary McAleese being argued out in pro- and anti-Revisionist terms. Her victory may be proof that Revisionism, after over sixty years, has failed to significantly shift the Irish public's perception of the past, but a wider examination of popular expressions of history – in local museums or summer schools, for example – would have provided enough proof of this already.

Notes

1 Brendan Bradshaw, interview in *History Ireland*, 1/1 (1993), p. 53.
2 Francis T. Holohan, 'History teaching in the Irish Free State 1922–35', *History Ireland*, 2/4 (1994), p. 53.
3 Douglas Gageby, 'The Media 1945–70', in J. J. Lee (ed.), *Ireland 1945–70* (Dublin: Gill & Macmillan, 1979), p. 127.
4 John Sheehan, 'Education and Society in Ireland 1945–70', Ibid., pp. 61–72.
5 Brendan Bradshaw, interview in *History Ireland*, 1/1 (1993), p. 53.
6 Séamus Ó Buachalla, *Education Policy in 20th Century Ireland* (Dublin:Wolfhound, 1988).

7   Quoted in John Horgan, *Seán Lemass: The Enigmatic Patriot* (Dublin: Gill & Macmillan, 1997), p. 8.

8   Tom Dunne, 'Dangers Lie in the Romanticising of 1798,' *The Irish Times*, 6 Jan. 1998, p. 19.

9   Elma Collins, interview in *History Ireland*, 5/1 (1997), p. 13.

10 Brendan Smith, 'Writing a School History: Ireland and the Normans', in *History Ireland* 1/3 (1993), p. 47.

11 Brendan Smith, *Ireland and the Normans: Progress or Decline?* (London: Longmans, 1993), p. 49.

12 See Bill Rolston in *Let in the Light: Censorship, Secrecy and Democracy* (Brandon, 1993).

13 Brenda Power, 'Eoghan Harris: Out of the Shadows', in *Magill*, Nov. 1997, p. 22.

14 Ibid.

15 Eoghan Harris quoted in Brenda Power, Ibid.

16 Breandán O hEithir, *The Begrudger's Guide to Irish Politics* (Bantry: Poolbeg, 1986), pp. 3–4.

17 Brendan Bradshaw, interview in *History Ireland*, 1/1 (1993), p. 54.

18 Tom McGurk, 'Raising the ghosts of Ballyseedy reveals a moral nation once again.' in *The Sunday Business Post*, 16 Nov. 1997, p. 18.

19 See Helen Wallis' review of Finlay Macleod (ed.), Togail Tir, in *Journal of the International Map Collectors' Society*, 44 (1991), p. 37.

20 Máirín Ní Dhonnchada and Theo Dorgan (eds.), *Revising the Rising* (Derry: Field Day, 1991).

21 Christine Kinealy, interview in *The Sunday Business Post*, 2 Nov. 1997, pp. 28–9.

22 See for example, Brian Murphy 'Is Revisionism in Irish history built on insecure foundations?', *Irish Times*, 24 Sept. 1992, p. 18, or John Waters, 'Turning a blind eye to history's continuing open sore,' *Irish Times*, 15 Aug. 1995, p. 16.

23 Paul Bew, interview, *History Ireland*, 2/4 (1994), p. 14.

24 *The Irish Times*, 18 Sept. 1997, p. 8.

25 Quoted in *The Sunday Business Post*, 26 Oct. 1997, p. 18.

26 Editorial, Ibid., p. 18.

27 Steve Bruce, 'Cultural Traditions: a double-edged sword?' in *Causeway*, 1/4 (1994), p. 21.

12
The Media and the State: Television and the Press 1949–99

John Horgan

The 1948 general election signalled the end of an uninterrupted sixteen-year period of Fianna Fáil rule, and the introduction of a decade of electoral volatility. This was a decade characterised, too, by a series of enthusiastic but often unsuccessful attempts by government to reorganise the media landscape, and by the first tentative steps towards the establishment and political regulation of the new and reputedly all-powerful medium of television. Fianna Fáil's second 16-year period in office (1957–73) coincided with the emergence of the electronic media generally as a *champ de bataille* between government and the media. By the Eighties and Nineties, governments of quite differing political hues found themselves dealing, for the most part inadequately and hesitantly, with the new challenges of de-regulation, the future of public service broadcasting, concentration of ownership, globalisation, and the economic colonisation of many forms of Irish media.

The sixteen years before 1948 had indeed been characterised, in so far as the media were concerned, by a stability which mirrored that of Mr de Valera's governments. The appearance of the *Irish Press* in September 1931, while Fianna Fáil were still in opposition, was a landmark. The new paper, the first daily paper to be established since the foundation of the State in 1922, filled a yawning gap in the media marketplace: the *Irish Times*, although it had to some extent come to terms with Mr de Valera's pragmatism in office, could never bring itself to encourage people to vote for him at election times; the *Irish Independent*, cautious and conservative to a fault, never espoused Mr de Valera's political opponents in Cumann na nGael (later Fine Gael) openly, but there was never any doubt where its real sympathies lay. *The Irish Press*, effectively, levelled the playing field, and played a major part in maximising the support for Mr de Valera at the 1932 election and consolidating it thereafter. Mr de Valera retained his position as its Controlling Editor, even as head of government, and despite the claim in the new paper's prospectus that it would not be a 'party organ'. This was to produce some piquant anomalies: in 1932, Mr de Valera as head of government censored Mr de Valera as controlling editor when the government forbade the publication of controversial letters from the Governor-General, who claimed that he had been slighted by Mr de Valera; a year later, when a military tribunal sent the Political Correspondent of the Irish Press to gaol for a month for refusing to reveal his sources of information in a political trial, Mr de Valera refused to commute the reporter's sentence, but paid him what was doubtless a welcome visit in Mountjoy Prison.

The change of government in 1948, however, put an entirely different cast on things. *The Irish Press* came under the able stewardship of Mr Sean Lemass, who was Mr de Valera's second-in-command and fresh from a sixteen-year stint as Minister for Industry and Commerce. Lemass assumed the role of managing director of the paper, which adopted its new role as poacher with gusto. Lemass himself frequently contributed spirited political commentaries to the paper under a pseudonym. One of these columns so angered the Minister for Social Welfare and Leader of the Labour Party, William Norton, that he sued for libel, receiving only derisory damages. The main function of the paper, however, apart from attacking the government, was quietly to take sides in the policy argument that was developing within Fianna Fáil. That party's old guard were still firmly wedded to the ideas of economic self-sufficiency, and to tariffs and import substitution as the main planks of economic policy. Lemass, convinced by the failures of the immediate post-war years that Irish industry was a weak reed which needed to be exposed progressively to competition if it was to thrive, was moving towards a position that was much more open on trade, and much more critical of past mistakes. Discreetly, almost subliminally, the Irish Press weighed in behind him, and was to play an important role in marshalling support for his policies in the late 1950s and early 1960s.[1]

Within the new government, as it happened, the media were to assume a prominent place on the political agenda. This was chiefly due to the concerns of the Minister for External Affairs and leader of the small Clann na Poblachta party, Mr Sean MacBride, a former associate of Mr de Valera's who had come to believe that Fianna Fáil had lost its original energy and momentum, particularly in relation to the question of partition. MacBride, a barrister by profession, had also worked as a journalist for the French Havas news agency, and had even at one stage been employed briefly, under an assumed name, by a unionist newspaper in London.

MacBride had a high but somewhat unrealistic expectation of the power of the media to generate change in political attitudes, particularly abroad, and made one of the principal planks in his platform the establishment of a new organisation, the Irish News Agency, whose main task, as he first enunciated it, would be to publicise the problem of partition abroad. For all that this idea had been current in one form or another since the War of Independence (1918–21), when the IRA had shown itself adept at enlisting foreign journalistic and diplomatic support for the cause of Irish Independence, MacBride's proposal was poorly thought out and riven with flaws. It also marked a total break with de Valera's policy in this respect, which had been based on the almost equally unrealistic belief that a national short-wave radio service, aimed at the diaspora and at public opinion abroad, would energise international opinion on Ireland's side.

MacBride had originally suggested the idea to de Valera at the end of the Second World War, at a time when belief in the propaganda value of various media had been heightened by Hitler's use of radio in particular. De Valera and his chief media advisor Frank Gallagher, a former editor of the Irish Press and thereafter Director of the Government Information Bureau, were cool about the proposal, arguing that nobody would believe in the impartiality of the statements issuing from any such agency under government control. MacBride's enthusiasm vaulted over such quibbles, and in speeches to the Dail on the setting up of the Agency, he managed to maintain simultaneously that it would not be a propaganda body, and that it would be the spokesman abroad for the Irish government's position on partition.

The agency survived, against the odds, for some seven years and three governments. That it survived at all was partly due to the adroitness of its first managing director, Conor Cruise O'Brien (then a civil servant in MacBride's department of External Affairs), and partly to the calibre of its staff, who were drawn from the cream of Dublin journalism, and paid – by the standards of the time – exceptionally well. It never performed adequately any of the functions for which it had been designed. Its chief activity became the export of general Irish news stories to foreign (usually British) publications, who returned the compliment by printing them only in the Irish editions of their newspapers. This was an almost entirely circular process, with little added value in propaganda or indeed any other terms. It finally succumbed to the combined assaults of the mandarins of the Department of Finance, who saw that it would never become economically viable, and the doughty members of the National Union of Journalists in Ireland, whose own tidy little business in exporting Irish news to UK publications had been seriously undermined by the Agency's activities.[2]

The short-wave radio experiment, initiated by de Valera as a means primarily of projecting Ireland to the American audience, died a slow and lingering death.[3] It was suffocated partly by the disinterest of non-Fianna-Fáil governments, who saw it merely as a hangover from the *ancien régime*; partly by organisational weaknesses (its relay of Irish radio broadcasts to the US was simultaneous with their broadcast in Ireland, which meant that the programmes reached the US at a time when most of the inhabitants of that continent were in bed); and partly by technological developments, as the emergence of FM radio and television dealt a death blow to the sale of short-wave radios in the US.

In the embers of that short-wave service, however, there were sparks that were to be fanned into flame. Two developments, in particular, were of considerable political and cultural significance, and these owed their existence almost entirely to the short-wave initiative. One was the news service, and the other was the cultural extension of radio via the orchestra and the 'Rep', or the Radio Eireann Repertory Company. Both of these developments found a home in the existing Radio Eireann service, which was at that stage completely under government control, and staffed and organised as an integral part of the department of Posts and Telegraphs.

The relationship of broadcasting to the State during this period was anomalous. The news service had traditionally been innocuous and non-controversial, in part because of the legacy of the war years, when strict censorship was the order of the day. Radio Eireann's role was also stringently demarcated by its explicit function as a public service organisation with the specific brief of protecting and promoting native Irish culture, notably language and music. It fulfilled this task with enthusiasm, at whatever cost to its ratings, in an era when Irish listeners could in many cases easily switch to the BBC, Radio Luxembourg, and other stations. It was not heedless of the consequences, and carried out surveys to establish which stations attracted Irish audiences, but was too embarrassed to publish the results, which showed that by the mid-1950s no more than 0.1 per cent of the potential listenership tuned in to Irish language broadcasts.[4]

It was a Fianna Fáil Minister for Posts and Telegraphs, however, who began the process of inching Radio Eireann towards a greater degree of openness. After he became Minister on Fianna Fáil's return to power in

1951, Erskine Childers (who had been Advertising Manager of the Irish Press in 1931) set about the creation of a new structure which, although wholly advisory in character, at least offered the possibility of an input into broadcasting policy that was neither political nor bureaucratic. In a way that was still weak and ineffectual, it none the less presaged the developments that were to find legislative expression in the 1960s, and the eventual removal of broadcasting from the direct control of government.

The main impetus for change in the late 1950s, however, came, ironically, from within the depths of the civil service itself. Leon O Broin, Secretary of the department of Posts and Telegraphs, saw television looming on the horizon, and did his best to alert his political masters to its significance and its implications. His fellow-mandarins in the Department of Finance took fright, possibly seeing in it a newer and even more expensive version of the Irish News Agency. It would, one of them wrote, be ridiculous to think of a television service in a country which had manifested no interest in it and whose people would probably be opposed to the spending of considerable sums of public money on such a luxury available, of course, to a very limited number because of geographical and financial reasons.[5]

Politicians were hesitant at best: aware of the powerful pressures of religious and cultural interests, they were obsessed with questions of control, and seriously considered farming out the television service to private commercial interests, both as a way of finessing the cards played by the clerical/cultural lobbies, and as a way of saving the exchequer money.

The Government of Sean Lemass, who succeeded de Valera as Taoiseach in 1959, took an early decision to establish television as a new service under a public authority. This decision, which was against the weight of the advice they had been tendered and against Lemass's personal view, was influenced primarily by fears that Irish culture would disappear from the agenda of a purely private television service. Indeed, since the 1930s Lemass had been in favour of private involvement in national broadcasting, and governments of this hue, although officially wedded in later years to the concept of public service broadcasting, were readily persuaded that the national broadcasting service was anti-government, and occasionally sought to rebalance the broadcasting equation more in favour of private interests, most dramatically in 1991.[6] Lemass himself was only dissuaded at the last minute from marking the new station's cards in a series of official government directives, and confined himself to enumerating the desiderata in a memorandum to his Minister for Posts and Telegraphs, Joseph Brennan, which made his own views quite clear. Subjects which might be covered, he opined, included:

1. The 'image' of Ireland and of the Irish to be presented, including the avoidance of stage-Irishisms, playboyisms etc. The 'image' should be of a vigorous, progressive nation, seeking efficiency.
2. The handling of Social Problems, either general or local. The desirable course would be to encourage objective presentation of facts and constructive comment. The 'God-help-us' approach should be ruled out.
3. The presentation of features and comments on events abroad involving criticism of the policies of other governments. The attitude to events in Iron Curtain countries would require particular definition.
4. The coverage of events in Northern Ireland, with particular reference to criticism of the policies of the Northern Ireland administration, and the encouragement of anti-Partition sentiment.
5. The presentation of plays and features which emphasise sex.
6. The policy to be followed in covering sporting events, and the prominence to be given to national games.
7. The utilisation of the service for religious instruction, and the facilities to be given to non-Catholics.
8. The utilisation of the service for instruction in scientific subjects, and the subjects which are suitable for such instruction.[7]

The surprising omission of the Irish language from this politically correct agenda of conservative Irish Republicanism was hardly an error: Lemass had little sympathy for it except in symbolic terms. In outline, however, it presaged accurately enough an era of close government attention to the new medium, particularly on political, economic and social matters. Cultural matters were not ignored: the official archives are replete with representations from spokespeople for various cultural organisations complaining about the alleged bad effect television was having on Irish culture, and the Commission on the Restoration of the Irish Language (1965) in an interim report had made clear its belief that television and radio should play a much more prominent role in the language revival movement. But increasingly issues such as freedom of expression, editorial independence, and the coverage of news and current affairs on the new medium came to dominate state–media relationships.

The 1960 Broadcasting Act, which established the Irish television service, in fact took two steps in one. It not only created a statutory basis for the new service, but also established a new relationship between broadcasters, government and the public. Removed from the tutelage of the department of Posts and Telegraphs and the well-meaning but ineffective Advisory Committees, both radio and television began slowly to flex their muscles. It was, after all, the decade of the Sixties, when the rising international economic tide, allied to Lemass's expansionist and export-focused industrial policy, was creating a sea-change in Irish life. Some, at least, of the emigrants who had left in the 1950s were returning to new jobs and better prospects than ever before. There was a palpable air of optimism, of challenges to established authority, and a sense that change was possible in many social and political fields.

The conflicts between government and broadcasters in the 1960s[8] reflect the strong desire of the governments of that time that the new medium should be used to promote, rather than criticise, national policy. The problem was that the new governing mechanism for television (and radio), an Authority established under statute, did not envisage direct contact between politicians and broadcasters. None the less, politicians frequently contacted the Authority, or its individual members, and even station executives, to express concerns about a whole range of subjects. This practice was eventually codified in a 1967 memorandum by the Minister for Posts and Telegraphs designed to ensure that contacts between ministers and the station took place only via designated senior officials, thus reducing the possibility of inconvenient leaks about government interference.

Lemass personally made no bones of his conviction that the role of the new medium should not lose sight of overriding national considerations or indulge itself in the 'undue representation of our faults' under 'the pretext of objectivity'.[9] He was not slow to mark the new Broadcasting Authority's cards, even in minor matters, but he was especially sensitive to critical programmes on economic matters and on emigration. He described one current affairs programme as increasingly 'a medium for the uncritical presentation of the views of persons associated with various camps and crank projects'[10] and urged Telefís Éireann, via his press secretary, to 'take the whine out of their voice'.[11]

His view of what should be done was simple and old-fashioned: if any programme projected the wrong view, Telefís Éireann should immediately prepare and transmit a corrective programme. He was persuaded against insisting on such a course of action by the television authorities, who correctly argued that news of such an initiative would compound the original problem instead of solving it. For their part, the controllers of the new service managed to avoid taking any disciplinary or other overt action which would have led to questions about the station's credibility as a commentator on and analyst of public affairs.

It was inevitable that these mini-controversies, which took place in private, should be accompanied by more explosive exchanges in public. The most dramatic of these took place in 1966, almost on the eve of Lemass's resignation as Taoiseach and in the midst of a major confrontation between the government and the National Farmers Association. It was an open secret that the government was dismayed by the latitude being given to the protesting farmers by the broadcasters, and had done its best to bring the station to heel. Lemass, questioned about this in the Dail, gave a typically blunt assessment of the relationship he thought should subsist between broadcasters and government:

> Radio Telefís Éireann was set up by legislation as an instrument of public policy and as such is responsible to the Government. The Government have overall responsibility for its conduct and especially the obligation to ensure that its programmes do not offend against the public interest or conflict with national policy as defined in legislation. To this extent the Government reject the view that RTE should be, either generally or in regard to its current affairs and news programmes, completely independent of Government supervision. As a public institution supported by public funds and operating under statute, it has the duty, while maintaining impartiality between political parties, to present programmes which inform the public regarding current affairs, to sustain public respect for the institutions of Government and, where appropriate, to assist public understanding of the policies enshrined in legislation enacted by the Oireachtas. The Government will take such action by way of making representations or otherwise as may be necessary to ensure that Radio Telefís Éireann does not deviate from the due performance of this duty.... There is, I think, a very special obligation on Government to ensure that the decision to entrust this responsibility to an independent authority does not conflict with the public interest.[12]

This was to remain the official statement of government policy, and was publicly implemented again under his predecessor, when the Minister for External Affairs, Frank Aiken, succeeded in preventing the sending of an RTE reporting team to North Vietnam. It was not long, however, before these skirmishes paled into insignificance beside the problems created by the eruption of violence in Northern Ireland in 1968-9, when the attempt by broadcasters to come to grips with a situation led to new crises in government–media relationships. Sean Lemass's statement from 1966, although it evoked strong protests from many Irish journalists inside and outside the broadcasting organisation, was in fact little more than an exegesis of Section 31 of the 1960 Broadcasting Act, which gave the government the important residual power to insist that the state broadcasting service should broadcast anything the government believed to be essential, and to prevent the broadcasting of any material the government found objectionable. This power was not the object of any journalistic criticism when the Act became law: for a quarter of a century after the eruption of political violence in the North, it was to be the linchpin of controversy.

The emergence of the civil rights movement in the North, the re-appearance on the scene of the IRA in 1969, and the rapidly escalating conflict pushed the politics of partition back onto the media agenda in a way that had not happened since Lemass's brief visit to Northern Ireland to meet the Northern Prime Minister, Terence O'Neill, in 1965. The problem was that there were, effectively, no guidelines to deal with a situation in which a legitimate political party – Sinn Féin – was the acknowledged public face of an illegal paramilitary organisation – the IRA. The situation was complicated by the fact that Sinn Féin's ideology was unambiguously directed, not just to the extirpation of Unionism and the re-unification of the island, but to the destruction also of the Dublin government and political system, which it saw, in a semi-theological way, as illegitimate inheritors of the Republican tradition, established on the flawed basis of the 1921 Anglo–Irish Treaty.

In this confused and volatile situation, the government became increasingly apprehensive about the prominence being given to Sinn Féin statements on the broadcast media. It was not only a law-and-order issue: it was something which went to the root of the government's self-understanding as the legitimate, democratic heir to the tradition of Pearse and the other 1916 leaders. Accordingly, when in September 1971 Telefís Éireann carried interviews with two IRA spokesmen, the government issued for the first time a Directive under Section 31 of the 1960 Act instructing the authority to 'refrain from broadcasting any matter that could be calculated to promote the aims or activities of any organisation which engages in, promotes, encourages or advocates the attaining of any political objective by violent means'. The Authority sought clarification, which was refused. In November 1972, following the broadcasting of a lengthy summary of an interview with an IRA spokesman, the government dismissed the Broadcasting Authority in its entirety and replaced it. This inaugurated a period of low-level guerilla warfare between broadcasters and government. The new Authority was positioned uneasily in the middle, anxious to ensure the continued credibility of its broadcasts, but perennially sensitive to the government's power of the purse – decisions about whether, when and by how much the annual licence fee should be raised, with major implications for the station's income, were (and remain) entirely a matter for Cabinet.

A change of government in 1973 removed Fianna Fáil from office after another uninterrupted sixteen-year period. The new Labour Minister for Posts and Telegraphs, Conor Cruise O'Brien, was if anything even more hostile to militant Republicanism than his predecessor had been (he once intimated that he would like to introduce legislation which would allow him to take action against the editor of the Irish Press for publishing letters from pro-Republican sources in his columns). He was also, however, more sensitive both to broadcasting procedures and to the concept of public accountability. Accordingly, the 1976 Broadcasting Amendment Act, which he initiated, clarified the terms under which directives would be given to the broadcasters, making them less ambiguous, and also enacted that no government could dismiss the Authority without the prior approval of both houses of parliament (the Dáil and Seanad). The Act also instituted a Broadcasting Complaints Commission, although in a milk-and-water form which made little difference to broadcasting practice.

The arguments about political censorship of broadcasting, however, although it involved centrally important questions of principle and practice, was one essentially carried on by a political and journalistic elite. In the years between 1971 and 1994 (when the directive ceased to be renewed on an annual basis) not one member of either house of parliament queried government policy. Fifteen years after the ban had first been instituted, more than a third of the respondents to a Dublin survey indicated that they had never heard of it.[13] When it was finally allowed to lapse in 1994, it was less because of the existence of a new climate of rapprochement between government and broadcasters, more because it was seen as a political obstacle in the movement towards the first major IRA ceasefire. Its legacy, apart from a series of sometimes grotesque case-histories, has been an enhancement of the propensity to self-censorship evident in any organisation subject to government control (however remote and intermittently exercised) which has taken a further five years to begin to dissipate.

In the meantime, other developments were taking place – developments which had a far higher public profile than the arguments about Section 36, for the very simple reason that they more immediately affected a far higher proportion of the viewing public. These were the issues related to viewer and listener choice which, although originally discussed only in terms of the national provision of broadcasting services, formed the basis for a further series of government decisions into the Eighties and Nineties which moved government–media relationships onto a new plane.

The cultural and social changes which underpinned these developments were in themselves significant. In 1963, two years after the introduction of a native television service, there were still three radio licences to every two television licences. By 1969 there were 161,000 radio licences and 433,000 television licences. By 1989 (when the stand-alone radio licences had been abolished) there were 782,000 television licences.[14] There are currently (1998) 990,000 licences. In addition, a wide swathe of residents along the eastern coast of the island and parts of the midlands had free (if qualitatively variable) access to UK television channels from transmitters in Wales or Northern Ireland. As early as 1966, indeed, the government had insisted (against the wishes of the Irish broadcasting organisation) that new tower blocks of public housing in the northern suburbs of Dublin should be fitted with special aerials so as to enable them to receive the UK channels. Elsewhere in the country, reception was confined to programming generated by Radio Telefís Éireann or RTE (as Telefís Éireann had been renamed in the 1976 legislation).

Pressure for choice of viewing escalated throughout the 1970s, and a Broadcasting Review Committee (1971–4) recommended that RTE be given a second channel. The new Minister, Conor Cruise O'Brien, counterproposed that a second national television channel should be set up, whose function should be to re-broadcast BBC 1 programmes throughout the state. His parallel intention was that RTE should be re-broadcast throughout Northern Ireland as an act of reciprocity by the British government, but the total plan was swamped in public protest and effectively undermined by an RTE survey (1974) which showed that the majority of respondents wanted a second RTE channel. This was duly provided, but not under his stewardship.

In the meantime, the spread of cabling in Dublin, and the increasingly sophisticated use of aerial and re-transmitter technology, introduced UK broadcasting channels to an ever-widening Irish audience. This mirrored a trend which had long been evident in the print media, and which was to be the subject of more intense controversy in the Nineties: the penetration of the Irish print-media market by UK-published newspapers, which have for many years accounted for almost one in four of morning papers, and one in three of Sunday papers sold in the state.

The playing-field thus levelled for television remained comparatively undisturbed until the late Nineties, when, with the licensing of a second Irish television station (in private ownership) and an acknowledgement of the major challenges facing Irish public service broadcasting in the mew millennium, government–broadcasting relationships assumed a new intensity. In the meantime, the battleground shifted towards radio where, not least because of the dramatically lower capital costs involved, the possibility of providing wider listener choice involved government and broadcasters, public and private, in a series of running skirmishes throughout the last three decades of the century.

Overshadowed by the advent of television, RTE radio had, by the late 1960s, become something of a backwater. It was set in its ways, and had little in the way of real competition. It was a service that, despite small oases of quality, not least in cultural programming, was obstinately middle-aged and middle-of-the-road. If government and broadcasters did anything, it was generally because they were pushed, rather than on foot of any interventionist strategy. Interventionism, such as it was, emerged as a response to pressure group politics and activities rather than as part of any overall coherent broadcasting policy. The decision to establish Radio na Gaeltachta in March 1972, for instance, was fuelled partly by Fianna Fáil's fear of losing votes in key west of Ireland constituencies, and partly by the dangerous attraction of pirate radio in the Irish language, which, unlike its music-driven English-language counterpart, was overtly libertarian, communitarian and anti-authoritarian in tone. There is a particular irony in this: the proposal for a separate Irish-language radio station had been made intermittently since the 1920s, but had been ignored by successive governments. This was due partly to natural departmental inertia, partly to the fear that such a station might prove a focus for alternative politics, and partly to the national ideological fiction that, since all Irish people spoke Irish anyway, Irish-language broadcasting could most appropriately be integrated with the general national service rather than being ghettoised in a service of its own. The later establishment of an Irish-language television service, Telefís na Gaeilge (1996) was due to similar forces, including the broadcasting from a pirate Irish-language television station in one of the major Irish-speaking areas in 1987. Telefís na Gaeilge, as it happened, placed a fresh burden on the national broadcasting station, which has been obliged to supply it with a certain quantity of free programming.

The growth of the pirate radio phenomenon in English, which began in the 1970s,[15] and was initially largely urban in character, was driven in part by a genuine search for alternatives, in part by an aggressive (often UK-financed) entrepreneurism that saw the opportunity for massive and quick profit-taking. It was also, of course, illegal, but the 1926 Wireless Telegraphy Act, the main weapon in the government's armoury, was old, rusty and quite likely to explode in the hands of anyone who attempted to utilise it.

By the time that the government decided that something had to be done, the situation was almost out of control. The most successful pirate stations were attracting hundreds of thousands of listeners, and millions of pounds worth of advertising. The political risks involved in banning them, in the absence of any equally popular (but legal) alternative, were so foreseeable as to induce legislative paralysis. RTE, belatedly aware of the problem, introduced a new 'pop' radio channel, Radio 2 (later renamed 2FM) in May 1979, but rather than stemming the tide, this only slowed it marginally.

In 1985, the then Coalition government led by Garrett FitzGerald established an Interim Radio Commission to advise on the future shape of radio, but that Commission's deliberations were sidelined by an intra-governmental dispute about the future control of local broadcasting. RTE, in a pre-emptive strike, had put forward a proposal for a whole series of local or regional stations under its control. This proposal was strongly backed by the Labour Party, the minority party in government, which had links with trade unions in RTE. Fine Gael, the majority partner in government, was far more oriented towards privatisation, but was unable to persuade its Labour partners to shift their ground, all the more so because this particular issue became a surrogate for a number of other issues on which the parties were divided. Fianna Fáil then made it an issue in the 1987 general election, reasoning correctly that they had nothing to lose: indeed, their overt support for the legalisation of private commercial radio was a major plank of their appeal to younger voters. Back in government in 1987, they rapidly legislated to rationalise the status quo with the support of Fine Gael, now liberated from its relationship with Labour.

The decade that followed saw the gradual emergence and evolution of structures designed to put government–media relationships on a new footing, but progress was slow and often dogged by controversy. The model originally chosen for private commercial broadcasting was the Independent Radio and Television Commission (October 1988), which was charged with the task of establishing a network of local and regional radio stations, and awarding a franchise for a second, private television network. Some commentators suggested that, in a total population of little more than three and a half million people, this was optimistic and, as events turned out, they were proved at least partly right. Many local stations did in fact get off the ground, the first of them in Dublin in July 1989. Some of the regional stations have achieved substantial listenership in their target areas with a format modelled partly on mid-range music choices and partly on traditional local print media.

Nationally, the story has been quite different. An initial attempt to establish a national alternative to RTE radio (Century Radio) was seriously under-capitalised and under-researched. It was launched in September 1989, and collapsed in November 1991, in the midst of a controversy which showed plainly that the government was prepared, if the occasion arose, to change the rules in favour of private commercial interests. It was hardly a coincidence that a number of those who had put capital into Century Radio initially had also been associated with Fianna Fáil, especially as donors. In the event, the Minister for Communications, Ray Burke, proposed a radical reorganisation of the financing of broadcasting, which would have involved turning the national 2FM service, which had by then established a successful popular music service and was attracting substantial advertising, into a purely public service station with no advertising. Under this scenario, Century would become the only national popular music station; £3 million of the annual licence fee revenue would be diverted to the private commercial stations generally; and a 'cap' would be put on RTE advertising so as to divert revenue from this source into the commercial sector. The minister was forced to back down under political pressure from his coalition partners, and in the face of a threat by RTE journalists to 'black' an EEC summit in which he and other Cabinet ministers were participating in Dublin. Its successor, Radio Ireland (1997), staggered into its second year on the airwaves only courtesy of an expensive re-launch which saw it re-christened as Today FM. TV3, the projected alternative to RTE television – more properly the projected domestic alternative, as cable and satellite are now providing an ever-wider choice to many Irish homes – was awarded its original franchise in April 1989, but did not come on the air until late 1998, after bouts of capital starvation and re-investment.

In the meantime two other developments, each of them linked to the trend towards media globalisation, provided government with a series of new challenges which, as had now become the norm, were only partially and hesitantly accepted. One was the need to find a new sense of direction, purpose, and perhaps new forms of organisation and financing for public service broadcasting as it entered the era of globalisation; the other was a growing concern about the future of the indigenous print media, fuelled by the collapse of the Irish Press group in 1995, by concerns about the increasing market share controlled by one major player (Independent Newspapers), and by its increasing presence in the Irish newspaper marketplace, not only as wholesaler but as owner of UK media interests.

The development of government policy in relation to broadcasting during this period was marked by a sea-change. As has been noted, government interventionism in the past had been largely related to questions of content, and were often low-level in character. The Nineties, however, were marked by a number of important structural initiatives by the state, the details of which are still in the process of being worked out. Michael D. Higgins, as Minister for Broadcasting in the 1994–7 coalition governments, published a Green Paper in March 1995 in which, for the first time, important initiatives in relation to existing structures were outlined. Principally, the Green Paper suggested the creation of a Super-Authority which would combine many of the existing functions of the current RTE Authority and the IRTC, take over certain housekeeping functions from the Department, and centralise arbitration functions and complaints procedures. Even more controversial was the suggestion that the new Authority should have power to change internal RTE structures and assess its performance in key areas. Taken together, these marked a high point in interventionism by the state: the argument, as ever, is about the extent to which such powers, created for positive reasons by a government which had a bias in favour of public service broadcasting, could be used for malign purposes by governments of a different hue.

These proposals were strongly resisted by RTE, but taken up in a modified form by Higgins' successor, Sile de Valera; but they have not yet appeared even in draft legislative form, and are unlikely to do so for some time. Mr. Higgins's other major domestic intervention, however, is already on the statute books. This was the 1993 Broadcasting Bill in which – persuaded at least in part by doubts about RTE's ability to provide innovative and creative programming – he sequestered a fixed percentage of the RTE budget for independent film-makers. This decision is being modified slightly by his successor, but the principle remains intact. One of his other important initiatives, however, was on the international level. During intergovernmental negotiations leading up to the drafting and passage of the EU's Amsterdam Treaty, he succeeded in inserting an important protocol defining and protecting the rights of public service broadcasting organisations, in the teeth of considerable opposition from European commercial broadcasting interests who felt that they were entitled to a proportion of licence fee income in so far as their output was oriented towards public service.

A question which began to mature in the later Nineties was that of digitalisation, which had not been dealt with to any great degree in the Green Paper or in the discussions surrounding it. As the century closed, however, it became evident that this new technological development and the capital required to fuel it, raised important questions of regulation, deployment and ownership. These questions are still at an early stage of discussion, but the government has already signalled its acceptance of RTE's contention that, as the state broadcasting service, it should be centrally involved in the process, and has agreed that RTE should control 40 per cent of the shares in a new company which will be set up to oversee Ireland's entry into the digital age.

Throughout the Nineties the indigenous print media landscape was also undergoing dramatic changes, and government was being drawn, generally unwillingly, into the hot-house atmosphere of circulation wars, ownership problems and questions of political influence. The indigenous industry had established its own pressure group, National Newspapers of Ireland (1985), mainly to campaign for better fiscal treatment from the government and for changes in the libel laws, in neither of which did it particularly succeed. In 1995 the Irish Press group, plagued for years by under-capitalisation and poor management, succumbed. Four years earlier, it had become involved in a joint venture with an American newspaper magnate, Ralph Ingersoll, as part of its attempt to raise fresh capital. The relationship soured, and ended in the courts. In the intervening period, and just before the collapse of the group, the Irish Independent group had taken a minority stake in the Irish Press, less as a white knight and more as a prophylactic against the projected involvement of the UK *Daily Mail*, which would have provided the Independent group newspapers with powerful competition on their home turf.

These developments in turn prompted political calls for an official investigation into the state of the newspaper industry, as the Independent Group now controlled a huge slice of the indigenous market. It had a minority stake in the loss-making *Sunday Tribune*, which had already been the subject of adverse comment by the Competition Authority; a 50 per cent stake in the tabloid *Daily Star* (the other 50 per cent being owned, as part of a highly successful joint venture, by Express newspapers); it owned two Sunday newspapers, one morning newspaper, Dublin's only evening newspaper, and a swathe of profitable provincial weeklies; and it had a 50 per cent stake in Princes Holdings, a company that held potentially highly profitable franchises for the distribution of television and other services via MMDS technology.

The government therefore established a Commission on the Newspaper Industry (1995–6), more as a holding exercise than anything else. It was reluctant to challenge the Independent group's power, partly for obvious political reasons, partly because the penetration of the Irish print media marketplace by UK-based publications meant that a court might decide that the Independent group did not hold a dominant position in the total market-place within the terms of anti-monopoly legislation. Any challenge it might make to the Independent group, therefore, would unleash a lengthy legal battle without any guarantee of a successful outcome.

The Report of the Commission drew attention to the dangers of concentration of media ownership and the dangers of cross-ownership, but was unable to come to any firm conclusions about the role of the Independent group in particular. Its report, however, had little or no effect on the central issues it addressed. *The Sunday Business Post*, a national newspaper originally started by Irish journalists, went through French and German ownership before ending up in the hands of a UK conglomerate; and the powerful UK Mirror Group in 1998 bought into the profitable Irish regional newspaper market in Donegal. The Report was very rapidly overshadowed by events surrounding the general election of 1997 when the daily *Irish Independent*, in a total break with tradition, urged its readers, in a front-page editorial to vote for the Fianna Fáil opposition. Fianna Fáil formed the next government – despite receiving the second lowest share of the total national vote in the party's history – but both party and paper were almost immediately mired in a controversy involving allegations of political favouritism and hidden donations to party funds.[16]

One element of the controversy involved Princes Holdings, whose quest for profitability had been hindered by government unwillingness to legislate against pirate deflectors of UK television signals; at a key pre-election meeting between company executives and representatives of the outgoing government, the newspaper's dissatisfaction with government policy in this regard was made abundantly clear. Another element involved political donations: it was revealed in 1998 that a company controlled by the Independent's chairman, the millionaire Dr. A. J. F. O'Reilly (although the company concerned was not part of the Independent group), had made a substantial donation to a senior Fianna Fáil figure in highly controversial circumstances. Shortly afterwards it was also disclosed that the Independent group itself had made regular donations to political parties over a number of years, although the amounts and recipients were not identified. Recent legislation ensures that all such donations over a certain limit will now have to be publicly identified by the recipients.

As the new century approaches, therefore, the relationship between state and media has moved from stability, through uncertainty, into turbulence. The decreasing amount of controversy about content suggests that broadcasters have established an important and relatively widespread freedom of action under existing legislation. A new range of controversies about the financing, structures and accountability of broadcasting, however, also have implications for content, but of a less direct kind than heretofore.

Notes

1   For more detail on this see Catherine Curran, 'Fianna Fail and the origin of the Irish Press', *Irish Communications Review*, 6 (1996).
2   For more detail on this see Horgan, 'Government, Propaganda, and the Irish News Agency', in *Irish Communications Review*, 3 (1993), pp. 31–43.
3   Cf. *The Irish World Service – the story of Ireland's short-wave station*, unpublished MA in Journalism thesis, Paul Cullen, Dublin City University, 1991.
4   Cf Robert Savage, *Irish Television: The Political and Social Origins* (Cork: Cork University, 1996), p. 6.
5   Savage, *Irish Television*, p. 9.
6   Cf. the events surrounding the collapse of Century Radio, p. 299.
7   Lemass to M. Moynihan (Secretary to the government), National Archives of Ireland, S 14996D, 30 March 1960.
8   For more detail on this era see Doolan, Dowling and Quinn (eds.), *Sit Down and Be Counted* (Dublin: Wellington Books, 1969).
9   Lemass to Michael Hilliard (Minister for Posts and Telegraphs), National Archives of Ireland, D/T, S 14996D, 12 April 1960.
10   Lemass to Pádraig Ó hAnnrachain (head of Government Information Bureau), National Archives of Ireland, D/T S 3532 C/63, 13 September 1962.
11   Lemass to Ó hAnnrachain, National Archives of Ireland, D/T S 3532 C/63, 4 January 1963.
12   Parliamentary debates, Dáil Éireann, Vol 224, Col. 1045–6 and 1048, 12 October 1966.
13   Unpublished survey by Niall Meehan and Jean Horgan, School of Communications, Dublin City University, 1987.
14   Figures (rounded) from Dermot Keogh, *Twentieth-Century Ireland: Nation and State*, (Dublin: Gill and Macmillan, 1994), p. 253.
15   Cf. Peter Mulryan, *Radio Radio: the story of independent, local, community and pirate radio in Ireland* (Dublin: Borderline, 1988), *passim*.
16   For further information on the Independent Group, cf. Horgan, 'The Life of O'Reilly', *British Journalism Review*, (9) (2) (1998), pp. 29–35.

Part IV
Afterword

13

From 'Frugal Comfort' to Ten Thousand a Year: Trade and Growth in the Irish Economy[1]

Cormac Ó Gráda

Part 1. Introduction

Our interpretations of the past are always creatures of the present. In the late 1990s, after a decade of unprecedented prosperity, economists have been busy trying to account for Irish economic success. Luminaries from afar, such as Paul Krugman and Jeffrey Sachs, write about 'the good news from Ireland' and 'Ireland's growth strategy: lessons for economic development', while *The Economist* muses about 'what can the Irish teach the rest', and runs a cover story on Ireland under the heading, 'Europe's Shining Light'. A decade ago, however, gloom and doom were the dominant themes in Irish economic commentary and historiography. The contrast is reflected in the bleak titles of a survey of the Irish economy in *The Economist* in January 1988 ('The Poorest of the Rich') and of a 1989 contribution by Rudiger Dornbusch, another superstar of the dismal science ('Credibility, debt, and unemployment: Ireland's failed stabilization').[2]

Even a decade ago the case for the Republic of Ireland being a failed economic entity was a strong one. For several decades before independence in 1921 living standards and productivity in Ireland had been converging on levels in Britain and most of Western Europe, though admittedly at the cost of heavy emigration. Between the 1920s and the 1980s, however, Ireland lost ground to its neighbours. The estimate of Irish GDP on the eve of the First World War which underpins these comparisons also informed Joseph Lee's critique of Irish economic performance since independence in *Ireland: Politics and Society* (1989). Lee argued that Irish living standards in the 1910s matched those of north European economies such as Norway and Finland, but that thereafter Ireland slid down the European income league table. Lee's work, published in the wake of a period of fiscal retrenchment and rising unemployment, was one of several to argue that independent Ireland had failed to deliver the goods. Today Lee's emphasis on the institutional and cultural constraints on economic performance may seem somewhat dated, yet on the issue of under-performance during the first half century or so of independence he was broadly correct.[3]

Several assessments of Ireland's economic record, including Lee's, invoke cross-country comparisons of income levels and output growth. This makes sense, with the proviso that the comparisons allow for 'catchup', that is, the presumption that Ireland, like other poorer European economies, should have converged on their richer neighbours. One such assessment of the record between 1950 and 1988 by Kevin O'Rourke and myself matches Ireland's record against that of a sample of most other West European economies, and finds it wanting. This is partly because a relatively good showing between the late 1950s and the mid-1970s was negated by effects of the fiscal response to the oil crises of the 1970s. Adding the past decade or so to the sample relocates Ireland on or above the convergence line estimated from such a sample. Between 1987 and 1995 the ratio of Irish to UK output per head, adjusted for deviations from purchasing power parity, rose from 61 to 97 per cent, while the private consumption ratio rose somewhat less impressively, from 57 to 84 per cent.[4]

Why, after more than a half century of under-performance, has the Irish economy finally found its feet? A recent authoritative study suggests five factors, without attempting to rank them: shifting demographic structure, increasing human capital, infrastructural investment, a benign macroeconomic environment, and the opening up of the economy to imports and foreign capital.[5] This chapter takes a longer view of the last of these. It sets the retreat from the protectionist regime installed in the 1930s in context (Part 2) and assesses its consequences (Parts 3 and 4). It then compares trends in the two Irish economies before and after trade liberalization (Part 5), and briefly concludes (Part 6).

Part 2. The Rise and Fall of Protectionism

Running a newly independent economy is a learning experience, and sovereignty is therefore likely to exact an economic cost. Its size will depend on the starting conditions and on how well the constituent parts of the larger economy had been getting along before they broke up. If the breakup is peaceful, the cost may be small; the breakup of Czechoslovakia in the early 1990s is probably in that category. The more good-natured the separation, the more likely the two economies will remain integrated. Moreover, if the breakup is anticipated by all parties, much of the damage may be incurred beforehand (e.g. such as the outflow of labour and capital from Quebec since the 1970s). But if the split is the consequence of long-standing ethnic hatreds and feelings of discrimination and being colonised, the stakes may be very different. In such cases, on the one hand, the economic cost of keeping two unwilling partners together may bulk large; on the other, if the rhetoric of independence is one of economic nationalism and exploitation, separation may be followed by costly nationalistic economic policies. The newly independent government's freedom for manoeuvre is conditioned by the past.

The first decade of Irish independence fits the harmonious, low-cost scenario. The pro-treaty Cumann na nGaedheal administrations of 1923–32 opted for fiscal retrenchment, low tariffs,[6] and monetary probity. The electorate sought something more, however, and in 1932 voted in a political party, Fianna Fáil, dominated by the losing side in the civil war of 1922–3. Straight away Fianna Fáil embarked on a policy of import-substituting industrialisation (ISI), which would prove very costly in time. Its case for ISI rested on the convictions that farming could never provide the employment needed to sustain a vibrant, growing community, and that free trade could not produce the industries needed to increase employment. Others have since offered different rationalisations for ISI-based strategies. In post-1945 Latin America a key influence was the conviction that in the long run the terms of trade favour industry over agriculture.[7] The small size of the Irish market made irrelevant another argument for favouring manufacturing over farming: that manufacturing is subject to scale economies absent in agriculture.[8] In the 1980s both the World Bank and the International Monetary Fund made financial aid packages conditional on countries shedding ISI-oriented policies. Irish economic history has not been kind to the case for ISI either: of all the reasons given for the Irish economy's poor performance before the 1960s, the failure of ISI to deliver the goods is perhaps the single most plausible one.

The inability of ISI to generate sustained output growth was already evident in the trend of industrial production in the late 1930s, but the Second World War intervened before the message could sink in. After 1939 the big drop in living standards brought about by enforced 'national self-sufficiency' captured well a scenario depicted by economist

John Maynard Keynes to a prestigious Dublin audience in April 1933.[9] However, the pattern of initial growth spurt followed by near-stagnation was repeated in the decade or so after 1945. Industrial output recovered as capital stock was replaced and consumer demand rose, only to stagnate once again when the domestic market had been fully sated. The contrast between 1931–6, when net industrial output rose by 31 per cent, and 1936–8, when it rose by only another 6 per cent, is matched by that between 1945–53 and 1953–58, when industrial production rose by 87 and 7 per cent respectively. By the early 1950s government officials realised full well that the scope for further investment in import-substituting production was almost exhausted. A 1953 memorandum from the Department of Industry and Commerce admitted that 'many forms of production are now at the limits of existing market needs'. Trade liberalisation was not yet deemed an option, however; further state investment in order to increase population and purchasing power was the preferred solution.[10]

It bears noting that though Fianna Fáil's inspiration for ISI was largely home-grown, some rise in protectionism after 1932 was inevitable regardless of which party was in power, because the 1930s were years of trade destruction everywhere. Nor was the semi-autarky forced on the Irish Free State during the Emergency of 1939–45 a product of the commercial policy chosen earlier. There are grounds, therefore, for arguing that the real economic damage was done after 1945.

The blame was widely shared: Fianna Fáil failed to take the opportunity to liberalise after 1945, but the inter-party government (1948–51) ushered in a consensus about protection which would hold until the late 1950s. Indeed, by 1948 industrialists may well have found in the new Minister for Industry and Commerce, Fine Gael's Daniel Morrissey, a welcome change from a formidable and increasingly testy Seán Lemass of Fianna Fáil. Lemass is remembered as the architect of ISI, but the tone of his remarks to manufacturers in the early post-war period was sometimes far from friendly. One example is his reminder to a delegation of industrialists in February 1945 that 'of the very large number of plans received relating to export development, very few [had] been received from firms which might be considered as wholly national'. On that occasion he singled out clothing mills for particular criticism, ruling out restrictions on imports until they produced cloth of sufficient quality and variety and in particular 'cheap cloths for the workingman's type of suit'. Less than a year later, Lemass rejected pleas from the Federation of Irish Manufacturers for the right to nominate harbour commissioners with the remark that 'the Bill was not for the purpose of adding to the prestige of the Federation'. Even more cutting was his request in December 1946, in the context of post-war proposals to liberalise world trade, for the Federation's views on how such proposals would affect Irish industry, 'together with a suggested list of tariffs which might be reduced in the event of Ireland having to make a contribution to the general world reduction to artificial barriers to trade'. Shortly before the general election of 1948 the Federation was moved to organise a protest meeting in the Mansion House against Lemass's Industrial Prices and Efficiency Bill.[11] Yet his disappointments were not enough to prompt him to scupper protection.

In March 1948 it was Daniel Morrissey, not Lemass, who told officers of the Federation of Irish Industry that 'so far as he was concerned personally, no Irish industrialist need have the slightest qualms or fears'. A few months later Morrissey would reassure another FII delegation about the new trade agreement just negotiated with the United Kingdom. Its Article 2, he explained, entitled the government to impose tariffs or quotas for balance of payments reasons on goods normally not subject to them. In practice, however, he felt that 'we could use that Article for any purpose we saw fit'. Morrissey also sought to reassure the industrialists that the Prices Commission, established in the wake of an earlier (1938) trade agreement, was now a dead letter.[12] Again, in 1950 it was Morrissey who held that £60 million worth of goods imported in 1948 and 1949 could have been produced domestically, and one of the main functions of the Industrial Development Authority (IDA) as originally constituted by Morrissey in 1949 was to review requests for protection. Lemass likened the new IDA to a redesigned version of the Tariff Commission, a Cumann na nGaedheal creation of the 1920s. By this time Lemass believed that many of the firms created since 1932 were engaged in profiteering and that new industries should be able to survive without protection. But he would not have questioned Morrissey's view that 'the origin of many of our economic and social problems is [the] low proportion of our population employed in industry'. Nor would he have objected to decisions such as that of granting a licence in 1949 to the Dundalk subsidiary of a Yorkshire shoemaking concern to produce 'utility' footwear for export to Britain.[13] But few commentators in the 1940s would have seen export-oriented industrialisation as a panacea. It is symptomatic that at a time when whisky and linen accounted for the bulk of Irish-manufactured exports to the United States, a senior member of the Marshall Plan mission to Ireland saw its prospects for further dollar earnings in tourism, 'smoked salmon, Belleek, special linen products, unusually (*sic*) printed books and cards'.[14]

The second inter-party administration was no less protectionist than the first. In late 1955 one of its ministers stressed its anxiety 'to use the protective arm in support of the establishment, maintenance, and extension of worthwhile industries'; a year later, another referred in the Dáil to the link between 'increased employment, reduced dependence on imports and expansion of exports', and his scheme empowering the IDA to make grants of up to £50,000 to new industrial concerns excluded proposals to produce commodities for which 'the requirements of the public are sufficiently met by undertakings already established'. Such statements echoed a conventional wisdom well expressed in the majority report of the Commission in Emigration, which published its deliberations in 1956.[15] It was not until the late 1950s that the consensus on protectionism collapsed. Significantly, Lemass's famous speech to the party faithful in Clery's ballroom in downtown Dublin (11 October 1955) contained no mention of removing tariffs; as T. K. Whitaker noted later, the key theme of that speech was a Keynesian commitment to increasing employment through public investment on 'socially useful projects'.[16]

It is worth keeping the removal of protective tariffs and the removal of restrictions on foreign capital inflows distinct. The determination to allow in foreign capital preceded the decision to liberalise commodity trade by several years. In 1953 Lemass had invited U.S. industrialists to Ireland, and his successor, William Norton, would do the same three years later. In January 1957 Lemass wrote to a friend:[17]

> I am now of the opinion that, in regard to future industrial expansion, we must start thinking in terms of attracting into this country large external firms to establish export factories here, and frame our tax and other laws to encourage and facilitate this result. I cannot say the effort will succeed but I would prefer to make it before planning further state activity in the industrial field.

Lemass and Fianna Fáil were slow to commit themselves to thoroughly 'reopening' the economy. But the writing was on the wall: as *Economic Development* (November 1958) put it, 'the coming of freer trade in Europe in one form or another must be faced in due course'. Thereafter Lemass would repeatedly claim that protection had made industry complacent and inefficient: one of the attractions of the various trade liberalisation options being discussed was that they would force it to be competitive and reduce its capacity to profiteer.[18]

In the wake of the Anglo-Irish trade agreement of 1938, which envisaged some relaxation of the protectionist regime built up since 1932,

Ireland's fledgling industrialists protested vehemently through the newly founded Federation of Irish Manufacturers.[19] Yet when Ireland applied to join the EEC on the United Kingdom's coat-tails in 1961, neither capital nor labour in protected sectors offered much resistance. Why did the policy shift to trade liberalisation in the later 1950s and early 1960s proceed so smoothly and not provoke more protest? In Latin America, after all, the realisation that ISI was not working did not produce a retreat from autarky: it took decades before it yielded to pressure from outside.[20]

In the Irish case part of the answer must be the dismal state of the economy in the late 1950s. National income had hardly grown since the postwar recovery of 1945–50; the labour force fell from just short of 1.3 million in 1946 to just over 1.2 million in 1957, as emigration reached rates not achieved since the 1880s. Agriculture depended largely on a British market where public policy kept prices artificially low, while a small industrial sector relied on a stagnant home market. Twice, in 1952 and 1956, drastically deflationary budgets were introduced to 'solve' balance of payments problems. To make matters worse, most other economies in Western Europe were doing well, with Ireland's nearest rivals in the misery stakes being Spain and Portugal. The first half of what economic historians now dub the 'Golden Age' of 1950–73 passed the Irish economy by. The prevailing gloom was reflected in sources ranging from *Dublin Opinion* to the *Irish Banking Review*, and received official sanction in T. K. Whitaker's *Economic Development* (1958), which conceded that 'after 35 years of native government people are asking whether we can achieve an acceptable degree of economic progress'.

In the 1950s the labour movement's growing sense of disillusionment with manufacturing as a source of dynamism and extra employment did not make it a propagandist for free trade. Instead, it still placed its hopes on the expansion of the state capital programme and in particular the construction of more houses and schools. Yet it offered little resistance to the retreat from protection.[21] Capital's reaction was also surprisingly muted. Indeed, the leadership of the Federation of Irish Manufacturers seems to have accepted the prospect of freer trade from 1957 on, proclaiming through its official organ, *The Second Arm*, that it had 'adopted no wait and see attitude, but [was] actively engaged in studying the question in all its aspects, keeping in mind the idea of a readaptation fund for those industries that may be deeply affected by free trade in action'. Some members urged continued support for protection, but the leadership merely hoped that Ireland, as a backward region, might be allowed the benefits of a free trade area without incurring all the obligations immediately. In September 1959 the Federation's council called for substantial financial assistance from the government for those sectors most likely to suffer. The Federation's new outward-looking attitude was also reflected in the efforts of its president, Dr. J. I. Fitzpatrick who, in the course of an American tour during the summer of 1958, sought 'every opportunity' to advise U.S. industrialists of Ireland's potential as an exporting base.[22]

Perhaps the prospect of adaptation grants reassured industrialists; perhaps too there was a feeling that free trade was 'all talk', and that change, though bound to happen, wouldn't happen overnight. In the early 1960s Lemass operated on the belief that the economy had about a decade to adjust to foreign competition, and he lent hope to encourage 'sensitive' industries by demanding a longer transitional period than that laid down in the Treaty of Rome in Ireland's official membership application to Brussels. The unilateral, across-the-board reductions of 10 per cent in tariffs in 1963 and 1964 showed that he meant business, but one should note too the gradual character of the reductions negotiated in the Anglo-Irish Free Trade Agreement of 1965.

The 'all-encompassing', consensual approach adopted by Lemass probably also helped in the trade liberalisation campaign. Lemass was behind the creation of the Irish National Productivity Committee (1959), the Employer Labour Conference (1962), the National Industrial Economic Council (1963) and the Committee on Industrial Organisation (1961). All these bodies involved government, employer and labour representatives. The creation of the Committee on Industrial Organisation (CIO) was explicitly linked to the need to adjust to freer trading conditions, while one of the functions of the Employer Labour Conference was to study the implications of Common Market membership for Irish labour relations and social policies.

Part 3.   Trade Liberalisation

The challenge to arguments linking trade and growth is that, according to the simplest version of conventional trade theory, liberalisation affects only output levels, not long-term growth. In the words of *The Economist* (21 March 1998), 'Economists are still busy trying to understand whether, and how, freer trade boosts economic growth.' Nevertheless, several empirical cross-section analyses stress the growth effects of openness. According to Jeffrey Sachs and Andrew Warner, 'Open economies tend to converge, but closed economies do not. The lack of convergence in recent decades results from the fact that the poorer countries have been closed to the world.'[23] By the same token, reducing controls on commodity and factor flows should increase output growth. Such empirical generalisations offer more support for the role of openness in the Irish success story than textbook trade theory.

The trade regime imposed in the 1930s and 1940s was first relaxed and then gradually abolished in the 1960s. The ratio of merchandise trade (imports plus exports) to GDP rose in tandem, from about 25 per cent in 1945 to 106 per cent in 1974–89. It is now (1996–8) about 127 per cent. Over the same half century or so, the ratio of foreign-owned capital to GDP rose from insignificance to well over one.[24] Modelling and estimating the impact of these shifts on Irish macroeconomic performance is beyond the scope of this chapter. Such a project would face several difficulties, not least that of measuring the aggregate degree of protection at different points in time. Louden Ryan's pioneering study found that the average tariff in the Irish Free State quintupled, from 9 to 45 per cent, between 1926 and 1936. But this ignores the important fiscal role of tariffs; an informal manipulation that excludes conventional excise items from the import data produces an increase in the average tariff from 3 per cent in 1926 to 17 per cent a decade later. On the other hand, biasing the structure of tariffs towards finished products and away from intermediate inputs would mean that what economists call the effective rate of protection was higher than the nominal rate; this was certainly so in the Irish case. To complicate matters further, non-tariff barriers, in particular quotas and prohibitions, bulked large. Indeed, businessmen generally preferred quotas to tariffs; in 1945 a spokesman for the FII suggested that 'Irish industry did not require tariffs that the extent of its protection should be that afforded by quotas to offset the disadvantages in the methods of production'.[25] Moreover, in Ireland a complex tariff regime was compounded by controls on capital imports. The Control of Manufactures Acts (1932) sought to preserve the Irish market for Irish capital, so that, in the words of a resolution from the fledgling Federation of Irish Industries, 'Irishmen with Capital, may, with some degree of safety, engage in the economic remaking of their own state.' Though definitely a nuisance for would-be alien investors, in practice many non-nationals were allowed in. By 1950 about 250 licences had been issued to non-nationals seeking to set up industrial concerns aimed at the domestic market.[26] Since the 1960s, policy shifts have produced an outward-looking trade regime, yet a regime which contained, and still contains, its own distortions.

Table 13.1.   Imports (M) and exports (X)
of footwear as shares of gross output (GO)

Year	M/GO	X/GO
1950	3.8	3.0
1960	4.2	17.9
1970	15.1	25.5
1980	138.0	50.2
1990	560.8	83.0
1995	953.3	170.3

Source: *Census of Industrial Production* and
Trade Statistics, relevant years.

In the 1960s and 1970s the indigenous manufacturing sector was badly mauled by trade liberalisation. Penetration of the domestic market by imports was significant for product lines ranging from apparel and clothing to soap and detergents, and from leather handbags to carpets. The pace of the penetration was uneven; on accession to the EEC, domestic producers were still holding their own in several sectors (such as vehicle assembly) which would suffer during the 1970s and 1980s. Table 13.1 describes the effect of trade liberalisation and direct investment on the highly protected footwear industry. In the 1950s and 1960s Ireland imported and exported little footwear, but the numbers since suggest the development of a healthy, if somewhat lopsided, two-way trade.

The policy about-turn transformed the composition of Irish industrial output, and seems to have helped boost total factor productivity, employment and economic growth. Foreign investment's role was central; by 1973 overseas firms would account for almost one-third of all employment in manufacturing. And yet in the 1970s criticism of policy towards the multinationals mounted. The landmark Telesis Report (1982) argued that the grants regime was too generous and provided the wrong kind of signal to prospective investors. Its finding that too many of the branch plants established by American companies were cosmetic 'spit-and-polish' operations infuriated the IDA, but there was certainly something to it, and industrial policy in subsequent years shifted the emphasis from capital grants and preferential tax treatment for manufacturing, for example, to more infrastructural investment in communications and the environment. The potential of multinational services was also recognised. By the early 1990s the IDA had shifted from making inflated promises about employment prospects to contrasting the modest losses in manufacturing employment in Ireland with huge losses

Table 13.2. Labour's percentage share in value added in certain industries

Industry	(NACE)	Ireland		UK		NI
		1984	1990	1984	1991	1984
Pharmaceuticals	(257)	8.2	9.9	27.5	28.2	
RTV equipment	(345)	15.7	8.4	39.3	38.1	
Office machinery	(33)	12.4	10.9	29.8	40.2	48.4
Instruments engineering	(37)	26.5	26.7	48.1	46.3	52.1

Source: Ó Gráda, *A Rocky Road*, p. 122.

elsewhere in Europe in the 1970s and 1980s. The subtext seemed to be that manufacturing's job-creating potential was weak. Since then, against the odds, employment in manufacturing has been increasing impressively. The linkages between multinationals and indigenous producers have grown, and the performance of the indigenous manufacturing sector has improved.

Part 4. But it was not quite Free Trade

That the census of industrial production and GDP data exaggerate the output gains from the multinationals is now well known. This is because tax incentives have encouraged multinationals to employ transfer pricing to maximise their value added in Ireland. The contrast in the census of production between the net output per worker in Irish and foreign-owned manufacturing industries offers good *prima facie* evidence of this. Some of the huge gap between Irish and foreign owned concerns in 1990 – £26,500 against £69,100 – could be put down to differences in technology and product mix, comparing clothing with, say, engineering or pharmaceuticals. However, transfer pricing is the most plausible explanation for the huge output per worker in multinational-owned pharmaceuticals (£204,000) and 'other food preparations' (£427,000). Another sign of transfer pricing is the enormous drop in the share of wages and salaries in net industrial output from over half in the 1950s and 1960s to 40–45 per cent in the 1970s and less than 30 per cent today.[27] The results of comparing labour's share in a few selected industries in Ireland, Northern Ireland, and the UK (see Table 13.2) are also striking. Using disaggregated industrial categories and the NACE classification minimises, though it does not eliminate, the distortions caused by different output mixes.

Since transfer pricing seems to be part of the price of attracting multinationals, the Irish economy is probably not a loser by it. But the huge profits repatriated by the multinationals are a reminder that this is not classic free trade. In the 1960s commercial policy shifted from being heavily biased against imports to favouring exports: incentives based on capital subsidies and low taxes on business replaced others based on protection. The point is important because Ireland's late industrialisation could not have been achieved with a regime of free trade. The poor record of the manufacturing sector before independence is instructive in this respect. Moreover, wages in Ireland and Britain had been converging since the famine. In the 1950s easy access to the British labour market meant that labour in Ireland, though a backward economy, was not so cheap. Multinationals required other incentives to make them locate in Ireland. Industrialisation was built on a uniquely generous combination of grants and tax reliefs: in the early 1980s the IDA absorbed 12 per cent of all public investment and 2 per cent of GDP. However, the successes of the last decade or so have taken place in tandem with a decline in state aids as a proportion of GDP. EU calculations put state aids at 6.4 per cent of GDP in 1986–8, 4.9 per cent in 1988–90, and 3.5 per cent in 1992–4. Today the Irish percentage is not high by EU standards, and Ireland's competitive edge is based less on distortionary tax breaks than on a low rate of corporation profits tax applied across the board rather than to exporters of manufactured product alone.[28]

How has Ireland fared in the comparative advantage stakes? In relatively free trading conditions an economy's comparative advantage should be reflected in its trading pattern. Don Thornhill's analysis of Ireland's revealed comparative advantage (RCA) in manufacturing between the 1960s and 1980s[29] exploits this presumption. It defines a country's RCA in an industry as the ratio of its share of total world exports in that industry to its share in global manufacturing trade. A ratio greater than one reveals Irish comparative advantage. Thornhill's finding that Ireland had a comparative advantage in meat and dairy products comes as no surprise, but the implied comparative advantage in sectors such as organic chemicals, essential oils, scientific instruments, other food preparations (mainly cola concentrates) and medical and pharmaceutical products was surely, in part at least, the product of distortions induced by transfer pricing and a benign tax regime. Thornhill's results may thus simply reflect the importance today of footloose industries which are attracted to a particular location not by its resource base, but by factors such as low labour costs, grants, taxes and historical accidents. This makes comparative advantage very difficult to predict;

an unanticipated growth spurt or an unplanned clustering of investments may allow a critical mass to build up, resulting in acquired comparative advantage.

Whatever may be said about a decade or two ago, the recent success of the high-tech sector is undoubted: so much so that a sector such as computer software might be deemed a former Irish infant industry, now grown up, perhaps? It is too soon to tell, but one possible implication of the Irish developmental experience is that subsidising exports is a better 'catching-up' strategy than taxing imports. Traditional international trade theory would not argue this way: it is very critical of the intellectual case for infant industries.[30] However, the Irish experience suggests a more benign scenario, in which subsidies to export-oriented multinationals may generate dynamic gains that ISI-oriented protection cannot deliver. They might do so in particular by economising on scarce capital and managerial and marketing skills, and by generating external economies such as a highly trained labour force.

The multinationals, and industry generally, have had an important impact on Ireland's occupational profile. Between the early 1960s and early 1990s industry's share of total civilian employment fell by over a third in Britain and by a quarter in the EU; it rose in Ireland during the 1960s and has held its own in the 1990s. Thus one way of interpreting the IDA's efforts is as an attempt to buck the dominant trend in Western Europe, where industrial employment has fallen almost everywhere since the 1970s. Perhaps after half a century of trying to modernise, 'backward' Ireland's comparative advantage is finally in high-tech manufacturing and services?

Part 5.   North and South

Until recently the main purpose of comparisons of economic performance in the two Irelands was to highlight Southern under-achievement. Two excellent studies by geographer Desmond Gillmor and economist Dermot McAleese invoked Northern Ireland to provide pictures of what the Southern agricultural and manufacturing sectors should have looked like in the absence of protection. Gillmor applied a simple dissimilarity index to the agricultural categories listed in Table 13.3. The index, computed by adding the absolute value of the percentage differences in each category's output and then dividing the sum by two, can range from 0 (complete correspondence) to 100 (complete divergence). Given differences in location, demand and climate, some variation is inevitable even under free-trade conditions. For example,

Table 13.3.   Agricultural output in the two Irelands: sectoral shares

		1926	1938	1960	1985	1995
Tillage	North	21.6	12.0	9.1	6.6	9.5
	South	14.6	19.0	20.4	11.3	12.9
Milk	North	19.4	17.3	17.0	27.8	28.8
	South	24.1	24.0	23.1	36.5	34.4
Cattle	North	23.2	14.9	21.1	40.8	35.3
	South	24.3	22.4	30.3	38.8	37.8
Sheep	North	4.3	3.5	5.8	4.1	8.2
	South	5.0	6.6	7.0	4.0	4.4
Pigs	North	9.3	29.9	28.3	10.5	8.1
	South	16.0	13.5	11.4	5.7	6.6
Poultry	North	22.3	22.4	18.7	10.2	10.0
	South	15.9	14.6	7.7	3.7	3.9
Index		13.3	24.3	27.9	13.4	11.5

Source: Gillmor, 'The political factor'; Ó Gráda, *Rocky Road*, p. 89; *NI Abstract of Statistics*, 15, p. 134; *Statistical Abstract* (1996), p. 76.

dairying was more important in the South throughout, poultry breeding in the North. Still, the index captures very well the divergence between North and South that followed in the 1930s and the convergence in the wake of EEC accession. By this reckoning, in the 1990s the two agricultures were more alike than they had been in the 1920s. Similarly, McAleese deemed the gap in the degree of specialisation in manufacturing in the two Irelands in the early 1960s to be a reflection of ISI, and the subsequent convergence to be due to trade liberalisation.[31]

Both studies implied that the South's tariff regime distorted its output mix and reduced its volume. They help explain why between the 1920s and the 1960s the South fell behind the North in terms of output and living standards.

More recently it is the relative strength of the South's performance that is striking. Between 1985 and 1997 Southern GNP grew almost twice as fast as Northern GDP, and by the latter date both Southern output per worker and output per capita had edged ahead of Northern Ireland. However, it has taken the recent success of the South's economy some time to sink in. Only a few years ago one Belfast economist's conviction that the Republic's economy was performing poorly led him to claim that 'on current trends rapid convergence towards continental western Europe, or even Great Britain, is not likely'. In the same publication another strongly pro-union economist held that there was a '25–30 per cent cross-border gap in living standards' between North and South. The latest available macroeconomic data do not support such economic begrudgery. In 1994 household expenditure in Northern Ireland was 84 per cent of UK levels, the same as the Republic's percentage share of private consumption in the UK a year later. True, Northern living standards are higher when gauged by expenditure on consumer durables such as colour televisions, video recorders and cars. But the gap in living standards is being fast eroded.[32]

The shifting North–South balance lends a certain poignancy to an 'orange marxist' interpretation of the partition of Ireland in 1920, which depicts it as a product of Southern economic backwardness rather than of political loyalties or sectarian tensions *per se*. The contrast confidently drawn between 'bustling progressive industrial Ulster', and 'backward', 'stagnant', 'peasant southern Ireland', always dubious as a rationalisation of partition, seems ironic now.[33]

Though the Northern Ireland economy has outperformed the Southern for most of its independent existence, its pace of convergence towards the United Kingdom mean has been sluggish. In 1971 Northern Ireland GDP per head was 78 per cent of the UK average; today it is about 83 per cent. Since 1970 the South has been luckier than the North in two respects. First, it escaped the worst of the post-1969 Troubles. Second, it was more fortunate in its choice of multinational investors. But Northern Ireland's problems reach back further. A recent critique of the Northern policy response in the 1950s and 1960s to the challenges of peripherality and the rather 'rustbelt' character of its manufacturing arm pointed to the practice of 'subsidising physical capital investment rather than enhancing TFP growth'. Such a response persisted into the 1990s, and indeed this criticism has some resonance for the South also.[34]

Financial relations between Ireland and the United Kingdom fuelled endless nationalist rhetoric before 1921 and provoked the Economic War of 1934–8. The fiscal ties between Northern Ireland and the rest of the United Kingdom are also a controversial topic. Labhrás Ó Nualláin's 1952 study of financial relations between Northern Ireland and the rest of the United Kingdom found 'some substance' in the claim that between 1921 and 1950 the North's fiscal contribution exceeded public expenditure in the province. However, in the late 1940s Northern Ireland was 'quite definitely not bearing a proportionate share of the Imperial liabilities and expenditure'. The author's unabashedly anti-partitionist interpretation was that this was Whitehall's price for upholding an administration 'willing to hold fast to the status quo and resist all attempts to upset it'. Ó Nualláin's calculations identified the beginnings of a net transfer which had become enormous: about one-quarter of personal expenditure in the province[35] by the 1990s. Graham Gudgin's sadder but kinder interpretation of the outcome is that it was the product of the North's relative backwardness and the UK's progressive welfare and taxation systems.[36]

6. Conclusion

This chapter began with a comment about the influence of the present on the past. Predictions for the future can similarly be over-influenced by the euphoria or gloom of the present. In the 1950s and 1980s Cassandra would have had a field day in Ireland; today it is the turn of Dr. Feelgood. Yet even the measured musings of some of the country's best economists foresee GNP growth rates of between 4 and 5 per cent annually well into the new millennium.[37] If achieved, by 2010 living standards in Ireland will be as high as in all but the richest of European economies; and Ireland will have experienced a generation of economic growth probably never previously paralleled in its history. Such transformations are never the product of policy changes alone. It takes sweat and mortar as well as architects to build castles. But in the final reckoning the policy shifts described above will have been one of the key elements in Ireland's success story.

Bibliography

Birnie, Esmond (1995). 'Economic consequences of the peace', in J. W. Foster (ed.), *The Idea of the Union*. Belfast: Belcouver Press.

Bradley, John, John FitzGerald, Patrick Honohan, and Ide Kearney (1997). 'Interpreting the recent Irish growth experience', in David Duffy, John FitzGerald, Ide Kearney, and Fergal Shortall (eds.), *The Medium Term Review 1997–2003*. Dublin: ESRI.

Gillmor, Desmond (1989). 'The political factor in agricultural history: trends in Irish agriculture 1922–85', *Agricultural History Review*, 37(2): 166–79.

Girvin, Brian (1994). 'Trade unions and economic development', in Donal Nevin (ed.), *Trade Union Century*. Cork: Mercier, pp. 117–32.

Gudgin, Graham (1995). 'The economics of the union: romance and reality', in J. W. Foster, *The Idea of the Union*.

Guiomard, Cathal (1995). *The Irish Disease*. Dublin: Oak Tree Press.

Horgan, John (1997). *Seán Lemass: The Enigmatic Patriot*. Dublin: Gill & Macmillan.

Kennedy, K. A., T. Giblin, and D. McHugh (1988). *The Irish Economy in the Twentieth Century*. London: Routledge.

Keynes, John Maynard (1933). 'National self-sufficiency', *Studies*, 22: 177–93.

Lee, J. J. (1989). *Modern Ireland 1912–1985*. Cambridge: Cambridge University Press.

Murphy, Gary (1996). 'Fostering a spurious progeny? The trade union movement and Europe, 1957–1964', *Saothar*, 21.

Ó Nualláin, Labhrás (1952). *Ireland: Finances of Partition*. Dublin: Clonmore & Reynolds.

Ó Gráda, C. (1994). *Ireland: A New Economic History 1780–1939*. Oxford: Oxford University Press.

Ó Gráda, C. (1997). *A Rocky Road: the Irish Economy Since Independence*. Manchester: Manchester University Press.

Ó Gráda, C. and K. O'Rourke, Irish economic growth 1950–1988', in N. F. R. Crafts and G. Toniolo (eds.), *Economic Growth in Europe since 1945*. Cambridge: Cambridge University Press, pp. 388–426.

Krugman, Paul (1997). 'Good news from Ireland: a geographical perspective', in Alan W. Gray (ed.), *International Perspectives on the Irish Economy*. Dublin, pp. 38–53.

Sachs, J. D. (1997). 'Ireland's growth strategy: lessons for economic development', in Gray, *International Perspectives*, pp. 54–63.

Notes

1 My thanks to Joe Durkan and Brendan Walsh for extensive comments on an earlier draft, and to Robert Grier of IBEC for arranging my perusal of the IBEC archive. 'Frugal comfort' for all was Éamon de Valera's aspiration in his famous St. Patrick's Day speech in 1943; GNP per head in the Republic today is about £10,000.

2 Paul Krugman, (1997). 'Good news from Ireland: a geographical perspective', in Alan W. Gray (ed.), *International Perspectives on the Irish Economy* (Dublin, 1997) pp. 38–53; Sachs, 'Ireland's growth strategy', in Gray (ed.), *International Perspectives*; *The Economist*, 16 January 1988, 27 April 1996, 17 May 1997; R. Dornbusch, 'Credibility, debt, and unemployment: Ireland's failed stabilization', *Economic Policy*, 8 (1989), pp. 173–201.

3 e.g. K. A. Kennedy, T. Giblin, and D. McHugh, *The Irish Economy in the Twentieth Century* (London: Routledge 1988); Christopher Johns, 'Last in the class?', *Studies*, 82 (325) (1993), pp. 9–23; Cormac Ó Gráda and K. O'Rourke, *Irish Economic Growth 1950–1988*, in N. F. R. Crafts and G. Toniolo (eds.), *Economic Growth in Europe since 1945* (Cambridge: Cambridge University Press, 1996), pp. 388–426; Cathal Guiomard, *The Irish Disease* (Dublin: Oak Tree Press, 1995); J. J. Lee, *Ireland 1912–1985: Politics and Society* (Cambridge: Cambridge University Press 1989). A few of Lee's critics countered that his base-year estimate of Irish GNP was too high; for Tom Garvin (in a review of Lee in *Irish Historical Studies*, no. 105 (1990), p. 87) 'far too high, perhaps by a factor of two'. However, Garvin's accompanying assertion that Irish income per head had quadrupled during decades surveyed by Lee is hard to credit: a quadrupling would have required an average annual growth rate of well over 2 per cent over six decades which included the 1920s and 1930s (a period of near stagnation), the Emergency years (years of economic contraction), and the 1950s (another dismal decade of near-zero growth). If GDP failed to grow before 1960, then a quadrupling of output would have required an average growth rate of over seven per cent for the rest of the period. Combining unofficial

estimates of GDP for the 1920s and 1930s with the official data available from 1938 on corroborates Lee's more sombre reading.

4 Cormac Ó Gráda, *A Rocky Road: the Irish Economy Since Independence* (Manchester: Manchester University Press, 1997), ch. 1; Organisation for Economic Co-operation and Development, *Economic Survey Ireland*, 1988/9 and 1997. The slower rise in the consumption ratio is a reflection of the growing importance of repatriated profits.

5 John Bradley, John FitzGerald, Patrick Honohan and Ide Kearney (1997), 'Interpreting the recent Irish growth experience', in David Duffy, John FitzGerald, Ide Kearney and Fergal Shortall (eds.), *The Medium Term Review 1997–2003* (Dublin: ESRI), p. 64.

6 Cumann na nGaedheal's limited experimentation with protective tariffs included one on ready-made clothing, with much the same results as those imposed by Fianna Fáil later. Cormac Ó Gráda, *Ireland: A New Economic History* 1780–1939 (Oxford: Oxford University Press 1994), pp. 386–8; Seán P. O'Shea, 'The Irish wholesale ready-made clothing and cap industry', in P. O'Neill's *Commercial Who's Who* (Dublin, 1936), pp. 187–91.

7 Alan M. Taylor, 'On the costs of inward-looking development: price distortions, growth, and divergence in Latin America', *Journal of Economic History*, 58(1) (1998), pp. 1–28.

8 Kiminori Matsuyama, 'Agricultural productivity, comparative advantage, and economic growth', *Journal of Economic Theory*, 58 (2) (1992).

9 John Maynard Keynes, 'National self-sufficiency', *Studies*, 22 (1933), p. 189.

10 National Archives (NA), DT/S13101 c/1.

11 IBEC Archive, Box 14 (minutes of meetings 10 January 1946; 13 December 1946; 12 December 1947); Box 15 (meeting 12 February 1945).

12 IBEC Archive, Box 15 (Meetings with Morrissey, 8 March 1948 and 4 August 1948).

13 Parliamentary Debates Dáil Éireann (PDDÉ), 9 Mar 1950, vol. 11 cols. 15845, 1601 1616; NA, TID/1207/2933.

14 Wiliam Howard Taft, 'Mr. Taft on Industry and tourism', in *Ireland's Economy: Radio Eireann Talks on Ireland's Part in the Marshall Plan* (Dublin, 1949), p. 28.

15 *Irish Times*, 3 October 1955 (Brendan Corish); PDDÉ, vol. 160, Col. 1942 (William Norton); Commission on Emigration and Other Population Problems, *Reports* (Dublin, 1956), paragraphs 396–7.

16 T. K. Whitaker, 'From protection to free trade: the Irish experience', *Administration*, 21(4) (1973), p. 416.

17 Cited in John Horgan, *Sean Lemass: The Enigmatic Patriot* (Dublin: Gill & Macmillan, 1998), p. 167.

18 e.g. IBEC Archives, Box 14 (FII council meeting, 26 November 1937); NA/ICTU/4002 (Meeting with Taoiseach 1959).

19 NA, TID2215/9 contains several pleas from concerned manufacturers. The FIM grew out of a meeting of manufacturers in Dublin on 7 May 1932. A provisional committee circulated a memorandum, suggesting that the shift in policy following Fianna Fáil's victory opened the way for 'an organization solely composed of manufacturers and dealing exclusively with their interests'. The Federation came into being on 14 November 1932 (IBEC Archive, Box 13).

20 Taylor, 'On the costs of inward-looking development', *Journal of Economic History*, pp. 5–9.

21 Gary Murphy, 'Fostering a spurious progeny? The trade union movement and Europe, 1957–1964', Saothar, (1996), 21, p. 67.; see too Brian Girvin, 'Trade unions and economic development', in Donal Nevin (ed.), *Trade Union Century* (Cork: Mercier, 1994), pp. 117–32.

22 *The Second Arm*, 4 (5) (Sept-Oct 1957), 7; 5 (1) (Jan–Feb 1958), p. 5; 5 (4) (July-Aug 1958), 9; IBEC Archive, Box 13 (minutes of FII national council, 9 October 1959); Ó Gráda, *Rocky Road*, p. 50. In April 1958 the Federation created a select committee to investigate the likely consequences of Irish membership of the European Free Trade Agreement (EFTA). The committee prepared a questionnaire, but as the likelihood of EFTA membership receded it ceased to function. It was revived in early 1960, and commissioned a pilot survey of the woollen and worsted weaving industry by UCD economists Gerard Quinn and Garret Fitzgerald.

23 J. D. Sachs and A. Warner, 'Economic reform and the process of global integration', *Brookings Papers in Economic Activity* (1995), p. 3; Sebastian Edwards, 'Openness, productivity and growth: what do we really know?', *Economic Journal*, 108 (1998), pp. 383–96; Dan BenDavid and Michael Loewy, 'Free trade, growth, and convergence', *National Bureau of Economic Research Working Paper*, 6095 (1998).

24 No data on the value of the foreign-owned capital stock are available. However, in 1996 profits accruing to non-nationals totalled £4,521 million and royalties another £2,145 million. Given that GDP was £36.9 billion, assuming that these sums represented 10 per cent on the capital invested implies a ratio of 1.8. The data is taken from *National Income and Expenditure 1996* (Dublin, 1997).

25 W. J. L. Ryan, 'Measurements of tariff levels in Ireland', *Journal of the Statistical and Social inquiry Society of Ireland*, 18 (1948/9): pp. 109–33; D. McAleese, *Effective Tariffs and the Structure of Industrial Protection in Ireland* (Dublin, 1971); Ó Gráda, *Ireland*, pp. 406–9; IBEC Archive, Box 14 (memo of officers' meeting, 13 December 1945). For more on the ambiguities of measuring protection, see Lance Pritchett and Geeta Sethi, 'Tariff rates, tariff revenue, and tariff reform: some new facts', *World Bank Economic Review*, 8(1) (1994): pp. 1–16. On the gap between nominal and effective rates under ISI in Latin America, see Sebastian Edwards, 'Openness, trade liberalization and growth in developing countries', *Journal of Economic Literature*, 31 (1992), p. 1363.

26 NA, TID/1207/3253; IBEC Archive, Box 13, resolution passed 23 June 1933. See also Mary E. Daly, 'An Irish Ireland for business? The Control of Manufactures Acts, 1932 and 1934', *Irish Historical Studies*, 24 no. 94 (November 1984), pp. 246–72. The FII was established in the wake of Fianna Fáil's victory.

27 The scope of U.S. corporations to employ transfer pricing is constrained by tax monitoring on the part of the U.S. internal revenue. Note too that a similar, though less dramatic, rise in capital's share is seen in economies such as those of the United Kingdom and the United States.

28 Data on the IDA's spending is given in OECD surveys of the Irish economy. See too *European Commission, Fifth Survey on State Aid in the EU in the Manufacturing and Certain Other Sectors* (Brussels, 1997), Table 3; E. W. Bond and S. E. Guisinger, 'Investment incentives as tariff subsidies: a comprehensive

measure of protection', *Review of Economics and Statistics*, 67 (1) (1985), pp. 91–7. Tax deductions, due in large part to the imputed value of the special 10 per cent corporation tax applied to manufacturing accounted for half of state aid.

29 D. J. Thornhill, 'The revealed comparative advantage of Irish exports of manufactures 1969–1982', *Journal of the Statistical and Social inquiry Society of Ireland*, 25M (1987/8), pp. 91–146.

30 Robert E. Baldwin, 'The classical case against infant industry tariff protection', *Journal of Political Economy*, 77 (1969), 295–305; Douglas A. Irwin, *Against the Tide: An Intellectual History of Free Trade* (Princeton: Princeton University Press, 1996), pp. 116–37.

31 Desmond Gillmor, 'The political factor in agricultural history: trends in Irish agriculture 1922–85', *Agricultural History Review*, 37 1989 (2): pp. 166–79; D. McAleese, 'Do tariffs matter? Industrial trade and specialization in a small open economy', *Oxford Economic Papers*, 29(1) (1977), pp. 117–27; Ó Gráda, *A Rocky Road*, pp. 79–81.

32 Desmond Birnie, 'Economic consequences of the peace', in J. W. Foster (ed.), *The Idea of the Union* (Belfast: Belcouver Press 1995), p. 117; Graham Gudgin, 'The Economics of the Union: Romance and Reality', in J. W. Foster, *The Idea of the Union*. p. 86; *Economic Trends*, 27 (1997).

33 Paul Bew and Henry Patterson, *The British State and the Ulster Crisis* (London, 1985), p. 3.

34 N. F. R. Crafts, 'The Golden Age of economic growth in postwar Europe: why did Northern Ireland miss out?', *Irish Economic and Social History*, 22 (1995), p. 25.

35 EEC/EU net transfers to the Republic averaging 4.6 per cent of GDP between 1973 and 1997 were modest by comparison.

36 Labhras Ó Nualláin, *Ireland: Finances of Partition* (Dublin: Clonmore and Reynolds, 1952), pp. 186–7; Gudgin, 'The economics of the Union', in Foster (ed.), *The Idea of The Union*.

37 David Duffy, John FitzGerald, Ide Kearney, and Fergal Shortall (eds.), *The Medium Term Review 1997–2003*.

Index